Aiding Forensic Investigation Through Deep Learning and Machine Learning Frameworks

Alex Noel Joseph Raj
Shantou University, China

Vijayalakshmi G. V. Mahesh
BMS Institute of Technology and Management, India

Ruban Nerssison
Vellore Institute of Technology, India

Ang Yu
Carolina University, USA

Jennifer Gentry
Carolina University, USA

IGI Global
PUBLISHER of TIMELY KNOWLEDGE

A volume in the Advances in Digital Crime, Forensics, and Cyber Terrorism (ADCFCT) Book Series

Published in the United States of America by
IGI Global
Information Science Reference (an imprint of IGI Global)
701 E. Chocolate Avenue
Hershey PA, USA 17033
Tel: 717-533-8845
Fax: 717-533-8661
E-mail: cust@igi-global.com
Web site: http://www.igi-global.com

Library of Congress Cataloging-in-Publication Data

Names: Raj, Alex Noel Joseph, 1979- editor. | Mahesh, Vijayalakshmi G. V., 1978- editor. | Nersisson, Ruban, 1980- editor. | Yu, Ang, 1978- editor. | Gentry, Jennifer, 1974- editor.
Title: Aiding forensic investigation through deep learning and machine learning frameworks / Alex Noel Joseph Raj, Vijayalakshmi G.V. Mahesh, Ruban Nersisson, Ang Yu, and Jennifer Gentry, editors.
Description: Hershey PA : Engineering Science Reference, [2022] | Includes bibliographical references and index. | Summary: "This book provides an outline of deep learning and machine learning frame works/methods for its use in forensic science to produce accurate and reliable results in aiding investigation process by covering the challenges, latest developments, advancements, future and emerging approaches/algorithms, deep learning architectures data handling and analysis"-- Provided by publisher.
Identifiers: LCCN 2022012077 (print) | LCCN 2022012078 (ebook) | ISBN 9781668445587 (hardcover) | ISBN 9781668445594 (paperback) | ISBN 9781668445600 (ebook)
Subjects: LCSH: Forensic sciences--Data processing. | Criminal investigation--Data processing. | Deep learning (Machine learning) | Machine learning.
Classification: LCC HV8073 .A549 2022 (print) | LCC HV8073 (ebook) | DDC 363.25--dc23/eng/20220502
LC record available at https://lccn.loc.gov/2022012077
LC ebook record available at https://lccn.loc.gov/2022012078

This book is published in the IGI Global book series Advances in Digital Crime, Forensics, and Cyber Terrorism (ADCFCT) (ISSN: 2327-0381; eISSN: 2327-0373)

British Cataloguing in Publication Data
A Cataloguing in Publication record for this book is available from the British Library.

Advances in Digital Crime, Forensics, and Cyber Terrorism (ADCFCT) Book Series

ISSN:2327-0381
EISSN:2327-0373

Editor-in-Chief: Bryan Christiansen, Global Research Society, LLC, USA, Agnieszka Piekarz, Independent Researcher, Poland

MISSION

The digital revolution has allowed for greater global connectivity and has improved the way we share and present information. With this new ease of communication and access also come many new challenges and threats as cyber crime and digital perpetrators are constantly developing new ways to attack systems and gain access to private information.

The **Advances in Digital Crime, Forensics, and Cyber Terrorism (ADCFCT) Book Series** seeks to publish the latest research in diverse fields pertaining to crime, warfare, terrorism and forensics in the digital sphere. By advancing research available in these fields, the **ADCFCT** aims to present researchers, academicians, and students with the most current available knowledge and assist security and law enforcement professionals with a better understanding of the current tools, applications, and methodologies being implemented and discussed in the field.

COVERAGE

- Information Warfare
- Malicious Codes
- Database Forensics
- Cyber Warfare
- Network Forensics
- Criminology
- Vulnerability
- Hacking
- Computer Virology
- Identity Theft

IGI Global is currently accepting manuscripts for publication within this series. To submit a proposal for a volume in this series, please contact our Acquisition Editors at Acquisitions@igi-global.com or visit: http://www.igi-global.com/publish/.

The Advances in Digital Crime, Forensics, and Cyber Terrorism (ADCFCT) Book Series (ISSN 2327-0381) is published by IGI Global, 701 E. Chocolate Avenue, Hershey, PA 17033-1240, USA, www.igi-global.com. This series is composed of titles available for purchase individually; each title is edited to be contextually exclusive from any other title within the series. For pricing and ordering information please visit http://www.igi-global.com/book-series/advances-digital-crime-forensics-cyber/73676. Postmaster: Send all address changes to above address.

Titles in this Series

For a list of additional titles in this series, please visit:
http://www.igi-global.com/book-series/advances-digital-crime-forensics-cyber/73676

Dark Web Pattern Recognition and Crime Analysis Using Machine Intelligence
Romil Rawat (Shri Vaishnav Vidyapeeth Vishwavidyalaya, India) Shrikant Telang (Shri Vaishnav Vidyapeeth Vishwavidyalaya, India) P. William (Sanjivani College of Engineering, Savitribai Phule Pune University, India) Upinder Kaur (Akal University, Talwandi Sabo, India) and Om Kumar C.U. (School of Computer Science and Engineering (SCOPE), Vellore Institute of Technolog, India)
Information Science Reference • © 2022 • 281pp • H/C (ISBN: 9781668439425) • US $250.00

Using Computational Intelligence for the Dark Web and Illicit Behavior Detection
Romil Rawat (Shri Vaishnav Vidyapeeth Vishwavidyalaya, India) Upinder Kaur (Akal University, Talwandi Sabo, India) Shadab Pasha Khan (Oriental Institute of Science and Technology, Bhopal, India) Ranjana Sikarwar (Amity University, Gwalior, India) and K. Sakthidasan Sankaran (Hindustan Institute of Technology and Scienc, India)
Information Science Reference • © 2022 • 336pp • H/C (ISBN: 9781668464441) • US $250.00

Media and Terrorism in the 21st Century
Elnur Ismayil (Istanbul Medeniyet University, Turkey) and Ebru Karadogan Ismayil (Uskudar University, Turkey)
Information Science Reference • © 2022 • 299pp • H/C (ISBN: 9781799897552) • US $215.00

World Politics and the Challenges for International Security
Nika Chitadze (International Black Sea University, Georgia)
Information Science Reference • © 2022 • 427pp • H/C (ISBN: 9781799895862) • US $215.00

For an entire list of titles in this series, please visit:
http://www.igi-global.com/book-series/advances-digital-crime-forensics-cyber/73676

IGI Global
PUBLISHER of TIMELY KNOWLEDGE

701 East Chocolate Avenue, Hershey, PA 17033, USA
Tel: 717-533-8845 x100 • Fax: 717-533-8661
E-Mail: cust@igi-global.com • www.igi-global.com

Table of Contents

Detailed Table of Contents

Deep learning (DL) is a rising field that is applied in forensic science and criminal investigation (FSCI). FSCI specialists are confronting many difficulties because of the volume of of information, little bits of confirmations in the turbulent and complex climate, conventional lab structures, and once in a while, deficient information which might prompt disappointment. The application of DNA sequencing technologies for forensic science is particularly challenging in systems biology. DL is at present supporting practically every one of the unique fields of FSCI with its various methodologies like analysis of data, pattern recognition, image handling, computer vision, data mining, statistical examination, and probabilistic strategies. In this manner, DL is helping forensic specialists and examiners by defining legitimate proof, 3D remaking of crime locations, taking care of proof viably, and dissecting it to arrive at obvious end results at different degrees of investigation and criminal justice.

Ayaz Ahmad, National Institute of Technology, Patna, India
Supriya Prashant Diwan, Government College of Engineering, Karad, India
Sudhansu Sekhar Nanda, Kirloskar Institute of Advanced Management Studies, India
Lingaraj Sethi, Odisha University of Technology and Research, India
Prashanta Kumar Patra, Odisha University of Technology and Research, India

Digital forensic methods for cybercrime investigation in a cloud computing environment (i.e., cloud forensic) is a broad term that encompasses a number of different fields, including digital forensics and cloud computing. The authors hope to gain a better understanding of cloud computing and identify challenges and opportunities in forensic science. They present research that may be used to establish strategies for the creation of measures, standards, and technological research to minimise the issues that cannot be solved with current technology and methodologies. Among the topics covered in this chapter are cloud computing, digital forensics, cybercrimes, and cloud forensics. Also covered are an overview and principles of cloud computing as well as digital forensics, cybercrimes, and challenges, as well as opportunities in the field of cloud forensics. The state of the art in the cloud forensic domain is also presented, as is a literature review on related work to digital forensics techniques in the cloud computing environment.

Ramesh Naidu P., Nitte Meenakshi Institute of Technology, India
Dankan Gowda V., B. M. S. Institute of Technology and Management, India
Kumaraswamy S., Global Academy of Technology, Bengaluru, India
Pankaj Dadheech, Swami Keshvanand Institute of Technology, Management, and Gramothan, India
Ansuman Samal, Siksha 'O' Anusandhan (Deemed), India

The internet of things (IoT) is a revolutionary technology that links living and non-living devices all around the world. As a result, the frequency of cyber-attacks against IoT deployments is expected to rise. As a result, each system must be absolutely secure; otherwise, consumers may opt not to utilize the technology. DDoS assaults that recently attacked various IoT networks resulted in massive losses. There is only one way to detect stolen data from software and malware on the IoT network that is discussed in this chapter. To categorize stolen programming with source code literary theft, the tensor flow deep neural system is offered. To communicate raucous information while simultaneously emphasizing the value of each token in terms of source code forgery, tokenization, and measurement, the malware samples were gathered using the Malign dataset. The results show that the methodology proposed for analyzing IoT cyber security threats has a higher classification efficiency than current methodologies.

Dankan Gowda V., B. M. S. Institute of Technology and Management, India
Puneeth Kumar B. S., St. Joseph's College (Autonomous), India
Shekhar R., Alliance University, India
Pankaj Dadheech, Swami Keshvanand Institute of Technology, Management, and Gramothan, India
Thangadurai N., Sankalchand Patel University, India

As the number of connected devices grows, the internet of things (IoT) poses new security challenges for network activity monitoring. Due to a lack of security understanding on the side of device producers and end users, the majority of internet of things devices are vulnerable. As a result, virus writers have found them to be great targets for converting them into bots and using them to perform large-scale attacks against a variety of targets. The authors provide deep learning models based on deep reinforcement learning for cyber security in IoT networks in this chapter. The IoT is a potential network that connects both living and nonliving things all around the world. As the popularity of IoT grows, cyber security remains a shortcoming, rendering it exposed to a variety of cyber-attacks. It should be emphasized, however, that while there are numerous DL algorithms presently, the scientific literature does not yet include a comprehensive catalogue of them. This chapter provides a complete list of DL algorithms as well as their many application areas.

Madhab Paul Choudhury, National Institute of Technology, Jamshedpur, India
Madhab Paul Choudhury, National Institute of Technology, Jamshedpur, India
Chandrashekhar Azad, National Institute of Technology, Jamshedpur, India

Machine learning techniques are being used to create an intrusion detection system (IDS) for detecting and classifying cyber-attacks at the network-level and the host-level in a timely manner. Various datasets are available for research by cyber security researchers. However, no previous study has shown the detailed analysis of the performance of various machine learning algorithms on various available datasets. As the nature of malware is changing dynamically with the changing attacking methods, the detailed analysis of the available data sets is necessary to find out the cause of the malware datasets, and accordingly, necessary steps can be executed for maintaining the security of the network. A deep neural network (DNN) is being explored to develop an effective intrusion detection system. The optimal network parameters and network topologies for DNNs are chosen through the following hyper parameter selection methods with KDD Cup 99 dataset. The DNN model can be applied on KDD Cup 99 and on other datasets also such as NSL-KDD, UNSW-NB15, Kyoto to conduct the experiment.

Hui Wang, Auckland University of Technology, New Zealand
Wei Qi Yan, Auckland University of Technology, New Zealand

Face recognition is an important biometric in video surveillance. However, the conventional algorithms of face recognition are also susceptible to various conditions. The contribution of this chapter is to explore face recognition by using deep learning, including detecting the location of human faces on the given images at various distances and multiple angles. In the distances, the influence of the distance from the camera to a face and the size of the face in the images is explored. There are 500 images collected from various videos as the input and they are applied to train the proposed models. The accuracy of face recognition from the videos excluding training dataset is at 90.18%. The results indicate that this method is able to recognise human faces with partial occlusion and various distances.

Anitha Ruth J., SRM Institute of Science and Technology, India
Uma R., Sri Sairam Engineering College, India
Vijayalakshmi G. V. Mahesh, B. M. S. Institute of Technology and Management, India
P. Ramkumar, Sri Sairam College of Engineering, India

Deep learning technologies, such as neural networks, have tackled complicated issues from large-scale data processing to computer vision and human-level control. Editing photographs with software designed for commercial purposes makes it easy for anyone to manipulate images in order to create fictitious ones. Generative adversarial networks (GANs) are currently being utilised to generate superficially realistic photographs, as opposed to the old methods that were previously used to create phony images. The GANs images are referred to as deep fakes. To the unaided eye, they appear to be real photographs. As a result, it's impossible to spot

As the internet of things and cloud computing create new technological revolutions in the field of healthcare, the issues such as security, privacy, authentication, the integrity of patient data, and medical images become sensitive. This chapter proposes a cryptographic technique for the secure storage of medical images based on biometric key generation. Cryptographic algorithms can be used to enhance the security of cloud storage systems. The proposed biometric-based encryption scheme takes the advantage of biometric features of the fingerprint and iris of the user to meet the desired security characteristics. A 256-bit bio-key is generated based on the distance between the fingerprint features and used in the advanced encryption standard (AES) for image encryption. The experiments conducted on the set of medical images also prove the effectiveness and security aspects of the proposed biometric key-based image encryption. The encryption method is also tested on the set of medical images and compared with other encryption schemes.

Classroom management relies heavily on the ability to keep track of student attendance. Attendance checks by calling names or handing out a sign-in sheet are time-consuming and vulnerable to fraud, especially the latter. Data science and image processing are the focus of this regarding counting the number of people present at a gathering for various objectives, such as determining a person's duty status, determining a person's physical presence in a classroom, determining a person's security clearance to enter a meeting hall, etc. It takes a lot of time and effort to maintain a database for future use when generating attendance records using the standard technique. With the help of the latest technology, attendance can be entered automatically. It is a frequently used face recognition technique that generates a binary code for each cell and compares it to the reference image. With the use of deep learning, this LBP method has been reworked in order to automate attendance generation.

Preface

This book attempts to provide an outline of deep learning and machine learning frame works/methods for its use in forensic science to produce accurate and reliable results in aiding investigation process. Further it discusses the challenges, latest developments, advancements, future and emerging approaches/algorithms, deep learning architectures data handling and analysis. The book also tries to provide suitable solutions to the challenges.

Forensic science involves application of scientific methods to examine, analyze and investigate the evidence to aid Law enforcement. The evidence includes an array of inputs obtained from different sources in the crime scene that include: fingerprints, dental signatures, DNA, ballistics, autopsies, patterns, toxicology, chemical analysis, traces (blood samples/DNA samples), forensic radiology (postmortem computed tomography (PMCT)), handwriting analysis and digital data: information acquired from mobile phones, computer systems, computer network traffic analysis, emails, storage devices etc. This evidence is examined, assessed and validated for accurate results to draw the conclusion.

Artificial intelligence with its potential subsets Machine learning (ML) and Deep learning (DL) can transform the domain of forensic science with its capability in handling diverse data, recognizing the patterns, analysis, interpretation and presenting the results. The ML and DL frameworks with developed mathematical and computational tools facilitates the investigators in providing reliable results.

This book provides an effective platform for forensic investigators, law practitioners, students, academicians, engineers and researchers working in the field of pattern recognition, cyber security, digital forensics, forensic science, biometrics, computational intelligence, artificial intelligence, image analytics, video analytics, surveillance, etc., The book provides insights about the current research trends which have flourished due to the availability of Machine and Deep Learning models.

There are total of twelve chapters arranged in orderly manner. Few chapters provide a review on Forensic Science and Criminal Investigation through Deep Learning Framework, Network and Computer Forensics. Other chapters discuss about Network Forensic Tools, Digital Forensic Techniques, Cyber Security, Deep Learning based AI modeling, Intrusion detection, Face Detection and Recognition,

Speech analysis of speakers and medical encryption techniques. The abstracts of all the chapters are presented below.

Chapter 1 provides a review on Forensic Science and Criminal Investigation (FSCI) through Deep Learning Framework. The chapter analyses the use Deep Learning (DL) in the space of Forensic Science and Criminal Investigation (FSCI). The current situation of FSCI specialists is confronting many difficulties because of gigantic measure of information, little bits of confirmations in the turbulent and complex climate, conventional lab structures and once in a while deficient information which might prompt disappointment. The application of DNA sequencing technologies for forensic science is particularly challenging in systems biology. DL is at present supporting practically every one of the unique fields of FSCI with its various methodologies like Analysis of Data, Pattern recognition, Image handling, Computer vision, Data mining, Statistical examination and probabilistic strategies. In this manner, DL is helping Forensic specialists and examiners by defining legitimate proof, 3D remaking of crime locations, taking care of proof viably and dissecting it to arrive at obvious end results at different degrees of investigation and criminal justice.

Chapter 2 presents about digital forensic techniques and principles in cloud environment. Digital forensic methods for cybercrime investigation in a cloud computing environment (i.e., cloud forensic) is a broad term that encompasses a number of different fields, including digital forensics and cloud computing. It provides a better understanding of cloud computing and identify challenges and opportunities in forensic science. Present research that may be used to establish strategies for the creation of measures, standards, and technological research to minimize the issues that cannot be solved with current technology and methodologies is also a part of our analysis of the current research landscape. Among the topics covered in this chapter are cloud computing, digital forensics, cybercrimes, and cloud forensics. Also covered are an overview and principles of cloud computing, as well as digital forensics, cybercrimes, and challenges, as well as opportunities in the field of cloud forensics. A state-of-the-art in the cloud forensic domain is also presented, as is a literature review on related work to digital forensics techniques in the cloud computing environment.

In **Chapter 3**, IoT-deep learning based detection of cyber security threats are presented. The Internet of Things (IoT) is a revolutionary technology that links living and non-living devices all around the world. As a result, the frequency of cyber-attacks against IoT deployments is expected to rise. As a result, each system must be absolutely secure; otherwise, consumers may opt not to utilize the technology. DDoS assaults that recently attacked various IoT networks resulted in massive losses. There is only one way to detect stolen data from software and malware on the IoT network that we've discussed in this chapter. To categorize stolen programming with source code literary theft, the Tensor Flow deep neural system is offered. To communicate raucous information while simultaneously emphasizing the value of each token in terms of source code forgery, tokenization, and measurement. The malware samples were gathered using the Malign dataset. The results show that the methodology proposed for analyzing IoT cyber security threats has a higher classification efficiency than current methodologies.

Chapter 4 presents deep learning models for cyber security in IoT networks. As the number of connected devices grows, the Internet of Things (IoT) poses new security challenges for network activity monitoring. Due to a lack of security understanding on the side of device producers and end users, the majority of Internet of Things devices are vulnerable. As a result, virus writers have found them to be great targets for converting them into bots and using them to perform large-scale attacks against a variety of targets. We provide deep learning models based on deep reinforcement learning for cyber security in IoT networks in this chapter. The IoT is a potential network that connects both living and nonliving things all around the world. As the popularity of IoT grows, cyber security remains a shortcoming, rendering it exposed to a variety of cyber-attacks. It should be emphasized, however, that while there are numerous DL algorithms presently, the scientific literature does not yet include a comprehensive catalogue of them. This chapter provides a complete list of DL algorithms as well as their many application areas.

Chapter 5 gives information about deep learning based AI modeling, intrusion detection. Machine learning techniques are being used to create an intrusion detection system (IDS) for detecting and classifying cyber attacks at the network-level and the host-level in a timely manner. Various datasets are available for research by cyber security researchers. However, no previous study has shown the detailed analysis of the performance of various machine learning algorithms on various available datasets. As the nature of malware is changing dynamically with the changing attacking methods, the detailed analysis of the available data sets is necessary to find out the cause of the malware datasets and accordingly necessary steps can be executed for maintaining the security of the network. A deep neural network (DNN) is being explored to develop an effective intrusion detection system. The optimal network parameters and network topologies for DNNs are chosen through the following hyper parameter selection methods with KDD Cup 99 dataset. The DNN model can be applied on KDD Cup 99 and on other datasets also such as NSL-KDD, UNSW-NB15, Kyoto to conduct the experiment.

In **Chapter 6**, deep learning-based face detection and recognition framework is presented. Face recognition is an important biometric in video surveillance. However, the conventional algorithms of face recognition are also susceptible to various condition. The contribution of this chapter is to explore face recognition by using deep learning, including detecting the location of human faces on the given images at various distances and multiple angles. In the distances, the influence of the distance from the camera to a face and the size of the face in the images is explored. There are 500 images collected from various videos as the input and apply them to train the proposed models. The accuracy of face recognition from the videos excluding training dataset is at 90.18%. The results indicate that this method is able to recognize human faces with partial occlusion and various distances.

Chapter 7 investigates on deep fake images using CNN frame works. Deep learning technologies, such as neural networks, have tackled complicated issues from large-scale data processing to computer vision and human-level control. Editing photographs with software designed for commercial purposes makes it easy for anyone to manipulate images in order to create fictitious ones. Generative Adversarial Networks (GANs) are currently being utilized to generate superficially realistic photographs, as opposed to the old methods that were previously used to create phony images. The GANS images are referred to as Deep fakes. To the unaided eye, they appear to be real photographs. As a result, it's very impossible to spot a phony image produced with GANs. The social network is made less safe as a result of the uploading of these bogus photographs. It is therefore critical that the digital image's legitimacy be detected before it is uploaded. So, it is important to detect the digital image's authenticity before it is uploaded. Thus, in this chapter, we suggest a few pre-trained Deep learning frameworks that may be used to effectively detect Deep fake images.

A work on implementation of machine learning aided speech analysis for speaker accent identification applied to Audio forensics is presented in **Chapter 8**. Accent recognition a sub set of speech recognition is crucial in audio forensics as it provides the authenticity of the speech that can be presented to the judicature as an evidence. The challenge here is to design a speaker accent identifying system that can provide significant information to match with the standards of the court of justice This process requires robust descriptors to represent speech signal with good discrimination ability. This chapter proposes to use Mel Frequency Cepstral Coefficients to identify and represent the human utterances by transforming the frequency from normal scale to Mel scale. The work utilized Support vector machine, k nearest neighbor neighbors, XG Boost, Linear discriminant analysis, Quadratic discriminant analysis and Decision tree algorithms to recognize the accent of the speaker. The experiment conducted on the accent recognition dataset demonstrated the ability of Mel Frequency Cepstral Coefficients and kNN classifier in identifying and discriminating six accents belonging to different speakers with better accuracy and least errors.

Chapter 9 proposes and presents a cryptographic technique for the secure storage of medical images based on biometric key generation. Cryptographic algorithms can be used to enhance the security of cloud storage systems. The proposed biometric-based encryption scheme takes the advantage of biometric features of the fingerprint and iris of the user to meet the desired security characteristics. A

256-bit bio-key is generated based on the distance between the fingerprint features and used in the Advanced Encryption Standard (AES) for image encryption. The experiments conducted on the set of medical images also prove the effectiveness and security aspects of the proposed biometric key-based image encryption. The encryption method is also tested on the set of medical images and compared with other encryption schemes.

Deep learning based automatic student authentication is provided in **Chapter 10**. Classroom management relies heavily on the ability to keep track of students' attendance. Attendance checks by calling names or handing out a sign-in sheet are time-consuming and vulnerable to fraud, especially the latter. Data science and image processing are the focus of this. Counting the number of people present at a gathering for various objectives, such as determining a person's duty status, determining a person's physical presence in a classroom, determining a person's security clearance to enter a meeting hall, etc. It takes a lot of time and effort to maintain a database for future use when generating attendance records using the standard technique. With the help of the latest technology, attendance can be entered automatically. It is a frequently used face recognition technique that generates a binary code for each cell and compares it to the reference image. With the use of deep learning, this LBP method has been reworked in order to automate attendance generation.

Further the book discusses the challenges, latest developments, advancements, future and emerging approaches/algorithms, deep learning architectures data handling and analysis in forensic investigation. The book also tries to provide suitable solutions to the challenges. Based on its coverage of the various domains, the book provides required materials to students, academicians and researchers working on ML and DL frameworks as applied to Forensic investigation.

Alex Noel Joseph Raj
Shantou University, China

Vijayalakshmi G. V. Mahesh
BMS Institute of Technology and Management, India

Ruban Nersisson
Vellore Institute of Technology, India

Ang Yu
Carolina University, USA

Jennifer Gentry
Carolina University, USA

Acknowledgment

The completion of this book would not have been possible with the support of several people. We would like to express our sincere thanks to all who contributed in many ways.

We sincerely thank the IGI global team who were happy to accept our proposal and provided timely help at all stages in solving various administrative issues.

We thank the invited authors and reviewers for their continuous support and efforts in making this book into this wonderful technical resource for Aiding Forensic Investigation Through Deep Learning and Machine Learning Frameworks.

We would like to acknowledge the support provided by our institutions and we would like to sincerely thank Shantou University, China, Vellore Institute of Technology, Vellore, India BMS Institute of Technology and Management, Bengaluru, India and Carolina University, North Carolina, United States for their unrelenting confidence in our abilities.

Our families too need a special mention. Finally, we thank the Almighty for giving us this wonderful opportunity.

Chapter 1
A Review on Forensic Science and Criminal Investigation Through a Deep Learning Framework

Pinaki Pratim Acharjya
https://orcid.org/0000-0002-0305-2661
Techno College of Engineering Agartala, Agartala, India

Santanu Koley
Haldia Institute of Technology, India

Subhabrata Barman
Haldia Institute of Technology, India

ABSTRACT

Deep learning (DL) is a rising field that is applied in forensic science and criminal investigation (FSCI). FSCI specialists are confronting many difficulties because of the volume of of information, little bits of confirmations in the turbulent and complex climate, conventional lab structures, and once in a while, deficient information which might prompt disappointment. The application of DNA sequencing technologies for forensic science is particularly challenging in systems biology. DL is at present supporting practically every one of the unique fields of FSCI with its various methodologies like analysis of data, pattern recognition, image handling, computer vision, data mining, statistical examination, and probabilistic strategies. In this manner, DL is helping forensic specialists and examiners by defining legitimate proof, 3D remaking of crime locations, taking care of proof viably, and dissecting it to arrive at obvious end results at different degrees of investigation and criminal justice.

DOI: 10.4018/978-1-6684-4558-7.ch001

INTRODUCTION

Since the last decade of the 20th century, we witnessed a world-changing digital revolution. Mobile phones, Internet and many of the various digital technologies have become a part of our daily lives. At first, we were unaware of how significant those tools will be in the future but today they play an essential role in our daily lives and so do in our professional lives. This makes it obvious that most of our valuable information is going to be stored in digital form. In this age of Information Technology, the needs to change and enforce the laws are also changing. As a result, conventional crimes, especially those involving finance and commerce, are constantly evolving in response to technological advancements. In almost any investigation, a detailed analysis of computer systems and digital devices is becoming increasingly necessary in deciding the evidence. This is where Digital forensic comes into the picture, to respond to law enforcement's clear and expressed needs in order to make the most of this emerging medium of electronic evidence, where machine learning can play a vital role by automating the time taking processes.

Digital forensics can be defined as a branch of forensic science dedicated to recover and investigate digital data. It is an evolving field that is always advancing to catch with the changes in devices and how they are used for the identification, preservation, analysis, and recovery of data from computer systems and various other digital storages. The "Big digital forensic evidence" is today's major challenge for law enforcement agencies. The amount of data that needs to be analyzed is rising all the time. An issue that needs to be solved is how to easily detect relevant file artifacts. In order to encourage further research in this field, we delve deeper into the role of machine learning in digital forensics applications in this paper, and provide an overview of the work already done in this direction.

Artificial Intelligence (AI) and DL have great advantages and hold a bright future ahead. But the same technology can inevitably be used to craft, automate and execute some serious crimes that can also be deadly for people. AI and DL has been around since a long time but it is now that we have enough computational power to effectively develop strong artificial neural networks (ANN) in a sensible time frame with the help of strong hardware and software support. Companies like Google, Amazon, Samsung, etc. are heavily investing in AI technologies and funding the research. Artificial Intelligence (AI) and DL hold great forensic importance. It is a new field to dive in for forensic investigators and the scope of research is really big. Since Artificial intelligence (AI) is becoming widely available to more and more people, the potential of the technology to be used for malicious purposes also increases significantly. To counter this and be prepared for forensic challenges regarding crimes committed with AI or DL, forensic evaluation and analysis of the technology is necessary.

This chapter demonstrates a review on the importance and implementation of DL for forensic science, forensic analysis and criminal investigation in order to have a better understanding of where DL stand in today's cyber security domain when it comes to collecting digital evidence. This chapter started by talking about Digital Forensics and its past to illustrate the fields of digital forensics where DL methods have been used to date. This paper also lists out some important artifacts findings that can be taken as a reference for cases in future to prove or determine DL techniques used on provided evidence.

LITERATURE SURVEY

A comprehensive description and development of a novel method for object detection in images using Deep Neural Networks were provided by Christian et al. In the research, a machine learning model was developed to successfully classify images and localize various object positions detected in the image. The research comprehensively explains how deep neural networks outperformed other classification techniques and it presented neural networks as a more powerful and robust algorithm suitable for classification problems because of its deep architecture. The validity of the approach used in the model developed is analyzed by using it on VOC as the test dataset. The experiment conducted with the model on this dataset utilizes boundary boxes to detect a significant object in these test images and its conclusive accuracy is compared with three related approaches which include: sliding window version of a DNN classifier (Du et. al., 2018), a 3-layer compositional model by (Jin et al., 2010) and the DPM by (Felzenszwalb et al., 2010) and (Girshick et al., 2013) to evaluate the achieved results of the model.

(Ng et al., 2015) developed a model for crowd analysis for digital forensics over video surveillance during the 2015 Emotion Recognition in the Wild contest. Due to the large number of resources required to train the neural networks from scratch on a pre-trained deep CNN using a small dataset of a static image from movies, the Transfer Learning approach was deployed. The pre-trained model was originally trained on a large dataset of 1.2 million images thereby contributing to the accuracy of the model. The overall accuracy of the model after being trained and tested on the new dataset for emotion recognition on static images is 48.5%, which is quite low and inefficient. A proposed solution to this accuracy drawback is the expansion of the labelled dataset to a reasonable extent while retraining the model.

An object detection model on digital images, based on a novel CNN was developed by (Joseph et al., 2017). The architecture of the model involves a single CNN to classify boundary boxes of objects in a resized input image of 448 x 448, unlike other object detection framework that uses a sliding window approach which the

CNN is applied on several spaced locations on the entire image. The model was trained on several datasets including VOC 2007 & 2012 and ImageNet 2012 thereby making the model generalized on several categories of objects. However, this model still has a drawback in that it still struggles with a small and clustered image like a flock of birds in the sky.

Similar research based on the YOLO-CNN was conducted by (Rayson et al., 2017). The researchers developed a real-time end to end automatic license plate recognition system in support of the state-of-the-art YOLO-CNN algorithm for object detection. The final layer of the model was trained and fine-tuned using a large public dataset. The dataset was prepared with three different digital cameras used to take photographs of the license plates at different angles, thereby preparing a large dataset with a variety of images in terms of image quality which contributes to the level of accuracy achieved by the model. The experimentation was done using the Darknet Framework on GPU due to the computational power required to train YOLO on a large dataset. The accuracy achieved with the developed model is 78.33%. The research model was not created from scratch for object detection, they retrained CR-NET, YOLOV2, and Fast YOLO which are pre-trained state-of-the-art models for object detection (Transfer Learning) and compare their results.

A novel approach for object detection and localization in digital images for forensic crime scene investigation was developed by (Saikia et al., 2017). Crime scene reconstruction starts with the identification of shreds of evidence at a crime scene, therefore the research presents a Faster Region-based Convolutional Neural Network (R-CNN) to optimize existing DL algorithms for object detection. The R-CNN model was pre-trained with the MS-COCO dataset. It was tested on two different test sets; the ImageNet Room objects and Karina dataset. The accuracy of the model turns out to be excellent on the ImageNet dataset but low on the Karina dataset due to poor image quality of the videos.

An evaluation and comparison of models design for age estimation from facial features extracted from digital images and videos was conducted by (Rodríguez-Félix et al., 2018). The researchers developed a model to support digital forensic expert with an automated investigation of images of child abuse and child pornography. To solve the prominent problem of the non-availability of datasets, they went further to develop a dataset generator that creates a structured dataset from images contained in various semi-structured datasets. The comparative analysis compares the accuracy of the following machine learning models (online and offline) based on their mean absolute error: Amazon Recognition (Artificial Neural Network), Deep Expectation, DEX (CNN), Kairos (Support Vector Machine, SVM), and Microsoft Azure Cognitive Service (DL).

(Tallón-Ballesteros et al., 2014) proposed research on various categories of glasses that could be found shattered or broken at a crime scene as a primary source of evidence if a proper and accurate identification of these glass types is achieved. A dataset from glass identification of the USA Forensic Science Service which is available on the University of California, Irvine (UCI) repository was used. They performed a comparative analysis of four machine learning classification algorithms (Decision Tree, Naïve Bayes, Artificial Neural Network, and K-Nearest Neighbours).

An image mining system to detect illicit images with criminal behaviours for digital forensics was developed by (Brown et al., 2005). Using SVM and a Bayesian classifier algorithm, the researchers developed a model to filter relevant features of images based on grammar queries from the user. The model developed was trained to classify appropriate and inappropriate images based on clad and nude content respectively, using a training set of 214 images in three different colour spaces to train the SVM model. The performance result of the model is quite remarkable considering the time of the research with 92% true positive results and 79% true negative detection rate; however, incorrect classification can be corrected by fine-tuning the grammar-based query and feedback feature provided by the system for communication with the user.

A different dimension to digital image forensics was introduced by (Muhammad et al., 2017) whereby the validation of the authenticity of images is conducted through the recognition of the particular camera used to take the image. A justification for this approach is the affordances of a large variety of mobile phones today with highly sophisticated cameras and it becomes highly expensive in terms of time and computational power to carry out digital forensic analysis on a single PC. They carried out the source camera identification methodology presented on a 6000-image dataset taken by six (6) mobile phone cameras using Hadoop for feature extraction and Manhout Random Forest Classifier for image classification, thereby achieving a very efficient forensic analysis process in terms of speed and an accuracy of 85% to 95% across various mappers.

An application of CNN for art painting identification to detect copyrighted images used without content provider's permission for commercial purposes was created by (You et al., 2017). The research is an instance of *Scale-Invariant Feature Transform* (SIFT); a state-of-art handcrafted image descriptor. It deployed an artwork dataset of 100 main art images distorted in various forms to expand the dataset to 30000 distorted images. The resultant model was trained on 25000 distorted images and tested on 5000. The model produced a CNN with a 2% test error rate.

An extensive analysis and evaluation are carried out on different CNN architectures on a computer aid detection problem for thoracoabdominal lymph node (LN) and interstitial lung disease (ILD) detection by (Shin et al., 2016). The AlexNet CNN (seven-layered), Cifar-CNN (three-layered) and GoogleNet CNN (eleven layered) are the CNN evaluated in the research. Two major challenges using CNN to classify medical images include the unavailability of an extensive dataset for training and testing. However, they utilize publicly available thoracoabdominal lymph node and interstitial lung disease image datasets labelled by radiologists, and secondly, CNNs are trained on natural images, unlike medical images which are 2D or 2.5D images. Pre-trained CNN can still classify medical images effectively by using the approach of transfer learning which involves fine-tuning the higher layers of these CNN. The conclusive accuracy of various CNN evaluated in the research creates a state-of-the-art machine learning model that can be used to develop high-performance CAD systems in further research works.

(Di Francesco et al., 2015) presented a method to prevent counterfeit images from being detected by state-of-the-art forgery detectors by modifying certain micro-pattern in these images. The research developed a strategy for counter-forensics which overrules the operation of techniques used for forgery detection which uses the statistical distribution of micro-patterns in images which are optimized through high-level filtering and summarized in some image descriptor used for the final classification. We review the statistical algorithm proposed for counter forensics of images or videos which they describe as Greedy Sampling Algorithm, they analyzed its efficiency when it has limited knowledge or perfect knowledge of the feature used by a forgery detection algorithm for classification (genuine or not). They propose the success of the research in the paper by analyzing the experimental result of the counter-forensics algorithm on 100 images; thereby the output images are indistinguishable by the forgery detector. However, the result is remarkable when the algorithm presented has complete knowledge of the feature extraction technique used by the detector compared to the limited knowledge scenario which consumes more CPU time.

ORIGINS OF FORENSIC SCIENCE IN CRIMINAL INVESTIGATION

The history of forensic science awaits exploration as forensic science as a discipline was not much spoken about until recently. On increasing the cognizance of the subtle importance of forensic science in the past, one cannot but amp up the reverence for this field of science. The word forensic has its origin from the Latin word *"forensis"* which stands for a forum. Forensic Science is basically used in tandem with any discipline that has associations with the legal system. In a nutshell, forensic science is the application of scientific methods and principles to questions of law. Or, in layman's terms, forensic science is a discipline used by a forensic investigator to solve crimes.

Although it is uncertain exactly where the concept of forensic science originated, most historical experts agree it was very likely in China around the 6th century or earlier. This belief is based on the earliest known mention of the concept, found in a book titled "Ming Yuen Shih Lu," printed in that period.

During the 7th century, the concept of utilizing fingerprints as a means of identification was first established. According to historical records, a street merchant was able to verify the identity of a particular customer who owed him money by capturing his fingerprints on a bill. A judge accepted the prints as undeniable evidence, providing a very early example of forensic science in action. In 1659, the Merriam-Webster Dictionary officially recognized and printed the word "forensic". The term had been used in medical writings for many years, but until then was not considered to be an "official" word in the English language. In modern times the term is well-known and part of everyday language.

Throughout the years, science became more prominent in legal settings, and scientific discoveries were commonly used to decide the outcome of important legal matters. By the late 1700s, forensic science was being used as a factor to determine guilt or innocence in major criminal cases, including charges of murder. One of this science's primary functions is to study DNA, the genetic coding found on all living things. DNA samples can be acquired from any human or animal and then be tested, and compared to other samples for similarities. This process is highly respected, and a major consideration for cases in which the identity of an individual must be established.

As modernization was coming, different scientists made significant developments in various fields of Forensics and came to be known as the Father of those particular fields.

Mathieu Joseph Bonaventure Orfila (Forensic Yard, 2020) was a Spanish Toxicologist and Chemist. He studied and published a book on the effects of poisons on animals and the ways of detecting a particular poison, a work that established 'Toxicology' as a legitimate scientific endeavor. For his publication in Forensic Toxicology in the 19th century he is known as the *Father of Modern Toxicology*.

Alphonse Bertillon (1813-1914) devised the scientific system of personal identification. He started to develop scientific anthropometry which is a systematic procedure of taking a series of body measurements as a means of differentiating one individual from another. This has been later replaced by the Fingerprints. However, for his achievements of creating the Bertillon system and identifying criminals through scientific processes, he is considered as the *father of criminal investigation.*

Francis Galton (1822-1911) developed the method of classification of Fingerprints. He is responsible for the present system of identification by Fingerprints. He laid a foundation for acceptance of fingerprints as evidence in courts by publishing many articles, books, scholar articles, interviews, etc. Later, Henry Faulds used a classification system to classify various fingerprints in police force etc, and the classification system is still in use.

Hans Gross (1847-1915) was an Austrian criminologist popularly known as the *Father of Criminalistics.* His publication 'Criminal investigation' in 1893 helped to establish the forensics in terms of transferring of evidence from criminal to victim.

Edmond Locard (1847-1915) was a French criminologist. He discovered the basic principle of Forensic Science i.e., Locard's exchange principle which states that 'Every contact leaves a trace'.

Albert S. Osborn (1858-1915) is also known as the *father of questioned document examination.* He made significant contributions to the field of questioned document examination. His first contribution was the book publication titled *"Questioned Documents"* in 1910 and the second edition of the same book in 1929. Leone Lattes (1887-1954) devised a relatively simple procedure for determining blood group from a drop or from the dried bloodstain. The procedure developed by Dr Leone Lattes is still in use today. She is credited as the '*Father of Bloodstain identification*'.

Calvin Hooker Goddard (1891-1955) devised the technique of comparison of a fired bullet with a test bullet. It is also possible to determine if the particular weapon has been used for firing of a bullet. It would be possible to get the exact identity of the weapon and the bullet from where it was fired. He is also known as the '*Father of Forensic Ballistics*'.

Sir Alec Jeffreys (1950-present) is a British Geneticist and developed the DNA profiling and genetic fingerprinting technique and is used currently all over the world in Forensic Science for the purpose of the law.

DEVELOPMENT OF FORENSIC SCIENCE IN INDIA

Anthropometry Bureau

This was established in Calcutta in 1892 (Tewari and Ravikumar, 2000). This bureau had adopted Bertillon's method of personal identification. This center has got records of criminals such as photographs and other detailed descriptions of appearance.

Fingerprint Bureau

William Herschel the collector of Hugli in West Bengal found that markings on the fingertips of an individual are unique and never change during their lifetime. He applied his knowledge and skill in devising a system of registration of finger and thumb impression. Edward Henry followed this principle of recording fingerprints of criminals and thereby a fingerprint bureau was established in 1897 at Calcutta.

Department of Explosives

During the British rule explosions and explosive related activities became common and to detect the type of explosives and cause of explosions the department of explosives was set up in Nagpur and later established in 5 other regions of India i.e., Calcutta, Bombay, Madras, Agra, Gwalior.

Government Examiner of Questioned Document (G.E. QD)

During the struggle for independence, the government of West Bengal created this post (to identify the handwritings of secret documents) in 1904. It was later shifted to Shimla in 1906 under the control of the criminal investigation department. During that time, Mr. CR Hardless was appointed to this post.

Serologist to Government of India

When the science of examining human blood in India was started, it had also become possible to examine seminal stain in a criminal investigation in certain specific cases where it felt mandatory.

Serology department was first established in Calcutta in 1910. Although the department was not developed, it did support the criminal investigations in India. It was renamed as Office of Serologist and Chemical examiner to the government of India.

Footprint Section of C.I.D

It was established in Calcutta in 1915. The main duty was to collect, preserve and analyze the footprint for identification of criminals.

Forgery Section of C.I.D

In 1917 this section was set up under C.I.D by the government of West Bengal. They detect cases of currency /coins and forgery notes/documents. Later on, government security printing press was established in Nasik.

Ballistics Division

In 1930, it was established in Calcutta for the examination of firearms as the incidents of firearms were increasing. Later, the ballistics division was added in many states' forensic laboratories.

Mobile Forensic Laboratory

Most of the states in India have got this Facility. The main function is to help police personnel in their investigation at a crime scene by helping them to locate, to collect and preserve the evidence. The team will also provide a photographic facility to record a crime scene and valuable evidence. Another important duty is to guide the police to collect an adequate and correct sample for comparison and also provide leads for further investigations.

Scientific C.I.D Section

Some police are trained scientifically to help the department where technical photography, scientific surveillance and investigations and other technical needs are existing.

TYPES OF FORENSIC INVESTIGATION

The following table displays everything in detail:

Table 1. Types of forensic investigation

Types of Forensic Investigation	Characteristics
Forensic Accounting / Auditing	A forensic accounting (Kishor and Bholane, 2006) investigation aids the victims of fraud or financial crimes. Also known as financial investigation, this kind of analysis uses intelligence-gathering techniques, accounting, business, and communication skills to provide evidence to attorneys involved in criminal and civil investigations. They investigate by combing through a large number of relevant figures, searching for irregularities or illegal financial practices. Crimes can vary from tax evasion to theft of company assets. They also look into insurance claims and high payouts. Forensic accounting services can include: • Searching for hidden assets • Calculating lost wages • Tracing misappropriated funds • Performing fraud investigations

Continued on following page

Table 1. Continued

Types of Forensic Investigation	Characteristics
Forensic Computer or Cyber Forensics	Computer investigations are similar to electronic discovery (or e-discovery). These forensic investigations recover data from computers and hard drives to solve a crime or find evidence of misconduct. Computer investigators can uncover things like sale of black-market goods, fraud, and sex trafficking. Some common situations that call for computer investigation are divorce, wrongful termination, employee internet abuse, unauthorized disclosure of corporate information, and other illegal internet activity. Forensic computer investigations can find information on cell phones and hard drives including emails, browsing history, downloaded files, and even deleted data. One of the first cases in which computer forensics (Chaturvedi et al., 2020) lead to a conviction involved the messages exchanged in an online chat room.
Crime Scene Forensics	Crime scene investigations document and gather any physical evidence found at a crime scene in order to solve a crime or determine whether a crime has taken place. This kind of investigation also includes the analysis of what investigators collect to ensure the evidence is credible and relevant. There are a wide range of crime scene investigators like ballistics experts, who study the trajectory of ammunition and match bullets to potential firearms, who specialize in teeth and bite-marks to identify missing persons or victims of mass disaster.
Forensic Archaeology	Forensic archaeology focuses on human remains that are severely decomposed. They mainly focus on clues they can glean from the bones, including carbon dating to determine their age. From these clues, they can sometimes establish cause-of-death. If a mass grave is discovered or in the event of large casualties, forensic archaeologists can identify the victims using facial reconstruction software.
Forensic Dentistry	Forensic dentists are vital when a victim can't be identified by any other means or when a culprit bites a victim. Since teeth have distinct patterns, the marks left behind can identify a suspect or victim. The shape of the jaw can also indicate age, gender, and DNA can be extrapolated from teeth like with bone marrow and hair. Even if the victim wasn't bitten, physical evidence found at a crime scene may still be useful for forensic dentists. For example, a pencil with bite marks or a half eaten apple might have deep enough impressions to reveal someone's identity.
Forensic Entomology	Forensic entomology is the study of any insects found at a crime scene. Alive or dead, these bugs can reveal where a crime took place, whether the victim had been given drugs, and the time of death. Some insects are only found in specific areas so finding them on a body can suggest whether a body was moved. The presence of larvae in a body can also suggest how long a victim has been dead. If the crime isn't a murder, insects will still occupy untreated wounds in abuse cases or identify the origin of illegally imported goods, like cannabis.

Continued on following page

Table 1. Continued

Types of Forensic Investigation	Characteristics
Forensic Graphology	Forensic graphologists study the handwriting on ransom notes, poison pen letters, suicide notes, and blackmail demands. Though age and gender cannot be determined by handwriting alone, it can indicate the writer's state of mind at the time the note was penned. Handwriting can give insights about: • Mood • Motivation • Integrity • Intelligence • Emotional stability Slant, size of writing, and the weight of the hand all reflect information about the writer. The phrases and slang the writer uses can also say a lot about location and motive. Forensic graphologists are also used to verify the validity of documents such as insurance claims or police statements.
Forensic Pathology	Ultimately, it is the forensic pathologist's job to find out cause-of-death, especially when it is suspected that the death was not due to natural causes. They perform an autopsy, which involves observing both the outside and inside of the victim. On the outside there may be signs of blows, bruises, bullet entry points, or asphyxia. On the inside, the pathologist will look at things like the organs and stomach contents. By observing these things, a pathologist can determine whether the death was a suicide, murder, or due to natural causes.
Forensic Psychology	Forensic science is the general term used for all of the scientific processes involved in solving a crime. Some types of forensic science include: • DNA coding • Toxicology (drugs and the effects) • Serology (bodily fluids) • Ballistics (everything related to firearms) a big part of forensic science is the collection, storage, and analysis of fibres, DNA, bodily fluids, and other physical evidence. The roles of forensic scientists have become vital to the sentencing of criminals due to the reliability and accuracy of the evidence they provide. It is also a section of forensics that is constantly growing and changing as technology advances
Forensic Toxicology	Forensic toxicology studies toxic substances, environmental chemicals, and poison. The drug tests needed for certain job applications are an example of the most basic forensic toxicology. Today, a large part of a forensic toxicologist's job is studying both illegal and legal drugs. Using urine, blood, or hair, they look at the way these substances are absorbed, distributed, and eliminated by the body. They will also look at their effects. For a murder, substances use shows itself in the brain, liver, and spleen.

BASIC LAWS AND PRINCIPLES OF FORENSIC SCIENCE

The laws and principles of all the natural sciences have formed the base of Forensics. In fact, the application all the sciences to analyze the evidence to answer crime mysteries have helped develop several laws and principles of Forensic science (Forensic Yard, 2021). There are 7 basic principles of forensic science which include

- Law of Individuality
- Law of Progressive change
- Principle of Comparison
- Principle of Analysis
- Locard's principle of Exchange
- Law of Probability
- Law of Circumstantial facts.

Law of Individuality

This law states that, "*Every object whether natural or man-made has a unique quality or characteristic in it which is not duplicated in any other object.*"

The law of Individuality has been verified in different fields and the most common among them is the fingerprints. Millions and Billions of fingerprints have been studied and yet not a single fingerprint has matched with other whether it is of twins or two fingers of same person.

Any two objects such as grains of sand, salt, seeds, twins or man-made objects such as currency notes, coins, laptop, suits, typewriter, etc. they may seem similar to each other yet a unique characteristic is always present between them.

Law of Progressive Change

This law states that, "*Everything changes with the passage of time.* "

In simple words, nothing is permanent and the rate of change varies on different objects. This law has a significant effect on crime scene investigations because of the changes occurring in the crime scene and criminal with the passage of time. The criminal, evidence, objects involved may become unrecognizable.

If the crime scene is not secured in time, a change in weather, presence of animals/ humans, etc. changes rapidly. For example, road accident on a busy highway may be unrecognizable or lose all necessary evidence if not secured on time.

The objects such as bullet fragments may develop rust, shoes may develop wear and tear marks, wooden objects may destroy due to presence of termite, knife may develop additional patterns, etc. Therefore, quick action is required in all segments of criminal investigations.

Principle of Comparison

This law states that, "*Only the likes can be compared.* "

It highlights the need to provide like samples and specimens for comparison with the questioned evidences.

In a murder case, the expert is of the opinion that the person was killed by stabbing with a sharp piece of rod. It will be unnecessary to send a knife for comparison.

If a bullet recovered from the body is fired from the shotgun, it will be useless to send a pistol for comparison.

Principle of Analysis

This principle states that, "*There can be no better analysis than the sample analysed.*"

This principle highlights the need for correct sampling and packaging of evidences to avoid tampering & destruction and for effective analysis and results. Incorrect sampling may mislead the investigation.

In a rape case, the investigating officer collected the clothes of the victim which had semen and blood stains on it.

Locard's Principle of Exchange

This principle states that, "*Whenever two entities come in contact with each other, they exchange the traces between them.*"

This principle was stated by French scientist known as Edmond Locard, and therefore it is known as Locard's principle.

According to Locard, when a criminal or a murder weapon or any of his objects comes in contact with the victim or the surrounding, they leave some traces in that area whereas also picks up the traces from the places or person they have been in contact with. If those traces are identified by the expert, and track it to its original source, the criminal can be linked with the crime scene and the victim.

This principle is demonstrated in almost all the cases where there is a contact such as fingerprints, foot marks, tyre marks, bullet residues, hair sample, etc.

Law of Probability

This law states that, "*All identifications definite or indefinite, made consciously or unconsciously are on the basis of probability.*"

The term probability is mostly misunderstood. It determines the chances of occurrence of a particular event in a particular way out of total number of ways in which an event can take place or fails to take place with equal facility.

For example, an unknown woman is found murdered in a farm. The dead body of that woman had a gold-plated tooth, healed foot fracture and a tattoo on her left arm. A woman with the similar characteristics was also reported missing. There are high chances that the unknown corpse is of that missing woman.

The probability of that corpse being of another woman will be 1 in millions and the identity of that unknown corpse is established.

Law of Circumstantial Facts

According to this law, "*Facts do not lie, men can and do*."

Facts cannot be wrong, it cannot lie, it cannot be wholly absent. Therefore, the importance of circumstantial facts is good for oral evidence.

In a case where a person is in armed forces is known to carry his duty till 10 Pm and resumes in the morning at 9 am. He secretly slips out of the unit at night kills a person and returns back secretly to join the duty on time. By circumstantial evidence, he can prove his presence in the unit at that time and escape the punishment.

DEEP LEARNING (DL)

DL is a subclass of Artificial Intelligence (AI), and it is a machine learning method that teaches computers and devices how to operate logically. The name DL comes from the fact that it penetrates many layers of the network, including a secret layer. The further one dives, the more compound information that can be gleaned. To reproduce intelligence in the same way that humans do, DL techniques rely on a range of composite

Figure 1. Concepts of DL at a Basic Level.

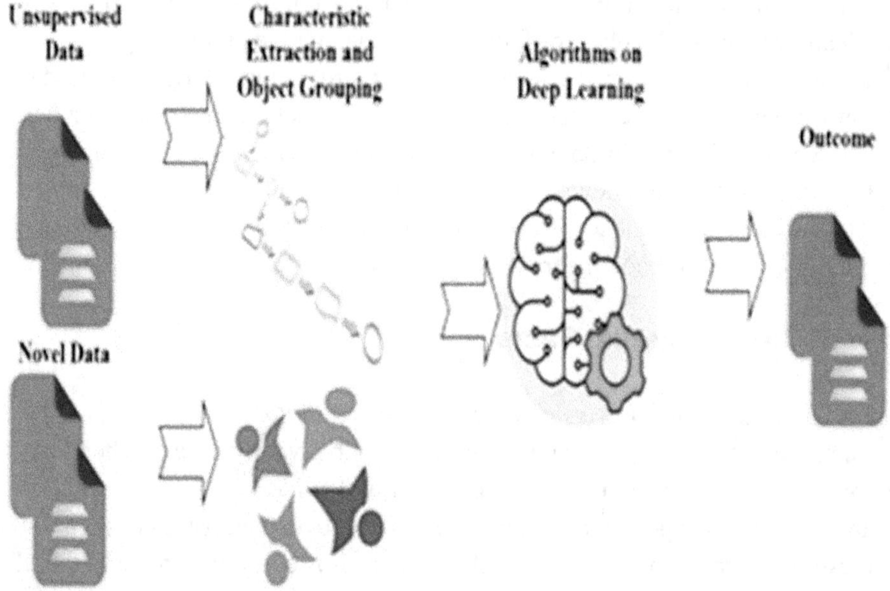

algorithms. These many procedures instruct computers to create meaningful designs and are consequently classified into several sorts. Aside from credit to ML, pattern recognition is a crucial component of DL; computers do not require extensive programming. During DL, machines may work with images, text, or audio recordings to perform and act on a few tasks in a human-like fashion.

Virtual Assistants, Chatbots, Healthcare, Entertainment, News Aggregation, Composing Music, Image Coloring, Robotic, Image Captioning, and Advertising are some of the industrial uses of DL. Special achievements can be achieved if well-structured computers can efficiently imitate human performance in a given amount of time. DL emphasizes machine learning techniques that unearth enormous amounts of data. As a result, it aids computers in recognizing characteristics and adapting to change. Supports periodic data set identification changes, recognizes the causes, and disseminates a trustworthy data conclusion. DL is now working on more dependable compound function development. It is unsurprising that this particular place is accumulating a great deal of significance, attracting a lot of attention from new experts.

As it gains acceptance around the world, DL is becoming an increasingly vital part of human life. It makes daily life easier than previously, and it will continue to do so in the future, whether it's a self-driving car or the DL component of language recognition, which is driving countless computerizations in the modern period.

Nonetheless, the importance of DL can be enhanced by the fact that the world now produces a significant amount of data, necessitating a large-scale structure. The most acceptable application of DL is to increase the volume and accessibility of information. All of the data collected from this data is used to generate 100 percent accurate results via repetitive learning prototypes.

Figure 2. Elementary DL Concepts.

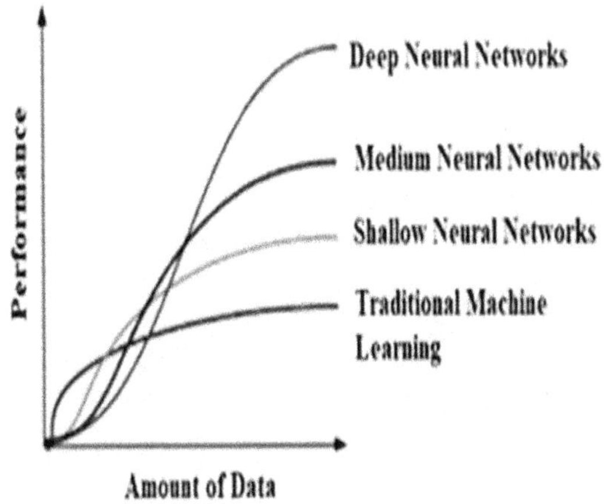

Consistent estimates emerge from frequent evaluation of large datasets, which eliminates judgment errors and inconsistencies. In the future, DL will continue to develop a name for it, both commercially and personally, and will continue to produce a great number of job opportunities.

TECHNIQUES OF DEEP LEARNING

Some complex problems are extremely tough for human minds to solve. In dealing with such challenges, certain features of the DL approach remain equally accurate and effective. Here's how many different types of DL Methods are discarded:

Classic Neural Networks (CNN)

CNN is also known as Fully Connected Neural Networks (FCNN), which is widely recognized as a result of multilayer perceptions, in which neurons remain connected at constant levels. Fran Rosenblatt, (Wang and Raj, 2017) an American psychologist invented it in 1958. There are hidden layers in addition to the input and output layers. The story is depicted in the diagram below.

Figure 3. Basic architecture of classic three-layer neural network.

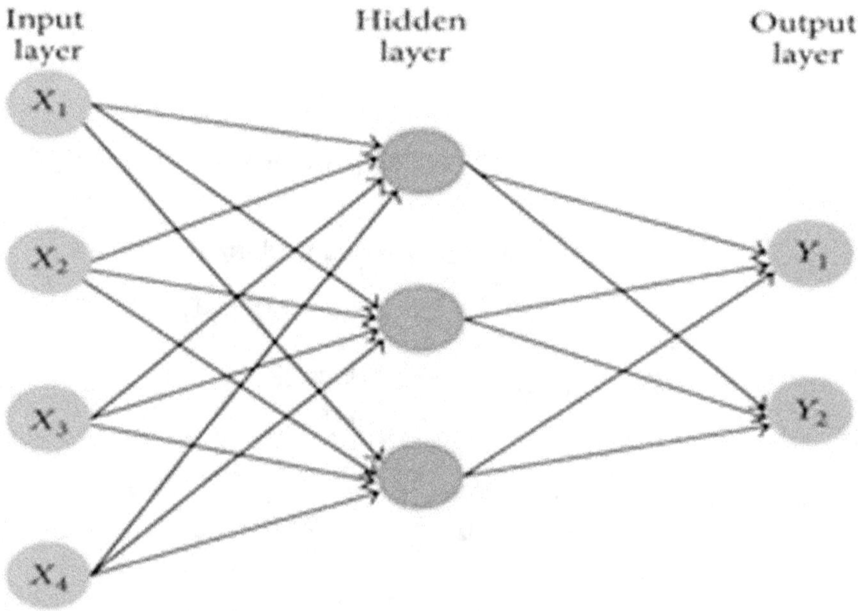

This includes the transformation of the model to the required binary data contribution. This model involves three functions (Albawi et al., 2017), namely:

Linear Function

To be correct, it identifies a solitary row that multiplies the input by an unchangeable factor.

Non-Linear Function

Any conclusion in use is necessarily non-linear in nature. Contrasting a decision means diversity, as well as following one of them. Additional options in the decision position are unexpectedly closed. Thus, it is not surprising that neural networks are essential for non-linearity, as they have to make decisions to control the flow of calculations.

Sigmoid Curve

This is a capacity that makes an interpretation of from 0 to 1 as a S-molded bend between its sections. The exaggerated digression (tan h) notices to the S-molded bend which differs from - 1 towards 1 (Han et al., 2021).

Rectified Linear Unit (ReLU)

ReLU is a solitary point work that profits 0 if the information cost is not exactly the predefined esteem along these lines making a straight numerous if the info esteem is more prominent than the predetermined worth. The best way to deal with some table datasets is to design lines and segments in CSV arrangement and issue relapse by genuine expense input (Ying et al., 2019). Any model is best with maximum flexibility, just like Artificial Neural Networks (ANNs)

Convolution Neural Networks (CNN)

CNN is a modern then immense conceivable sort of normal ANN model. Subsequently, intended to address more noteworthy complexity, preprocessing and information total. It holds references after the succession of neurons exist in the visual cortex of a creature's cerebrum.

It (Isono et al., 2020) perhaps measured as the highly effective adaptable model for concentrating in image along with non-pictorial information. There are following associations:

1. It consists of a solitary input layer, usually a 2D collection of neurons meant for data analysis of the main image, which is related to the pixels of the image.
2. Some CNNs have a 1D surface (layer) of the final product neuron that processes digital photos at inputs via an extended linked dividing surface area.
3. CNNs additionally have a third layer, perceived as an example layer, to tie the quantity of neurons in the equivalent network layers.
4. For the most part, CNNs have single or different associated layers that convey the example to the final yield layer.

This network model can assist and extract suitable data about image in a method of fewer components or parts. As soon as the data to be taken as input is introduced into the convolutional model, there are four phases associated with the formation of CNN:

Figure 4. Convolution Neural Networks (CNN) working procedure.

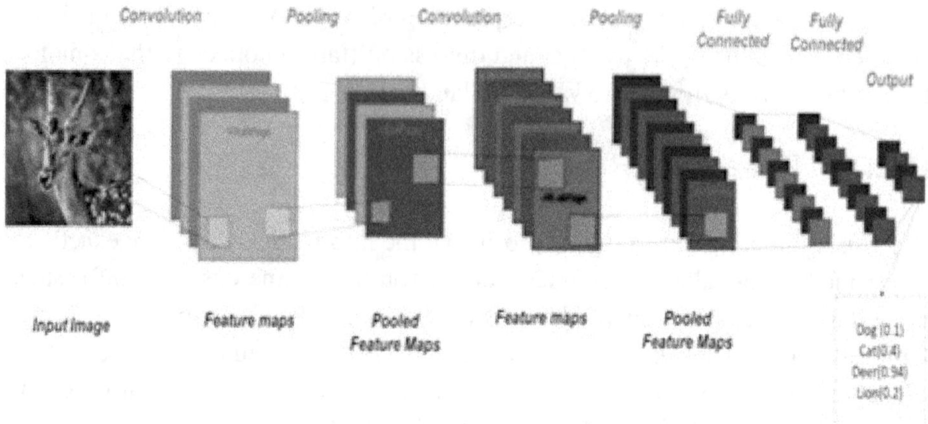

Convolution

The technique produces include maps from input information, followed by a capacity that chips away at this guide.

Max-Pooling

This assists CNN understand an image built on specific variations.

Flattening

Therefore, the data engendered is then compressed for a CNN to examine. Therefore, the data generated for a CNN test are compressed.

Full Connection

This is over and again assigned as a secret layer that joins the misfortune work for a model.

CNNs with picture identification, picture investigation, picture division, video examination, and normal language handling are adequate for obligation. On the other hand, where the CNN network can be a valuable estimate, there may be additional settings:

Photo datasets revolve around OCR document analysis at this moment. One-dimensional can be added by changing any two-dimensional input data for quick analysis. The model wants to be concerned with its structural design in order to produce the output.

Recurrent Neural Networks (RNNs)

RNNs are primarily conceived to aid the prediction sequence. This type of networks relies completely on arrangements of data of variable input spans.

RNN determines (Heck and Salem, 2017) the acquired information as an input value for existing estimates as opposed to its previous class. Therefore, it very well may be gainful to acquire momentary memory in an organization, impact the employable authority of stock value deviations, or extra time-arranged information plans.

Figure 5. Recurrent Neural Network (RNN) structure.

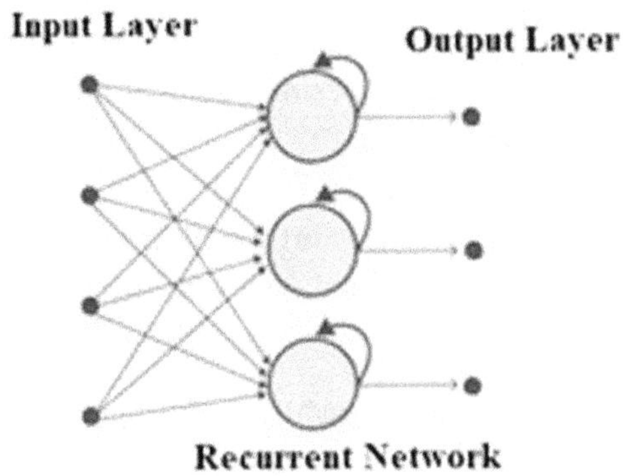

There are two common types of RNN techniques work extensively to assess a problem. Such type of systems namely:

LSTMs

They are convenient to predict data in time progressions through memory. The input, output and forget are three different gates.

Gated RNNs

They are similarly valuable in anticipating information of time arrangements through memory. The first is an update and the second is a reset within the dual gates.

RNNs work finest within:

1. **One to one:** A sole input associated with only output, such as an image organization.
2. **One to many:** The solitary input is associated with the output frameworks, identified with picture inscribing that contains various contentions from a sole picture.
3. **Many to one:** A grouping of data sources that produce a solitary output, for instance: word feeling order.
4. **Many to many:** Succession of data sources creating legacy of outputs like video recording. It rehearses language interpretation, discussion displaying just as more widely.

Generative Adversarial Networks

Generative Adversarial Network is an intersection of two DL techniques for neural organizations, to be specific: a generator and a discriminator. Albeit the generator network gathers counterfeit data, the discriminator administrations segregate among real and wrong information.

Commonly networks are feasible (Bin et al., 2021), in light of the fact that the generator creates fake information separate from the genuine information - other than the discriminator sees interminably genuine just as incredible information without

Figure 6. Recurrent Neural Network (RNN) structure.

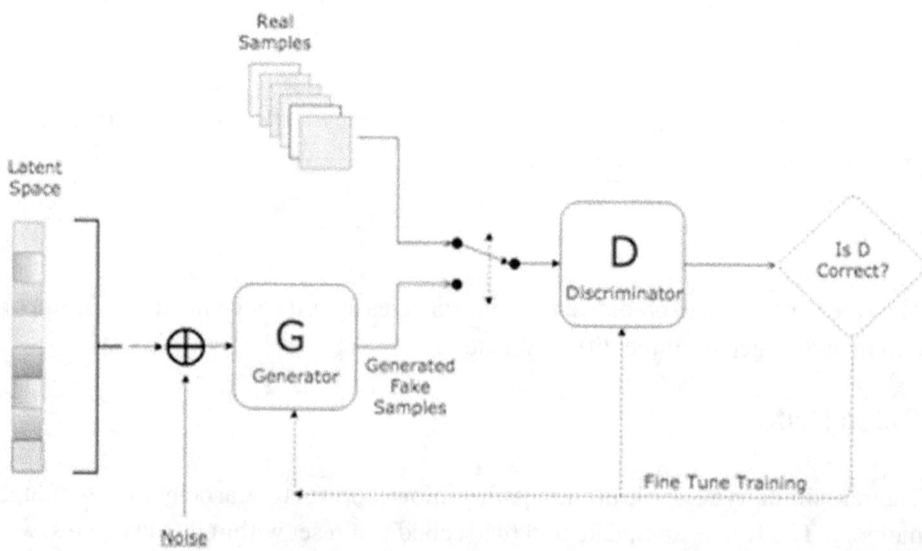

segregation. There are circumstances where the need to make a library of images is vital, the generator organization will make recreated information in solid pictures. A short time later, a de-convolution neural organization is made.

Here, an image detector network is introduced to distinguish among original then bogus images. Initially through an attempt of 50% exactness, the detector wants to establish the value of its cataloging because the generator will make its artificial image improved within generations. Such competition will complete the subsidy on the efficiency and speed of the network.

These drives are finest in image and text formation, improvement of images, innovative drug detection methods.

Self-Organizing Maps

Self-organized maps (SOMs) are unproven data support efforts that reduce the quantity of arbitrary variables within a prototypical. The output quantity is mobile as a two-dimensional model, since the individual synapses are connected to its I/O nodes.

Since the individual data points participate in the model illustration, (Yin, 2008) keeps track of the weight of the adjacent nodes or the Best Matching Units (BMUs). Built near the BMU, the value for the weight deviates. Since weights are

Figure 7. Basic model of self-organizing map neural network.

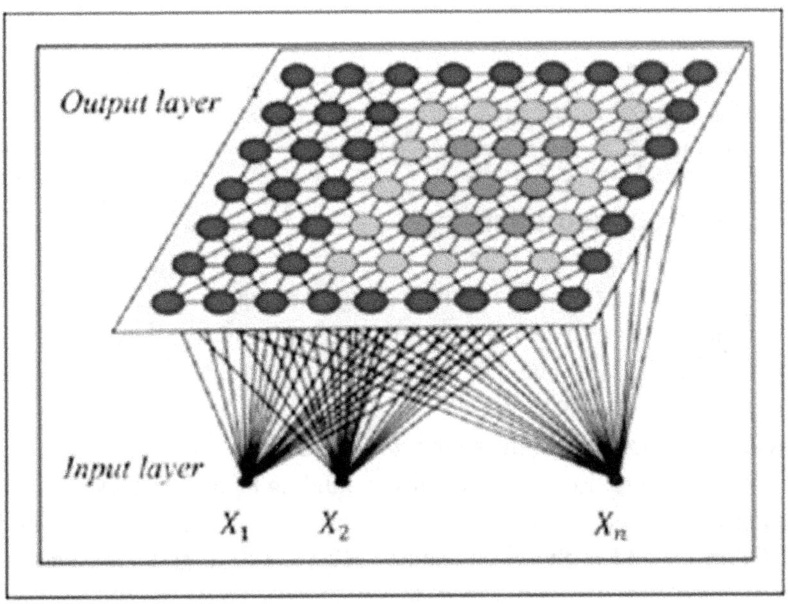

recognized like a property of a node, the cost indicates the place where the node is placed within network.

Boltzmann Machines

Aforementioned network model does not appear in either determined order then as a result the nodes are linked in a rounded pattern (Hinton, 2011) as shown in the figure. From such uniqueness, these DL methods are produced model limitations. Unlike its predecessors in the fully determinant network model, the Boltzmann machine model is characterized as stochastic.

Figure 8. Boltzmann machine.

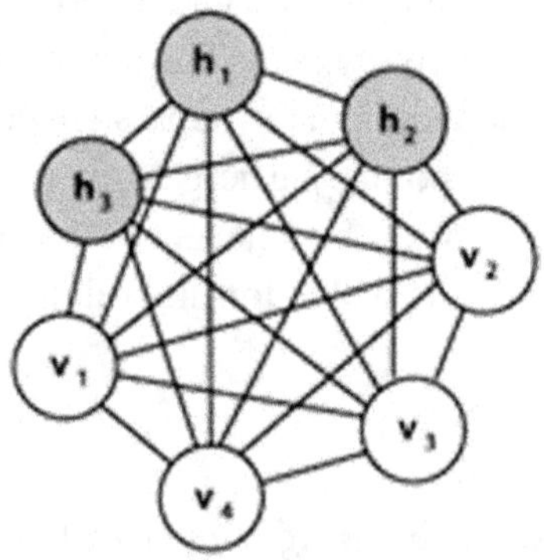

It makes relentless efforts in monitoring the system, introducing binary endorsement platforms, detailed dataset analysis, step-by-step approach to AI structure formation.

Deep Reinforcement Learning

Such learning denotes the method where an agent reaches out with the environment for considering the state of deep reinforcement learning to adjust its state. Agents can be witnesses and fair measures, as a result, help agents give a network its purpose through state cooperation (Mousavi et al., 2016).

This network model contains an input layer, an output layer, then various secret layers, while the condition of the actual surrounding is the input layer. Such model endeavor in a consistent work to expect the approaching compensation of individual accomplishment held in the circumstance accepted. It attempts its best in board games namely chess, poker, self-drive vehicles, mechanical technology, stock administration, resource evaluating and so forth.

Figure 9. Deep Reinforcement Learning.

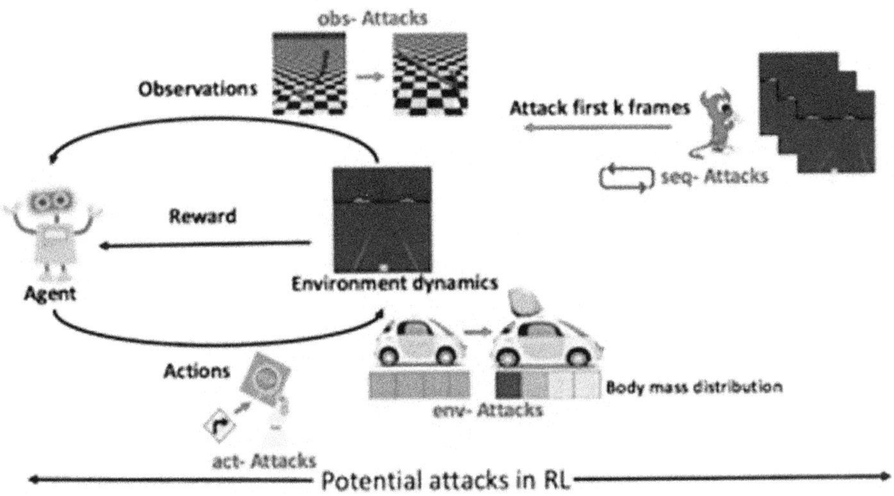

Auto Encoders

Among the highest level of regular routine areas for the DL practice, this model works mechanically remain on its bits of feedbacks, already satisfying an enactment capacity and completing yield deciphering (Yusiong and Naval, 2019). Along these lines, building up a boundary peril creates less sorts of information and augments the increase of the inward information structure.

There are different Kinds of Auto-encoders:

Sparse

Where secret layers surpass the input level produces space to diminish over fitting with the objective of speculation. This confines the expense work, accordingly totally keeps away from the auto encoder in the wake of exaggerating its hubs.

De-Noising

Now, an advanced type of input is randomly converted to 0.

Figure 10. Basic structure of Auto encoder.

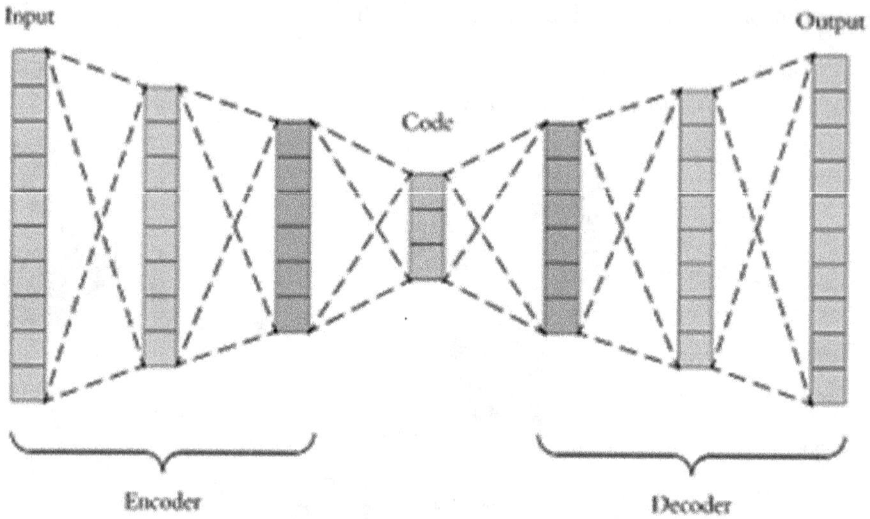

Contractive

It is adding a penalty factor to the damage function for over fitting the hidden layer and copying the data to hide the input layer.

Stacked

In an auto encoder, when additional hidden layers are added, it takes two stages of encoding at one stage of decoding.

It makes the best effort in character identification, establishes a mandatory recommendation model, and improves the structure of huge datasets.

Back Propagation

In DL, the back-prop method is mentioned by way of a necessary tool for neural networks to find little mistakes in data estimates. Propagation, alternatively, refers to the communication of data in a certain way through a devoted network. The whole structure can strive to deliver signals in the way of instantaneous progress of the conclusion and in contrast leads behind any data related to the limitations of the network.

Initially, the network evaluates the constraints and resolves the data, next, it is weighed by a loss function, thirdly, the recognized error is propagated backwards to self-adjust any inappropriate constraints. It tries its finest in data debugging.

Figure 11. Different types of Auto encoder.

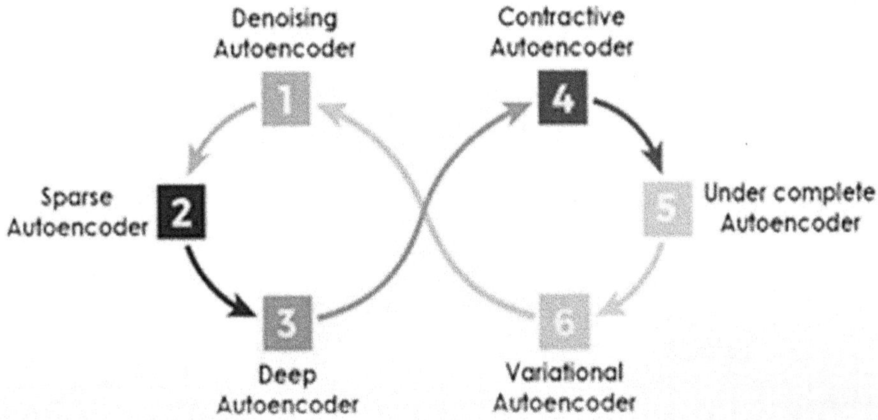

Figure 12. Back-prop procedure.

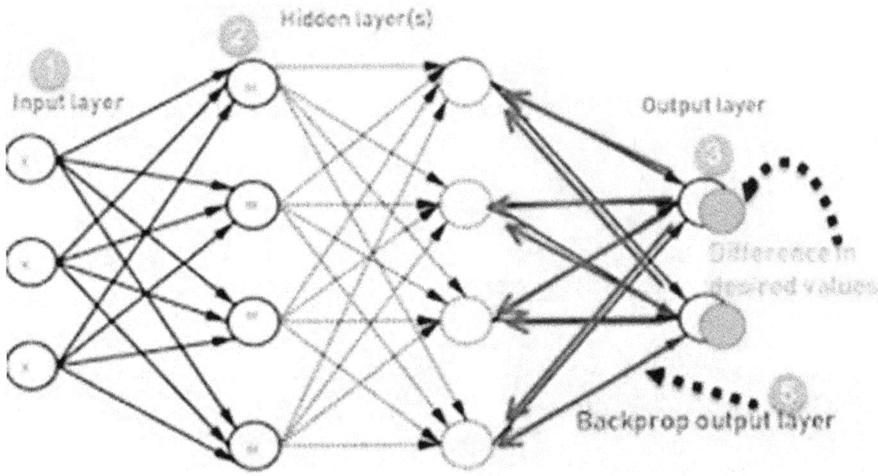

Gradient Descent

A gradient mention to an opal that has quantifiable perceptions then might point to an association between variables in a mathematical context. In this method of DL, the connection between the errors that occurred with the data parameter in the neural network perhaps identified as "x" then "y". Variables are already changing frequently in a neural network, so the error may be magnified otherwise reduced by small size deviations.

Figure 13. Gradient Descent with dimensions.

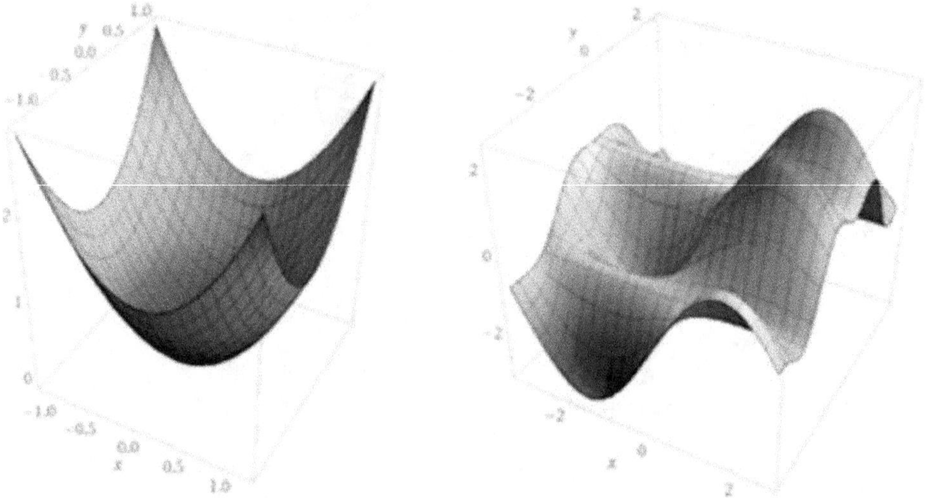

Numerous experts have envisioned the method as a stream route coming down the approach gradient. A similar strategy is to get the neutral best resolution. Subsequently some local minimum resolutions exist in a neural network, where data can be stuck then slowly, leading to inappropriate storage. There is a practice of refraining from such measures.

DEEP LEARNING APPLICATIONS

This segment defines the basis of this discussion on a number of grounds that are realistic with the DL Algorithm.

Automatic Speech Recognition (ASR)

Google has publicized that Google Voice Search has improved its services, using Deep Neural Networks (DNN) in 2012 as a necessary technology to model words in a language. DNN has exchanged Gaussian blending models that have been in the industry for 30 years. Similarly, DNN has shown that it is more intelligent to measure what words a user is generating at each prompt in a timely manner and by doing so they clearly bring enhanced speech recognition accuracy.

In 2013, DL ASR and ML together increased the total pair. DL is primarily related to the practice of different levels of non-linear revolution for the production of speech

Figure 14. An Automatic Speech Recognition (ASR) technique.

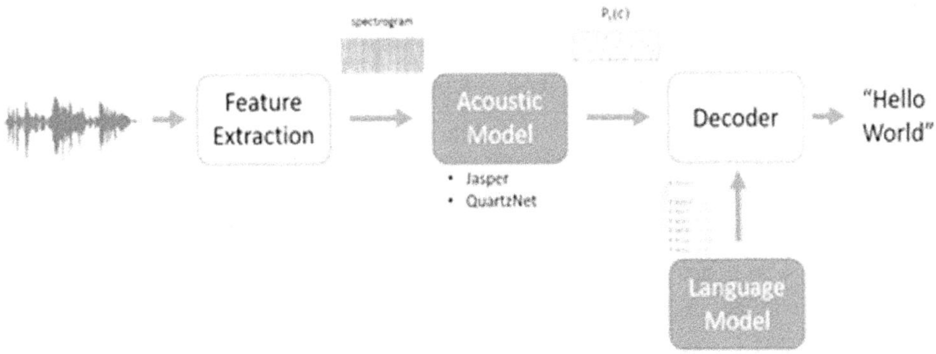

structures, although there are examples-based figure exercises for speech structures through thin layer learning that have high levels but are characteristically empty.

Image Recognition

Deep max-pooling involuntary neural networks are practiced to understand mitosis in breast histology images. Mitosis is really hard to recognize. Indeed, mitosis is a compound process in which the nucleus of a cell undergoes numerous changes. In this style, DNN is used as a conventional pixel classifier that enables raw pixel values

Figure 15. Traditional vs. DL Image Recognition technique.

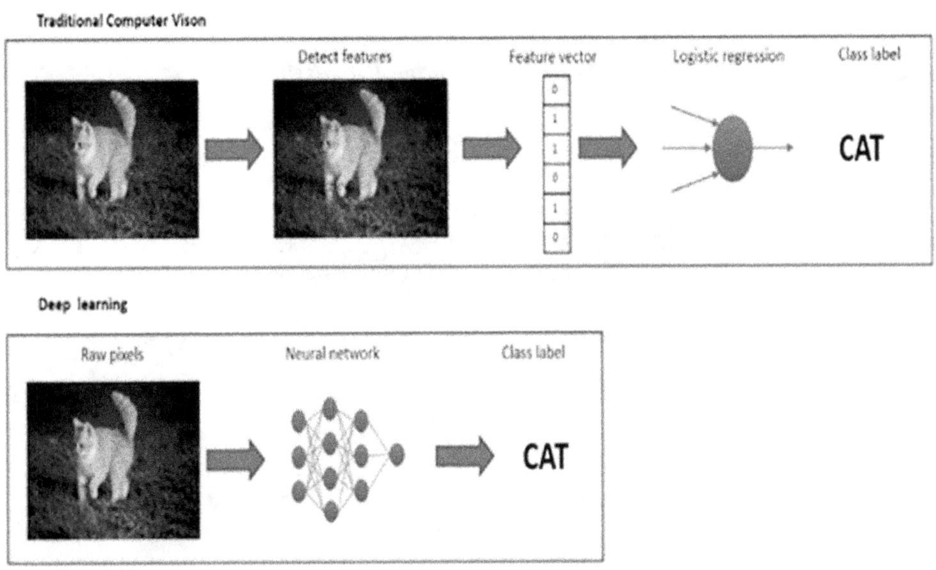

and does not require any human input. Subsequently, DNN inevitably acquires a set of graphic structures from the training data. DNN knowingly overcomes a completely challenging system through a well-established and controlled computational effort on a widely accessible dataset: a typical laptop has insufficient minutes to process a 4MPixel image.

The ImageNet LSVRC-2010 Encounter completes a large and deep CNN to categorize 1.2 million high-resolution images into 1000 diverse categories. According to the assessment data, they have accomplished top-1 and top-5 error rates of 37.5% and 17.0%, which has improved significantly in earlier practices. From all tests Introduction of faster GPUs as well as use of larger datasets can enhance the results.

Natural Language Processing

Nowadays, an assortment of language and information retrieval applications uses DL methods in a large scale.

Utilizing deep architecture, DL techniques hide structures from training information and features are suitable for any work of different levels of abstraction. A succession of Deep Structured Semantic Models (DSSM) was planned for Web search was introduced in 2013. Precisely, the use of DNN to rank several credentials (documents) for a specific query described here:

Initially a non-linear scheme is achieved so that the query can be mapped to a shared semantic space alongside the document. Previously, specified the importance of specific documents, the query was designed as cosine parallels among their vectors in that semantic space.

Figure 16. Basic structure of Natural Language Processing.

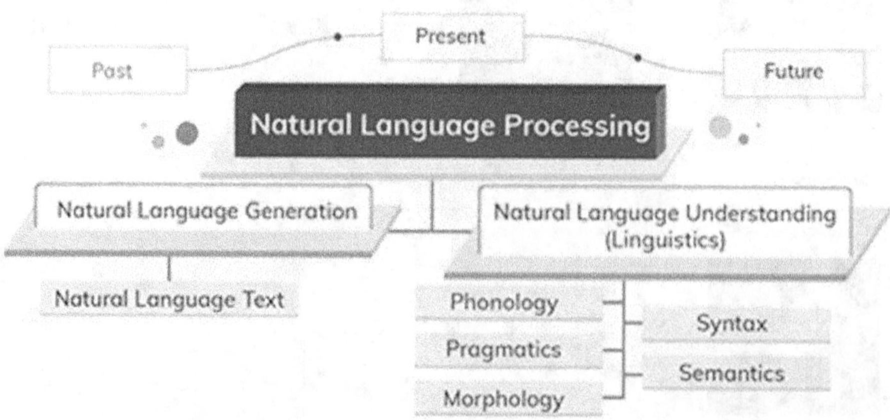

Neural network presentation is individually very efficient. They use click-through data as a temporary possibility of the document being clicked. Here it is given that the question is capitalized as required. New models in a web document position job are evaluated through an attested and actual data set.

Drug Discovery and Toxicology

Quantitative Structure Analysis / Predictive Analysis (QSAR / QSPR) are an attempt to formulate mathematical models related to the physical and chemical properties of composites in their chemical composition. Multi-task learning is effective for QSAR using several neural network presentations. They utilized a counterfeit neural organization to concentrate on a capacity that anticipated the activity of a composite for a long time simultaneously. The plan has been joined through elective procedures and has recently been depicted to represent those neural organizations, including performing various tasks, which can convey provocative great outcomes in the pattern of shapes through irregular forest.

Figure 17. Steps of Drug Discovery using DL.

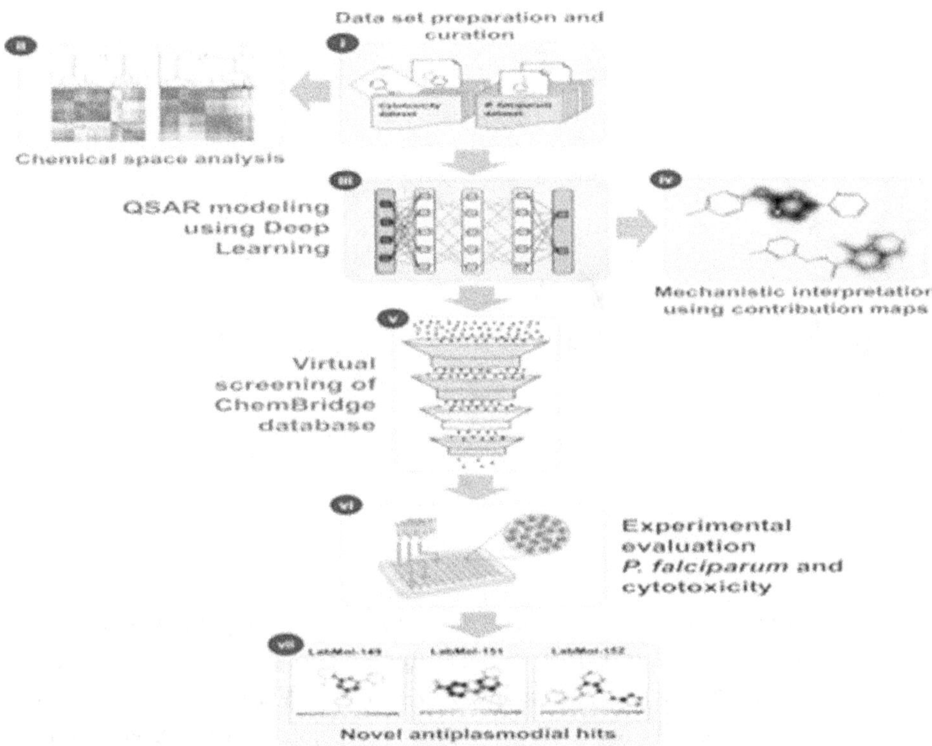

In 2015, AtomNet has been presented as unique construction based, profound CNN which intended to anticipate the bioactivity of little particles for drug disclosure submissions. This paper additionally shows how to apply the convolutional ideas of component area and various leveled structure to the demonstrating of bioactivity and compound communications. AtomNet outflanks past docking approaches on an assorted arrangement of benchmarks by a huge degree, accomplishing an AUC more noteworthy than 0.9 on 57.8% of the objectives in the DUDE standard.

Customer Relationship Management

A structure for independent control of a client relationship, the board framework been outlined. Initially, an altered adaptation of the broadly acknowledged Recency-Frequency-Monetary Value arrangement of measurements can be utilized to characterize the state space of customers or givers are investigated. Second, a strategy to decide the ideal direct promoting activity in discrete and nonstop activity space for the given individual, in view of his situation in the state space is portrayed.

Figure 18. Customer Relationship Management in DL.

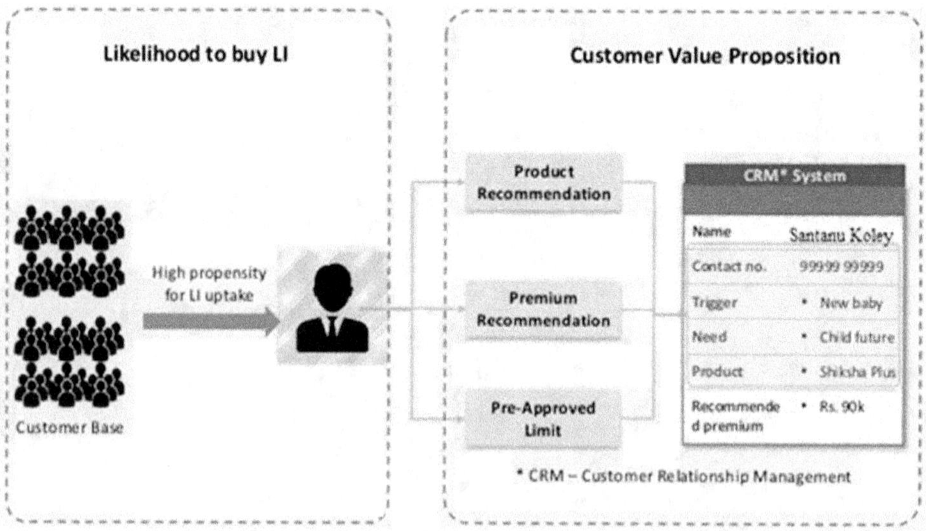

The system includes the utilization of sans model Q-figuring out how to prepare a profound neural organization that joins a customer's situation in the state space to accolades related with conceivable advertising exercises. The assessed esteem work over the customer state space can be deciphered as client lifetime esteem (CLV), and subsequently considers a fast module assessment of CLV for a given customer. Test results are introduced, in light of Knowledge Discovery and Data Mining Tools Competition, mailing dataset of gift requesting.

Recommendation Systems

Programmed music suggestion has turned into an undeniably important issue as of late, since a ton of music is presently sold and devoured carefully. Most recommender frameworks depend on collective sifting. In 2013, proposed to utilize an idle factor model for suggestion, and anticipate the inert variables from music sound when they can't be gotten from utilization information. Conventional methodology is looked at utilizing sack of-words portrayal of the sound signs with profound convolutional neural organizations and the expectations is assessed by quantitatively and subjectively on the Million Song Dataset. The outcome shows that the new advances in DL make an interpretation of to the music proposal setting, with profound convolutional neural organizations essentially outflanking the conventional methodology.

Figure 19. Recommendation System structure in DL.

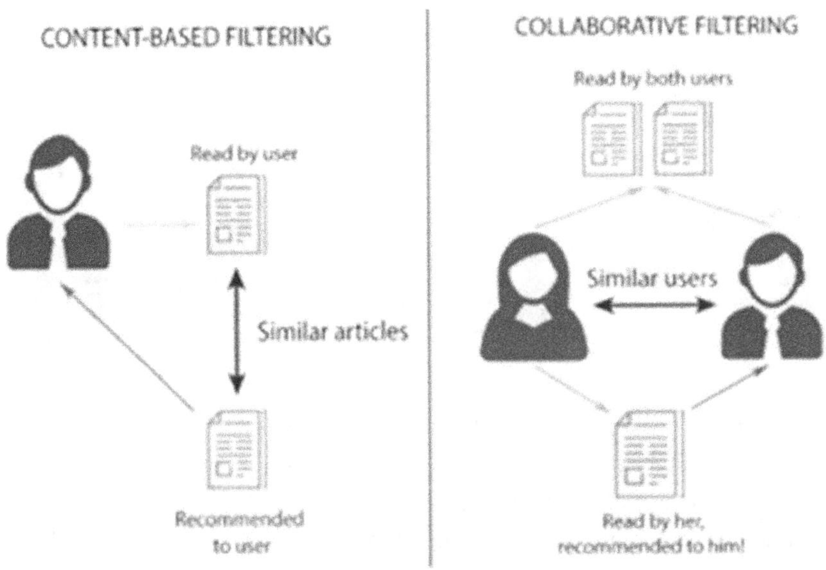

Ongoing internet-based administrations depend vigorously on programmed personalization to prescribe significant substance to an enormous number of clients. This expects frameworks to scale quickly to oblige the flood of new clients visiting the web-based administrations interestingly. In 2015 proposed a substance-based suggestion framework to address both the proposal quality and the framework adaptability. They additionally proposed to utilize a rich list of capabilities to address clients, as indicated by their web perusing history and search inquiries. They utilize a DL way to deal with map clients and things to a dormant space where the similitude among clients and their favored things is expanded. Versatility investigation show that the multi-view DNN model can without much of a stretch scale to incorporate large number of clients and billions of thing passages.

Bioinformatics

The explanation of genomic data is a significant test in science and bioinformatics. Existing information bases of realized quality capacities are deficient and inclined to mistakes, and the bimolecular analyses expected to further develop these data sets are slow and expensive. While computational strategies are not a substitute for trial confirmation, they can help in two ways: calculations can support the duration of quality explanations via naturally proposing errors, and they can anticipate beforehand unidentified quality capacities, speeding up the pace of quality capacity disclosure.

Figure 20. Deep Learning in Bioinformatics.

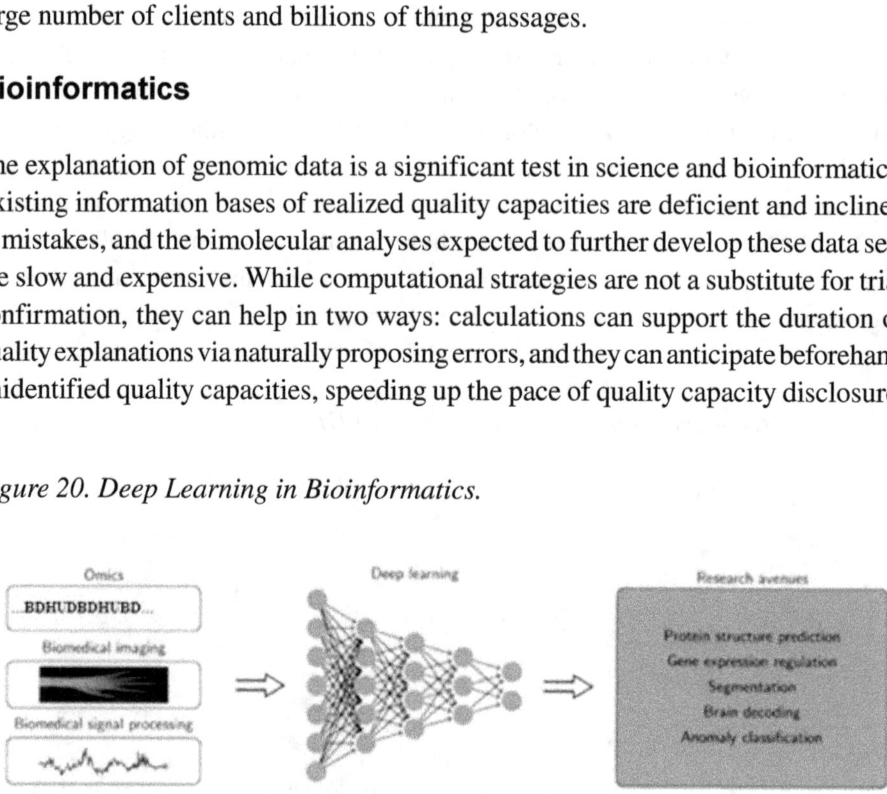

The objective utilizing profound auto encoder neural organizations is created. With probes quality explanation information from the Gene Ontology project, it shows that profound auto encoder networks accomplish preferred execution over other standard AI techniques, including the famous shortened particular worth deterioration.

DEEP LEARNING-BASED SOURCE IMAGE FORENSICS

With the development of modern techniques, digital imaging has become an important component in our daily life. It is easy for us to capture digital images with devices such as smart phones and digital reflex cameras, embellish them by using photo-editing software, and then upload them to social network platforms to share the important moments of our life with our friends. The ease with which we handle digital images, however, is a double-edged sword. Forged images are becoming more and more widespread in our life and seeing is no longer believing (Zhu et al., 2004; Farid, 2006), especially with the advent of techniques based on artificial intelligence (AI) such as generative adversarial networks (GAN) (Cao et al., 2019) that can be exploited by malicious actors to spread "fake news" (Beridze and Butcher, 2019).

In order to verify the authenticity and integrity of a digital image, a number of techniques, known collectively as "digital image forensics" (Piva, 2013), were developed during the last years. Within this research area, source image forensics tries to answer the general question "where is this digital image from?", and to do so multiple sub-topics can be explored, represented in the following figure [Figure 21] as source camera identification, recaptured image forensic, computer graphics (CG) image forensic, GAN-generated image detection, and source social network identification.

In the past the task of source image forensics has been dealt with several algorithms based on statistical analysis and pattern recognition. More recently, improvements in computing capabilities sparked a renewed interest in techniques based on machine learning. In particular, DL-based schemes have been successfully applied in the field of source image forensics, and have proved their effectiveness in various competitions (Guan et al., 2019; Stamm et al., 2018).

Techniques based on artificial neural networks have been known for many years and have gone by many names. A series of breakthroughs in 2006 (Hinton et al., 2006; Bengio et al., 2007; Ranzato et al., 2007), however, made the use of deep neural networks viable and gave rise to the field known as DL (LeCun et al., 2015; Goodfellow et al., 2016).

After that, methods based on DL have consistently achieved remarkable results on a series of tasks such as handwritten digital recognition and image classification, often beating competing approaches based on conventional schemes. A number of specialized techniques have been developed in the field of computer vision, including convolutional neural networks (CNN), recurrent neural networks (RNN), and generative adversarial networks (GAN). Among them, CNNs have been shown to be effective when dealing with image-related tasks, and have been subsequently adopted as a basis for numerous digital image forensics methods.

Figure 21. The structure of the presented view.

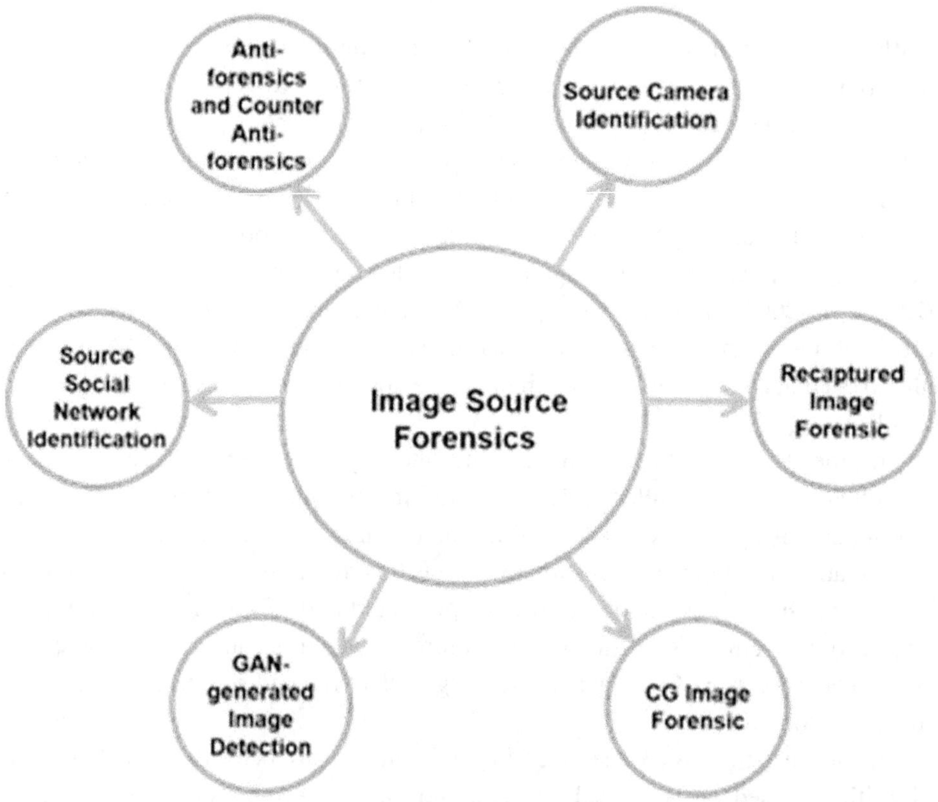

Basic components of CNNs consist mainly of convolutional layers, pooling layers, and activation functions, which are stacked together to construct the architecture of CNNs. According to (Khan et al., 2019) recent innovations in CNNs building and training can be categorized as structural reformulation, parameters optimizations, regularization, and loss function. Among those, structural reformulation plays the most important role in improving the performance, and can be divided into seven different classes: spatial exploitation, depth, multi-path, width, channel boosting, feature map exploitation, and attention based CNNs. Typical CNN architectures such as AlexNet (Krizhevsky et al., 2012), VGGNet (Simonyan and Zisserman, 2014), GoogleNet (Szegedy et al., 2015), ResNet (He et al., 2016), DenseNet (Huang et al., 2017), Xception (Chollet, 2017), SENet (Jie et al., 2017), Siamese Network (Chopra et al., 2018), are well known. We refer the interested reader to the review by (Khan et al., 2019), (Gu et al., 2018) for further details about deep learning.

The impressive results obtained by DL-based methods in image source forensics motivate us to provide a comprehensive review of those approaches in such a way as to allow a neophyte to come into this field with some help. In this paper, we did our best to collect all the related paper which have been published in journals, conferences, and arXiv. We observed that all of them have some common modules, and we propose a unifying framework where all these schemes fit, thus simplifying their comparison. The framework is visually represented in Figure 22. First, the input, a full resolution image, is usually cropped into small and fixed-size pixel patches. Then, all patches are processed, or a patch selection strategy can be applied to choose the patches that are more useful for the following task. Next, these patches can be pre-processed by a spatial filter to improve their signal-to-noise ratio (SNR). After that, they are fed to a convolutional neural network (CNN). Classification of a single patch can be achieved either by having a softmax layer at the end of the network, or by training a separate classifier on the features extracted by the last layer of the CNN. At the end, the classification result for the original image can be obtained by voting among the pixel patches. It should be noted that our general framework includes all the ideas used in the methods that we have reviewed; until now, however, no single method is using all those techniques. In Figure 22, optional parts are denoted by a dotted contour. Starting from the general framework, we have divided the reviewed algorithms in the following five separate sub-sections, according to their main contributions:

1. Adoption of traditional convolutional neural networks (T.CNN) for source camera identification tasks;
2. Improvement of performance by using data enhancement (D.A.), including data augmentation and data preprocessing;
3. Improvement of performance through fusion and ensemble (F./E.);
4. Improvement of performance by means of patch selection (P.S.);
5. Adoption of different classifiers (C.).

The most significant network parameters of the reviewed works are summarized in Table 1 and Table2. Then, in Tables 3 and 4, we have summarized the experimental settings and the performance achieved by those architectures, as well as by some conventional CNNs.

The remaining part of this review is organized as follows. First of all, in Section 2 the DL-based methods that deal with the most important topic of this area, i.e., source camera identification is described. In Sections 3 to 6 an overview on the methods dealing with the remaining sub-topics: recaptured image forensic, CG image forensic, GAN-generated image detection, and source social network identification, respectively is presented. In Section 7 anti-forensics and counter-anti-forensics algorithms based on DL methods is described. A description of the results obtained

Figure 22. The framework of the deep learning-based algorithms for source forensics. (Section X.X) indicates the subsection where the related technique is described in detail.

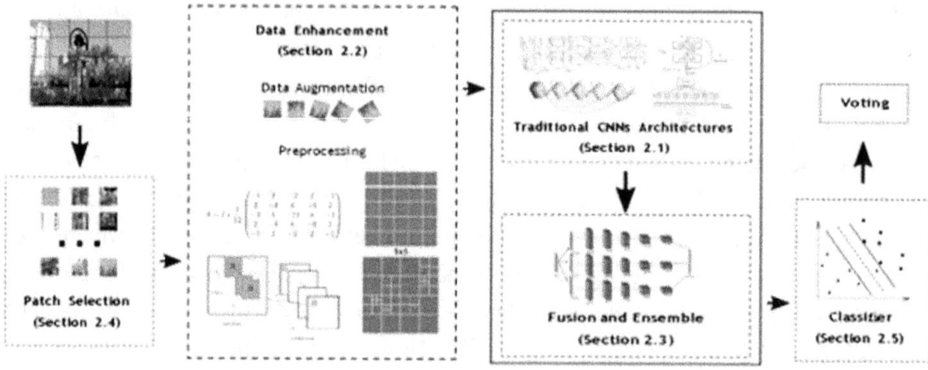

by the described techniques will be given in Section 8. Finally, in Section9, we will provide our analysis and conclusion on deep learning-based source image forensics.

SOURCE CAMERA IDENTIFICATION

One of the hot topics in multimedia forensics is source camera identification, the purpose of which is to trace where an image is from Identifying the source camera is an important step in pointing out the owner of illicit images (e.g., crime scenes, terroristic act scenes, etc.) and ensuring the security and trustworthiness of such digital data.

Traditional Convolutional Neural Networks (T.CNN)

Early works focused on applying to the problem of source camera identification traditional convolutional neural networks consisting of stacked convolutional layers. To the best of our knowledge, DL-based schemes for source camera identification were firstly introduced by (Baroffio et al., 2016). This path-breaking method used a simple architecture with five layers, including three convolutional steps and two fully connected layers, working on 48 × 48 patches. The authors tested their network for both instance-level and model-level camera identification, obtaining accuracies of 29.8% and 72.9%, respectively. Moreover, model-level camera identification increased to 94.1%on full resolution images with a voting strategy on the respective image patches. Focusing on images captured by mobile phones, which nowadays are the most popular image acquisition devices, (Freire-Obregón et al., 2019) proposed a six-layer CNN architecture, including two convolutional layers, one max pooling layer and three fully connected layers. The activation function used in this work was the Leaky Rectified Linear Unit (L-ReLU) which, as reported by the authors, led to slightly better performance than those obtained by using ReLU activations. Then, (Huang et al., 2018) presented an architecture similar to the one proposed by (Baroffio et al., 2016), and the authors were able to improve over the accuracy obtained by (Freire-Obregón et al., 2019) by using Batch Normalization and more convolutional layers. Following along the line of deeper CNN architectures, (Yao et al., 2017) (code available at https://github.com/grasses/Camera-Identification) put forward a 13-layer convolutional neural network. The proposed method is robust against JPEG compression and noise adding; however, it is not resistant to re-scaling operation.

(Chen et al., 2017) investigated the use of a residual neural network (ResNet) with 26 layers for source camera identification, and proved its effectiveness with multiple experiments: the accuracies obtained for brand-, model-, and device-level identification were 99.12%, 94.73%, and 45.81%, respectively. According to their paper, ResNethas better performance than AlexNet, GoogleNet, and the scheme from (Baroffio et al., 2016). (Ding et al., 2019) extended this last method by combining ResNet architecture with a multi-task learning strategy, further improving the performance. The three tasks (brand-level, model-level, and sensor-level classification) are integrated into one framework and share the weights of the CNN architecture.

Several works (Marra et al., 2018; Stamm et al., 2018; Kamal et al., 2018; Kuzin et al., 2018; Ferreira et al., 2018), applied to source camera identification new architectures from computer vision such as DenseNet, XceptionNet. (Marra et al., 2018) used XceptionNet to obtain overall accuracies of 95.15% for pixel patches and 99.31% for the full resolution image by using a voting strategy.

All the works cited so far are intended to solve source camera identification in a closed-set scenario, where there is the assumption that we have a perfect knowledge of all the devices that could possibly capture the query images, which means that the acquisition devices for test data are the same used for acquiring training data. A more realistic case, however, is the open-set scenario, where information about query images is not completely known. Recently, a number of DL methods for this more challenging scenario have been proposed. (Bayar and Stamm, 2018) presented two different schemes to address the open-set problem for camera model identification, which aims to judge whether the device that captured the query image is known or unknown. The first one uses, in place of a classification layer, a confidences core mapping with a thresholding strategy to evaluate whether the true source camera model is known or unknown. The other approach uses a different classifier on features extracted by a CNN. (Mayer and Stamm, 2018) tried to measure similarity among images by using a siamese network. Features are extracted from the last layer of a CNN and fed into a siamese network to learn a measurement of source similarity, which allows for verifying if two query images are captured by same device or not.

It should be noted that the evolution of CNN architectures proposed for Source Camera Identification tasks closely follow the one of architectures proposed for computer vision tasks. This is somewhat to be expected as CNNs are well-suited for that kind of tasks, and thus a great deal of research on neural architectures produced by the community was focused on solving those problems.

Given the encouraging results obtained so far, it is logical to assume that the forensics community will keep on building on new CV architectures.

Data Enhancement (D.E.)

Data enhancement, including data augmentation and pre-processing, has been widely used as an effective way to improve the performance when dealing with computer vision tasks. These techniques have also been adopted for source camera identification schemes. (Bondi et al., 2017), (Bondi et al., 2017) normalized the images by subtracting the pixel-wise mean value, which is a popular way to center the data and helps the network to learn faster. (Kamal et al., 2018) applied five different data augmentation operations: random crops, random rotations, image manipulations (including JPEG compression, gamma correlation, and resizing), images addition, and empirical mode decomposition. It should be noted that the authors increased the training set size by collecting more images from Flickr (https://www.flickr.com/).The results demonstrated that adding more images has a great impact to performance: considering that DL-based methods are data-driven, increasing the number of training examples definitely leads to higher detection accuracies. Team GPU_muscle (Stamm et al., 2018; Kuzin et al., 2018) collected more than 500 GiB of photos from various resources (Flickr, Yandex. Fotki, Wikipedia Commons, mobile reviews, and others) and obtained an accuracy of more than 98% by training traditional CNNs. In addition, using manipulated images such as enhanced images with gamma correction, JPEG compressed images, and images transformed by resampling operation, to some extent, enhances the robustness of the CNN model.

Preprocessing techniques to improve the signal-to-noise ratio (SNR) of input data have been introduced following the intuition that the main difference between computer vision and image source identification tasks lies in the importance of image contents. Usually, computer vision tasks are seriously dependent on the image contents, whereas the opposite is true when dealing with source camera identification. In the latter case, the correct class to be attributed to an example is heavily dependent on the noise component introduced by camera acquisition. Based on this observation, some research (Bayar and Stamm, 2017; Tuama et al., 2016;

Zuo, 2018; Wang et al., 2018; Yang et al., 2017) proposed to reduce the interference of the image contents using two kinds of preprocessing. The first technique is based on the idea of applying a denoising filter F to the input Image I, and then subtracting the result of that operation from I itself, thus obtaining the noise N:

$$N=I-F(I). \qquad (1)$$

(Tuama et al., 2016) chose a wavelet-based denoiser, as filters of that kind have been widely used in model-based schemes based on Photo Response Non-Uniformity (PRNU) for source camera identification. (Bayar and Stamm, 2017) evaluated the effect of a median filter with 3 × 3 windows (MFR). These second preprocessing technique is based on the idea that the noise can be easily obtained by using a spatial filter G:

$$N = I * G \qquad (2)$$

(Tuama et al., 2016) also tested the effectiveness of a high-pass (HP) filter. According to that work, HP filters yield better results than wavelet-based denoiser when used in CNN-based schemes. (Ding et al., 2019) evaluated the case of gaussian filter residuals with three scales (3 × 3, 5 × 5, 7 × 7) and verified their effectiveness.

Following the idea of spatial filters, (You et al., 2017), (Yang et al., 2017) presented self-learning filters as a way to further improve the SNR. Self-learning filters can be trained together with the rest of the network. Inspired by SPAM features (Pevny et al. 2010), (Bayar and Stamm, 2018) (code available at https://gitlab.com/MISLgit/constrained-conv-TIFS2018) proposed a novel constrained convolution which ensures that learned high-pass filters are within a given bound. In particular, the central weight of the convolutional kernel is set to−1 and the sum of the other weights is equal to 1. Instead of designing the filter, (Wang et al., 2018) used local binary patterns (LBP) to code the image. The images are first processed by LBP coding operation in the preprocessing step, and then fed into CNN architecture. Self-learning filters, constrained convolutions, and LBP coding are reported to outperform high-pass filters.

Recently, (Zuo, 2018) evaluated how the performance of CNN models is impacted by the use of two preprocessing techniques: laplacian gaussian smoothing filters and non-local means denoising filters. Results indicate that the CNN model without pre-procession provides better performances. The possible explanation from perspective of the training data and strategy are given. It should be noted, however, that the dataset used was only composed of images captured by three camera models, and that the number of epochs during training phase was small due to limitations in the available computing power. For these reasons, extended experiments should be conducted to verify the effect of preprocessing in future.

The analysis of data enhancement techniques used in source camera identification tasks highlight an important difference with respect to classical DE methods used in machine learning. Commonly used augmentation algorithms used by the ML community focus on helping the network become rotation- or scale-invariant by presenting image contents in different conditions. In source camera identification tasks, on the contrary, most DE technique aims to reduce the influence of image contents by filtering out information deemed not useful. As those two classes of enhancement methods are not mutually exclusive, future works could attempt to combine them to come up with a more comprehensive way to make the network more robust.

Fusion and Ensemble (F./E.)

Fusion and ensemble strategies aim to enhance performance by fusing multiple models and features together. (Yang et al., 2017) constructed a content-adaptive fusion network by merging three models together, thus significantly increasing the overall accuracy with respect to the single models. (Bayar and Stamm, 2017) combined constrained convolutions and MFR at the first layer of the CNN architecture and obtained a slight improvement over a constrained CNN. (Kamal et al., 2018) used the ensemble feature of DenseNet201 trained using three image scales (64 × 64, 128 × 128, 256 × 256), which is beneficial to the CNN model. (Ferreira et al., 2018) proposed to integrate Inception Net and XceptionNet architectures to boost performance.

Patch Selection (P.S.)

It is well known that the PRNU noise that can be extracted from an image is related with its contents. Smooth, non-saturated areas with high luminance are good for PRNU estimation. Furthermore, content-adaptive processes such as CFA demosaicing and JPEG compression can be applied during image acquisition. Therefore, choosing different areas in the image could have some effect on the performance. Based on this fact, a good strategy for choosing the best pixel patches to be used for CNN training can be essential to obtain higher performance. (Bondi et al., 2016) (code available at https://github.com/polimi-ispl/camera-model-identification-with-cnn) only select for training the pixel patches whose average values are close to half of the image dynamic range. Another criterion for patch selection, which aims to find the better textured pixel patches with the half of the image dynamic, was proposed by (Kamal et al., 2018), (Bondi et al., 2017). In this approach the quality value for a pixel patch is computed from its variance and mean. Pixel patches with higher measure value are used to train the CNN model. (Güera et al., 2018) proposed a CNN-based solution to estimate, for each pixel patch, a value representing the camera-model-attribution reliability. (Yang et al., 2019) adopted a different approach where pixel patches were separated into three subsets according to their mean and variance. Then, a different CNN model would be trained on each subset. Finally, query pixel patches would be classified using the model corresponding to their characteristics.

It appears that, currently, the dynamic range of a patch is considered to be the best descriptor for its usefulness for the task at hand. Experimental results confirm that such an approach is sensible. It would however be interesting to explore more diverse descriptor, perhaps taking into account the peculiarities of the neural network that will be subsequently used to classify the selected patches.

Classifier (C.)

Some computer vision works (Tang, 2013; Chen and Wang, 2014; Abdulnabi et al., 2015) claim that using a separate SVM classifier on the features learned by a CNN instead of a softmax layer can improve classification performance. In the same way, some image forensics researchers have recently explored if the adoption of different classifiers can improve the performance. In particular, (Huang et al., 2018), (Kamal et al., 2018), (Bondi et al., 2017), (Bondi et al., 2017) and (Bayar and Stamm, 2017), (Bayar and Stamm, 2017) proposed two-stage learning strategies by feeding the features extracted by a CNN model into a different classifier such as a Support Vector Machine (SVM), Extremely Randomized Trees (ERT), cosine similarity measure, nearest means core, and deep learning architecture with squeeze and excitation block. The results confirm that these classifiers can achieve better performance with respect to simple softmax layers.

Summary

The most significant network parameters and the experimental settings of the reviewed works are summarized in Table 1, where we have identified twelve main architectures (using the short name A1, A2, …, A12). Then, in Table 3 we have summarized the experimental settings and the performance achieved by those architectures, as well as by some conventional CNNs.

RECAPTURED IMAGE FORENSIC

Recaptured image forensic deals with the task of establishing whether an image has been recaptured or not, that is if it has been generated by capturing a printed picture or a screen display with an acquisition device. (Yang et al., 2018) presented an effective and practical DL-based method to address this problem: Laplacian Convolutional Neural Networks (L-CNN). In this technique the Laplacian filter is embedded into the first layer of a CNN to improve the noise signal ratio introduced by recapture operations. In that paper five different kinds of high-pass filters have been evaluated. Experimental results showed that performance obtained using Laplacian filter is better than the one obtained by using other high-pass filters, or by not using filters at all. According to the paper, L-CNNs achieve 96% detection accuracy even when applied to 64 × 64 image patches. To the best of our knowledge, this is the first work based on deep learning to detect recaptured images. (Choi et al., 2017) tested an in e-layer CNN on 64 × 64 patches and obtained a detection result on the original images by using a voting strategy. The authors report lightly improved results over model-based methods. (Li et al., 2017) proposed a new framework by combining CNNs with RNNs. Instead of using a Laplacian filter in the first layer, the authors considered the convolutional operation as the preprocessing. The weights of the convolutional operator can be automatically learned during the training phase. Features extracted from trained CNN model were then fed into a recurrent neural network to classify the images. Aforementioned algorithms were evaluated on a small-scale dataset. Recently, (Agarwal et al., 2018) developed a diverse large-scale dataset for evaluating recaptured image forensic techniques. The dataset consists of 14,500 recaptured images and 14,500 original images. Those images were captured by various devices such as cameras, displays, scanners, printers. The authors also proposed an eight-layer CNN with 16 different kinds of Gaussian filtering residuals in the first layer. The reported detection accuracy was up to 99.9% for 64 × 64 pixels patches, which is a great improvement over model-based schemes.

The most significant network parameters and the experimental settings of the reviewed works are summarized in Table 2, where we have identified four main architectures (using the short name B1, B2, B4). Then, in Table 4 we have summarized the experimental settings and the performance achieved by those architectures, as well as by some conventional CNNs.

We can notice how most of the techniques proposed for recaptured image forensics are based on some kind of manual of automatic filtering. As an image's subject is not useful for establishing whether the image has been recaptured, those filters attempt to discard that information while, at the same time, highlighting the traces left by their capturing operation.

Table 2. Summary of the reviewed architectures for source camera identification is described below. CC and IC denote Constrained and Instant convolutional operations, respectively. GAP denotes the presence of a global average pooling operation. BN denotes the presence of batch normalization operations.

Architecture	Input Size	Preprocessing	NLayers	Convolutional Part		BN	GAP	Fully Connected Part		
				Activation	Pooling			NLayers	Activation	Dropout
A1	48×48×3	-	3	ReLU	Max	-	-	1	ReLU	C
A2	32×32×3	-	2	L-ReLU	Max	-	-	2	L-ReLU	C
A3	36×36×3	-	3	ReLU	Avg	C	-	1	ReLU	C
A4	64×64×3	-	13	ReLU	Max		-	2	?	C
A5	256×256×3	-	1Conv, 12Residual	ReLU	-	-	C	-	-	-
A6	64×64×3	-	4	?	Max	-	-	1	ReLU	-
A7	64×64×3	-	10	?	Max	-	-	1	ReLU	-
A8	256×256×2	IC+CC	4	TanH	Max, Avg	C	-	2	TanH	-
A9	256×256	HP	3	ReLU	Max	-	-	2	ReLU	C
A10	256×256×3	LBP	3	ReLU	Max	C	-	2	ReLU	C
A11	64×64×3	-	6	ReLU	Avg	C	C	-	-	-
A12	64×64×3	-	1Conv, 3Residual	ReLU	Avg	-	C	-	-	-

COMPUTER GRAPHICS IMAGE FORENSIC

Another possible source of a digital image is represented by Computer Graphics algorithms, so proper methods to detect this kind of origin have also been developed. In this field, (Yu et al., 2017) evaluated VGG-based architectures for CG image detection and found that their performance could be improved by dropping max-pooling layers. The authors explained that pooling layers could lead to a loss of association between adjacent pixels. Therefore, they presented a six-layer CNN without any pooling layer and achieved detection accuracies of over 98% on 32 × 32 patches. (He, 2018) tested several training strategies for VGG-19 and ResNet-50 architectures. Specifically, transfer learning technique was applied during the training phase and a fine-tuned ResNet-50 model was found to have the best performance. The authors report an average detection accuracy of about 96.1% on DSTok dataset. Building on the hybrid CNN-RNN approach of (Li et al., 2017), (He et al., 2018) presented a similar framework with a dual-path CNN to identify CG images. In this approach, 96 × 96 patches are firstly converted to the YCbCr color space. Then, the luminance component is processed by a Schmidt filter bank to generate 13 different kinds of filtered responses. Lastly, the pair of chrominance components Cb, Cr and the filtered responses of the luminance component are separately fed

Table 3. Summary of the reviewed architectures for recaptured image forensics (RF), CG image detection (CGI), GAN-generated images detection (GAN), and Source social networks identification (SSN). Lap denotes Laplacian filter, GR denotes the Guassian residuals. Col + Tex is the combination of Cb, Cr and the texture filtering responses by Schmidt filter bank. Filters denote a combination of three kinds of high-pass filters used for steganalysis and DCT-His denotes the histogram of DCT coefficients.

Architecture		Input Size	Preprocessing	NLayers	Convolutional Part		BN	GAP / Stats	Fully Connected Part		
					Activation	Pooling			NLayers	Activation	Dropout
RF	B1	N × N × 3	Lap	5	ReLU	Avg	C	GAP	-	-	-
	B2	64 × 64 × 1	GR	6	L-ReLU	-	C	-	1	L-ReLU	-
	B3	32 × 32 × 3	Conv	2	ReLU	Avg	C	-	1	?	-
	B4	64 × 64 × 3	-	6	ReLU	Max	-	-	2	ReLU	C
CGI	C1	32 × 32 × 3	-	6	ReLU	-	-	-	2	ReLU+BN	-
	C2	96 × 96	Col + Tex	4	ReLU	Avg	C	-	1	?	C
	C3	650 × 650	Filters	5	ReLU	Avg	C	GAP	-	-	-
	C4	NxN	Conv	3	ReLU	Max	C	-	1	ReLU	C
	C5	100 × 100 × 1	-	2	ReLU	-	-	Stats	1	ReLU	C
GAN	D1	N × N × 3	Lap	3	L-ReLU	Max	-	-	2	L-ReLU	-
SSN	E1	64 × 64	DCT-His	2	ReLU	Max	-	-	1	ReLU	C
	E2	64 × 64	PRNU	4	ReLU	Max	-	-	1	ReLU	C

into a four-layer CNN. Using this technique, the authors improved over the results obtained by (Yu et al., 2017) by 4 percentage points. (Yao et al., 2018) designed a five-layer CNN where the inputs are preprocessed by using high-pass filters. In this work, the authors explored three high-pass filters that were first introduced in the field of steganalysis: SQUARE5x5, SQUARE3x3, and EDGE3x3. (Cui et al., 2018) evaluated the use of ResNet-50 using the PRNU noise as input, and their architecture achieved a detection accuracy of 98% on Columbia Photographic Images and Photorealistic Computer Graphics Dataset. Instead of using fixed filters in the preprocessing step, (Quan et al., 2018) (code available at https://github.com/weizequan/NIvsCG) proposed a CNN with 32 convolutional operations in the first layer so that the weights of convolutional operator can be learned during the training phase. The results reported in their paper show that the performance of this

Table 4. The experimental settings for different algorithms are shown here. In this table, DA, FE, PS, C denotes respectively data augmentation, fusion and ensemble, patch selection, and classifiers. The ratio between training and test data is shown in the column "Train: Test". For the performance-patch/voting, the numbers between parentheses denote the number of models/sensors in the test set. It should be noted that the evaluation matrix for 8, 20 is that 0.7 × (accuracy of unaltered images) + 0.3 × (accuracy of manipulated images). Some works evaluated the performance on multiple datasets; only the most representative ones are shown in this table.

Architecture		Input Size	D.A.	F./E.	P.S.	C.	Train:Test	Dataset	Perf. (Patch)		Perf. (Voting)	
									Model	Sensor	Model	Sensor
[54]	A1	48 × 48 × 3	-	-	-	Softmax	7:3	Dresden (Gloe and Böhme, 2019)	72.9% (27)	29.8% (74)	94.1% (27)	-
[55]	A2	32 × 32 × 3	-	-	-	Softmax		MICHE-I [94]	98.1% (3)	91.1% (5)	-	-
[56]	A3	36 × 36 × 3	-	-	-	SVM	8:2	Dresden (Gloe and Böhme, 2019)	-	-	-	99.9% (10)
[57]	A4	64 × 64 × 3	-	-	C	Softmax	3:2	Dresden (Gloe and Böhme, 2019)	93% (25)	-	>98% (25)	-
[58]	A5	256 × 256 × 3	-	-	-	Softmax	7:3	Dresden (Gloe and Böhme, 2019)	94.7% (27)	45.8% (74)	-	-
[60]	A6	64 × 64 × 3	-	-	-	Softmax	8:2	VISION [95]	-	80.77% (35)	-	97.47% (35)
	DenseNet-40	32 × 32 × 3							-	87.96% (35)	-	95.06% (35)
	DenseNet-121	224 × 224 × 3							-	93.88% (35)	-	99.10% (35)
	XceptionNet	299 × 299 × 3							-	95.15% (35)	-	99.31% (35)
[62]	DenseNet-201+SE-Block	256 × 256 × 1	C	C	C	SE-Block	3:2:1	SPC2018 [38]	98.37% (10, weighted)	-	-	-
[67]	A6	64 × 64 × 3	-	-	C	SVM		Dresden (Gloe and Böhme, 2019)	93% (18)	-	>95% (18)	-

Continued on following page

Table 4. Continued

Architecture		Input Size	D.A.	F./E.	P.S.	C.	Train:Test	Dataset	Perf. (Patch)		Perf. (Voting)	
									Model	Sensor	Model	Sensor
[68]	A7	64 × 64 × 3	-	-	C	Softmax		Dresden (Gloe and Böhme, 2019)	94.93% (18)	-	-	-
[69]	A8	256 × 256 × 2	C	C	-	ET	4:1	Dresden (Gloe and Böhme, 2019)	98.58% (26)	-	-	-
[70]	A9	256 × 256	-	-	-	Softmax	8:2	Dresden (Gloe and Böhme, 2019)	98.99% (12) 98.01% (14)	-	-	-
[72]	A10	256 × 256 × 3	C	-	-	Softmax	8:2	Dresden (Gloe and Böhme, 2019)	98.78% (12) 97.41% (14)	-	-	-
[74]	A12	64 × 64 × 3	C	C	C	Softmax	4:1	Dresden (Gloe and Böhme, 2019)	-	97.03% (9)	-	-
[73]	DenseNet-161	480 × 480 × 3	C	-	-	Softmax	-	SPC2018 [38]	98% (10, weighted)	-	-	-
[73]	A11	64 × 64 × 3	C	C	C	Softmax	4:1	Dresden (Gloe and Böhme, 2019)	-	94.14% (9)	-	-
[64]	Inception-Xception	299 × 299	-	C	C	Softmax		SPC2018 [38]	93.29% (10, weighted)	-	-	-
[59]	ResNet-modified	48 × 48 × 3	C	-	-	Softmax		Dresden (Gloe and Böhme, 2019)	-	-	79.71% (27)	53.4% (74)

method is better than the conventional methods, like Geo (Ng et al., 2005), SPAM (Pevny et al., 2010), and Mfra (Peng et al., 2017), which indicate the effectiveness of CNN-based method on computer graphics (CG) image forensic. (Rahmouni et al., 2017), (code available at https://github.com/NicoRahm/CGvsPhoto) presented a novel statistical features extraction (SFE) layer and embed it between the last convolutional layer and the first fully connected layer. The SFE layer would extract four features: mean, variance, maximum, and minimum. The authors also explored feeding those features into different classifiers such as LDA and SVM. According to their paper, the best results are obtained by the CNN model trained in an end-to-end way. Continuing on this path, (Nguyen et al., 2018) improved detection performance by using a more powerful feature extractor: VGG-19. In this approach, the outputs of the convolutional operations before first three max pooling layers were extracted and the final features were calculated by computing their mean and variance. Then, three groups of those final features were fed into a fused 1-DCNN with two convolutional and three fully connected layers. Sharing a similar idea with the last two methods, (De Rezende et al., 2018) explored using other feature extractors and different classifiers: softmax, k-nearest neighbors, XGBoost, and SVM. In the end, ResNet-50 was chosen and the outputs of its 49th layer were used as features. The authors report that combining ResNet50 with a SVM classifier with RBF kernel achieved the best performance.

The most significant network parameters and the experimental settings of the reviewed works are summarized in Table2, where we have identified five main architectures (using the short name $C1$, $C2$,, $C5$). Then, in Table 4 we have summarized the experimental settings and the performance achieved by those architectures, as well as by some conventional CNNs.

It can be noted that many recent works adopt approaches based on the extraction of statistical features from filtered images. All of them, however, only compute simple indicators such as mean and variance. It would be interesting to explore the possibility of using more sophisticated statistical features and whether those variants could yield an improvement on photo-realistic CG images.

GAN-GENERATED IMAGE DETECTION

In recent years, a number of DL techniques capable of generating fake multimedia contents have been developed. Those methods, collectively called “deepfakes”, include auto encoders (AE) and generative adversarial networks (GAN). This pose significant challenges to the forensics community, as the contents generated by those techniques are much more realistic than the ones generated by computer graphics algorithms. Numerous researches and competitions (Tolosana et al., 2020) have focus on the detection of deepfake multimedia, such as the MFC2018 and DFDC launched by NIST and Facebook, respectively, and some surveys on this topic have been published. (Verdoliva, 2020) presented an overview of media forensics and deepfakes. (Nguyen et al., 2019) came up with a survey of algorithms used to create deepfakes and, more importantly, methods to detect deepfakes proposed in the literature to date. (Tolosana et al., 2020) provided a thorough review of techniques for manipulating face images including DeepFake methods, and methods to detect such manipulations.

The most recent topic related to source image forensics is the detection of content generated by means of GANs. Here, (Marra et al., 2018) evaluated the performance of several image forensic detectors and popular computer vision CNN architectures on GAN-generated images detection. More specifically, the authors used four image forensic detectors: the method proposed by (Fridrich and Kodovsky, 2012), the one by (Cozzolino et al., 2017), the one by (Bayar and Stamm, 2016), and the one by (Rahmouni et al., 2017). The reviewed CNN architectures were: DenseNet (Huang et al., 2017), InceptionNetv3 (He et al., 2018), XceptionNet (Chollet, 2017), and the Cycle-GAN (Zhu et al., 2017) discriminator. Experimental results showed that XceptionNet has the highest average detection accuracy even for images that have under gone Twitter-like compression. (Haodong et al., 2018) reported on an experimental investigation about the effectiveness of forensic detectors for GAN generated image detection, and in particular fake face images generated by Deep Convolutional Generative Adversarial Networks (DCGAN) (Radford et al., 2016) and Wasserstein Adversarial Networks (WGAN) (Arjovsky et al., (2017). Four approaches were evaluated in this work: GAN discriminator, face quality assessment, Inception score, and VGG-features with FLD. The best performance was obtained by using VGG-features with FLD. However, its generalization performances are limited when test set images are generated by different GAN schemes than the one used for training. Focusing on the differences in color composition between original and GAN generated images, (Li et al., 2018) presented a method where a feature set based on co-occurrences matrices is used to capture color image statistics. Firstly, the color image is transformed to RGB, HSV, and YCbCr spaces. Then, residual images would be generated for RGB, H, S, Cb, Cr channels, and co-occurrence matrices for all the residual images would be calculated. The extracted features would be finally fed into a binary classifier. The proposed method was evaluated on three public faces datasets; CelebA (Liu et al., 2015), HQ-CelebA (Karras et al., 2017), LFW (Huang et al., 2008) with four kinds of generated images (deep feature consistent variation alauto-encoder (DFC-VAE) (Hou et al., 2017), DCGAN, WGAN-Gradient penalty (WGAN-GP) (Gulrajani et al., 2017), Progressive Growing Generative Adversarial Networks (PGGAN) (Karras et al., 2017), and it was able to obtain better performance than the one of model-based texture feature set (Boulkenafet et al., 2016). McCloskey and Albright (McCloskeyet al., 2018) extracted features from color and saturation space to detect PG-GAN generated image. On one hand, the standard rg chromaticity space is applied and the bivariate histograms of r, g components are fed into a INHnetwork (Chenet al., 2018). On the other hand, two groups of saturation measurements are extracted as features and SVM is used to classify PG-GAN generated images. The dataset produced in conjunction with the US National Institute of Standards and Technology's Media Forensics Challenge 2018 was used to evaluate the performance of those two schemes. According to

Table 5. The experimental setting for different algorithms for recaptured image forensics (RF), CG image detection (CGI), and Source social networks identification (SSN) are described as follows. In this table, DA, FE, PS, C denotes respectively data augmentation, fusion and ensemble, patch selection, and classifiers. The ratio between training and test data is shown in the column "Train: Test ". For the performance-patch/voting, the numbers between parentheses denote the patch sizes, when applicable.

		Arch	Input size	D.A	F./E	P.S	C	Train: Test	Data Set	Perf (Patch)	Perf (voting)
RF		B1	N×N×3	C	–	–	Softmax	1:1	NTU-Rose LCD-R	99.74% [512] 99.30% [256] 99.48%[128] 95.23%[64]	
		B2	64×64×1	C				8:2			
		B3	32×32×3	C	–	–	Softmax	1:1	LS-D	99.90%	
									ASTAR	86.78%	93.29%
									NTU-Rose	96.93%	98.67%
									ICL	97.79%	99.54%
		B4	64×64×3	–	–	–	Softmax	1:1	ICL	85.73%	96.60%
CGI		C1	32×32×3	–	–	–	Softmax	3:1	Columbia		98%
		ResNet50	224×224	–	–	–	Softmax	5-fCV	DSTok	96.1%	
		C2	96×96	C	C	–	Softmax	13:4	3DLink	90.79%	94.87% (192)
		C3	650×650	C	–	–	Softmax	9:8	WIFS	99.95%	100%
		ResNet50	?	C	–	–	Softmax	7:1	Columbia	98%	
		C4	233×233	C	–	C	Softmax	3:1	Columbia	85.15%	93.20%
		C5	100×100×1	–	C	–	MLP	8:2	WIFS	84.80%	93.20%
		VGG19		–	C	C	MLP	5:2	WIFS	96.55%	99.89%
		ResNet50	224×224×3	–	–	–	SVM		DSTok	94%	
SSN		E1	64×64	C	–	–	Softmax	9:1	UCID	98.41%	
									PUBLIC	87.60%	95% (Avg)
									IPLAB	90.89%	
		E2	64×64	C	–	–	Softmax	9:1	UCID	79.49%	90.83%
									VISION	98.50%	
									IPLAB		83.85%

the report, saturation statistics provided better performance. (Mo et al., 2018) expected that the main difference between the original and GAN-generated images would be reflected on the residual domain. Therefore, they presented a three-layer CNN with a Laplacian filter preprocessing to identify fake face images generated by PG-GAN. From the perspective of artificial fingerprints, (Marra et al., 2018) explored a PRNU-based scheme for GAN-generated image detection. Three GAN architectures are considered in this work: Cycle-GAN, Pro-GAN, and Star-GAN. The results demonstrated that those GAN schemes would leave artificial fingerprints into the generated images.

The most significant network parameters and the experimental results of the reviewed works are summarized in Table 2, and in Table 5.

Based on our review of GAN-generated image detection works, we can broadly classify the proposed methods in three categories: existing detection methods; approaches based on the analysis of color characteristics of the images; and techniques based on the analysis of images' residual/noise. However, GANs are a very popular topic among machine learning researchers, and thus we expect GAN-generated images to become increasingly difficult to be detected. Existing techniques are likely to become obsolete in a short time, and for this reason forensics researchers will need to keep building new, effective detection methods.

SOURCE SOCIAL NETWORKS IDENTIFICATION

In recent years, social networks such as Facebook, Google+, and Twitter became more and more important in the daily life of a large part of the world population. According to Caldelli et al., 2017), on average 350 million photo are uploaded daily on Facebook and around 60 million monthly on Flickr. To the best of our knowledge, (Amerini et al., 2017) were the firsts to propose a CNN-based algorithm to identify from which social network a query image has been downloaded. The authors indicated that image manipulations applied by social networks usually include compressing as JPEG and resizing the original file, and that different social networks use different parameters for those operations. Therefore, it is possible to identify the source social network by looking at the discrete cosine transform (DCT) coefficients of the resulting image. Inspired by the work of (Wang and Zhang, 2016), the authors extracted from each image the histogram of the first nine DCT coefficients and fed them into as imple4-layer 1DCNN, obtaining great performance on source social network identification. (Caldelli et al., 2018) presented another scheme based on a 2D CNN with a preprocessing step. In the pre-processing stage, the PRNU noise of the image would be extracted. This noise would be then fed into a 6-layer 2D CNN. This technique obtains performance comparable with the one from the first method.

The most significant network parameters and the experimental settings of their viewed works are summarized in Table 2, where we have identified the two main architectures as *E*1 and *E*2. Then, in Table 4 we have summarized the experimental settings and the achieved performance.

The works presented in this section assume that images published on a social network will be re-encoded as JPEG after being processed by some unknown set of operations. Even if this is a sensible assumption, there is no guarantee that the specific processing pipeline used by a social network will stay the same over time. A simple software update on the backend software of a social platform could dramatically change how the images are processed, thus making an existing classifier obsolete. For this reason, all the methods described in this section require a constant update where social-network-processed images are continuously used to retrain the models. This is, however, inevitable due to the lack of knowledge about the inner working of social platforms.

ANTI-FORENSICS AND COUNTER ANTI-FORENSICS

Image anti-forensics is techniques that aim to make forensics algorithms fail by modifying the images in a visually imperceptible way. Their goal is to prompt the image forensics community to come up with more robust forensics schemes. Recent developments in DL research led to the development of generative adversarial networks (GANs), novel techniques that proved to be very effective in deceiving many existing image forensics approaches. (Güera et al., 2017) trained a DenseNet-40 model for source camera identification and verified its vulnerability to Fast Gradient Sign Method (FGSM) (Goodfellow et al., 2014) and Jacobian-based Saliency Map Approach (JSMA) (Papernot et al., 2016) attacks. (Marra et al., 2018) evaluated the vulnerability of DL-based source camera identification algorithms to adversarial attacks in a more comprehensive manner. In this work, four kinds of DL-based methods (shallow CNN, DenseNet-40, DenseNet-121, XceptionNet) and two schemes of adversarial attacks (FGSM, Projected Gradient Descent (PGD) (Madry et al., 2017)) are tested to study their behavior when classifying both pixel patches and full resolution images. According to the study, DL-based approaches are vulnerable to adversarial attacks. The authors report that, even if the robustness of DL-based methods can be improved by using adversarial training or training with JPEG-compressed images, the resulting networks are still vulnerable to targeted attacks. (Zhao et al., 2018) generated increasingly strong adversarial examples by using FGSM and Least-likely Class Method (LLCM) (Kurakin et al., 2016) and verified the vulnerability of DL-based image forensic algorithms. (Fan et al., 2018) proposed two kinds of gradient-based attacks against deep learning-based recaptured image forensic schemes: single attack and multiple attacks. In order to verify the effectiveness of the proposed approach, the authors performed the attack on DL-based methods which employed adversarial training (as proposed by (Szegedy et al., 2013) as a defense. The results indicated that single attack is ineffective on models that employ adversarial training, while multiple attacks with a slow learning rate will obtain better results. Besides generating adversarial examples, generative adversarial networks attracted extensive attention because of their ability to generate photorealistic pictures and to achieve image-to-image translations. Two kinds of attacks against CNN models for source forensics have been proposed by modifying the GAN framework. Focusing on source camera identification, (Chen et al., 2018) defined a new loss function for the generator comprised of three terms: the perceptional loss, the classification loss, and the adversarial loss. More specifically, the perceptional loss describes the mean absolute difference between the original image and its falsified copy. The classification loss was designed to measure the difference between the output of the camera model identification classifier for the falsified image and the ideal output for the target camera model. The adversarial loss represents the standard loss function of GANs. In order to fool deep learning-based methods for recaptured image detection, (Zhao et al., 2018) proposed a Cycle-GAN-based scheme by fusing the adversarial loss, the cycle consistency loss and the low frequency consistency loss. In addition to the loss function used in Cycle-GAN, a low frequency consistency loss based on a median filter is proposed to keep the generated image similar to the original one.

Counter anti-forensics (Barni et al., 2018) methods have been proposed as a defense against anti-forensics techniques by improving the robustness of image forensics methods in case of anti-forensics attacks. Meanwhile, with the advent of adversarial examples, numerous approaches have been developed in the field of computer vision to defend against adversarial attacks (Akhtar & Mian, 2018), (Kurakin et al., 2018). According to the review paper on the threat of adversarial attacks by Akhtar and Mian (Akhtar & Mian, 2018), until now defenses against adversarial attacks can be broadly divided into three categories. The first kind of defense is based on using modified examples either during training or during test. Adversarial training is based on this idea. The second kind resorts to modifying the networks by adding more layers, changing loss and soon. The last kind employs external models as network add-on when classifying unseen examples. It should be mentioned that DL and adversarial attacks greatly contributed to the cooperation between computer vision and image forensics communities, thus accelerating the development of related image forensics techniques. We will now introduce three preliminary works proposed by source image forensics researchers. (Zhao et al., 2018) combined adversarial training and regularization of input gradients as a defense against FGSM and LLCM attacks. Firstly, the regularization term of input gradients is added into the original loss function; then, the adversarial training strategy is applied to train the CNN model. (Carrara et al., 2017), (Carrara et al., 2019) used OverFeat, well-known and successful deep convolutional network architecture, for the image representations. The features were extracted from the pool 5 layer of the OverFeat and fed into a k-nearest neighbors (KNN) regressor to get a score. If the score is below threshold, the query image will be classified as an adversarial example and thrown away. From the perspective of image forensics, Schöttle et al.

(Schöttle et al., 2018) presented an adversarial example detection scheme based on simple steganalysis features. Images that are not classified as adversarial examples will be distinguished by the CNN model (Madry et al., 2017). It should be noted that those three approaches were only tested on some relatively old attack methods, such as FGSM, LLCM, FGS, PGD, which are easy to defend against according to the report by (Carlini & Wagner, 2017).

More effective attack algorithms have been proposed in the field of computer vision; it is thus necessary to further study those methods in order to verify their performance in case of more powerful attacks. Thanks to the effort of (Papernot et al., 2018) a Python library which implements sixteen different kinds of adversarial attacks are available for other researchers to test their proposed defense schemes.

Evaluation Measures and Datasets

In this section we will describe the evaluation protocol and the datasets used in there viewed papers.
The metric used in most of the papers is the accuracy:

$$\text{Acc}=\frac{TP+TN}{TP+FP+TN+FN} \tag{3}$$

Where *TP*, *TN* mean the number of correctly classified positive and negative cases, *FP*, *FN* represent the number of incorrectly classified positive and negative cases, respectively.

Besides, in order to fairly evaluate the performance for original and manipulated images in case of unbalanced datasets, a weighted accuracy is also used in some papers:

$$Acc_{weighted} - \frac{7}{10} Acc_{unaltered} + \frac{3}{10} Acc_{altered} \tag{4}$$

Where $Acc_{\text{unaltered}}$, Acc_{altered} denote the accuracyies in the case of unaltered images dataset and altered images dataset, respectively.

We will now introduce the publicly available image forensics datasets used for evaluating performance as shown in Tables 3 and 4. Datasets are organized according to the forensics topics. As some anti-forensics and counter anti-forensics methods use datasets introduced in the other sections, we will only report them once. Some of the datasets are freely downloadable from the authors' websites, while others can be obtained upon request.

Table 6. The statistical table for GAN-generated image detection. GAN shows the GAN model used to generate the images. Method represents the detection algorithm. Performance is the obtained accuracy unless otherwise specified. Only the best performance described in each paper is reported in this table.

GAN	Dataset	Method	Performance
Cycle-GAN (Zhu et al., 2017)	Cycle-GAN Data	Cycle-GAN Discriminator (Zhu et al., 2017)	83.58%
		Fridrich and Kodovsky, 2012	94.40%
		Cozzolino et al., 2017	95.07%
		Bayar and Stamm, 2016	84.86%
		Rahmouni et al., 2017	85.71%
		DenseNet (Huang et al., 2017)	89.19%
		InceptionNet V3 (He et al., 2018)	89.09%
		XceptionNet (Chollet, 2017)	94.49%
DC-GAN W-GAN	CelebA (Liu et al., 2015)	DCGAN Discriminator	95.51%
		VGG+FLD	>90% (DC-GAN) >94% (W-GAN)
DFC-VAE DCGAN WGAN-GP PGGAN	CelebAHQ (Karras et al., 2017) CelebA (Liu et al., 2015), LFW (Huang et al., 2008)	Co-Color	100%
PG-GAN	CelebAHQ (Karras et al., 2017)	Lap-CNN	96.3%
GAN	MFS2018 (Guan et al., 2019)	RG-INHNet Saturation Features	0.56 (AUC) 0.7 (AUC)
Cycle-GAN Pro-GAN Star-GAN	MFS2018 (Guan et al., 2019)	PRNU-based method	0.999 (AUC)

Source Camera Identification

Dresden Image Dataset (Gloe and Böhme, 2010) was built for the purpose of developing and bench marking camera-based digital forensic techniques. There are more than 14,000 images captured by 73 devices which belong to 25 different models. Dresden dataset was released in 2010, when smartphones were not yet a popular way to take pictures and therefore this dataset does not contain pictures taken with such devices.

VISION (Shullani et al., 2017) is a video and image dataset for source identification. It is currently composed by 34,427 images and 1914 videos, both in the native format and in their social version (Facebook, YouTube, and WhatsApp are considered), from 35 modern smartphones/tablets of 11 major brands.

SPC2018 (Bestagini, 2018) is a dataset published in 2018 for the IEEE Signal Processing Cup competition whose topic was camera model identification. This dataset consists of 2750 images from ten different camera models (including point-and-shoot cameras, cell phone cameras, and digital single-lens reflex cameras), with 275 images captured using each camera model.

Recaptured Image Forensic

LS-D (Agarwal et al., 2018) is a large-scale dataset for evaluating recaptured image forensic. Four kinds of recapture attacks are considered: (1) photographing a printed copy of an image; (2) scanning a printed copy of an image; (3) photographing a displayed image; and (4) capturing a screen-grab of displayed image. This dataset consists of 145,000 pairs of original and recaptured images. A diverse set of devices has been used to recapture the images: 234 displays, 173 scanners, 282 printers, and 180 recaptured cameras.

NTU-Rose (Cao and Kot, 2010) is a collection of images recaptured from LCDs with good quality. It is composed of 2700 recaptured images captured by using three digital still cameras and three LCDs. The number of the original images is 300, including 100 images taken by the three cameras, 100 images downloaded from Flick, and 100 tampered images.

ICL (Thongkamwitoon et al., 2015) is a dataset of images recaptured from a LCD and consists of 1035 original images taken by nine different cameras and 2520 images recaptured by using different devices. Camera settings were tuned in order to maintain a high image quality. Therefore, this dataset provides high-quality, high-resolution recaptured images.

ASTAR (Gao et al., 2010) is a smartphone images dataset for single image recaptured detection. The dataset is divided in three subsets. Subset A consists of 1094 real-scene images and 1137 recaptured images with real environment background. Subset B is built by cropping the real-scene images from Subset A, and by adding 1765 recaptured images without real environment backgrounds. Subset C consists of 587 pairs of single captured and recaptured images through transforming and cropping.

CG Image Detection

Columbia (Ng et al., 2005) consists of 800 CG images downloaded from Internet, 1200 images from personal collections, 800 original images from Google Image searches, and 800 recaptured CG images.

DSTok (Tokuda et al., 2013) includes CG and real photograph (PG) images collected from the Internet. There are 4850 pairs of CG and PG images. All of them were JPEG-compressed and the file sizes were between 12 KB and 1.8 MB.

WIFS (Rahmouni et al., 2017) is built for new CG and PG images. There are 1800 CG images and 1800 PG images. CG images were downloaded from the Level Design Reference Database, which contains more than 60,000good resolution video-game screenshots in JPEG format. Only five different video games were judged photo realistic enough to be included in WIFS, and thus only 1800 images were selected. PG images are high-resolution images taken from the RAISE dataset and directly converted to JPEG format.

3D link (He et al., 2018) consists of 6800 CG im+ages download from the 3D link website and 6800 PG images captured under various environmental conditions by using different camera models.

GAN-Generated Image Detection

MFS2018 (Guan et al., 2019) is a dataset released in 2018 for a media forensics challenge, which aims to help advance the state-of-the-art for image and video forensics techniques. For what concerns the works reviewed in this paper, only a subset of the dataset was used (GANCrop and GANFull).

Social Network Identification

UCID social (Caldelli et al., 2017) is a UCID-based dataset for social network identification. Images from UCID were first JPEG-compressed with different quality factors. Then, those compressed images were uploaded to and subsequently downloaded from Flickr, Facebook, and Twitter. The UCID social dataset is composed of 30,000 images, 10,000 images from each social network.

The PUBLIC social dataset (Caldelli et al., 2017) consists of 3000 uncontrolled images with different sizes, JPEG quality factors and contents. Those images were directly downloaded from different social networks, including Flickr, Facebook, and Twitter, 1000 images for each one.

IPLAB (Giudice et al., 2017) provides 2720 images in JPEG format. Ten social networks were considered for this dataset: Facebook, Google+, Twitter, Flickr, Instagram, Tumblr, Imgur, Tinypic, Whatsapp, and Telegram. Captured images were uploaded to the social networks either by using a web browser, or by using iOS and Android native apps.

CONCLUSION

This work has been explained on a number of technical approaches to improving IoT concepts in the field of security through IoT systems and in-depth learning applications. This work hopes to explore many features of the platform based on DL-based IoT technology and structure, architecture, DL. In addition, the effort is complete on how to tackle smart applications in domestic, wearable, car, city, retail, energy bustle, health and environment supportive living systems, agriculture and poultry farming, machine monitoring methods in various industries through in-depth learning. For many more philosophical observations, inspections streamline DL deposits for IoT. So that DL requests can be healthily appreciated, this learning reflects irregular testing and improves them on a variety of features such as characteristic extraction, recognition, cost, delay, calculation load, and so on. Nevertheless, QoS still has almost the potential to increase limitations, privacy and distribution, which can be talked about in future works. Overall, the results of this writing are expected to be realistic for scholars, engineers, healthcare professionals and policy makers who want to make some effort in the field of IoT.

REFERENCES

Abdulnabi, A. H., Wang, G., Lu, J., & Jia, K. (2015). Multi-task CNN model for attribute prediction. *IEEE Transactions on Multimedia, 17*(11), 1949–1959.

Agarwal, S., Fan, W., & Farid, H. (2018). A diverse large-scale dataset for evaluating rebroadcast attacks. In *Proceedings of the 2018 IEEE International Conference on Acoustics, Speech and Signal Processing (ICASSP)* (pp.1997–2001). IEEE.

Akhtar, N., & Mian, A. (2018). Threat of adversarial attacks on deep learning in computer vision: A survey. *IEEE Access: Practical Innovations, Open Solutions, 6*, 14410–14430.

Albawi, S., Mohammed, T. A., & Al-Zawi, S. (2017, August). Understanding of a convolutional neural network. In 2017 international conference on engineering and technology (ICET) (pp. 1-6). IEEE.

Amerini, I., Uricchio, T., & Caldelli, R. (2017). Tracing images back to their social network of origin: A cnn-based approach, In *Proceedings of the 2017 IEEE Workshop on Information Forensics and Security (WIFS)* (pp. 1–6). IEEE.

Arjovsky, M., Chintala, S., & Bottou, L. (2017). Wasserstein Generative Adversarial Networks. In *Proceedings of the International Conference on Machine Learning* (pp. 214–223). Academic Press.

Barni, M., Stamm, M. C., & Tondi, B. (2018). Adversarial Multimedia Forensics: Overview and Challenges Ahead. In *Proceedings of the 26th European Signal Processing Conference (EUSIPCO)*. IEEE.

Baroffio, L., Bondi, L., Bestagini, P., & Tubaro, S. (2016). *Camera identification with deep convolutional networks.* arXiv preprint arXiv:1603.01068, 460.

Bayar, B., & Stamm, M. C. (2016). A deep learning approach to universal image manipulation detection using a new convolutional layer. In *Proceedings of the 4th ACM Workshop on Information Hiding and Multimedia Security* (pp. 5–10). ACM.

Bayar, B., & Stamm, M. C. (2017). Augmented convolutional feature maps for robust cnn-based camera model identification. In *Proceedings of the 2017 IEEE International Conference on Image Processing (ICIP)* (pp. 4098–4102). IEEE.

Bayar, B., & Stamm, M. C. (2018). Towards open set camera model identification using a deep learning framework. *2018 IEEE International Conference on Acoustics, Speech and Signal Processing (ICASSP)*, 2007–2011.

Bayar, B., & Stamm, M. C. (2018). Constrained convolutional neural networks: A new approach towards general purpose image manipulation detection. *IEEE Transactions on Information Forensics and Security, 13*(11), 2691–2706.

Bengio, Y., Lamblin, P., Popovici, D., & Larochelle, H. (2007). Greedy layer-wise training of deep networks. In *Advances in Neural Information Processing Systems* (pp. 153–160). MIT Press.

Beridze, I., & Butcher, J. (2019). When seeing is no longer believing. *Nature Machine Intelligence, 1*(8), 332–334.

Bestagini, M. C. S. P. (2018). *IEEE signal processing cup 2018 database-forensic camera model identification.* doi, 10, H2XM2P.

Bin, K., Luo, S., Zhang, X., Lin, J., & Tong, X. (2020). Compressive data gathering with generative adversarial networks for wireless geophone networks. *IEEE Geoscience and Remote Sensing Letters, 18*(3), 558–562.

Bondi, L., Baroffio, L., Güera, D., Bestagini, P., Delp, E. J., & Tubaro, S. (2016). First steps toward camera model identification with convolutional neural networks. *IEEE Signal Processing Letters*, *24*(3), 259–263.

Bondi, L., Güera, D., Baroffio, L., Bestagini, P., Delp, E. J., & Tubaro, S. (2017). A preliminary study on convolutional neural networks for camera model identification. *Electronic Imaging*, *2017*(7), 67–76.

Boulkenafet, Z., Jukka, K., & Abdenour, H. (2016). Face spoofing detection using colour texture analysis. *IEEE Transactions on Information Forensics and Security*, *2016*(11), 1818–1830.

Brown, M. E., Treviño, L. K., & Harrison, D. A. (2005). Ethical leadership: A social learning perspective for construct development and testing. *Organizational Behavior and Human Decision Processes*, *97*(2), 117–134. doi:10.1016/j.obhdp.2005.03.002

Caldelli, R., Amerini, I., & Li, C. T. (2018). PRNU-based Image Classification of Origin Social Network with CNN. In *Proceedings of the 2018 26th European Signal Processing Conference (EUSIPCO)* (pp. 1357–1361). Academic Press.

Caldelli, R., Becarelli, R., & Amerini, I. (2017). Image origin classification based on social network provenance. *IEEE Transactions on Information Forensics and Security*, *2017*(12), 1299–1308.

Cao, H., & Kot, A. C. (2010). Identification of recaptured photographs on LCD screens. In *Proceedings of the 2010 IEEE International Conference on Acoustics, Speech and Signal Processing* (pp.1790–1793). IEEE.

Cao, Y. J., Jia, L. L., Chen, Y. X., Lin, N., Yang, C., Zhang, B., ... Dai, H. H. (2018). Recent advances of generative adversarial networks in computer vision. *IEEE Access: Practical Innovations, Open Solutions*, *7*, 14985–15006.

Carlini, N., & Wagner, D. (2017). Adversarial examples are not easily detected: Bypassing ten detection methods. In *Proceedings of the 10th ACM Workshop on Artificial Intelligence and Security*. ACM.

Carrara, F., Falchi, F., Caldelli, R., Amato, G., & Becarelli, R. (2019). Adversarial image detection in deep neural networks. *Multimedia Tools and Applications*, *78*, 2815–2835.

Carrara, F., Falchi, F., Caldelli, R., Amato, G., Fumarola, R., & Becarelli, R. (2017). Detecting adversarial example attacks to deep neural networks. In *Proceedings of the 15th International Workshop on Content-Based Multimedia Indexing*. ACM.

Chaturvedi, A., Awasthi, A., & Shanker, S. (2020). Cyber Forensic -A Literature Review. Trinity Journal of Management, IT & Media, *10*(1).

Chen, C., McCloskey, S., & Yu, J. (2018). Focus Manipulation Detection via Photometric Histogram Analysis. In *Proceedings of the IEEE Conference on Computer Vision and Pattern Recognition* (pp. 1674–1682). IEEE.

Chen, C., Zhao, X., & Stamm, M. C. (2018). Mislgan: An Anti-Forensic Camera Model Falsification Framework Using a Generative Adversarial Network. In *Proceedings of the 2018 25th IEEE International Conference on Image Processing (ICIP)* (pp. 535–539). IEEE.

Chen, S., & Wang, Y. (2014). *Convolutional Neural Network and Convex Optimization.* Department of Electrical and Computer Engineering University of California SanDiego.

Chen, Y., Huang, Y., & Ding, X. (2017). Camera model identification with residual neural network. In *Proceedings of the 2017 IEEE International Conference on Image Processing (ICIP)* (pp. 4337–4341). IEEE.

Choi, H. Y., Jang, H. U., Son, J., Kim, D., & Lee, H. K. (2017). Content Recapture Detection Based on Convolutional Neural Networks. In *International Conference on Information Science and Applications*. Springer.

Chollet, F. (2017). Xception: Deep learning with depth wise separable convolutions. In *Proceedings of the IEEE conference on computer vision and pattern recognition* (pp. 1251–1258). IEEE.

Chopra, S., Hadsell, R., & LeCun, Y. (2005). Learning a Similarity Metric Discriminatively, with Application to Face Verification. In *Proceedings of the 2005 IEEE Computer Society Conference on Computer Vision and Pattern Recognition (CVPR'05)*. IEEE Computer Society.

Cozzolino, D., Poggi, G., & Verdoliva, L. (2017). Recasting residual-based local descriptors as convolutional neural networks: An application to image forgery detection. In *Proceedings of the 5th ACM Workshop on Information Hiding and Multimedia Security* (pp. 159–164). ACM.

Cui, Q., McIntosh, S., & Sun, H. (2018). Identifying materials of photographic images and photorealistic computer generated graphics based on deep CNNs. *Comput. Mater. Contin.*, *55*, 229–241.

De Marsico, M., Nappi, M., Riccio, D., & Wechsler, H. (2015). Mobile iris challenge evaluation (MICHE)-I, biometric iris dataset and protocols. *Pattern Recognition Letters*, *2015*(57), 17–23.

De Rezende, E. R., Ruppert, G. C., Theóphilo, A., Tokuda, E. K., & Carvalho, T. (2018). Exposing computer generated images by using deep convolutional neural networks. *Signal Processing Image Communication*, *2018*(66), 113–126.

Di Francesco, A., Arosio, B., Falconi, A., Di Bonaventura, M. V. M., Karimi, M., Mari, D., ... D'Addario, C. (2015). Global changes in DNA methylation in Alzheimer's disease peripheral blood mononuclear cells. *Brain, Behavior, and Immunity*, *45*, 139–144. doi:10.1016/j.bbi.2014.11.002 PMID:25452147

Ding, X., Chen, Y., Tang, Z., & Huang, Y. (2019). Camera Identification based on Domain Knowledge-driven Deep Multi-task Learning. *IEEE Access*, *7*, 25878–25890.

Du, M., Liu, N., Song, Q., & Hu, X. (2018, July). Towards explanation of dnn-based prediction with guided feature inversion. In *Proceedings of the 24th ACM SIGKDD International Conference on Knowledge Discovery & Data Mining* (pp. 1358-1367). 10.1145/3219819.3220099

Fan, W., Agarwal, S., & Farid, H. (2018). Rebroadcast Attacks: Defenses, Reattacks, and Redefenses. In *Proceedings of the 2018 26th European Signal Processing Conference (EUSIPCO)* (pp. 942–946). Academic Press.

Farid, H. (2006). Digital doctoring: How to tell the real from the fake. *Significance*, *3*(4), 162–166.

Felzenszwalb, P., Girshick, R., Mcallester, D. A., & Ramanan, D. (2010). *IEEE Transactions on Pattern Analysis and Machine Intelligence*. Institute of Electrical and Electronics Engineers. doi:10.1109/TPAMI.2009.167

Ferreira, A., Chen, H., Li, B., & Huang, J. (2018). An Inception-Based Data-Driven Ensemble Approach to Camera Model Identification. In *Proceedings of the 2018 IEEE International Workshop on Information Forensics and Security (WIFS)* (pp. 1–7). IEEE.

Forensic Yard. (2022). *7 Basic Laws and Principles of Forensic Science*. Retrieved from https://forensicyard.com/laws-and-principles-of-forensic-science/

Freire-Obregón, D., Narducci, F., Barra, S., & Castrillón-Santana, M. (2019). Deep learning for source camera identification on mobile devices. *Pattern Recognition Letters*, *126*, 86–91.

Fridrich, J., & Kodovsky, J. (2012). Rich models for steganalysis of digital images. *IEEE Transactions on Information Forensics and Security, 2012*(7), 868–882.

Gao, X., Qiu, B., Shen, J., Ng, T. T., & Shi, Y. Q. (2010). A smart phone image database for single image recapture detection. In *International Workshop on Digital Watermarking*. Springer.

Girshick, R., Donahue, J., Darrell, T., & Malik, J. (2014). Rich feature hierarchies for accurate object detection and semantic segmentation. In *Proceedings of the IEEE conference on computer vision and pattern recognition* (pp. 580-587). 10.1109/CVPR.2014.81

Giudice, O., Paratore, A., Moltisanti, M., & Battiato, S. (2017). A classification engine for image ballistics of social data. In *International Conference on Image Analysis and Processing*. Springer.

Gloe, T., & Böhme, R. (2010). The Dresden Image Database for benchmarking digital image forensics. In *Proceedings of the 2010 ACM Symposium on Applied Computing* (pp. 1584–1590). ACM.

Goodfellow, I., Bengio, Y., & Courville, A. (2016). *Adaptive Computation and Machine Learning series, Deep Learning*. MIT Press.

Goodfellow, I. J., Shlens, J., & Szegedy, C. (2014). *Explaining and Harnessing Adversarial Examples*. arXiv 2014, arXiv:1412.6572.

Gu, J., Wang, Z., Kuen, J., Ma, L., Shahroudy, A., Shuai, B., ... Chen, T. (2018). Recent advances in convolutional neural networks. *Pattern Recognition, 77*, 354–377.

Guan, H., Kozak, M., Robertson, E., Lee, Y., Yates, A. N., Delgado, A., . . . Fiscus, J. (2019, January). MFC datasets: Large-scale benchmark datasets for media forensic challenge evaluation. In 2019 IEEE Winter Applications of Computer Vision Workshops (WACVW) (pp. 63-72). IEEE.

Güera, D., Wang, Y., Bondi, L., Bestagini, P., Tubaro, S., & Delp, E. J. (2017). A counter-forensic method for cnn-based camera model identification. In *Proceedings of the 2017 IEEE Conference on Computer Vision and Pattern Recognition Workshops (CVPRW)* (pp. 1840–1847). IEEE.

Güera, D., Zhu, F., Yarlagadda, S. K., Tubaro, S., Bestagini, P., & Delp, E. J. (2018). Reliability map estimation for CNN-based camera model attribution. In *Proceedings of the 2018 IEEE Winter Conference on Applications of Computer Vision (WACV)* (pp. 964–973). IEEE.

Gulrajani, I., Ahmed, F., Arjovsky, M., Dumoulin, V., & Courville, A. C. (2017). Improved Training of wasserstein GANs. *Proceedings of the 31st International Conference on Neural Information Processing Systems.*

Han, Z., Francesca, C., Nikolic, K., Mirza, K., & Toumazou, C. (2021, May). Signal identification of DNA amplification curves in custom-PCR platforms. In *2021 IEEE International Symposium on Circuits and Systems (ISCAS)* (pp. 1-5). IEEE.

Haodong, L., Han, C., Bin, L., & Shunquan, T. (2018). Can Forensic Detectors Identify GAN Generated Images? In *Proceedings of the APSIPA Annual Summit and Conference 2018* (pp. 722–727). Academic Press.

He, K., Zhang, X., Ren, S., & Sun, J. (2016). Deep residual learning for image recognition. In *Proceedings of the IEEE conference on computer vision and pattern recognition* (pp. 770–778). IEEE.

He, M. (2018). Distinguish computer generated and digital images: A CNN solution. Concurrency Comput. Pract. Exp., 31(12).

He, P., Jiang, X., Sun, T., & Li, H. (2018). Computer graphics identification combining convolutional and recurrent neural networks. *IEEE Signal Processing Letters, 25*(9), 1369–1373.

Heck, J. C., & Salem, F. M. (2017, August). Simplified minimal gated unit variations for recurrent neural networks. In *2017 IEEE 60th International Midwest Symposium on Circuits and Systems (MWSCAS)* (pp. 1593-1596). IEEE.

Hinton, G. (2011). Boltzmann Machines. In C. Sammut & G. I. Webb (Eds.), Encyclopedia of Machine Learning. Springer. https://doi.org/10.1007/978-0-387-30164-8_83.

Hinton, G. E., Osindero, S., & Teh, Y. W. (2006). A fast learning algorithm for deep belief nets. *Neural Computation, 18*(7), 1527–1554.

Hou, X., Shen, L., Ke, S., & Qiu, G. (2017). Deep Feature Consistent Variational Autoencoder. *Proceedings of the 2017 IEEE Winter Conference on Applications of Computer Vision (WACV).*

Huang, G., Liu, Z., Van Der Maaten, L., & Weinberger, K. Q. (2017). Densely connected convolutional networks, In *Proceedings of the IEEE conference on computer vision and pattern recognition* (pp. 4700–4708). IEEE.

Huang, G. B., Mattar, M., Berg, T., & Learned-Miller, E. (2008). Labeled faces in the wild: A database for studying face recognition in unconstrained environments. *Proceedings of the Workshop on faces in 'Real-Life' Images: Detection, alignment, and recognition.*

Huang, N., He, J., Zhu, N., Xuan, X., Liu, G., & Chang, C. (2018). Identification of the source camera of images based on convolutional neural network. *Digital Investigation, 26*, 72–80.

Isono, T., Yamakura, M., Shimaya, S., Kawamoto, I., Tsuboi, N., Mineo, M., ... Hirai, H. (2020, November). A 12.1 TOPS/W Mixed-precision Quantized Deep Convolutional Neural Network Accelerator for Low Power on Edge/Endpoint Device. In *2020 IEEE Asian Solid-State Circuits Conference (A-SSCC)* (pp. 1-4). IEEE.

Jie, H., Li, S., Albanie, S., Gang, S., & Wu, E. (2017). *Squeeze-and-Excitation Networks*. arXiv: 1709.01507.

Jin, L., Zhang, Y., Tan, W., & Liu, W. (2010). Effect of different treatment rapeseeds on activity of cellulose enzyme in sheep. *The Journal of Northeast Agricultural University, 17*(1), 57–61.

Joseph, R. M., Sun, J. S., Tam, E., & Carlson, J. R. (2017). A receptor and neuron that activate a circuit limiting sucrose consumption. *eLife, 6*, e24992. doi:10.7554/eLife.24992 PMID:28332980

Kamal, U., Rafi, A. M., Hoque, R., Das, S., Abrar, A., & Hasan, M. (2018).*Application of DenseNet in Camera Model Identification and Post-processing Detection*. arXiv 2018. arXiv preprint arXiv:1809.00576.

Karras, T., Aila, T., Laine, S., & Lehtinen, J. (2017). *Progressive growing of gans for improved quality, stability, and variation.* arXiv 2017, arXiv:1710.10196.

Khan, A., Sohail, A., Zahoora, U., & Qureshi, A. S. (2019). *A Survey of the Recent Architectures of Deep Convolutional Neural Networks*. arXiv 2019, arXiv:1901.06032.

KishorP.BholaneP. (2006). Forensic Accounting: A Brief Overview. *Journal of Business Issues*. http://ssrn.com/abstract=1642100

Krizhevsky, A., Sutskever, I., & Hinton, G. E. (2012). *Advances in Neural Information Processing Systems*. MIT Press.

Kurakin, A., Goodfellow, I., & Bengio, S. (2016). *Adversarial Machine Learning at Scale*. arXiv 2016, arXiv:1611.01236.

Kurakin, A., Goodfellow, I., Bengio, S., Dong, Y., Liao, F., Liang, M., Pang, T., Zhu, J., Hu, X., & Xie, C. (2018). Adversarial attacks and defences competition. In *The NIPS'17 Competition: Building Intelligent Systems* (pp. 195–231). Springer.

Kuzin, A., Fattakhov, A., Kibardin, I., Iglovikov, V. I., & Dautov, R. (2018, December). Camera model identification using convolutional neural networks. In *2018 IEEE International Conference on Big Data (Big Data)* (pp. 3107-3110). IEEE.

LeCun, Y., Bengio, Y., & Hinton, G. (2015). Deep Learning. *Nature, 521*, 436–444.

Li, H., Li, B., Tan, S., & Huang, J. (2018). *Detection of deep network generated images using disparities in color components.* arXiv 2018, arXiv:1808.07276.

Li, H., Wang, S., & Kot, A. C. (2017). Image recapture detection with convolutional and recurrent neural networks. *Electronic Imaging, 2017*(7), 87–91.

Li, R., Ni, R., & Zhao, Y. (2015). An effective detection method based on physical traits of recaptured images on LCD screens. In *International Workshop on Digital Watermarking*. Springer.

Liu, Z., Luo, P., Wang, X., & Tang, X. (2015). Deep learning face attributes in the wild. In *Proceedings of the IEEE international conference on computer vision* (pp. 3730–3738). IEEE.

Madry, A., Makelov, A., Schmidt, L., Tsipras, D., & Vladu, A. (2017). *Towards deep learning models resistant to adversarial attacks.* arXiv 2017, arXiv:1706.06083.

Marra, F., Gragnaniello, D., & Cozzolino, D. (2018). Verdoliva, L. Detection of GAN-generated fake images over social networks. In *Proceedings of the 2018 IEEE Conference on Multimedia Information Processing and Retrieval (MIPR)* (pp. 384–389). IEEE.

Marra, F., Gragnaniello, D., & Verdoliva, L. (2018). On the vulnerability of deep learning to adversarial attacks for camera model identification. *Signal Processing Image Communication, 65*, 240–248.

Marra, F., Gragnaniello, D., Verdoliva, L., & Poggi, G. (2018). *Do GANs leave artificial fingerprints?* arXiv 2018, arXiv:1812.11842.

Mayer, O., & Stamm, M. C. (2018). Learned forensic source similarity for unknown camera models. In *Proceedings of the 2018 IEEE International Conference on Acoustics, Speech and Signal Processing (ICASSP)* (pp. 2012–2016). IEEE.

McCloskey, S., & Albright, M. (2018). *Detecting GAN-generated Imagery using Color Cues*. arXiv 2018, arXiv:1812.08247.

Mo, H., Chen, B., & Luo, W. (2018). Fake Faces Identification via Convolutional Neural Network. In *Proceedings of the 6th ACM Workshop on Information Hiding and Multimedia Security* (pp. 43–47). ACM.

Mohammed, H., Clarke, N., & Li, F. (2016). An automated approach for digital forensic analysis of heterogeneous big data. *Journal of Digital Forensics. Security and Law*, *11*(2), 9.

Mousavi, S. S., Schukat, M., & Howley, E. (2016, September). Deep reinforcement learning: an overview. In *Proceedings of SAI Intelligent Systems Conference* (pp. 426-440). Springer.

Ng, H. W., Nguyen, V. D., Vonikakis, V., & Winkler, S. (2015, November). Deep learning for emotion recognition on small datasets using transfer learning. In *Proceedings of the 2015 ACM on international conference on multimodal interaction* (pp. 443-449). 10.1145/2818346.2830593

Ng, T. T., Chang, S. F., Hsu, J., & Pepeljugoski, M. (2005). *Columbia Photographic Images and Photo realistic Computer. Graphics Dataset*. ADVENT Technical Report Columbia University.

Ng, T. T., Chang, S. F., Hsu, J., Xie, L., & Tsui, M. P. (2005). Physics-motivated features for distinguishing photographic images and computer graphics. In *Proceedings of the 13th annual ACM international conference on Multimedia* (pp. 159–164). ACM.

Nguyen, H. H., Tieu, T., Nguyen-Son, H. Q., Nozick, V., Yamagishi, J., & Echizen, I. (2018). Modular convolutional neural network for discriminating between computer-generated images and photographic images. In *Proceedings of the 13th International Conference on Availability, Reliability and Security* (pp. 1-6). Academic Press.

Nguyen, T. T., Nguyen, C. M., Nguyen, D. T., Nguyen, D. T., & Nahavandi, S. (2019). *Deep Learning for Deepfakes Creation and Detection*. arXiv 2019, arXiv:1909.11573.

Papernot, N., Faghri, F., Carlini, N., Goodfellow, I., Feinman, R., Kurakin, A., Xie, C., Sharma, Y., Brown, T., & Roy, A. (2018). *Technical Report on the CleverHans v2.1.0 Adversarial Examples Library*. arXiv: 1610.00768.

Papernot, N., Mcdaniel, P., Jha, S., Fredrikson, M., Celik, Z. B., & Swami, A. (2016). The Limitations of Deep Learning in Adversarial Settings. *Proceedings of the IEEE European Symposium on Security & Privacy*.

Peng, F., Zhou, D. L., Long, M., & Sun, X. M. (2017). Discrimination of natural images and computer generated graphics based on multi-fractal and regression analysis. *AEÜ. International Journal of Electronics and Communications*, *71*, 72–81.

Pevny, T., Bas, P., & Fridrich, J. (2010). Steganalysis by subtractive pixel adjacency matrix. *IEEE Transactions on Information Forensics and Security*, *5*(2), 215–224.

Piva, A. (2013). An overview on image forensics. *International Scholarly Research Notices*, 2013.

Quan, W., Wang, K., Yan, D. M., & Zhang, X. (2018). Distinguishing between natural and computer-generated images using convolutional neural networks. *IEEE Transactions on Information Forensics and Security*, *13*(11), 2772–2787.

Radford, A., Metz, L., & Chintala, S. (2016). Unsupervised Representation Learning with Deep Convolutional Generative Adversarial Networks. *Proceedings of the 4th International Conference on Learning Representations*.

Rahmouni, N., Nozick, V., Yamagishi, J., & Echizen, I. (2017). Distinguishing computer graphics from natural images using convolution neural networks. In *Proceedings of the 2017 IEEE Workshop on Information Forensics and Security (WIFS)* (pp. 1–6). IEEE.

Ranzato, M., Poultney, C., Chopra, S., & LeCun, Y. (2007). Efficient learning of sparse representations with an energy-based model. In *Advances in Neural Information Processing Systems* (pp. 1137–1144). MIT Press.

Rayson, P. E., Mariani, J. A., Anderson-Cooper, B., Baron, A., Gullick, D. S., Moore, A., & Wattam, S. (2017). Towards interactive multidimensional visualisations for corpus linguistics. *Journal for Language Technology and Computational Linguistics, 31*(1), 27-49.

Rodríguez-Félix, D., Aragon-Noriega, E.A., Cisneros-Mata, M., Guevara-Aguirre, D., & Alcántara-Razo, E. (2018). *Management strategies for sustainable fisheries*. Academic Press.

Saikia, S., Fidalgo, E., Alegre, E., & Fernández-Robles, L. (2017, September). Object detection for crime scene evidence analysis using deep learning. In *International Conference on Image Analysis and Processing* (pp. 14-24). Springer. 10.1007/978-3-319-68548-9_2

Schöttle, P., Schlögl, A., Pasquini, C., & Böhme, R. (2018). Detecting Adversarial Examples – a Lesson from Multimedia Security. In *Proceedings of the 26th European Signal Processing Conference (EUSIPCO)* (pp. 947–951). Academic Press.

Shin, H. C., Roth, H. R., Gao, M., Lu, L., Xu, Z., Nogues, I., Yao, J., Mollura, D., & Summers, R. M. (2016). Deep convolutional neural networks for computer-aided detection: CNN architectures, dataset characteristics and transfer learning. *IEEE Transactions on Medical Imaging*, *35*(5), 1285–1298. doi:10.1109/TMI.2016.2528162 PMID:26886976

Shullani, D., Fontani, M., Iuliani, M., Al Shaya, O., & Piva, A. (2017). *VISION: A video and image dataset for source identification. EURASIP Journal on Information Security.*

Simonyan, K., & Zisserman, A. (2014). *Very deep convolutional networks for large-scale image recognition.* arXiv2014, arXiv: 1409.1556.

Stamm, M., Bestagini, P., Marcenaro, L., & Campisi, P. (2018). Forensic camera model identification: Highlights from the IEEE signal processing cup 2018 student competition. *IEEE Signal Processing Magazine*, *35*(5), 168–174.

Szegedy, C., Liu, W., Jia, Y., Sermanet, P., Reed, S., Anguelov, D., Erhan, D., Vanhoucke, V., & Rabinovich, A. (2015). Going deeper with convolutions. In *Proceedings of the IEEE Conference on Computer Vision and Pattern Recognition* (pp. 1–9). IEEE.

Szegedy, C., Vanhoucke, V., Ioffe, S., Shlens, J., & Wojna, Z. (2016). Rethinking the inception architecture for computer vision. In *Proceedings of the IEEE conference on computer vision and pattern recognition* (pp. 2818–2826). IEEE.

Szegedy, C., Zaremba, W., Sutskever, I., Bruna, J., Erhan, D., Goodfellow, I., & Fergus, R. (2013). *Intriguing properties of neural networks.* arXiv 2013, arXiv:1312.6199.

Tallón-Ballesteros, A. J., & Riquelme, J. C. (2014). Data mining methods applied to a digital forensics task for supervised machine learning. In *Computational Intelligence in Digital Forensics: Forensic Investigation and Applications* (pp. 413–428). Springer. doi:10.1007/978-3-319-05885-6_17

Tang, Y. (2013). *Deep learning using linear support vector machines*. arXiv 2013, arXiv:1306.0239.

Tewari, R. K., & Ravikumar, K. V. (2000). History and development of forensic science in India. *Journal of Postgraduate Medicine*, *46*(4), 303. PMID:11435664

Thongkamwitoon, T., Muammar, H., & Dragotti, P. L. (2015). An image recapture detection algorithm based on learning dictionaries of edge profiles. *IEEE Transactions on Information Forensics and Security*, *2015*(10), 953–968.

Tokuda, E., Pedrini, H., & Rocha, A. (2013). Computer generated images vs. digital photographs: A synergetic feature and classifier combination approach. *Journal of Visual Communication and Image Representation, 24*, 1276–1292.

Tolosana, R., Vera-Rodriguez, R., Fierrez, J., Morales, A., & Ortega-Garcia, J. (2020). *DeepFakes and Beyond: A Survey of Face Manipulation and Fake Detection*. arXiv 2020, arXiv:2001.00179.

Tuama, A., Comby, F., & Chaumont, M. (2016, December). Camera model identification with the use of deep convolutional neural networks. In *2016 IEEE International workshop on information forensics and security (WIFS)* (pp. 1-6). IEEE.

Verdoliva, L. (2020). *Media Forensics and DeepFakes: Sn overview*. arXiv 2020, arXiv:2001.06564.

Wang, B., Yin, J., Tan, S., Li, Y., & Li, M. (2018). Source camera model identification based on convolutional neural networks with local binary patterns coding. *Signal Processing Image Communication, 68*, 162–168.

Wang, H., & Raj, B. (2017). *On the origin of deep learning*. arXiv preprint arXiv:1702.07800.

Wang, Q., & Zhang, R. (2016). Double JPEG compression forensics based on a convolutional neural network. *EURASIP J. Inf. Secur.*

Yang, P., Ni, R., & Zhao, Y. (2018). Recapture image forensics based on Laplacian convolutional neural networks. In *International Workshop on Digital Watermarking*. Springer.

Yang, P., Ni, R., Zhao, Y., & Zhao, W. (2019). Source camera identification based on content-adaptive fusion residual networks. *Pattern Recognition Letters, 119*, 195–204.

Yao, H., Qiao, T., Xu, M., & Zheng, N. (2018). Robust multi-classifier for camera model identification based on convolution neural network. *IEEE Access: Practical Innovations, Open Solutions, 6*, 24973–24982.

Yao, Y., Hu, W., Zhang, W., Wu, T., & Shi, Y. Q. (2018). Distinguishing Computer-Generated Graphics from Natural Images Based on Sensor Pattern Noise and Deep Learning. *Sensors (Basel), 18*, 1296.

Yin, H. (2008). The self-organizing maps: background, theories, extensions and applications. In *Computational intelligence: A compendium* (pp. 715–762). Springer.

Ying, Y., Su, J., Shan, P., Miao, L., Wang, X., & Peng, S. (2019). Rectified exponential units for convolutional neural networks. *IEEE Access: Practical Innovations, Open Solutions, 7*, 101633–101640.

You, Y., Gitman, I., & Ginsburg, B. (2017). *Large batch training of convolutional networks*. arXiv preprint arXiv:1708.03888.

Yu, I. J., Kim, D. G., Park, J. S., Hou, J. U., Choi, S., & Lee, H. K. (2017). Identifying photorealistic computer graphics using convolutional neural networks. In *Proceedings of the 2017 IEEE International Conference on Image Processing (ICIP)* (pp. 4093–4097). IEEE.

Yusiong, J. P. T., & Naval, P. C. (2019, April). Multi-scale autoencoders in autoencoder for semantic image segmentation. In *Asian Conference on Intelligent Information and Database Systems* (pp. 587-599). Springer.

Zhao, W., Yang, P., Ni, R., Zhao, Y., & Li, W. (2018). Cycle GAN-Based Attack on Recaptured Images to Fool both Human and Machine. In *International Workshop on Digital Watermarking*. Springer.

Zhao, W., Yang, P., Ni, R., Zhao, Y., & Wu, H. (2018). Security Consideration for Deep Learning-Based Image Forensics. *IEICE Transactions on Information and Systems*, *2018*(101), 3263–3266.

Zhu, B. B., Swanson, M. D., & Tewfik, A. H. (2004). When seeing isn't believing. *IEEE Signal Processing Magazine*, *21*(2), 40–49.

Zhu, J. Y., Park, T., Isola, P., & Efros, A. A. (2017). Unpaired image-to-image translation using cycle-consistent adversarial networks. In *Proceedings of the IEEE International Conference on Computer Vision* (pp. 2223–2232). IEEE.

Zuo, Z. (2018). *Camera Model Identification with Convolutional Neural Networks and Image Noise Pattern, 2018*. Available online: http://hdl.handle.net/2142/100123

Chapter 2
Digital Forensic Techniques and Principles in a Cloud Environment

Ayaz Ahmad
National Institute of Technology, Patna, India

Lingaraj Sethi
Odisha University of Technology and Research, India

Supriya Prashant Diwan
Government College of Engineering, Karad, India

Prashanta Kumar Patra
Odisha University of Technology and Research, India

Sudhansu Sekhar Nanda
https://orcid.org/0000-0003-0974-181X
Kirloskar Institute of Advanced Management Studies, India

ABSTRACT

Digital forensic methods for cybercrime investigation in a cloud computing environment (i.e., cloud forensic) is a broad term that encompasses a number of different fields, including digital forensics and cloud computing. The authors hope to gain a better understanding of cloud computing and identify challenges and opportunities in forensic science. They present research that may be used to establish strategies for the creation of measures, standards, and technological research to minimise the issues that cannot be solved with current technology and methodologies. Among the topics covered in this chapter are cloud computing, digital forensics, cybercrimes, and cloud forensics. Also covered are an overview and principles of cloud computing as well as digital forensics, cybercrimes, and challenges, as well as opportunities in the field of cloud forensics. The state of the art in the cloud forensic domain is also presented, as is a literature review on related work to digital forensics techniques in the cloud computing environment.

DOI: 10.4018/978-1-6684-4558-7.ch002

INTRODUCTION

Emerging study areas in the field of cloud computing security include digital forensics and cloud computing service and infrastructure security. 'Cloud Forensic,' a term for using digital forensic concepts and procedures in a cloud context, has several challenges, and little study has been conducted in this crucial field. Cloud forensics faces a number of thorny issues, including crime scene reconstruction, isolating cloud instances, data provenance, and evidence segregation. In order to deal with cybercrimes in the cloud environment, digital investigators have a difficult task: reconstructing criminal events concerning an incident that took place and presenting digital evidence to the court as acceptable proof for the committed cloud-based crime (Ruan et al., 2018). Digital forensics are not yet supported by cloud computing services and infrastructures. Cloud computing's dynamic nature makes conventional digital forensic methodologies, methods, and tools ineffective.

Today, cybercrime is a major concern to governments, businesses, and people throughout the globe because of the damage that may be done to their digital systems, such as computer networks and storage devices. Occasionally, these defense measures may not stop attackers from breaking the security of systems, thus techniques and processes to find and track attackers and criminals who assaulted the systems are necessary in a serious way. An investigative science that deals with finding and tracking down the perpetrators is known as "digital forensic," and it's utilized to gather evidence from the crime scene to recreate the events that took place and submit it as acceptable evidence in a court of law (Fiterman and Durick, 2019). A theory of distributed systems has transformed the traditional thinking on cybercrime because of the introduction of new technologies like cloud computing. On-demand or cost-per-use cloud computing infrastructures are spreading over the globe to offer services for businesses and consumers. Cybercrime strategies have evolved to adapt to the changing cloud computing scenario. To combat these emerging forms of cloud-based criminality, digital investigators must also adapt and develop their tools and approaches. The importance of digital forensic investigation in the cloud will be shown by examining two fictional cybercrime situations in a cloud setting (Hemdan and Manjaiah, 2020). The online banking service and the malevolent user in the cloud are two examples of the two possibilities.

Online Banking Service

The following is an example of a criminal situation that might occur while using online banking services: "Bank XYZ's online banking service has Alex as a client. As part of the banking service, the concerned virtual guest resource is running Windows Server 2012 R2 Webserver Edition in a datacenter that has installed

VMware ESXi server 5. In the customer's opinion, an application-level weakness in the guest operating system was hacked and exploited by hackers in order to acquire his personal information, including his name, login, password, credit card number, and other vital details regarding his account. Forensic proof for a criminal investigation or civil action is foremost on the bank's agenda, even when the issue has been discovered (J. Dykstra and A. Sherman. 2018). It has been discovered that the issue would not have allowed the guest server to be accessed indefinitely. However, despite the fact that the bank has already blocked inbound web access from the virtual guest, the system must remain up and running in order to support other essential business functions ", it's a.

Malicious User in the Cloud

An example of a harmful behavior that might occur in the cloud is shown as follows: This is a VM that Bucky is running in the cloud. Malicious behavior has been seen in the actions of John. In order to get access to cloud infrastructure, he leased a second virtual machine (VM). To steal data from other VMs in the cloud, John planned to utilize Bucky's VM as a launchpad. Investigators will be able to access key data from one of the attackers' VMs. When the investigation was completed, the investigator discovered that the Owner's VM logs each visitor's IP address (Anwar and Anwar, 2019). Using customer data, the investigator discovered that Bucky's VM had been used to carry out the assault. In the end, the investigator obtained the IP address's network records from the appropriate cloud service provider. On the other hand, two possibilities exist. After the incident, John was able to collaborate with the cloud service provider. As a result, the cloud service provider sent a manipulated log to the investigator, who had no means of verifying the logs' accuracy. John will be unnoticed in this situation (Dykstra and Sherman, 2017). It is also possible for John to terminate her leased virtual machine without leaving any record of the assault, regardless of the cloud service provider's integrity. As a result, the cloud provider was unable to furnish the investigator with any helpful logs. Bucky will be held accountable if the investigator is unable to uncover the truth. There is a need to offer new approaches that may effectively perform digital forensics processes in the cloud in order to identify the real attacker in the aforementioned harmful attack scenario.

Figure 1. Imaginary Cloud Attack for Malicious Purposes.

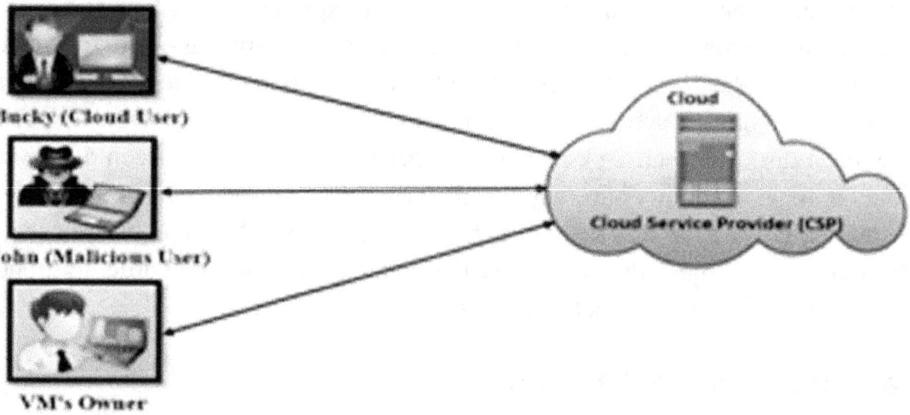

CLOUD COMPUTING

We'll go over some of the basics of cloud computing and digital forensics here, along with some examples of common cybercrimes.

There are a variety of ways to describe cloud computing, including the following: *An on-demand network access to an on-demand pool of customizable resources (such as a network and servers) is provided by cloud computing as a concept for allowing the provisioning and release of resources with little management effort or service provider engagement.*

Cloud Computing Characteristics

Figure 2 shows the NIST's definition of cloud computing, which highlights five key criteria

Figure 2. NIST's definition of cloud computing

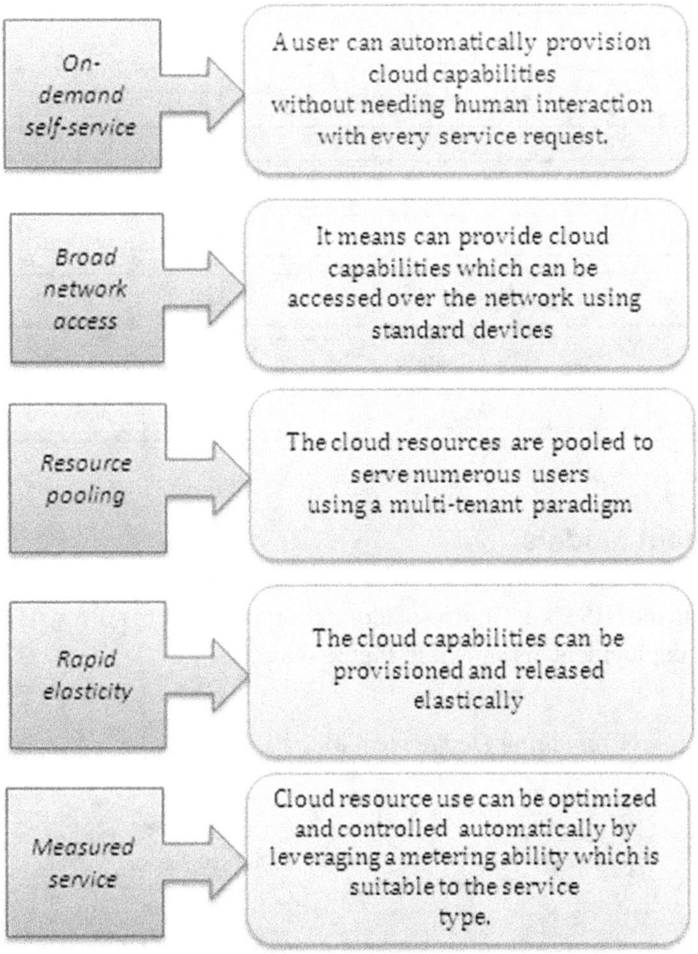

Deployment and Service models for cloud computing are shown in Figure 3.

Figure 3. Cloud Computing Framework.

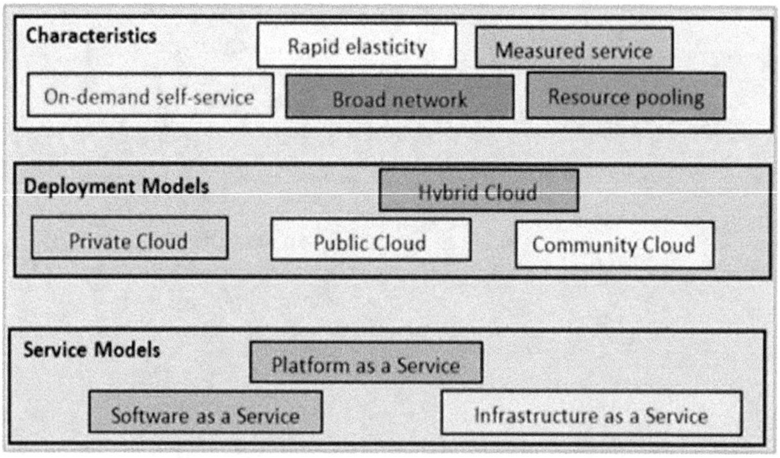

Deployment Models

According to the NIST's definition of cloud computing, there are four types of cloud computing deployment, as shown in Figure 4.

Figure 4. Cloud Computing Deployment Models.

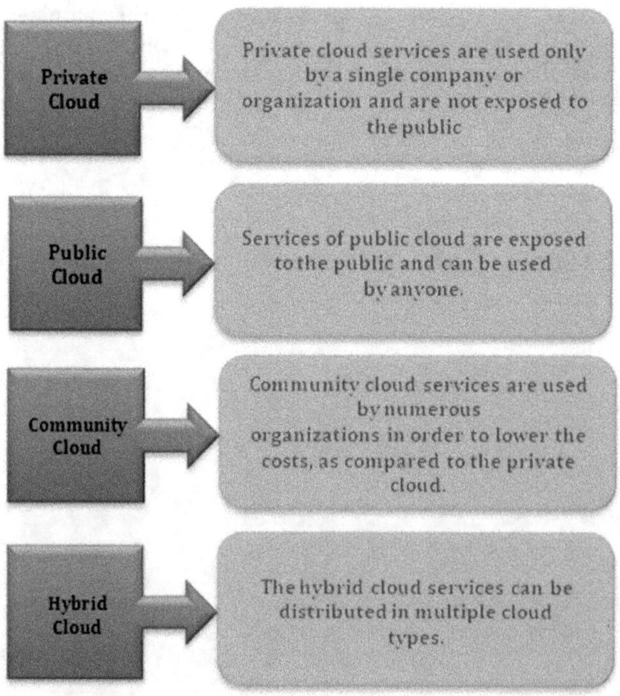

Service Models

According to the NIST's definition of cloud computing, there are three service models that are shown in Figure.5.

Software as a Service (SaaS)

It is possible for a SaaS user to access and utilize cloud-based apps provided by the cloud service provider (Biggs and Vidalis, 2018). Many computers throughout the world are connected to the Internet and can use these programs. An example of a SaaS is a cloud storage service like SkyDrive, Dropbox, or Google Drive.

Platform as a Service (PaaS)

In PaaS, the user may utilize the cloud provider's infrastructure to deploy applications written in a programming language or tool that the user chooses. Users have no control over the cloud infrastructure, but they do have control over their installed apps.

Infrastructure as a Service (IaaS)

User-definable cloud resources including networking, computation, and storage are available under IaaS. Users may also install and execute software, including operating systems and programs (Muniswamy-Reddy et al., 2020). Cloud infrastructure is out of the user's hands, although he or she has some degree of influence over the software, storage, and operating systems that are part of the cloud infrastructure. Amazon EC2 is an example of an IaaS service.

Figure 5. Service Models: (a) Software as a Service (SaaS), (b) Platform as a Service (PaaS) and (c) Infrastructure as a Service (IaaS).

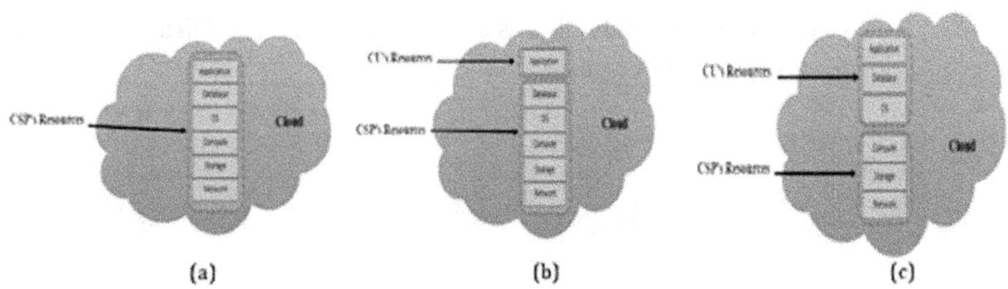

Digital Forensic Definition

Methods derived from and proven by science for the preservation and collection of digital evidence derived from digital sources in order to facilitate or further the reconstruction of events that have been found to be criminal, or to help anticipate unauthorized activity are known as scientific methods (Krautheim et al., 2018). There are several stages involved in digital forensic inquiry, as indicated in Figure 6, according to the digital forensic definition.

Figure 6. Procedure of Investigating Digital Crime

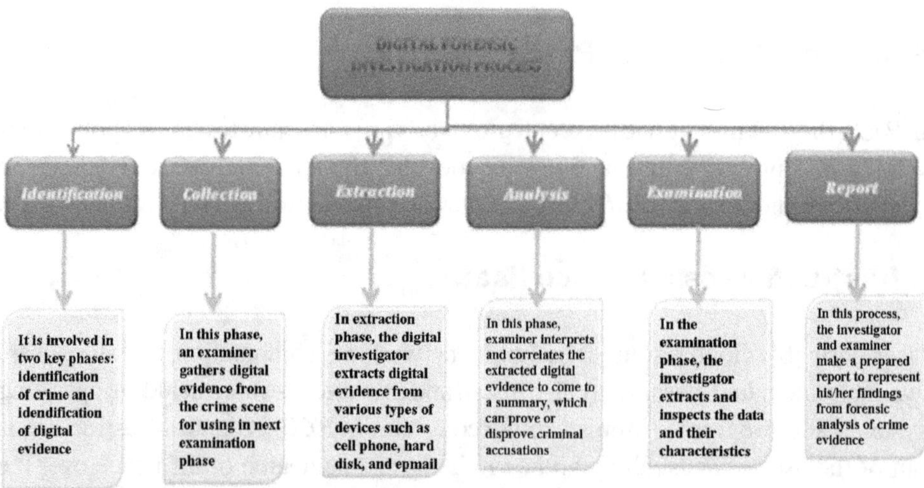

In order to bring cybercriminals to justice, digital investigators use digital evidence as a primary source of information. Many different types of digital evidence may be found on the internet (Santos et al., 2019). These include text files, audio files, images, and videos. If there is a link between a crime and its victim in court, the evidence utilized to show or establish this is known as evidence. Different sorts of digital evidence are shown in Figure 7.

Figure 7. Digital Evidence Types

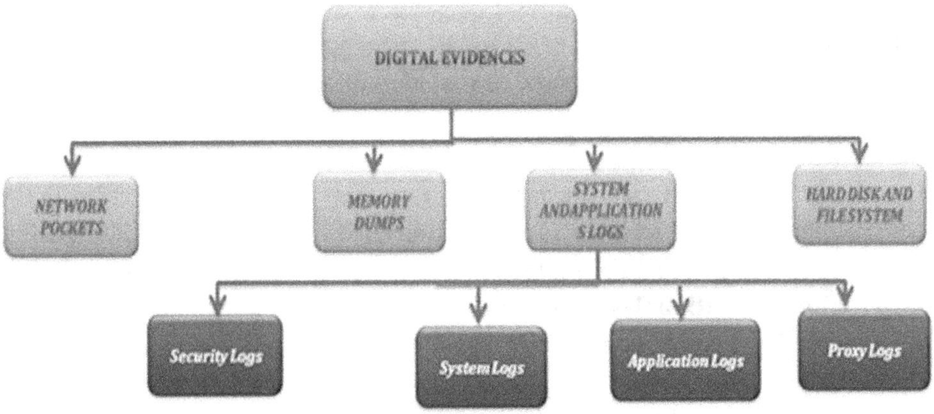

CLOUD FORENSICS

A new phrase was coined by Ruan and colleagues (Quick et al., 2021) to describe the growing demand for cloud digital forensics. An expert in this field said that it is an amalgamation between the fields of cloud computing and digital evidence collection. In "Cloud forensics is a subset of network forensics," it was also discussed. Forensic examinations of networks are the focus of network forensics. Cloud computing relies on a wide range of connectivity. Consequently, cloud forensics follows the same basic steps as network forensics, but with methods that are specific to cloud computing systems.

The Ruan Definition

It is possible to use digital forensics in cloud computing systems, which is known as the field of "cloud forensics". When it comes to creating digital evidence, it uses a hybrid forensic method (such as a thin client or a thick client) that is both remote and virtual. Internal and external investigations may be supported by cloud players (i.e. providers, consumers, brokers, carriers, auditors) interacting with each other. Legally, multi-jurisdictional and multi-tenant situations are generally referred to as multi-jurisdictional. (Ruan et al., 2013).

Cloud Forensics Challenges

A formula devised by the National Institute of Standards and Technology (NIST) (Quick and Choo, 2013) permits the formulation of all cloud forensics difficulties in a manner like this:

- **Actor/Stakeholder**: As the name suggests, this variable [a noun] refers to the people who are directly or indirectly impacted by the problem. Cloud users, researchers, and first responders are a few examples of stakeholders.
- **Action/Operation**: Using this variable [a verb], the stakeholder indicates the action they want to conduct. Decryption, imaging, and getting access are all examples of activities.
- **Object of This Action:** To execute the action on a particular item, use this variable. Data, audit logs, timestamps, proof, and so on are examples of objects.
- **Reason:** For this item, it's important to know exactly what obstacles the stakeholder encounters in order to do the task at hand.

The following are some examples of issues that may be described in a normalized way: If you are a forensic analyst, it is difficult to identify and attribute data that is destroyed in the cloud to a single user, since there is a limit to the number of backups that a cloud provider may keep. Because of the lack of compatibility across cloud service providers, it is difficult for investigators to correlate behavior. Because these reconstruction methods must be vetted or established, it is difficult for investigators and courts to rebuild virtual pictures or data.

A lack of interoperability across service providers, as well as a lack of customer control over proprietary architecture and/or technology utilized, makes the collecting and storage of forensic evidence difficult for investigators, law enforcement, and analysts (Dykstra and Sherman, 2018). Legal authorities have an uphill battle when trying to maintain the right chain of custody and ensure the protection of digital evidence such as digital data and metadata, as well as hardware. Because of the dispersed, shared infrastructure of cloud computing, it is difficult to establish and validate a chain of custody for law enforcement and courts.

The following list summarizes the various categories and their accompanying descriptions: An anti-forensic tactic is a collection of methods designed to thwart or mislead forensic investigation. Obfuscation, malware, and data concealing are just some of the strategies that may be used to jeopardize evidence in cloud forensics; malware can also bypass virtual machine isolation procedures (Salama et al., 2020). Initial triage of forensic artefacts acquired; processing massive volumes; etc. are some of the issues faced by incident first responders in cloud forensic investigations.

Management of roles: Forensic investigators working in the cloud face a variety of role management issues, such as tracing back a user's online identity and finding out who they really are, as well as separating cloud user credentials from those of actual people.

Cloud forensics has a number of standards hurdles, including the absence of even the most basic standard operating procedures (SOPs), practices, and tools, as well as interoperability issues amongst cloud service providers.

Figure 8. Cloud Forensics Challenges Categories

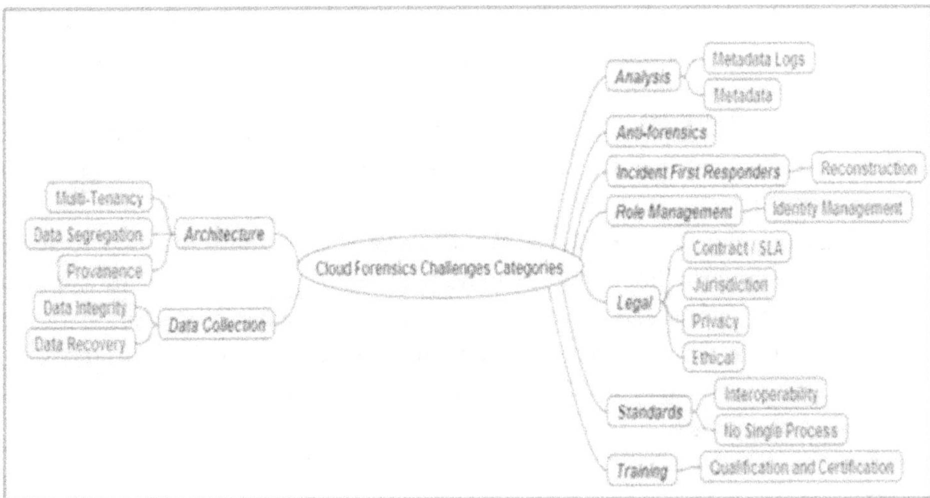

Cloud Forensics Opportunities

To use digital forensics in the cloud computing context, there are many options:

At a reasonable price: Using cloud computing forensic services, investigators may use the vast resources available without having to move digital evidence from the cloud to a local server for analysis, which consumes a lot of bandwidth (Federici, 2016).

There is a plethora of data in the cloud, making it possible for cloud forensics to retrieve any lost or deleted data as evidence of a crime. It's possible for cloud forensic services to employ scalability and flexibility to provide infinite storage, compute, and network resources using the pay as you go way of resource allocation.

Standards and guidelines (Shariati et al., 2019): Changes in cloud computing and cybercrime are prompting new standards and norms for cloud forensic science. "FaaS": "Forensics on demand" Forensic as a Service, a powerful cloud computing solution, is available to digital investigators and examiners (FaaS). Forensic investigators may make use of the vast cloud computing resources to provide FaaS. With this service, digital forensics may be used as a "on-demand" service, allowing for huge storage and processing capacity to be made available as needed for a digital investigation

(Saravanan and Maheswari, 2020) Cloud-based forensic servers will remain inactive until needed. On order to make documents available to digital investigators, it is possible to store them in the cloud. It's true that cloud computing capabilities might be utilized to sift, search, and hash evidentiary data. Among the numerous advantages of Forensics as a Service are the following: When a cloud server is hacked, it may be cloned and made instantly accessible to a cloud forensics server. This reduces the time it takes to gather evidence. Reduce service outages: Because of the cloud's hardware abstraction, it may not be necessary to buy specific hardware to continue collecting evidence in certain instances. The cloud's distributed file system enables for quick bit-for-bit copying, reducing the time it takes to send evidence (Meena et al., 2018). Forensic picture verification may be completed in a fraction of the time by using a cryptographic checksum or hash in certain cloud settings.

Decryption times can be slashed thanks to cloud computing's ability to share computing resources. Cloud storage options eliminate the need to estimate how much disc space is required for logging, enabling for a substantial quantity of log data to be saved and utilized throughout an inquiry. Log indexing and searches are now more efficient thanks to cloud resources, which provide limitless storage as well as real-time indexing and search capabilities.

CURRENT RESEARCH PROBLEMS IN CLOUD FORENSICS

Since the advent of cloud computing, nothing has been published on how digital forensics may be applied to these systems. Cloud forensics research is summarized in this part to better understand the existing difficulties and possible solutions. Cloud forensics difficulties and obstacles will be examined in this section: SLA, VMI, are all examples of methods used to collect and acquire forensic data.

Collection and Acquisition of Forensic Data

In cloud forensics, data gathering and acquisition from cloud infrastructure is a difficult task. By offering a web-based management panel like AWS's management console, cloud service providers (CSPs) may play a dynamic role in this step of the process. In an IaaS approach, (Narkhede et al., 2019) proposed a cloud management plane. Digital evidence that cannot be obtained via other means may be acquired from the console panel by both users and investigators. An additional degree of confidence is required — faith in the management plane is required for this solution. As long as they are able to access the system physically, they don't need this degree of confidence. six-layer trust model. It's easier to build confidence farther down the stack since there's less risk. Data gathering in cloud forensics is complicated by a number of difficulties. Many of these difficulties, such as the lack of control over cloud infrastructure, volatile data in the cloud, and legal and trust issues, multi-tenant systems, multi-tenancy, and high bandwidth.

Log Information

Log information is an important piece of digital evidence for forensic investigations. The cloud has been linked to logging, according to some experts. Decentralization, volatility, various tiers and levels, accessibility, dependency on the cloud service provider, and the lack of key information in logs are just few of the issues that cloud forensics faces when it comes to log information.

According to Marty and colleagues (Povar et al., 2020), a log management system has been presented that can address many of the problems associated with logs. The suggested method has three stages. The first step is to activate logging on all infrastructure components so that logs may be collected. Transferring data from the source to the central log collector requires the second stage of setting up a synchronized, dependable, bandwidth-efficient, and encrypted transport layer. In the last stage, you must ensure that the logs include the information that you want.

Logging given by operating system and security logs was implemented by (Grispos et al., 2019). They used Eucalyptus to build up a cloud computing environment in order to study digital forensics in the cloud. They used two virtual PCs to perform a DDoS assault, and then examined the bandwidth and CPU utilization logs to see whether they could identify the DDoS attack. As a result of analyzing the Jetty logs on Cloud Controller (CC), it is feasible to identify an attacker's IP address, browser type, and requested content.

A single Eucalyptus user and their VM communication patterns may also be seen in these logs, which show how many VMs they manage. (Federici, 2016) suggested that the cloud service provider (CSP) might give the customer with read-only API access to process, network, and access logs from all three cloud service types (APIs). The user may supply valuable information to digital investigators by using these APIs. In PaaS, users have complete control over their application and may record a variety of access information. Log information may be stored in a single place on a central log server. Encrypting and signing log data before transmitting it to the central server ensures that log data is protected from eavesdropping and modification.

Robust Service Level Agreement (SLA)

The present Service Level Agreement (SLA) does not adequately specify the cloud service provider's (CSP) obligation at the time of various malicious acts or their involvement in the digital forensic investigation. Users and cloud service providers should be held to high standards of service level agreements (SLAs) (Meena et al., 2018). The CSP should create a long-term trust connection with consumers or users in order to tackle the transparency challenges. When it comes to cloud-based crimes, a clear service level agreement (SLA) should specify the providers' responsibilities, including how and to what degree they assist in the forensic investigation.

Virtual Machine Introspection (VMI)

It is possible to monitor and audit the running status of a virtual machine (VM) from an external source, such as the Virtual Machine Monitor (VMM) or another virtual machine. Memory, registers, disc, processor, network, and other hardware-level events are all included in what is referred to as the "runtime state" of an application. Forensic analysis can be performed in real time, while the target system remains untouched. For example, if the harmful events are hidden by some rootkit, the VMI procedure may still be used to detect the malicious events. The experiment was carried out using an open source VMI library, Xen (VIX). To avoid confusion, this tool is now rebranded as LibVMI and is no longer under active development under the original name.

Data Provenance in the Cloud

It is crucial to the cloud forensic inquiry because provenance tells the tale of an object's history. Provenance has been used to cloud forensics by a few researchers. The chain of custody in cloud forensics may be maintained by the use of secure provenance, which can offer the evidence's access history, analysis, and preservation. However, no cloud service provider (CSP) has yet to implement any of the proposed approaches for safe provenance.

Trusted Platform Module (TPM)

TPM (Trusted Platform Module) was offered as a solution by numerous academics in order to protect the integrity and confidentiality of the data. It was suggested by various academics (Dykstra, J., & Sherman, A. 2018) that a TPM be used to ensure cloud computing is trustworthy. You may receive hardware encryption, machine authentication and signature with TPM, as well as secure key storage and attestation, by using this technology. For clients, it may guarantee the operating virtual instance's integrity, as well as the integrity of log files and the safe deletion of information. On the other hand, according to Dykstra et al. a running process may be altered without being detected by the TPM. In addition, CSPs now have a wide range of hardware, and only a handful feature TPM. As a result, CSPs will be unable to maintain a uniform hardware environment in the future while using TPM.

Isolating a Cloud Instance

The cloud instance must be separated if a crime occurs there, since isolation helps safeguard evidence from taint. As numerous nodes might contain several instances, this operation gets more difficult.

- **Instance Relocation Technique:** Moving an instance requires transferring secondary storage data, virtual memory content, and any active processes. Moving might be done manually or automatically. All of the administrator's control is available in manual mode. In CSP's automated mode, the instance is moved across nodes.
- **Instance Relocation Technique:** Moving an instance requires transferring secondary storage data, virtual memory content, and any active processes. Moving might be done manually or automatically. All of the administrator's control is available in manual mode. In CSP's automated mode, the instance is moved across nodes. It's important to keep other people's data safe and secure when travelling about.
- **Server Farming Technique:** In which the user and node may be re-routed to each other.
- **Sandbox Technique:** A sandbox may also be used to isolate an instance. Sandboxing applications may be installed in the cloud operating system to create a sandbox. Create a virtual cage around an instance and monitor the communication channels.
- **Man in the Middle (MITM) Technique:** Using an MITM between the cloud instance and the hardware may do this. Using this method, log data may be retrieved from the network, RAM, CPU, and hard disc. In order to reap the benefits of this strategy, the CSP should adopt this method for use in its cloud computing infrastructure.

Forensic Analysis for Cloud Storage Services

Secret materials like terrorist papers and child pornography may be stored in the cloud, while all evidence from the local storage can be erased to leave the criminals clean.

RESEARCH TOOLS AND TEST ENVIRONMENTS

A wide variety of forensic tools and test settings are utilized by researchers and investigators working in the digital forensic investigation sector. Encase and FTK are two popular computer forensic tools. Cloud forensic research is needed to improve current forensic tools or develop new tools specifically for cloud forensics. Most cloud service models need remote analysis and inspection tools because of the necessity to outsource infrastructure in most cloud service models Memory and network dumps must be acquired and processed using digital forensics techniques.

Figure 9 summarizes the most commonly used digital evidence extraction and analysis techniques. A suitable cloud testing environment for an experiment test bed is essential for evaluating theoretical approaches.

Figure 9. Summary of Digital Forensic Tools

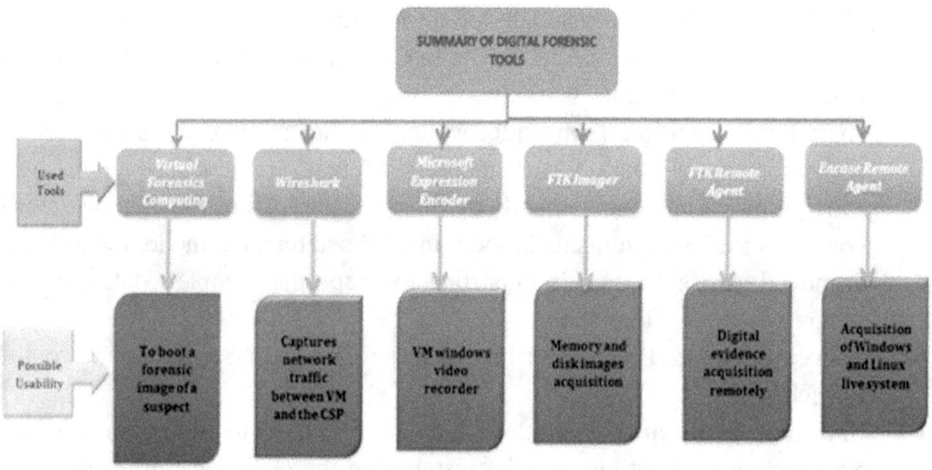

EVALUATION OF CURRENT FORENSIC TOOLS IN CLOUD

Digital forensics technologies like Accessdata FTK, Encase, and others are used by investigators. There are certain differences between cloud forensics and traditional computer forensics when it comes to the collecting of data. Data gathering from a cloud environment may be done using these technologies if certain modifications are made (i.e., Cloud). So far, only a few studies have examined the cloud-based capabilities of various forensic tools, such as (Saravanan and Maheswari, 2020). It is necessary to determine if cloud-based versions of forensic software like Encase and Accessdata FTK are feasible. A study by Dykstra et al. employed EnCase and

Accessdata FTK to gather digital evidence in the cloud using Amazon EC2. In order to gather data from three distinct strata, they carried out three tests and were successful in all of them as follows:

- **In the first experiment:** They were able to capture forensic evidence from the cloud's guest operating system layer remotely. Encase Servlets and FTK Agents were utilised to interact and gather data remotely.
- **For the second experiment:** It was done using the Eucalyptus cloud platform and the virtualization layer.
- **In the third experiment:** They used Amazon's export functionality to verify the data capture on the host operating system level. They discovered that, although data may be exported from S3, it cannot be exported from EBS.

CONCLUSION

Since cloud computing has taken off in recent years, there has been an urgent need to apply digital forensic science to this domain. To investigate crimes and occurrences in multi-tenant cloud systems, new methods are needed to ensure the validity and trustworthiness of the digital forensic process, which is critical in this new viewpoint. As well as an introduction to digital forensics in the cloud computing environment and its difficulties and current solutions, this chapter covered the fundamentals of cloud computing, digital forensics, cybercrimes, and cloud forensics.

ACKNOWLEDGMENT

We would like to acknowledge the support given by Department of Mathematics, National Institute of Technology, Patna, Bihar, India.

REFERENCES

Anwar, F., & Anwar, Z. (2011, December). *Digital forensics for eucalyptus. In 2011 Frontiers of Information Technology*. IEEE.

Biggs, S., & Vidalis, S. (2009, November). Cloud computing: The impact on digital forensic investigations. In *2009 International Conference for Internet Technology and Secured Transactions (ICITST)* (pp. 1-6). IEEE.

Dykstra, J., & Sherman, A. T. (2011). *Understanding issues in cloud forensics: Two hypothetical case studies*. UMBC Computer Science and Electrical Engineering Department.

Dykstra, J., & Sherman, A. T. (2012). Acquiring forensic evidence from infrastructure-as-a-service cloud computing: Exploring and evaluating tools, trust, and techniques. *Digital Investigation*, *9*, S90–S98.

Dykstra, J., & Sherman, A. T. (2013). Design and implementation of FROST: Digital forensic tools for the OpenStack cloud computing platform. *Digital Investigation*, *10*, S87–S95.

Federici, C. (2014). Cloud data imager: A unified answer to remote acquisition of cloud storage areas. *Digital Investigation*, *11*(1), 30–42.

Fiterman, E. M., & Durick, J. D. (2019). Ghost in the machine: Forensic evidence collection in the virtual environment. *Digital Forensics Magazine*, *2*, 73–77.

Grispos, G., Storer, T., & Glisson, W. B. (2012). Calm before the storm: The challenges of cloud computing in digital forensics. *International Journal of Digital Crime and Forensics*, *4*(2), 28–48.

Hemdan, E. E. D., & Manjaiah, D. H. (2015). Exploring digital forensic investigation issues for cyber crimes in cloud computing environment. *Proceeding of 1st International Conference on Computer Communication and Networks (i3CN)*.

Krautheim, F. J., Phatak, D. S., & Sherman, A. T. (2010, June). Introducing the trusted virtual environment module: a new mechanism for rooting trust in cloud computing. In *International conference on trust and trustworthy computing* (pp. 211-227). Springer. 10.1007/978-3-642-13869-0_14

Meena, D., & Gupta, H. (2013). Digital crime investigation using various logs and fuzzy rules: A review. *International Journal of Advanced Research in Computer and Communication Engineering*, *2*(4).

Muniswamy-Reddy, K. K., Macko, P., & Seltzer, M. I. (2010, February). Provenance for the Cloud. In FAST (Vol. 10, pp. 15-14). Academic Press.

Narkhede, S., Baraskar, T., & Mukhopadhyay, D. (2014, March). Analyzing web application log files to find hit count through the utilization of Hadoop MapReduce in cloud computing environment. In *2014 Conference on IT in Business, Industry and Government (CSIBIG)* (pp. 1-7). IEEE.

Povar, D., & Geethakumari, G. (2014, September). A heuristic model for performing digital forensics in cloud computing environment. In *International Symposium on Security in Computing and Communication* (pp. 341-352). Springer.

Quick, D., & Choo, K. K. R. (2013). Digital droplets: Microsoft SkyDrive forensic data remnants. *Future Generation Computer Systems, 29*(6), 1378–1394. doi:10.1016/j.future.2013.02.001

Quick, D., & Choo, K. K. R. (2013). Forensic collection of cloud storage data: Does the act of collection result in changes to the data or its metadata? *Digital Investigation, 10*(3), 266–277. doi:10.1016/j.diin.2013.07.001

Ruan, K., Carthy, J., Kechadi, T., & Baggili, I. (2013). Cloud forensics definitions and critical criteria for cloud forensic capability: An overview of survey results. *Digital Investigation, 10*(1), 34–43. doi:10.1016/j.diin.2013.02.004

Salama, U., Varadharajan, V., & Hitchens, M. (2012, June). Metadata based forensic analysis of digital information in the web. In *Annual Symposium of Information Assurance and Secure Knowledge Management* (pp. 9-15). Academic Press.

Santos, N., Gummadi, K. P., & Rodrigues, R. (2009). Towards Trusted Cloud Computing. *HotCloud, 9*(9), 3.

Saravanan, S., & Maheswari, B. U. (2014). Analyzing Large Web Log Files in A HadoopDistributedCluster Environment. *International Journal of Computer Technology & Applications, 5*, 1677–1681.

Shariati, M., Dehghantanha, A., & Choo, K. K. R. (2016). SugarSync forensic analysis. *The Australian Journal of Forensic Sciences, 48*(1), 95–117.

Chapter 3
IoT-Deep Learning-Based Detection of Cyber Security Threats

Ramesh Naidu P.
https://orcid.org/0000-0003-4941-9569
Nitte Meenakshi Institute of Technology, India

Dankan Gowda V.
B. M. S. Institute of Technology and Management, India

Kumaraswamy S.
https://orcid.org/0000-0002-0821-4869
Global Academy of Technology, Bengaluru, India

Pankaj Dadheech
https://orcid.org/0000-0001-5783-1989
Swami Keshvanand Institute of Technology, Management, and Gramothan, India

Ansuman Samal
Siksha 'O' Anusandhan (Deemed), India

ABSTRACT

The internet of things (IoT) is a revolutionary technology that links living and non-living devices all around the world. As a result, the frequency of cyber-attacks against IoT deployments is expected to rise. As a result, each system must be absolutely secure; otherwise, consumers may opt not to utilize the technology. DDoS assaults that recently attacked various IoT networks resulted in massive losses. There is only one way to detect stolen data from software and malware on the IoT network that is discussed in this chapter. To categorize stolen programming with source code literary theft, the tensor flow deep neural system is offered. To communicate raucous information while simultaneously emphasizing the value of each token in terms of source code forgery, tokenization, and measurement, the malware samples were gathered using the Malign dataset. The results show that the methodology proposed for analyzing IoT cyber security threats has a higher classification efficiency than current methodologies.

DOI: 10.4018/978-1-6684-4558-7.ch003

INTRODUCTION

IoT expansion has expanded significantly in social orders worldwide lately. As how much interconnected IoT hardware came to $27 billion out of 2017, these IoT gear will increment dramatically with buyer interest, with a limit expected to reach $125 billion by 2030. Explicit clever city applications are connected to monstrous, true gadgets, which actually have extremely critical metropolitan advantages. The enormous quantities of Iot gadgets in different assistance types, structures, applications and conventions (e.g., WIFI, wired, versatile, cell, Bluetooth) add to the test of potential IoT network the board. There are accordingly not kidding digital protection dangers and weaknesses to these Internet reconciliation conventions to assault data about ordinary resident exercises (Srinivasan et al., 2019). Such digital dangers may not be permitted on the LOT framework except if the approved customer or leader (for instance Miria botnet) is familiar with them. In splendid city adventures, there are two significant security issues. The chief test is the means by which to recognize zero-day attacks from a combination of IoT shows in the sharp cloud server ranch assuming that critical perils are stayed away from IoT systems (Joyia et al., 2017). The second is the best way to deal with recognize advanced attacks adroitly (for instance IoT malware attacks, etc.) in the IoT arrange already obliterating a shrewd local area. Today, most IoT sensors gather all data through the enormous measure of information gathered on cloud servers (Zanella et al., 2014).

As of now, the IOT network frameworks have insignificant assets and less elements (for example shrewd watches, keen lights, savvy locks, and so on) which are not utilized by IOT network applications. An amazing new technology known as the Thing Internet ties the whole world to the Internet. Personal, professional, and social goals may all be met with the support of Internet of Things (IoT) solutions (Karbab et al., 2017). The Internet of Things (IoT) is a global network of intelligent devices that does not need human involvement, which is great but it is susceptible to cyber-attacks. Intruder detection systems are an essential part of any network's defense against cyber attacks (IDS). A machine-learning network is used by many of the latest IDS to help them prepare for and identify cyber attacks (Jabbar et al., 2018). Centralized distributed computing development is facilitated by fog computing, which tackles scalability obstacles, poorer QoS (Quality of Service) high transmission capacity utilisation and distributed computing's high inactivity need in the IoT framework by using mist-based distributed computing. Consolidating and achieving IoT arrangements effectively is possible with the use of Mist to-hub. Figure 1 depicts the mist to-hub model design with applicable equal figuring for offering IDS measures, controls, and stocking closer to IoT network arte facts for circulated mist.

Figure 1. IoT network design based on fog-to-node communication

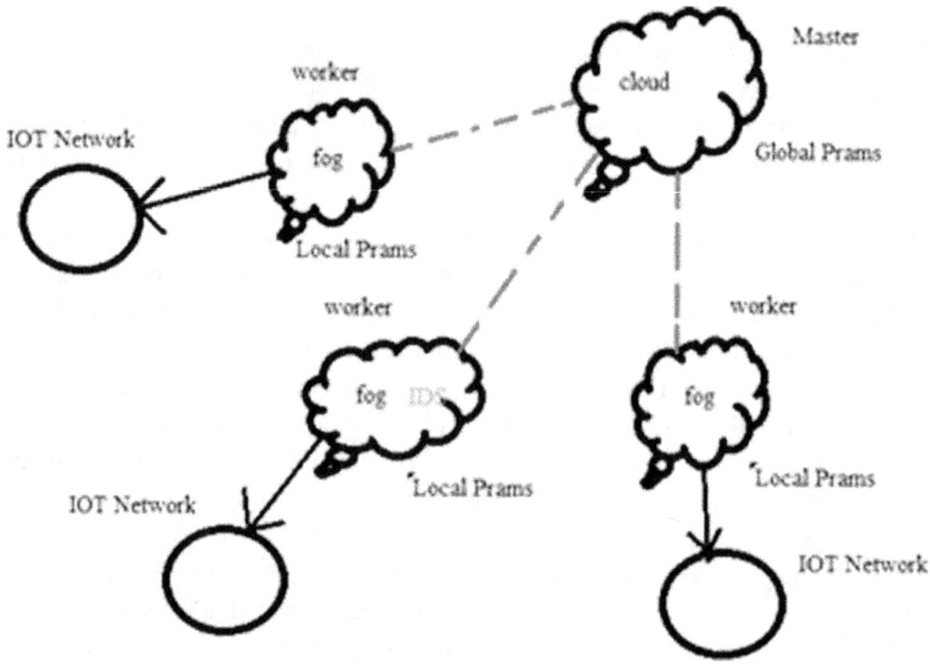

Free attacks may take advantage of IoT devices' constant network accessibility. Malware and pirated software may readily infect the IoT-cloud and compromise its security. Software piracy is the practise of creating new software by repurposing previously-owned source codes and passing them off as the original work of someone else (Chae et al., 2013). By thinking out techniques to reproduce the original reasoning and then structuring a similar reasoning in a different kind of source code, the saltine may copy the original reasoning. It poses a serious threat to Internet security, allowing unrestricted downloads of stolen software, open-source code, and pilfered variations to be developed and promoted. The IT sector is losing billions of dollars every year as a result of this (Akbulut and Dönmez, 2018). There is a 39 percent open theft rate in the BSA's 2016 report, which equates to $52.2 billion in annual losses for businesses. Studies have shown that anywhere from 5% to 20% of a product's source code has appropriated logic. In order to detect plagiarised programming, sharp unoriginality measures are necessary. Identifying clones, acknowledging similitudes with source code, analysing software bugs, and looking into software markers are all advised methods of written falsification (ShanmughaSundaram and Subramani, 2015). Techniques such as structural and textual analysis are the most used ones. These graphs are examined in terms of their underlying structure using the structure-based method. It can only be used for programming in a single Word structure (Ragkhitwetsagul, 2016). There are structural activities that make it difficult to capture the logic of an original software crack when it is reused in a different programming language (Imran et al., 2018). Intelligent software plagiarism and malware detection systems for safeguarding and protecting intelligent devices may be designed using IoT cloud industrial services. Layered IoT architecture is seen in Figure 2. Identifying physical factors and other smart objects in the environment is accomplished through the use of edge devices that interact with the environment, the network layer (consisting of networking devices that discover and connect devices on the IoT network in order to transmit and receive sensed data), and the application layer. Most cyber-attacks are aimed at the application and network levels of an IoT system.

Figure 2. A Layered Architecture for IoT Taking into account the three layers of IoT

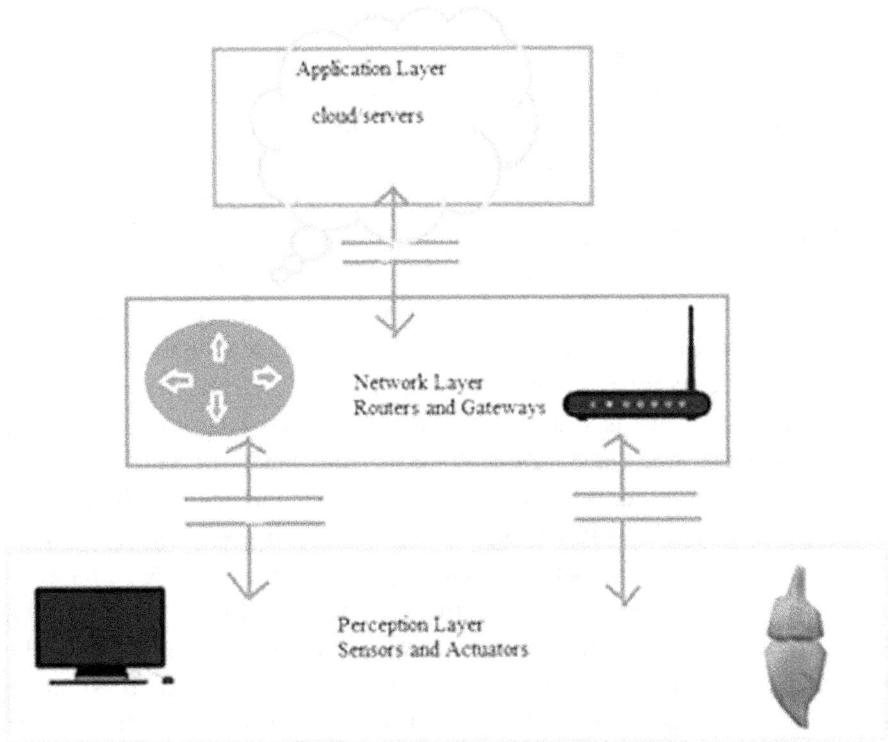

RELATED WORK

Deep learning methods were used in the fields of image processing, speech recognition, healthcare, and so on. These methods were better at getting results than other methods. An in-depth learning method is suggested to find out about distributed fog-to-thing attacks. It shows that cloud IoT networking is hard to use because it is centralized and not good for a big IoT network because it needs the edge of the network to be processed for cyber safety (Shabtai et al., 2009). The field of big data has shown a lot of awareness, so the huge IoT network that makes a lot of data can use fog-to-node methods for the IoT network. In this work, an encoder that stacks cars and a classifier called SoftMax use NSLKDD data sets to make predictions and classify the data (Yu et al., 2019). This work is compared to another low-level model of learning based on performance metrics like precision, false alarm rates, and detection rates. The author has also shown that the distributed parallel computing used in the fog to node model works well.

An SVM (Support Vector Machine) and a deep learning authentication encoder for network intrusion is what the author came up with. Deep learning isn't being used to cut down on the time it takes to train and test, or to improve efficiency by making the SVM classifier more accurate. When the author looked at other machine learning algorithms that aren't very deep like J48, she also looked at the proposed method of binary and multi-class classification. In terms of how well it worked and how accurate it was compared to other proposed methods, the proposed method was better (Bassey et al., 2019). A comparison was made between the shallow neural network and the deep neural network. KDDCup-'99 datasets were also used to compare and train the proposed study methods at a learning rate of 0. In their research, they found that deep learning is a new technology that could be very useful in the field of cyber security (Meidan et al., 2017). They also found that the deep-neural network model with three layers has been the best one. A deep learning model is used to find a Bidirectional Long Term Neural Network (BLSTMRNN), which is similar to LSTM, which is a model of an RNN. Data for four attack vectors used by the mirai botnet was made for this project by the person who did it (Miettinen et al., 2017). Using mirai, udp, dns, and ack as attack methods has been checked and proven to be safe, as well. The proposed method works well for vectors with 99 percent, 98 percent, and 98 percent accuracy, but it doesn't work well for vectors with ack attacks, which need more information. An illustrated literature survey and a short lesson on cyber security machine learning and profound learning methods are given. They are also shown. They talked about a lot of issues with IDS databases and how difficult it is to use machine learning and cyber security. They took care of a lot of issues (Aneja et al., 2018).

The author talked about how to train both of the methods for updating network data very quickly. This led to the retraining of the models, which meant that lifelong training was suggested as the next step in the process.

PROPOSED METHODOLOGY

Data Preprocessing

Using raw binary files, the images in colour are made. This turns the question of how to classify images into one about malware detection. The proposed research compared the best ways to turn malware binary files into a 256-color grayscale image with the best ways to do that now. It doesn't need any tools like a disassemble or a decompiler for reverse engineering. Gray images with only 256 colours won't be able to do as much as coloured images (Bai et al., 2018). Within a group of malware families, the stronger characteristics of malware images might be more important. Most malware detection methods that use machine learning algorithms have worked better with grey images in the past. The colour images have been turned into grayscale images, and extraction techniques have been used to classify the type of malware that was found. Function reduction methods are used to cut down on the amount of functionality that needs to be collected for classification (Gao et al., 2020). Using colour pictures to look for malware isn't the best way to use machine learning algorithms. This is because they give out exponential values. Deep learning algorithms can't keep up with huge malware datasets because these approaches can use filters to automatically remove noise (Li et al., 2018). Deep learning methods are used to get better results from the colour pictures. Four steps are needed to turn a binary file from malware into a colour image. When you start with raw binary files, the first thing to do is to make hexadecimal strings (0-15) from them. Second, you can slice a hexadecimal stream into an 8-bit slice, which calculates each eight-bit segment by an unsigned integer for each eight-bit segment (0-255). In the third step, the 8-bit vector is turned into a two-dimensional space matrix, which is how it looks (Gao et al., 2020). Third, each eight-bit integer is made up of red, green, and blue shaded colours. This makes two-dimensional spaces.

Deep Convolutional Neural Network (DCNN)

The DCNN can be used to do a very thorough analysis of malware data (DCNN). For the neural network model that was built, the Input layer is used to get training images from. The first thing to do is to reduce the noise and improve the signal characteristics by adding a convolution layer. Second, the pooling layer is used to cut down on the amount of data that needs to be stored, which saves important information. Second, the fully integrated layer is used to turn the two-dimensional array into one-dimensional and send it to the right classification. As a third thing, the different types of malware are marked by how each image is categorized.

Convolution Layer

By applying a convolution layer to reduce the picture of parameters, the key characteristics may be retrieved. Invariance of interpretation, rotation, and scale in the convolution layer. Because of its generalisation notion it helps to reduce the issue of overfitting. Equation 1, shows several maps as input to the convolutional layer.

$$x_j^l = f\left\{\sum_{i \in m_j} x_j^{l-1} * k_{ij}^l + b_j^l\right\} \tag{1}$$

A convolution kernel $\boldsymbol{k_{ij}^l}$ is used to combine an ith feature map (input) with a jth feature map (output). $\boldsymbol{b_j^l}$ is the bias and the activation function that are both consistent with the ith feature map.

Pooling Layer

The phrase "sub-sampling layer" refers to a pooling layer that provides maximum and average pooling options. Image distortion is minimised since it is unaffected by backward propagation. Equation 2 shows that the suggested DCNN function is improved while the features' factor is reduced.

$$x_j^i = f(down\left(x_j^{l-1}\right) + b_j^l \tag{2}$$

where down (.) executes a pooling operation and b is a bias value.

Fully Connected Layer

The output of the pooling layer is classified by the fully connected layer. Each neuron has a completely linked layer that connects it to the previous neuron. Improve model generalisation by reducing overfitting using this layer's usage Filters are used to reduce noise in the original picture during fine-tuning. For improved signal characteristics, it is necessary to specify the number and size of kernels.

Learning

The family names of the malware samples are used to appropriately classify them. Training the DCNN model presented in this study was accomplished by the use of SoftMax Cross-Entropy Loss. Equation 3 shows the Loss for the Training Data k.

$$Loss = -\log\left(\frac{\exp(f_{zt})}{\sum_k \exp(f_{zt})}\right) \tag{3}$$

fzt is the kth class rank, and fzt is the proper family score. In order to learn the model's parameters, the Adam optimizer, which aims to minimise the training data's loss, is used.

DEEP LEARNING WITH TENSORFLOW FRAMEWORK

As a high-level machine learning framework, TensorFlow may be utilised to do complicated calculations. Calling a certain API in TensorFlow may allow us to create various machine and deep learning methods. Complex calculations, training data, and monitoring the state-run of each function may all be done using multiple layers (Reshma et al., 2019).

Using the TensorFlow framework, the in-depth learning technique is intended to detect comparable source codes in various kinds of programming languages. Then, the comparable code taken from the pirated programme is utilised to identify it. To train the deep learning model, weighting values are supplied. This layer, also known as the completely linked layer, is designed to handle both input and output. There are three thick layers, each with 100 neurons, each with 50, and each with 30 neurons. With the input variable and input shape parameter, the first layer receives the data (Hasegawa et al., 2017). As a result of the complex network of connections between each neuron, information is constantly being sent into them from the layers above. The output variable for the plagiarised code is located in the fourth dense layer.

Use of drop-out layer in conjunction with activation and loss function, optimizer and learning error rate enhances the deep learning method Dropout layer may also be used to tackle the issue of overfitting (Meidan et al., 2018).

Data patterns may be deduced by using the rectifier (ReLU) activation approach for input variables. It may be represented in terms of the positive portion of its argument in equation (4).

$$f(x) = x^{+} = \max(0, x) \tag{4}$$

where the input to the comparable neurons is represented by the symbol x. When dealing with multi-class problems, sigmoid is a useful logistic approach. Equation 5 explains how it's defined mathematically.

$$S(x) = \frac{1}{1+e^{-x}} \quad (5)$$

In this case, S stands for the sigmoid function. Compiling and fine-tuning deep learning models need the Adam optimizer, also known as stochastic descent gradient. Discrete adaptive learning rates are calculated for each restriction.

Table 1. Comparison of the most advanced pirate detection methods available today

Proposed By	Source Code	Technique	Accuracy (%)
Bandara, Wijayrathna[46]	Java	KNN	86%
Son, J.-M	Java	LSA	99%
Cosma, G. and M.JOY	Java	Parse Tree	90%
Ullah, F[47]	C++, Java	LSA	80%
Ullah, F [6]	C++, Java, Python	MLR	86%
Our Proposed Approach	C++, Java, Python	Deep Neural Network	96%

The decaying means of pas squared gradients are shown in Equation 6 and 7.

$$m_t = \beta 1 m t_{-1} + (1 - \beta 1) gt \quad (6)$$

$$vt = \beta 2 vt\text{-}_{1+} (1 - \beta 2) g2 \quad (7)$$

Means of the first and second instant gradients are mt and vt, respectively. These formulae are used by the Adam optimization algorithm to determine the average of predecessor and successor moments(H. Gao, W. Huang, and Y. Duan. 2020).

Adam optimization algorithm In order to keep the initial gradient mt and square gradient vt's running exponential average up-to-date, these are estimations. Contributions from TensorFlow-based algorithms include:

- Design and enhance machine learning algorithms for huge data sets using this integrated GitHub framework and a wide range of APIs.
- The input, hidden, and output layers of this architecture use distinct activation functions to train the model automatically.
- In addition to providing dependable services, it is constantly improving and expanding the original concept.

- It is possible to execute these algorithms on a wide range of devices, from individual computers to whole networks.

IMPLEMENTATION

Machine learning techniques are being tested for their ability to identify IoT network assaults, as stated in the preceding portions of the experiment. In this chapter, detail the datasets, machine learning techniques, and implementation procedures that we employed.

Datasets

Large datasets are required to assess network flows and discriminate between normal and abnormal traffic due to the usage of machine learning algorithms in numerous applications for network security jobs. To build network datasets, researchers have conducted a number of experiments throughout the years. In most research including machine learning, data from simulated or actual networks is used to evaluate the results, as indicated in Table I. As a result of security concerns, many of these datasets remain secret. Nonetheless, some have been made public, such as DARPA 98 and KDD99. N-BaIoT and N-BaIoT The production of realistic IoT and network traffic statistics that incorporate novel Botnet situations is still rare, despite the existence of several datasets. In addition, some datasets do not include IoT-generated traffic, while others do not produce any new characteristics. There were certain instances where the testbed employed was not realistic, while there were others where the assault scenarios were not varied or interesting enough. The N-BaIoT dataset, produced by Meidan et al., was utilised in numerous subsequent research to train and evaluate IoT classifier algorithms. This dataset, despite its size and cleanliness, is uneven, with a smaller proportion of normal data than attack data. Moustafa et al. designed the Bot-IoT dataset, which has been utilised in our studies, to solve these issues. IoT network traffic and different assaults are included in the Bot-IoT dataset. Probing assaults, DoS attacks, and theft of information theft are all examples of BotIoT database attacks.

Machine Learning Algorithms

Machine learning classifiers (KNN, ID3, Random Forest, AdaBoost, Quadratic discriminant analysis, Multilayer perceptrons, and Naive Bayes) were tested on the Bot-IoT dataset (NB). In selecting these classifiers, the goal is to combine well-known techniques with a variety of desirable properties. The following is a quick rundown of the algorithms that were employed in this case.

Figure 3. Overview of Approach

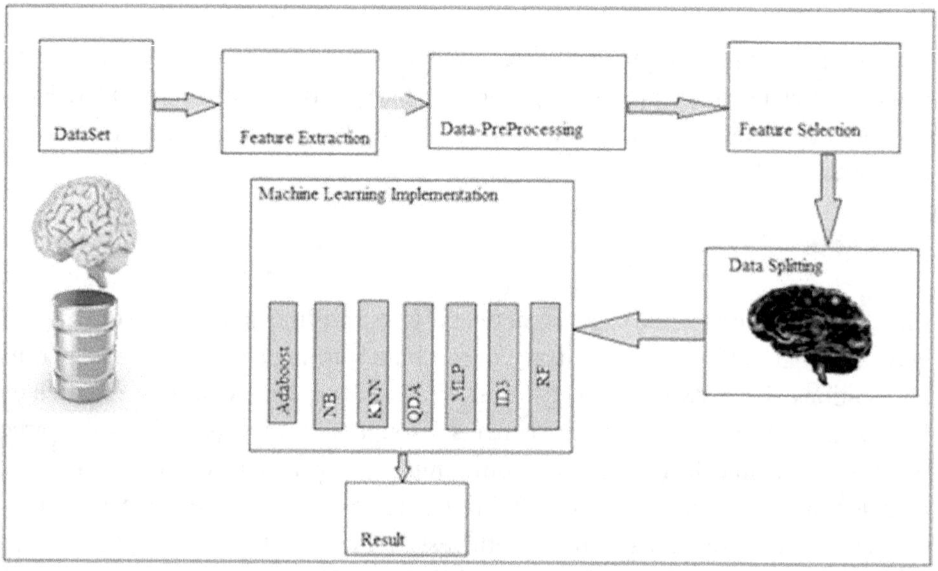

- **K-Nearest Neighbors (KNN):** When it comes to supervised learning, KNN is an excellent choice. New data points may be associated with comparable existing data points by searching through the available datasets. As a rapid training technique, KNN is very sluggish when attempting to estimate multidimensional data sets.
- **Quadratic discriminant analysis (QDA):** Supervised classification issues are well-suited to the QDA algorithm. Measured data may be assigned to one of several categories using discriminant analysis, a statistical method. There isn't a lot of data for a particular category, thus QDA is a good fit. To use Quadratic Discriminant Analysis, you'll need to have more samples than groups in your data.
- **Iterative Dichotomiser 3(ID3):** A dataset is fed into the ID3 algorithm, which then outputs a decision tree. One of its creators is Ross Quinlan. A classification technique known as a "decision tree" use a tree-like structure to make decisions. An algorithm with just conditional control statements may be shown this way. The nodes of the tree are the characteristics, and the "leaves" are the class values assigned to each record. ID3 is a forerunner

of the C4.5 method, which is often used in machine learning and natural language processing.

- **Random Forest (RF):** Decision trees are used in the RF machine learning technique. To construct a "forest," several distinct decision tree topologies are assembled in various ways. For example, this technique is capable of running on large datasets quickly, is low in weight compared to other approaches and is more resilient against noise and outliers than single classifier methods.
- **Adaptive Boosting (AdaBoost):** AdaBoost is a machine learning technique that focuses on classification problems and attempts to improve poor classifiers. One of the most widely used learning algorithms, Freund and Schapire's method was initially introduced in 1996. The capacity of the AdaBoost algorithm to cope with datasets that include missing values is by far its most critical feature.
- **Multilayer Perceptron (MLP):** Artificial neural network MLPs are a kind of feedforward MLP (ANN). Learning and generating new knowledge may be done using artificial neural networks (ANN), which are based on the way the human brain operates. It is not uncommon for MLPs to include more than three layers: an input, output, and hidden layer. Back-propagation, a supervised learning approach, is used to train MLP.
- **Naive Bayes(NB):** Popularly employed in supervision, it's known for its simplicity. Thomas Bayes' work is the foundation of the naïve Bayes technique. Intrusion detection systems could make use of NB to classify network traffic as "normal" or "anomalous." The traffic classification characteristics utilised by the NB classifier are handled individually despite the fact that these features may rely on one other. NB's simplicity, minimal sample demand, and ease of implementation make it user-friendly. It is impossible for NB to learn anything about the interconnections and interactions between features since it works with each feature on its own.

Implementation Steps

Feature extraction; data pre-processing; data splitting; feature selection; and implementation of machine learning algorithms are the five primary components of our technique.

- **Feature Extraction:** Raw network traffic data was processed with CICFlowMeter to extract flow-based characteristics (in pcap format). In all, CICFlowMeter generates 84 different network traffic characteristics. It is available from CIC as a network traffic flow generator. There is an option to download a CSV file of the dataset, as well as a visual document of the characteristics derived from the pcap file. The primary goal of this procedure was to add additional dataset characteristics to classifiers in order to increase their prediction skills.

- **Data pre-processing:** In order to make the dataset acceptable for machine learning, pre-processing methods are employed. This stage also involves eliminating data that is useless or damaged, which improves the dataset's correctness and makes it easier to analyse..
- **Splitting Data:** In order for machine learning to work, it need the availability of data. Testing the algorithm's performance needs additional data in addition to that necessary for training. 80% of the Bot-IoT dataset was considered training data, while the remaining 20% was considered testing data in our research.
- **Feature Selection:** IoT systems need a lightweight security solution with a low number of features that can be trained and tested with little resources. For the feature selection, In this chapter, used the Random Forest Regression approach. Using the random forest regressor, data may be condensed to manageable proportions. The model trains and responds more rapidly when the input data characteristics are reduced from more than 80 network traffic features to seven.
- **Implementation of Machine Learning Algorithms:** All of the experiments were carried out in Python using machine learning libraries provided by Python (scikit-learn, Matplotlib, Pandas, and NumPy). It was decided to conduct our evaluation of machine learning algorithms for the dataset in three stages: first, applied each algorithm to a different attack in the dataset separately. Then, used a set of features that combined the best characteristics of each attack (a list of these characteristics can be found in Table II). Finally, used the seven best characteristics found in the feature selection step to apply each algorithm to the entire dataset.

Table 2. Created for all kinds of assaults, the feature list

Flow IAT Mean	Flow Duration	Flow Pkts/s
Flow IAT Max	Fwd Pkt Len Max	TotLen Fwd Pkts
Fwd Pkt Len Mean	Tot Bwd Pkts	Fwd IAT Tot
Flow IAT Std	Flow Bytss	Tot Fwd Pkts

DEEP LEARNING METHODS FOR IoT SECURITY

In this part, we'll take a look at some of the strategies that make use of deep learning to improve IoT security. In light of this, we've come up with a few methods for enhancing IoT safety.

Feature Learning Process

When it comes to extracting features, the traditional method begins with the collecting of data and ends with feature extraction. Data collecting, data encoding, feature definition, and feature extraction will be divided into four processes for the purposes of this study. Data from IoT security databases are used to classify security aspects into static, dynamic, and causal categories in the multilayered hierarchical Bayesian network shown in figure 4.

Raw data, such as RF signals, device attributes, heat maps, and raw network packets, are acquired during the data collecting phase. There is a need to define how to handle raw data, which is sometimes quite vast, of mixed data kinds, and contains numerous unconnected items. One way to encode data is to break it down into smaller, more manageable units, such as individual pixels in a picture or individual network packets.

Figure 4. Feature Selection process

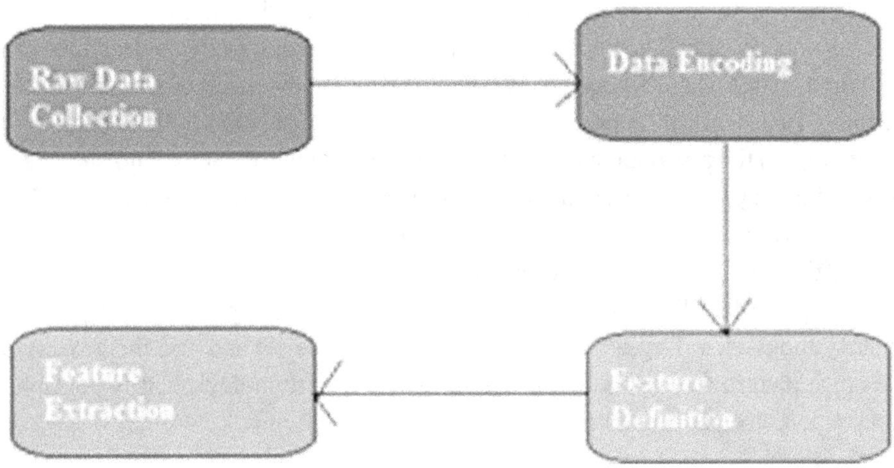

Each element is represented by the number xi. When defining features, data is grouped in such a way that the data object as a whole can be studied. Deep learning has recently introduced the concept of tensors, which may be used to arrange input pieces. Encoding raw data into a format suitable for a deep learning model's input is the first step. This procedure is referred to as D and the data after feature definition may be referred to as E.

$$X = D(x1,x2,x3,\dots\dots xn) \tag{8}$$

D is the process of arranging fundamental elements in predetermined sequences. Inputs are defined as features in the feature specification. Extracting features from structured data items is done using statistical approaches such as series analysis, frequency analysis or machine learning. The feature extraction is defined here as

$$V = F(X) = F\ (D\ (x1,\ x2,\ x3,..)) \tag{9}$$

The feature extraction techniques are referred to as F in this context. Feature vectors of fixed length V = v1, v2, v3..... are often the result of feature extraction. Data encoding and feature definition are presented in this work as two separate data preparation phases: (1) to extract relevant features from mixed raw inputs, and (2) to give structure to our data.

Deep Learning for Device Feature Extraction

Many linked devices in an IoT network make it difficult to identify a given device in an entire network. Techniques for identifying a particular IoT device are the topic of this section. The capacity to automatically acquire relevant features from raw inputs, such as autoencoders, is one of the most powerful components of deep learning. Deep learning approaches for extracting device features may be categorised depending on the raw data that they utilise for identification. Sensor noise patterns, radio frequency properties, and energy consumption may all be used to identify the uniqueness of a certain item. Deep learning allows for the extraction of higher-level information and the discovery of even the most minute variations across devices. As in camera identification, raw photos taken with a camera might be collected to identify the device. Begin by defining the raw picture set as I and then extracting the noise pattern from photos that are unique to a certain device. It is possible to determine noise patterns in most cases as follows:

$$N = I - F(I) \tag{10}$$

the denoised picture of I, and I is the original image with the original noise. It's common for a specific device's signal noise N to be unique, although it's not always the case. The residual noise is treated as a two-dimensional distribution and variables such as mean, max, skewness, and kurtosis are extracted using statistical techniques to extract signal noise patterns from a picture. Wavelet or Fourier transforms, when applied to the resulting two-dimensional two-dimensional noise signal, will reveal the frequency at which the noise level is occurring. According to, the signal noise matrix is immediately fed into the CNN, which tries to automatically extract features from noise with minimum human involvement, unlike approaches above.

EVALUATION

Performance measurements and a benchmark dataset are necessary to assess the effectiveness and efficiency with which deep learning approaches may be used.

Evaluation Measure

In machine learning, precision is a popular metric. How many real positive predictions are produced in comparison to the overall number of positive forecasts? (where either true or false). This is the number of false alarms in an intrusion detection system.

$$Precision = \frac{t_p}{t_p + f_p} \tag{11}$$

True positive examples (tp) and false positive examples (fp) are counted as tp and fp respectively. Recall is yet another frequent metric for evaluating an organization's success (also known as sensitivity). Recall is defined as the number of forecasts that were correct out of the total number of predictions that were correct. The following is a definition of recall:

$$recall = \frac{t_p}{t_p + f_n} \tag{12}$$

Since there are more positive cases than negative ones, get the value of the constant fn (false negatives). There are fn assaults that go unnoticed in an intrusion detection system. There is often an inverse connection between accuracy and recall that may be increased at the expense of the other.

The F1 score (sometimes referred to as F-Measure or F-score) is often used to assess classification accuracy in binary classification. To arrive at the final result, it takes into account both accuracy and recall. The harmonic average of accuracy and recall is what gives an F1 score its name. This is how the F1 score is calculated:

$$F1 = 2 * \frac{precision * recall}{precision + recall} \tag{13}$$

The F1 measure has a maximum score of 1, which means that both accuracy and recall are accomplished to the point of perfection. May use a graph called the receiver operating characteristic (ROC) curve to figure out the threshold for a binary classification system. The genuine positive rate is shown against the matching false positive rate with various threshold settings in a graphical representation. Using the area under the curve (AUC), a classification system's performance is measured. The AUC is a measure of separability since it indicates the magnitude of the area under the ROC curve. It can tell us how well the learning model is able to discriminate between the various classes. The classifier's ability to accurately anticipate a result based on the labels it has been given is directly proportional to its AUC. As a rule of thumb, the greater a model's AUC, the better its ability to classify data.

CONCLUSION

Deep learning is shown to have a significant influence on the Internet of Things environment in this research. One of the primary focuses of chapter is the use of deep learning technology to analyse the security issues associated with Internet of Things devices. The major subjects of discussion were deep learning-based device fingerprinting and profiling, as well as device classification. A functional layer was created in order to improve feature mapping for device identification in a semantically appropriate manner while maintaining functionality. Unprocessed traffic traces were transmitted to CICFlowMeter, which was used to determine flow-based characteristics from the raw traffic traces. The network flow is characterised by the 84 network traffic characteristics that CICFlowMeter provides. It was necessary to apply the Random Forest Regressor method to establish the importance of weight calculations during implementation in order to select which attributes would be used in the machine learning techniques. These calculations were carried out utilising two separate approaches. Previously, each attack type had its unique significance weights computed; in the second method, each attack type was grouped together and the importance weights for this group were calculated; in other words, the common qualities that are crucial for all assaults had been discovered. In the end, seven well-known machine learning algorithms were used to analyse the information. According to F-measure, the following are the algorithms that were utilised, as well as the performance ratios that were obtained: The values of Naive Bayes, QDA, Random Forest, ID3, AdaBoost, MLP, and K Nearest Neighbors were all between 0 and 1, but the value of F-measure was between 0 and 1. In this chapter, seven different supervised algorithms were investigated. The evaluation of the performance of certain unsupervised algorithms would be a worthwhile future endeavour to undertake. Apart than that, we employed a number of machine learning approaches on our own.

ACKNOWLEDGMENT

We would like to acknowledge the support given by BMS Institute of Technology and Management, Bangalore, India.

REFERENCE

Akbulut, Y., & Dönmez, O. (2018). Predictors of digital piracy among Turkish undergraduate students. *Telematics and Informatics*, *35*(5), 1324–1334. doi:10.1016/j.tele.2018.03.004

Aneja, S., Aneja, N., & Islam, M. S. (2018, November). IoT device fingerprint using deep learning. In 2018 IEEE international conference on internet of things and intelligence system (IOTAIS) (pp. 174-179). IEEE.

Bai, L., Yao, L., Kanhere, S. S., Wang, X., & Yang, Z. (2018, October). Automatic device classification from network traffic streams of internet of things. In *2018 IEEE 43rd conference on local computer networks (LCN)* (pp. 1-9). IEEE.

Bassey, J., Adesina, D., Li, X., Qian, L., Aved, A., & Kroecker, T. (2019, June). Intrusion detection for IoT devices based on RF fingerprinting using deep learning. In *2019 Fourth International Conference on Fog and mobile edge computing (FMEC)* (pp. 98-104). IEEE. doi:10.1109/WiMOB.2019.8923325

Chae, D. K., Ha, J., Kim, S. W., Kang, B., & Im, E. G. (2013, October). Software plagiarism detection: a graph-based approach. In *Proceedings of the 22nd ACM international conference on Information & Knowledge Management* (pp. 1577-1580). 10.1145/2505515.2507848

Gao, H., Huang, W., & Duan, Y. (2021). The cloud-edge-based dynamic reconfiguration to service workflow for mobile ecommerce environments: A QoS prediction perspective. *ACM Transactions on Internet Technology*, *21*(1), 1–23. doi:10.1145/3391198

Gao, H., Kuang, L., Yin, Y., Guo, B., & Dou, K. (2020). Mining consuming behaviors with temporal evolution for personalized recommendation in mobile marketing apps. *Mobile Networks and Applications*, *25*(4), 1233–1248. doi:10.100711036-020-01535-1

Gao, H., Liu, C., Li, Y., & Yang, X. (2020). V2VR: Reliable hybrid-network-oriented V2V data transmission and routing considering RSUs and connectivity probability. *IEEE Transactions on Intelligent Transportation Systems*, *22*(6), 3533–3546. doi:10.1109/TITS.2020.2983835

Hasegawa, K., Yanagisawa, M., & Togawa, N. (2017, July). Hardware Trojans classification for gate-level netlists using multi-layer neural networks. In *2017 IEEE 23rd International Symposium on On-Line Testing and Robust System Design (IOLTS)* (pp. 227-232). IEEE. 10.1109/IOLTS.2017.8046227

Imran, S., Khan, M. U. G., Idrees, M., Muneer, I., & Iqbal, M. M. (2018). An enhanced framework for extrinsic plagiarism avoidance for research article. *Technical Journal*, *23*(01), 84–92.

Jabbar, S., Malik, K. R., Ahmad, M., Aldabbas, O., Asif, M., Khalid, S., Han, K., & Ahmed, S. H. (2018). A methodology of real-time data fusion for localized big data analytics. *IEEE Access: Practical Innovations, Open Solutions*, *6*, 24510–24520. doi:10.1109/ACCESS.2018.2820176

Joyia, G. J., Liaqat, R. M., Farooq, A., & Rehman, S. (2017). Internet of medical things (IoMT): Applications, benefits and future challenges in healthcare domain. *Journal of Communication*, *12*(4), 240–247.

Karbab, E. B., Debbabi, M., Derhab, A., & Mouheb, D. (2017). *Android malware detection using deep learning on API method sequences*. arXiv preprint arXiv:1712.08996.

Li, X., Xiao, F., Li, L., Shen, J., & Qian, F. (2018, June). Detection Method of Hardware Trojan Based on Wavelet Noise Reduction and Neural Network. In *International Conference on Cloud Computing and Security* (pp. 256-265). Springer. 10.1007/978-3-030-00018-9_23

Meidan, Y., Bohadana, M., Mathov, Y., Mirsky, Y., Shabtai, A., Breitenbacher, D., & Elovici, Y. (2018). N-baiot—Network-based detection of iot botnet attacks using deep autoencoders. *IEEE Pervasive Computing*, *17*(3), 12–22. doi:10.1109/MPRV.2018.03367731

Meidan, Y., Bohadana, M., Shabtai, A., Guarnizo, J. D., Ochoa, M., Tippenhauer, N. O., & Elovici, Y. (2017, April). ProfilIoT: a machine learning approach for IoT device identification based on network traffic analysis. In *Proceedings of the symposium on applied computing* (pp. 506-509). 10.1145/3019612.3019878

Miettinen, M., Marchal, S., Hafeez, I., Asokan, N., Sadeghi, A. R., & Tarkoma, S. (2017, June). Iot sentinel: Automated device-type identification for security enforcement in iot. In *2017 IEEE 37th International Conference on Distributed Computing Systems (ICDCS)* (pp. 2177-2184). IEEE.

Ragkhitwetsagul, C. (2016, October). Measuring code similarity in large-scaled code Corpora. In *2016 IEEE International Conference on Software Maintenance and Evolution (ICSME)* (pp. 626-630). IEEE. 10.1109/ICSME.2016.18

Reshma, K., Priyatharishini, M., & Nirmala Devi, M. (2019). Hardware trojan detection using deep learning technique. In *Soft Computing and Signal Processing* (pp. 671–680). Springer. doi:10.1007/978-981-13-3393-4_68

Shabtai, A., Moskovitch, R., Elovici, Y., & Glezer, C. (2009). Detection of malicious code by applying machine learning classifiers on static features: A state-of-the-art survey. *Information Security Technical Report, 14*(1), 16-29.

ShanmughaSundaram, M., & Subramani, S. (2015). A measurement of similarity to identify identical code clones. *The International Arab Journal of Information Technology*, 735–740.

Srinivasan, C. R., Rajesh, B., Saikalyan, P., Premsagar, K., & Yadav, E. S. (2019). A review on the different types of Internet of Things (IoT). *Journal of Advanced Research in Dynamical and Control Systems*, *11*(1), 154–158.

Yu, J., Hu, A., Zhou, F., Xing, Y., Yu, Y., Li, G., & Peng, L. (2019, October). Radio frequency fingerprint identification based on denoising autoencoders. In *2019 International Conference on Wireless and Mobile Computing, Networking and Communications (WiMob)* (pp. 1-6). IEEE.

Zanella, A., Bui, N., Castellani, A., Vangelista, L., & Zorzi, M. (2014). Internet of things for smart cities. *IEEE Internet of Things Journal*, *1*(1), 22–32. doi:10.1109/JIOT.2014.2306328

Chapter 4
Deep Learning Models for Cyber Security in IoT Networks

Dankan Gowda V.
B. M. S. Institute of Technology and Management, India

Puneeth Kumar B. S.
St. Joseph's College (Autonomous), India

Shekhar R.
Alliance University, India

Pankaj Dadheech
https://orcid.org/0000-0001-5783-1989
Swami Keshvanand Institute of Technology, Management, and Gramothan, India

Thangadurai N.
Sankalchand Patel University, India

ABSTRACT

As the number of connected devices grows, the internet of things (IoT) poses new security challenges for network activity monitoring. Due to a lack of security understanding on the side of device producers and end users, the majority of internet of things devices are vulnerable. As a result, virus writers have found them to be great targets for converting them into bots and using them to perform large-scale attacks against a variety of targets. The authors provide deep learning models based on deep reinforcement learning for cyber security in IoT networks in this chapter. The IoT is a potential network that connects both living and nonliving things all around the world. As the popularity of IoT grows, cyber security remains a shortcoming, rendering it exposed to a variety of cyber-attacks. It should be emphasized, however, that while there are numerous DL algorithms presently, the scientific literature does not yet include a comprehensive catalogue of them. This chapter provides a complete list of DL algorithms as well as their many application areas.

DOI: 10.4018/978-1-6684-4558-7.ch004

INTRODUCTION

The newest developing promising technology known as the Internet of Things links everything on Earth via the internet. IoT (the technology) has the potential to enhance and assist in both our personal and professional lives, as well as our societal well-being. The internet of things, otherwise known as IoT, includes millions of smart devices all over the globe, all linked via the internet without human intervention. Unfortunately, because of this, it is vulnerable to cyber assaults just like any other network. A powerful tool for detecting cyber-attacks is an intrusion detection system (IDS) (Roopak et al., 2019). Machine learning has formed the core of all current IDS (including the state-of-the-art models). Fog computing extends cloud computing, where fog nodes are placed closer to IoT network devices to increase scalability, lower bandwidth usage, lower latency in QoS and overall enhance overall functionality. In fog-to-node computing, real IoT networks may achieve success. Figure 1 shows the architecture of a fog-to-node model, where fog nodes are dispersed and each node hosts distributed parallel computing that provides distributed fog systems with processing, control, and storing of IDS components that are more central to IoT network objects. In contrast to cloud services, fog nodes can identify a cyber-attack effectively and promptly. Internet of Things (IoT) refers to a collection of diverse technologies ranging from supercomputers to small devices with extremely little computational capacity, therefore protecting an IoT network poses major security challenges (Yuan et al., 2017). DDoS was a significant cyber-attack on the Internet of Things (IoT) that caused considerable damages. Attacks against web servers often use many hosts to overwhelming target systems, resulting in a total crash. This causes genuine users to be unable to use the system. It is expected that the denial-of-service attack would grow to around 17 million by 2020 as predicts. DL is a wider subfield of machine learning known as machine learning and machine learning (ML) is deeper than that, it is in fact a much larger network known as a deep neural network. This research, published in 2016, shows that deep learning methods such as deep belief networks and also convolutional neural networks (CNN) were developed in the 1980s and have since proved successful in a variety of areas such as image processing, natural language processing, and self-driving cars. One of the main challenges of deep learning techniques is the bigger the training dataset, the longer the training period.

Figure 1. Depicts the architecture of an Internet of Things network from fog to node.

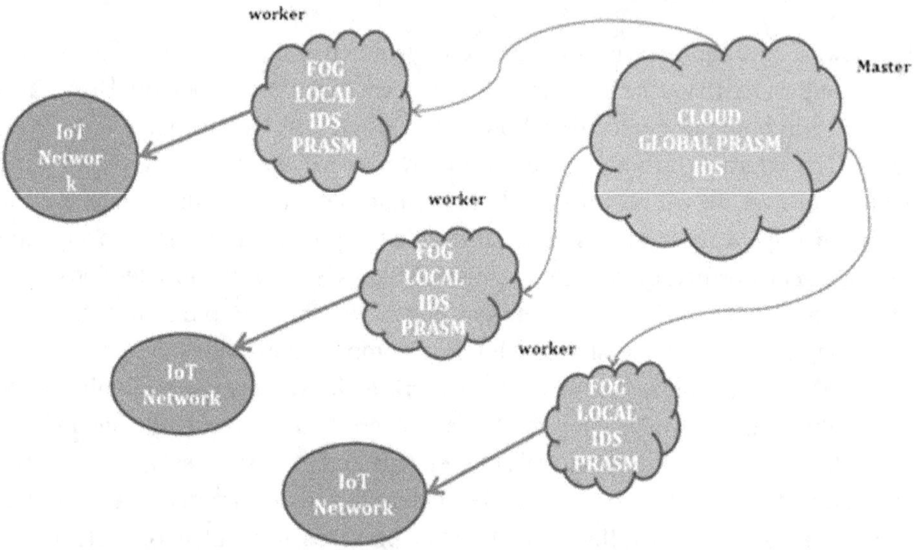

Figure. 2 shows the fundamental architecture of a deep learning model, which consists of one input layer followed by several hidden layers. The last layer of the model has one input and produces an output. CNN is a deep learning model that has been widely used in image and language processing (Sharif Razavian et al., 2014). The raw picture is immediately supplied to CNN models without any pre-processing, and the model then does various convolution operations on the image data (Hao et al., 2018). In the areas of NLP (natural language processing) and text processing, RNNs (Recurrent neural networks) have shown positive results. LSTM (Long Short-Term Memory) is a kind of RNN. Because LSTM is applied directly to raw data, it has a number of advantages.

Figure 2. The Deep Learning Model's Architectural Design

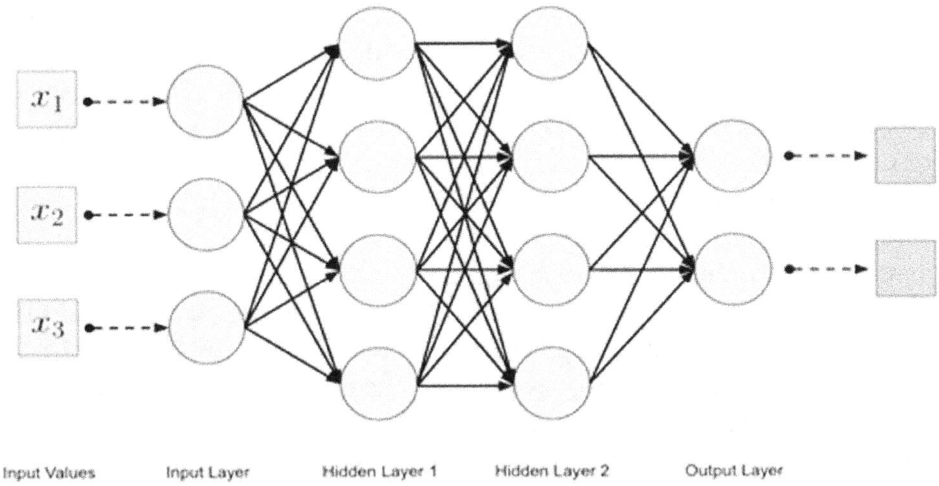

RELATED WORK

AI has seen significant development since the first models of deep learning were introduced. A powerful new application of deep learning techniques developed and quickly gained widespread use in a variety of scientific and engineering disciplines. A number of early application areas for deep learning have included such fields as health informatics, energy informatics, urban informatics, safety, security, hydrological systems modelling, economics, bioinformatics, and computational mechanics are some of the fields in which they may be found. In addition to deep learning, the other data-driven techniques, including ensemble and hybrid machine learning, will play an increasingly important role in data science (Hori et al., 2017). Although deep learning models and hybrid machine learning models may perform better than traditional machine learning models, some comparative studies have shown that these models struggle to consistently perform as well. Deep learning techniques are advancing rapidly due to a need for increased performance (Vigneswaran et al., 2018).

Bibliographies in research fields use established links and resources to help guide students toward relevant literature that explores subject matters as they develop, from subject discovery to creation, by thoroughly listing citations and explaining how to access such citations and resources (McDermott et al., 2018).

At the moment, however, a simple guide to deep learning techniques has not been shared. As a result, there is a vacuum in the study related to the introduction of deep learning techniques and describing how and in what situations they may be used. More specifically, this article's aim is to provide a comprehensive list of the most widely used deep learning algorithms, along with examples of notable applications for each (Vijayanand et al., 2018). There is a famous deep learning approach described in each part, along with examples of its pertinent applications. It is described in detail how deep learning methods and their building blocks work. Leveraging Deep Learning techniques, many areas have benefitted, including image processing, voice recognition, and healthcare. An attack detection technique based on deep learning is presented (McDermott et al., 2018).

IoT networks use centralized processing since it's not suitable for big IoT networks, because processing is required at the edge of the network for cybersecurity. Fog to node deep learning has proved in large data domains, thus for IoT a fog-to-node technique is suitable. This study uses stacked auto encoders coupled with SoftMax classifiers to train models using NSLKDD datasets (Patidar and Bains, 2020). A shallow learning model, which was developed on the basis of assessment criteria such as accuracy, false alarm rate, and detection rate, is then compared to the results of the experiment. The fog node model also displays improved accuracy and efficiency in attack detection when employed in distributed parallel computing environments, as shown in this chapter (Al Majeed et al., 2014). It was proposed to use an autoencoder that was self-taught and based on deep learning, as well as SVM (Support Vector Machine) to prevent network infiltration. In this case, deep learning is applied in an unsupervised manner to choose features. In a proposed methodology comparison, the author asserts that the approach may be used for both binary and multiclass classification, depending on the situation. In addition, he compares it to the J48, naive Bayesian, and random forest machine learning algorithms, among other things. It is claimed by the researchers that their technique produces better results in terms of performance, such as accuracy.

It is proposed that a deep learning model that makes use of a Bidirectional Long Short-Term Memory RNN be utilized for the detection of botnets in order to improve accuracy. An attack vector dataset has been prepared by the author for this project, which comprises four attack vectors whose use has been shown to be significant to the development of the Mirai botnet. A full and rigorous evaluation of this proposed approach has been conducted in terms of four attack vectors, including mirai, udp, dns, and ack, among others (Al-Rubaie, 2018). The suggested technique has shown good results in simulations for the mirai, udp, and dns attack vectors, but has shown less success against the ack attack vector (Al-Rubaie et al., 2016). The use of machine learning and deep learning methods to cyber security is covered in this book. The authors have not only spoken about the problems in obtaining accessible datasets for IDS training and testing, but they have also talked about the issues connected with machine learning and deep learning for IDS training and testing. Because network data is updated at a rapid pace, it is necessary to have a method of continually retraining the models.

DEEP LEARNING MODELS

Deep learning algorithms are being used in a variety of industries to handle complex problems. It is critical to understand that all deep learning algorithms use a variety of different types of neural networks to achieve a variety of different tasks. When doing sophisticated computations on a large amount of data, artificial neural networks (ANNs) are employed in deep learning. Human brain-based machine learning is a kind of machine learning that is distinct from the others. Deep learning methods, also known as machine learning techniques, are used to train systems by learning from examples (Aminanto et al., 2017). While deep learning is used in numerous areas, including health care, ecommerce, entertainment, and advertising, the healthcare and ecommerce businesses are the ones that employ it the most often. Deep learning techniques need both self-learning representations and artificial neural networks (ANNs) that imitate the way the brain computes information in order to function properly (Radanliev, 2018).

A methodology often used in machine learning processes begins with an algorithm extracting features from the input distribution using components that are not necessarily present in every distribution. The process of teaching computers to self-learn is similar to this: The algorithms create the models, and then those models are used to train the algorithm. In order to develop deep learning models, methods from different fields are used (Askar et al., 2011).

Despite the fact that no one network is regarded to be ideal, certain algorithms perform better in particular circumstances. When it comes to picking the best algorithms, you need to have a strong knowledge of all of the main algorithms.

Convolutional Neural Network (CNN)

CNNs, also known as ConvNets, are networks of computers that are built from numerous layers of computer hardware and software and are used for image processing and object recognition, among other things. The original CNN, which was named LeNet, was created by Yann LeCun in 1988. It was in use for identifying such things as ZIP codes and telephone numbers. To extract and analyse information from data, CNNs contain several layers. The CNN model features a convolution operation, with many filters in the stack to carry out the convolution process. CNN's use a ReLU activation function to execute element operations. Once the rectification process is completed, the result is a rectified feature map (Al-Garadi et al., 2018).

It is kept in a pooling unit after the rectified feature map has passed through a pooling layer for the second time. Pooling is a strategy for reducing the size of a feature map by using a down-sampling approach to reduce the number of features. A single, long, continuous, linear vector is created from the pooled feature map by applying a flattening layer to the feature map. When the flattened matrix of the pooling layer is provided as an input, the fully connected layer is able to execute the image classification and identification capabilities that it is capable of. Several image recognition tasks are carried out using CNNs, including categorizing satellite imagery, analyzing medical images, forecasting time series, and recognizing anomalies. A common data-mining approach is CNN, which is one of the most extensively used frameworks for data mining (Okpe et al., 2019). This approach is often used in the field of image processing. CNN layers may be classified into three types: convolutional, pooling, and fully connected layers (Figure 3). There are two phases in each CNN (called back-propagation and feed-forward) used for training. With regards to CNN architectures, the most popular ones are VGGNet, GoogLeNet, ZFNet, AlexNet, and ResNet.

Figure 3. CNN Architecture

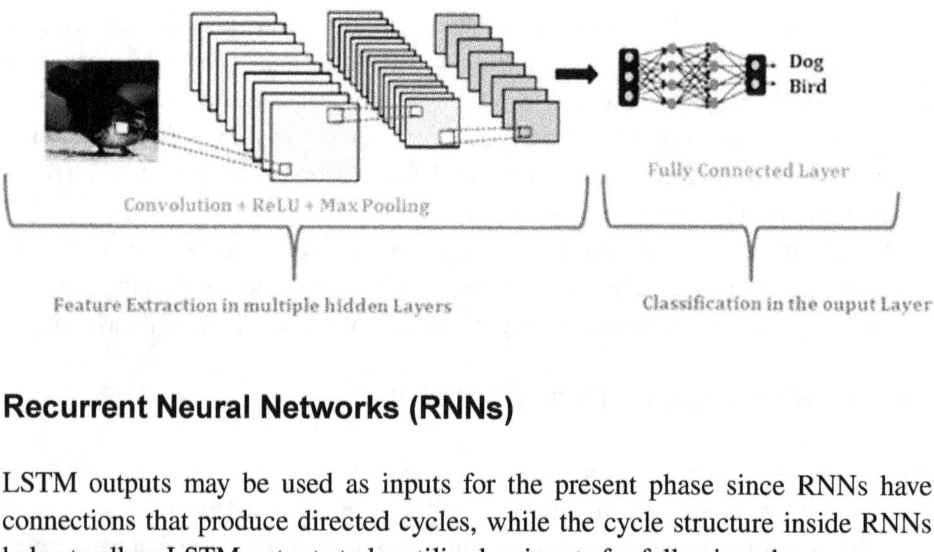

Recurrent Neural Networks (RNNs)

LSTM outputs may be used as inputs for the present phase since RNNs have connections that produce directed cycles, while the cycle structure inside RNNs helps to allow LSTM outputs to be utilised as inputs for following phases.

The output of the LSTM becomes an input to the current phase and may recall previous inputs due to the LSTM's internal memory (Anthi et al., 2019). Natural-language processing, handwriting recognition, and machine translation are just a few of the applications where RNNs come in handy. A RNN is tailored to identify patterns such as voice, handwriting, text, and such, and may be used to recognizing these patterns. using recurrent computations, the structure is progressively processed by an RNN and cyclical links in the structure are used An extended standard neural network, referred known as RNN, consists of time-invariant elements connected to each other in parallel rather than sequentially. Input data stored in a state vector is used to compute the output. The image in Figure 4 illustrates the structure of an RNN.

Figure 4. RNN Architecture

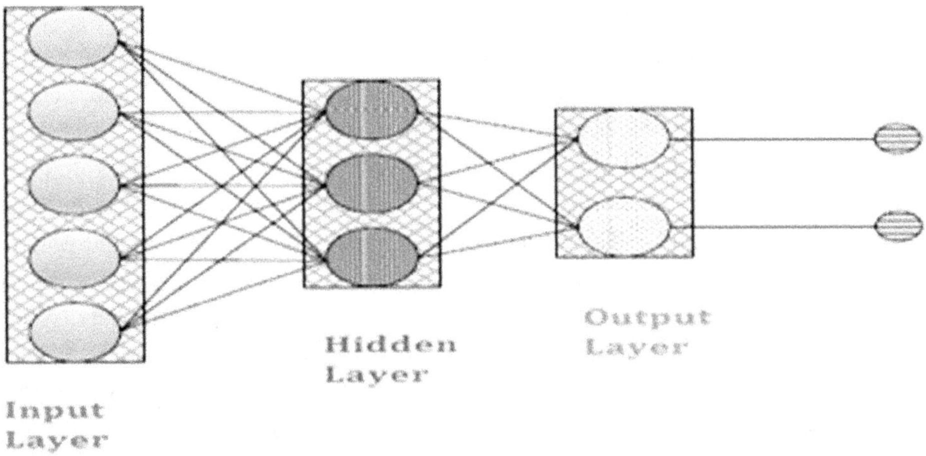

The RNN works at time t-1, the output takes the place of the input. In a similar way, the output at time t contributes to the input at time t+1. Recurrent neural networks may handle inputs of any duration. Historical information is accounted for in the calculation, and model size is not related to the size of the input.

Figure 5. Google's auto completing function is an illustration of how it works

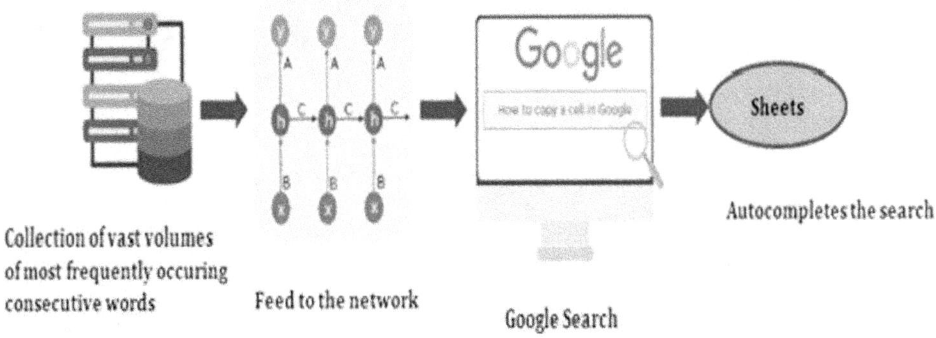

Long Short-Term Memory Networks (LSTMs)

It is possible to learn and remember long-term dependencies via the use of LSTMs, which are a kind of Recurrent Neural Network (RNN). It's in your nature to keep information for a long time. Over time, an LSTM (long short-term memory) or recurrent neural network (RNN) maintains data (Azmoodeh et al., 2019). Time-series prediction is aided by their ability to remember previous data. In the LSTM model, four interacting layers have a unique communication topology, similar to a chain. LSTMs are often utilized for voice recognition, music creation, and pharmaceutical research, but are also frequently used for time-series forecasts.

Using feedback connections in an RNN (LSTM) turns the general-purpose computer into an LSTM. This technique is ideal for both sequence and pattern recognition applications, as well as image processing tasks. An LSTM generally has three main components: an input gate, an output gate, and a forget gate. When LSTM has to make a decision on whether to allow the input to enter the neuron, or recall the prior computation, it can. A major benefit of the LSTM approach is that it utilizes the current input data to arrive at a conclusion. Figure 6 illustrates the LSTM algorithm's design.

LSTM has shown considerable use in environmental contexts, such as modelling the environment, such as hydrological prediction, air quality, and hazard forecasting. LSTM's capacity to generalize enables it to be effective in a wide range of application environments. the other application fields of LSTM include the demand for energy and consumption, as well as the wind energy sector, as well as solar power modelling (Elrawy et al., 2019). Additional research is necessary to investigate the new deep learning techniques and to see where they might be used.

Figure 6. LSTM Architecture

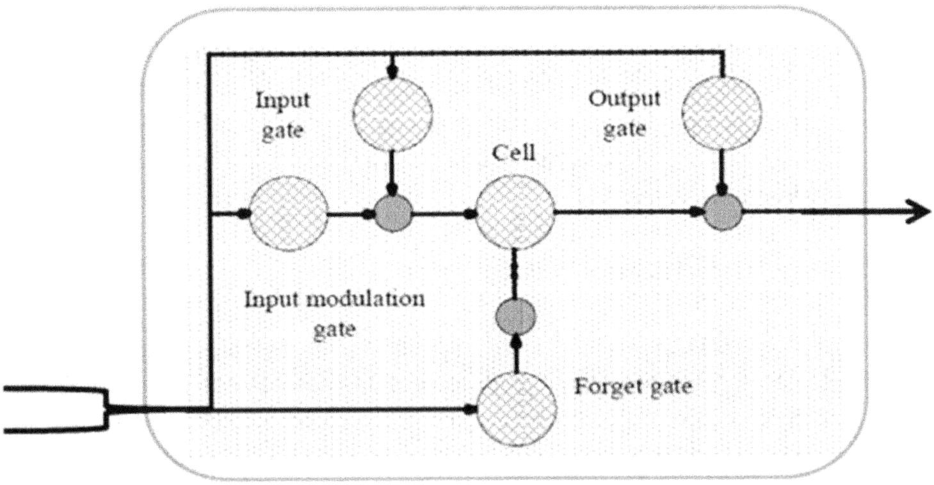

Generative Adversarial Networks (GANs)

Generate new instances that mirror the training data using generative deep learning (GANs) methods. GAN is built on two components: a generator and a discriminator. The generator is designed to generate false data, and the discriminator depends on that input. GANs have been more popular over time. Lenses are widely employed in the field of astronomy for making sharper pictures of celestial objects (Hajiheidari et al., 2019). They may also be used to further dark matter studies by simulating gravitational lensing. In order to update low-quality, 2D graphics in older games, video game makers utilize GANs (generative adversarial networks) to increase the resolution of such textures.

Figure 7. Illustrating how GANs operate

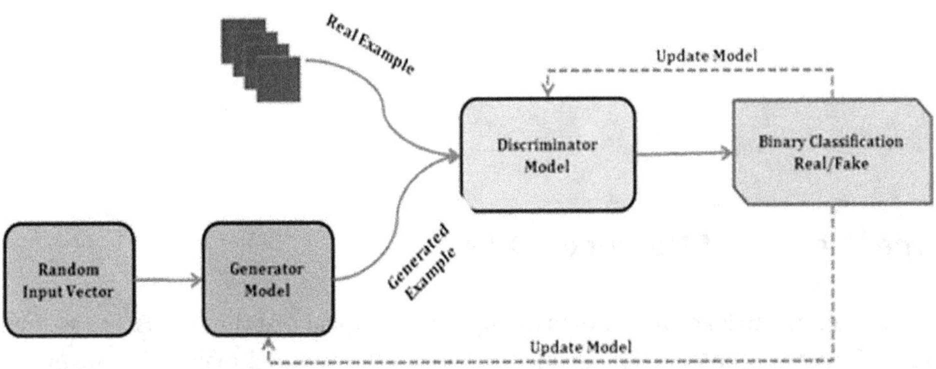

GANs assist in the production of believable 2D and 3D artwork, as well as photo-realistic depictions of human faces. GAN works: Real samples may be identified by a discriminator after it learns to distinguish between the generator's bogus data and the actual sample data. Discriminators learn quickly to discriminate between real and false data from fraudulent data generated by the generator. To update the model, both generators and discriminators rely on findings from the GAN, which transfers them to each other.

Denoising AutoEncoder (DAE)

It has proven possible to extend the original AE model to include an asymmetrical neural network (DAE) for learning features from noisy datasets (Radanliev, 2020). There are three levels to the DAE: the input layer, the encoding layer, and the decoding layer, which all work together. In order to amass valuable qualities, this might be established. Denoising AutoEncoders are created using the DEA method, an unsupervised approach (SDAE). This is a pre-trained feed-forward neural network technique with several hidden layers. Architecture of DEA technique is shown in Fig. 8.

Figure 8. DEA Architecture

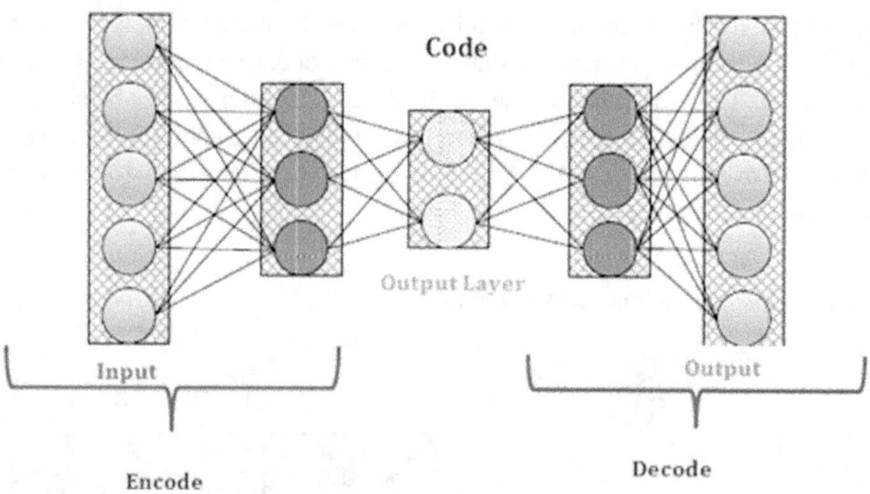

The Deep Belief Networks (DBNs)

When it comes to learning the data for high-dimensional manifolds, DBNs are often used. Except for connections inside each layer, this method makes use of several layers. Undirected connections are integrated in a multi-layered neural network that includes both directed and undirected interconnections (Nicolescu et al., 2019). A greedy strategy is used to teach Boltzmann machines (RBMs) in DBNs. A direct link exists between the RBM and the previous and subsequent levels. Restrictive Boltzmann machines (RBMs) are used to extract features from a feed-forward network and multiple layers of RBMs. There are just two layers in RBMs: the hidden layer and the visible layer. The architecture of the DBN technique is shown in Figure 9.

Figure 9. DBN Architecture

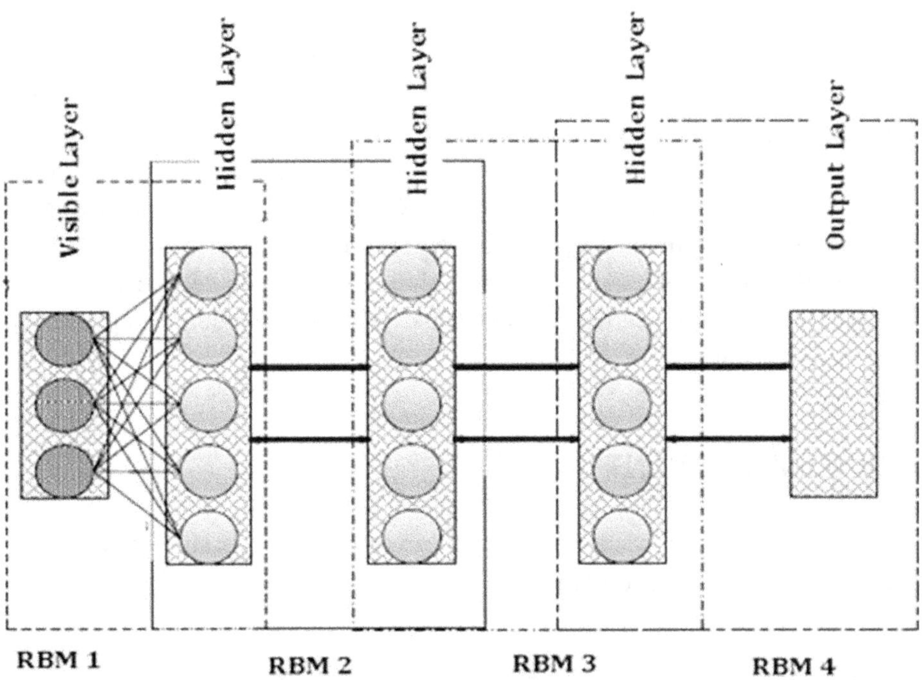

In terms of deep learning, DBN is one of the most accurate and efficient. Many other industries may benefit from the program's wide range of application areas, including those in engineering and science. Human emotion identification, time series prediction, renewable energy projection, economic forecasting, and cancer detection have all been used in the public sector in the recent decade.

CONCLUSION

The rapid growth of the Internet of Things, security issues are raised since most smart devices are easily hacked. Internet of Things (IoT) devices have been made easy pickings for botnet developers. Additionally, the ever-changing threat environment makes securing IoT networks difficult. Due to their application specificities, IoT devices follow predictable networking behaviors that are great for data analysis methods. Deep learning's emergence may aid in the development of IoT network monitoring solutions. However, large amounts of data are needed to train deep learning algorithms, which may not be readily accessible. The fast-changing nature of deep learning techniques may be challenging. A number of them have moved up the learning curve to master an area of application. Despite this, there remains a vacuum in current research; no one has yet summarized the techniques and applications of deep learning in a single article. This article focuses on deep learning techniques in order to give a comprehensive list of the most prevalent deep learning methods and to demonstrate notable applications. CNN, RNN, DAE, DBNs, and LSTM are some of the most common deep learning algorithms used by data scientists today. Feature selection is not required prior to training or testing in deep learning-based approaches. Each deep learning approach and its various building components are described in detail.

ACKNOWLEDGMENT

We would like to acknowledge the support given by BMS Institute of Technology and Management, Bangalore, India.

REFERENCES

Al-Garadi, M. A., Mohamed, A., Al-Ali, A. K., Du, X., Ali, I., & Guizani, M. (2020). A survey of machine and deep learning methods for internet of things (IoT) security. *IEEE Communications Surveys and Tutorials*, *22*(3), 1646–1685. doi:10.1109/COMST.2020.2988293

Al Majeed, S. M. S., Askar, S. K., & Fleury, M. (2014, March). H. 265 Codec over 4G Networks for Telemedicine System Application. In *2014 UKSim-AMSS 16th International Conference on Computer Modelling and Simulation* (pp. 292-297). IEEE. doi:10.1109/ICSSIT48917.2020.9214114

Al-Rubaie, M., & Chang, J. M. (2016). Reconstruction attacks against mobile-based continuous authentication systems in the cloud. *IEEE Transactions on Information Forensics and Security*, *11*(12), 2648–2663. doi:10.1109/TIFS.2016.2594132

Al-Rubaie, M., & Chang, J. M. (2019). Privacy-preserving machine learning: Threats and solutions. *IEEE Security and Privacy*, *17*(2), 49–58. doi:10.1109/MSEC.2018.2888775

Aminanto, R., Choi, H. C., Tanuwidjaja, P. D., & Yoo, K. (2017). Deep abstraction and weighted feature selection for Wi-Fi impersonation detection. *IEEE Trans. Inf. Forensics Secur.*, *13*(3), 621–636.

Anthi, E., Williams, L., Słowińska, M., Theodorakopoulos, G., & Burnap, P. (2019). A supervised intrusion detection system for smart home IoT devices. *IEEE Internet of Things Journal*, *6*(5), 9042–9053. doi:10.1109/JIOT.2019.2926365

Askar, S., Zervas, G., Hunter, D. K., & Simeonidou, D. (2011). Service differentiation for video applications over OBS networks. *16th European Conference on Networks and Optical Communications*, 200-203.

Azmoodeh, A., Dehghantanha, A., & Choo, K. K. R. (2018). Robust malware detection for internet of (battlefield) things devices using deep eigenspace learning. *IEEE Transactions on Sustainable Computing, 4*(1), 88-95.

Elrawy, M. F., Awad, A. I., & Hamed, H. F. (2018). Intrusion detection systems for IoT-based smart environments: A survey. *Journal of Cloud Computing*, *7*(1), 1–20.

Hajiheidari, S., Wakil, K., Badri, M., & Navimipour, N. J. (2019). Intrusion detection systems in the Internet of things: A comprehensive investigation. *Computer Networks*, *160*, 165–191. doi:10.1016/j.comnet.2019.05.014

Hao, W., Bie, R., Guo, J., Meng, X., & Wang, S. (2018). Optimized CNN based image recognition through target region selection. *Optik (Stuttgart)*, *156*, 772–777. doi:10.1016/j.ijleo.2017.11.153

Hori, T., Chen, Z., Erdogan, H., Hershey, J. R., Le Roux, J., Mitra, V., & Watanabe, S. (2017). Multi-microphone speech recognition integrating beamforming, robust feature extraction, and advanced DNN/RNN backend. *Computer Speech & Language*, *46*, 401–418. doi:10.1016/j.csl.2017.01.013

McDermott, C. D., Majdani, F., & Petrovski, A. V. (2018, July). Botnet detection in the internet of things using deep learning approaches. In 2018 international joint conference on neural networks (IJCNN) (pp. 1-8). IEEE. doi:10.1109/IJCNN.2018.8489489

Nicolescu, R., Huth, M., Radanliev, P., & De Roure, D. (2018). Mapping the values of IoT. *Journal of Information Technology*, *33*(4), 345–360. doi:10.105741265-018-0054-1

Okpe, O. A., John, O. A., & Emmanuel, S. (2018). Intrusion detection in internet of things (IoT). *International Journal of Advanced Research in Computer Science*, *9*(1), 504–509. doi:10.26483/ijarcs.v9i1.5429

Patidar, S., & Bains, I. S. (2020, August). Web security in IoT networks using deep learning model. In *2020 Third International Conference on Smart Systems and Inventive Technology (ICSSIT)* (pp. 848-855). IEEE.

Radanliev, P., De Roure, D. C., Nicolescu, R., Huth, M., Montalvo, R. M., Cannady, S., & Burnap, P. (2018). Future developments in cyber risk assessment for the internet of things. *Journal of Comput. Ind.*, *102*, 14–22. doi:10.1016/j.compind.2018.08.002

Radanliev, P., De Roure, D. C., Nurse, J. R. C., Mantilla Montalvo, R., Cannady, S., Santos, O., Maddox, L. T., Burnap, P., & Maple, C. (2020). Future developments in standardization of cyber risk in the Internet of Things (IoT). *SN Appl. Sci*, *2*(2), 201–212. doi:10.100742452-019-1931-0

Roopak, M., Tian, G. Y., & Chambers, J. (2019, January). Deep learning models for cyber security in IoT networks. In *2019 IEEE 9th annual computing and communication workshop and conference (CCWC)* (pp. 0452-0457). IEEE. 10.1109/CCWC.2019.8666588

Sharif Razavian, A., Azizpour, H., Sullivan, J., & Carlsson, S. (2014). CNN features off-the-shelf: an astounding baseline for recognition. In *Proceedings of the IEEE conference on computer vision and pattern recognition workshops* (pp. 806-813). IEEE.

Vigneswaran, R. K., Vinayakumar, R., Soman, K. P., & Poornachandran, P. (2018, July). Evaluating shallow and deep neural networks for network intrusion detection systems in cyber security. In *2018 9th International conference on computing, communication and networking technologies (ICCCNT)* (pp. 1-6). IEEE. 10.1109/ICCCNT.2018.8494096

Vijayanand, R., Devaraj, D., & Kannapiran, B. (2018). Intrusion detection system for wireless mesh network using multiple support vector machine classifiers with genetic-algorithm-based feature selection. *Computers & Security*, *77*, 304–314. doi:10.1016/j.cose.2018.04.010

Yuan, X., Li, C., & Li, X. (2017, May). DeepDefense: identifying DDoS attack via deep learning. In 2017 IEEE international conference on smart computing (SMARTCOMP) (pp. 1-8). IEEE. doi:10.1109/SMARTCOMP.2017.7946998

Chapter 5
Deep Learning-Based AI Modeling, Intrusion Detection

Madhab Paul Choudhury
National Institute of Technology, Jamshedpur, India

Madhab Paul Choudhury
National Institute of Technology, Jamshedpur, India

Chandrashekhar Azad
National Institute of Technology, Jamshedpur, India

ABSTRACT

Machine learning techniques are being used to create an intrusion detection system (IDS) for detecting and classifying cyber-attacks at the network-level and the host-level in a timely manner. Various datasets are available for research by cyber security researchers. However, no previous study has shown the detailed analysis of the performance of various machine learning algorithms on various available datasets. As the nature of malware is changing dynamically with the changing attacking methods, the detailed analysis of the available data sets is necessary to find out the cause of the malware datasets, and accordingly, necessary steps can be executed for maintaining the security of the network. A deep neural network (DNN) is being explored to develop an effective intrusion detection system. The optimal network parameters and network topologies for DNNs are chosen through the following hyper parameter selection methods with KDD Cup 99 dataset. The DNN model can be applied on KDD Cup 99 and on other datasets also such as NSL-KDD, UNSW-NB15, Kyoto to conduct the experiment.

DOI: 10.4018/978-1-6684-4558-7.ch005

INTRODUCTION

Insertion of malicious activity in a network is called threat. It is necessary to analyse the security ecosystem to identify any malicious activity that can hamper the activities of the network. If a threat is detected, then mitigation efforts must be enacted to properly neutralize the threat before it can exploit any present vulnerability. When threat is detected, and it should be mitigated that threat. Security programs must be able to detect threats quickly and effectively so that the attackers don't have enough time to root around in sensitive data. A number of network security system has been used for protecting network activity.

A firewall is a network security system that has been designed to prevent unauthorized access to or from private network. All messages entering or leaving the intranet pass through the firewall. It examines each message and blocks those that do not meet the specified security criteria. Firewall types are hardware and software. Packet Filter looks at each packet entering or leaving the network. An Intrusion Detection system (IDS) deploys sensors that monitor key points. An Intrusion Detection system (IDS) transmits small amounts of security-critical data back to the administrator for analysis after capturing it. When a cyber-attack occurs, the Intrusion Detection system (IDS) becomes able to detect the attack within some time. Intrusion Detection system (IDS) administrators can address and disrupt cyber-attacks when these occur. Afterward the Intrusion Detection system (IDS) can perform an assessment of the attack to determine the weakness of the network. Host-Based Intrusion Detection system (IDS) operates within a network on remote devices. Network-Based Intrusion Detection system (IDS) monitors activity across strategic points over an entire network. Stack Intrusion Detection system (IDS) can handle monitoring network packets in transit through the TCP/IP. Signature-Based Intrusion Detection system (IDS) searches a string of malicious bytes or sequences.

RELATED WORK

The research activity on the intrusion detection system has been discussed as follows: (Vinayakumar et al., 2019) have proposed the holistic approach to obtain a real time intrusion detection system using the deep learning technique. Here the information regarding the current network traffic attacks have been furnished. The authors have tried to scale the performance of a Network anomaly detection using KDD 99 and varied KDD cup 99 data set. With the KDD cup 99 datasets none of the machine learning classifiers are capable to improve the attack detection rate. DARPA/KDD Cup 88 data set have been failed to evaluate the classical intrusion detection system (IDS). But KDD Cup 99 is the most widely used reliable benchmark dataset in most of the study related to intrusion detection (ID) system evaluation and related other security related tasks. To resolve the inherent issues that exist in the KDD cup 99, one refined version NSL KDD has been used. Still this refined version is not able to solve the entire problem, so some more extra features have been added to KDD cup 99. This new dataset is called KYOTO dataset. The Kyoto datasets do not contain the false positives that minimize the number of alerts to the network administration. Most widely used dataset for HIDS is KDD Cup 98, KDD Cup 99.

(Moradi et al., 2004) have proposed a neural network-based system for Intrusion Detection and Classification of attacks to solve a multi class. For that reason, an output layer with three states have been used. Here three layers of neural network have been used. Under Matlab neural network toolbox has been used for MLP networks.

In identifying important features for Intrusion Detection using Support Vector Machines and Neural Networks, (Andrew H. Sung et al., 2003) have proposed an intrusion detection model used by DARPA. It has identified important issue features of intrusion detection system. Important and redundant input tends to produce more appropriate result. Intrusion Detection in Computer Systems by using artificial neural networks with deep learning approaches, (Hidalgo-Espinoza et al., 2020) have used a dataset Intrusion Detection Evaluation Dataset (CICIDS2017) developed by the Canadian Institute for Cybersecurity (CIC) in the laboratories dedicated to the information security. Building the dataset is to perform a massive amount of different controlled hacking attacks from different parts of the world to the dedicated servers. Here in the deep learning model, two different ARN architectures have been used as a shallow network for the usage of a Back Propagation Algorithm (BPA) and a deep network form by ANN architectures as a two-layered auto encoder and the Back Propagation Algorithm (BPA).

In this research paper named as A Multi-Dimensional approach towards Intrusion Detection System by (Thakur and Sanyal, 2012) have suggested a multi-dimensional approach towards intrusion detection. Network and system usage parameters like source and destination IP addresses, source and destination ports, incoming and outgoing network traffic data rate and number of CPU cycles per request have been divided into multiple dimensions. Here a mature function has been created and it has taken a value as input and has returned a value that determines the level of abnormality in the system usage. This is called the abnormality indicator. For n dimension it is referred to as Global Anomaly Indicator. It can detect the network anomaly in the detection phase.

(Liu and Lang, 2019) have suggested a novel hybrid algorithm, HOK-SMOTE which has used an ordered weighted averaging (OWA) approach for choosing the best features from the KDD cup 99 data set and K-Means SMOTE algorithm for imbalanced learning. Here an ensemble model has been compared against the hybrid algorithm. A lot of algorithms viz. Support Vector Machine (SVM), K Nearest

Neighbor (KNN), Gaussian Naïve Bayes (GNB) and Decision Tree (DT) have been integrated in this ensemble method. Thereafter weighted average voting method has been applied for prediction of outputs. (Priyadarsini et al., 2021) have presented a novel network Intrusion Detection System, which has played an important role in inspecting network security and has faced the current cyber-attacks on networks using the UNSW-NB15 dataset benchmark. The proposed system is a dynamically scalable multiclass machine learning-based network Intrusion Detection System (IDS). It consists of several stages based on supervised machine learning. It starts with the Synthetic Minority Oversampling Technique (SMOTE) method to solve the imbalanced classes problem in the dataset and then selects the important features for each class existing in the dataset by the Gini Impurity criterion using the Extremely Randomized Trees Classifier (Extra Trees Classifier). Results have shown that our proposed system performs better than related works in terms of accuracy, false alarm rate, Receiver Operating Characteristic (ROC), and Precision-Recall Curves (PRCs).

In the proposed framework by (Mouallaet al., 2021) three advanced deep learning algorithms have been applied to classify the intrusion: a convolution neural network (CNN), a long short-term memory (LSTM), and a hybrid convolution neural network with the long short-term memory (CNN-LSTM) model. The complexity of the network dataset has been dimensionality reduced. To improve the proposed system, the particle swarm optimization method (PSO) has been used to select relevant features from the network dataset. The obtained features have been processed using deep learning algorithms.

The objective of the research work by (Alkahtani and Aldhyani, 2021) is to improve the performance of Intrusion Detection System by applying machine learning techniques based on decision trees for detection and classification of attacks. The methodology has been adapted in three stages to process the datasets. The experiment has been conducted on KDDCUP99 data sets based on a number of features. The Bayesian three modes have been analysed for different sized data sets based upon total number of attacks. The time consumed by the classifier to build the model has been analysed and the accuracy has been done. (Shilpashree et al., 2019) have presented a study that has incorporated Information Gain Ratio (IGR) and has used K-means algorithm and support vector machine (SVM) algorithm for intrusion detection. In proposed framework NSL-KDD dataset has been ranked using Information Gain Ratio (IGR) and thereafter feature subset selection has been done using K-mean algorithm.

(Jha and Ragha, 2013) have made a comparative study of research on various machine learning models for intrusion detection system in terms of accuracy. They have used Decision Tree (DT), Naïve Bayes (NB) algorithm, k-Nearest Neighbor (kNN) and k-means algorithm, Recursive Feature Addition (RFA) with SVM,

Principal Component Analysis (PCA) and Ant Colony Optimization, Fuzzy Logic, Single hidden layer feed-forward neural network (SLFN), etc.

Various machine learning models have been attempted and evaluated by (Kok et al.,2019). These are Decision Tree, K-Nearest Neighbor Classifier, Logistic Regression, Naive Bayes, K-Nearest Neighbor Classifier, Logistic Regression, Deep Learning. To understand the current status of implementation of machine learning techniques for solving the intrusion detection problems, (Haq et al., 2015) have submitted a survey paper that consists of 49 related studies in the time frame between 2009 and 2014. This survey paper also has included a statistical comparison of classifier algorithms, datasets being used and some other experimental setups and the steps of feature selection.

(Othman et al., 2018), have introduced Spark-Chi-SVM model for intrusion detection. In this model, ChiSqSelector has been used for feature selection, and an intrusion detection model has been built by using support vector machine (SVM) classifier on Apache Spark Big Data platform. KDD99 data set has been used to train and test the model. A comparison between Chi-SVM classifier and Chi-Logistic Regression classifier has also been introduced here. The study by (Ahmad et al., 2021) has been conducted a systematic literature review of the different Machine Learning and Deep Learning based Network Intrusion Detection System and has investigated the published journal articles between 2017 to first quarter of 2020. A systematic literature review is a methodology followed to identify, examine, and extract needful information from the literature related to certain research topics.

(Awad, 2021) has focused on several data mining algorithms such as naïve Bayes, decision trees, support vector machines, decision tables, k-nearest neighbor algorithms, and artificial neural networks. Here an effort has been made with the association process in creating attack rules to identify anomaly detection in the network audit data, by using KDD99 dataset.

Conducting the analysis of the recent research it has been showed that the there is a trend in research work related to detect an anomaly in network. Several machine learning methods have been reported to have a very high detection rate of 98% while keeping the false alarm rate at 1%. However, at the state-of-the-art Intrusion detection system (IDS) solutions and commercial tools, there is no evidence of using anomaly detection approaches, and practitioners still think that it is an immature technology. That is the reason of conducting the proposed research work.

OBJECTIVES

Here in this paper a machine learning based algorithm has been proposed to detect whether an unauthorized person has entered into a given network to change network characteristics for malfunctioning or not. In this work KUDD CUP 99 data set has been used. Network characteristics of 42 numbers have been used. These are duration of network traffic, protocol type, service, flag, source bytes, destination bytes, no of wrong fragments, number of failed logins, number of logged ins, number of root shell, etc. Here an effort has been used to detect the parameters of network which are responsible for network hacking and by examining the range of values of network parameters, decision regarding the detection of network hacking can be made. Here 8 network labels have been used. These network labels are normal, back, buffer overflow, ipsweep, ftp-write, nmap, smurf, Neptune.

In this paper an effort has to be made to apply factor analysis under multivariate statistical model on the available data items for eliminating redundant items and to form a cumulative data item. Thereafter deep learning based neural network has to be applied on the cumulative data item as formed using factor analysis. K-means clustering algorithm has to be applied on the estimated data based on deep learning based neural network to get optimum number of clusters. Thereafter based on the clusters as formed and available network type data, confidence matrix has to be formed. The performance of confidence matrix has to be compared with the confidence matrix as formed without the application deep learning based neural network to verify the superiority of the deep learning based neural network model over the model without the application of deep learning based neural network model. The proposed methodology has been given in flow diagram as furnished in figure 1.

Figure 1. Flow Diagram of Proposed Model

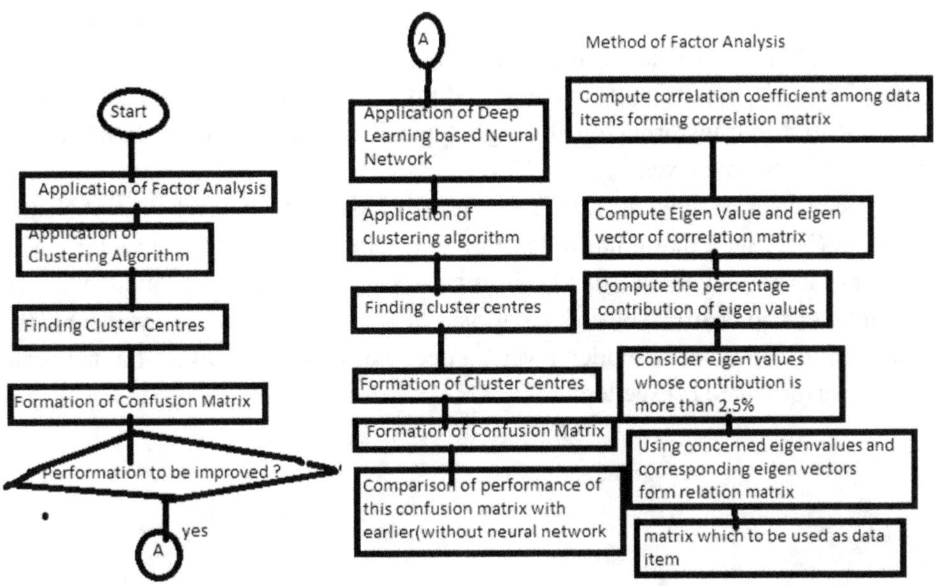

METHODOLOGY

Multivariate Statistical Tool

Multivariate statistical analysis is considered a useful tool for evaluating the significance of anomalies in relation to both any individual variable and the mutual influence of variables on each other.

Factor Analysis

Step 1: To calculate the correlation matrix for the features in the dataset.
Step 2: To calculate the eigenvalues and eigenvectors for the correlation matrix.
Step 3: To consider those eigenvalues whose contribution is more than 2.5%.
Step 4: To pick the eigenvectors corresponding to the selected eigenvalues and to form cumulative tem set for a particular data set.

Deep Learning Based Neural Network

The basic unit of a Neural Network (NN) is an artificial neuron, which is a simple simulation of biological neurons. Biological neurons take input from other neurons, form an action potential, and then output signals to subsequent neurons via synapses. Artificial neurons are also connected in an analogous way, and synaptic strengths are designated by numeric weights with higher weights indicating a stronger connection. Action potential is simulated by a nonlinear "activation function," which typically has a drastic output value change after input value exceeds a certain threshold. Neural Networks (NN) are typically composed of "layers" of artificial neurons, which take a signal from their counterparts in the preceding layer and output to the next after the afore mentioned transformation although, typically, there is no connection between neurons in the same layer.

A Deep Neural Network (DNN) is a specific case of the general class of Neural Network (NN) such that it has at least three layers in its structure: an input layer, an output layer, and at least one layer in between, designated as a "hidden" layer. Whereas a Deep Neural Network comprises of a number of hidden layers. Due the existence of a number of hidden layers, a deep network works like a human brain and its performance is excellent.

K-Means Clustering Algorithm

K-Means Clustering is an Unsupervised Learning algorithm, which groups the unlabeled dataset into different clusters. Here K defines the number of pre-defined clusters that need to be created in the process, as if K=2, there will be two clusters, and for K=3, there will be three clusters, and so on.
If k is given, the K-means algorithm can be executed in the following steps:

Step 1: Partition of objects into k non-empty subsets.
Step 2: Identifying the cluster centroids (mean point) of the current partition.
Step 3: Assigning each point to a specific cluster
Step 4: Compute the distances from each point and allot points to the cluster where the distance from the centroid is minimum.
Step 5: After re-allotting the points, find the centroid of the new cluster formed.

Confusion Matrix

A confusion matrix is a chart or table that summarizes the performance of a classification model or an algorithm for machine learning processes. Confusion matrices help with predictive analysis and can be effective tools for evaluating the functions a machine learning system performs correctly or incorrectly.

IMPLEMENTATION

Step 1: The KDD Cup 99 dataset have been taken from Kaggle which have been used as input data set.
Step 2: Redundant rows and unnecessary columns have been deleted to get revised dataset(matrix).
Step 3: The correlation coefficient among various network characters(columns) of the dataset has been computed.
Step 4: Now the eigen values and eigen vectors have been computed based on correlation matrix. The computed eigen values (d) are furnished in table 1A, table 1B and table 1C respectively. Since there are 26 items, table 1A contains first 10 values, table 1B contains next 10 values and table 1C contains last 6 values.

Table 1A. Eigen value (first part)

8.83	6.71	3.08	1.79	1.29	1.04	0.85	0.77	0.59	0.52

Table 1B. Eigen value (second part)

0.13	0.11	0.08	0.07	0.05	0.03	0	0	0	0

Table 1C. Eigen value (third part)

0.02	0.014	0.01	0.01	0.02	0

Step 5: Now it is necessary to calculate the percentage contribution of eigen value among all eigen values. The sum of all the eigen values s is computed as S== 26.00

The percentage of eigen values will be furnished in table 2A, table 2B and table 2C respectively

Table 2A. Percentage of Eigen values (first part)

33.95	25.78	11.83	6.9	4.99	3.99	3.27	2.94	2.3	2.01

Table 2B. Percentage of Eigen values (second part)

0.49	0.42	0.32	0.28	0.21	0.11	0.06	0.05	0.03	0.02

Table 2C. Percentage of Eigen values (third part)

0.01	0.003	0	0	0	0

It is known that if the eigen value percentage value is less than 2.5 then those corresponding datasets will be omitted.

Step 6: The major factors have been formed as the product of the square root of the eigen value with the square of eigen vector. The major factor values are furnished in table 3A, table 3B, table 3C respectively.

Table 3A. Major factor values (first part)

0.19	0.19	0.19	0.15	0.18	0	0	0	0	0.22

Table 3B. Major factor values (second part)

0.22	0.11	0.11	0.09	0.03		0.02	0.13	0.03	0.21	0.09

Table 3C. Major factor values (third part)

0	0.02	0.22	0.22	0.17	0.17

Step 7: The sum of each major factors will be computed as row wise to get the cumulative factor value. These cumulative factor values are furnished in table 4A, table 4B, table 4C respectively.

Table 4A. Cumulative value (first part)

0.35	0.37	0.37	0.45	0.37	0.91	0.93	0.52	0.5	0.36

Table 4B. Cumulative value (second part)

0.36	0.55	0.29	0.57	0.92	0.48	0.44	0.36	0.60	0.57

Table 4C. Cumulative value (third part)

0.52	0.36	0.36	0.38	0.38

Step 8: Now based on the cumulative factor value and column item, a relation has been formed to produce the actual data source value. Using the actual values and the relation as formed, the actual data source value has been produced.

Step 9: K-means algorithm has been used on the cumulative data value as computed in step 7.

Step 10: It has been observed that the number of clusters as 6 gives minimum intra cluster distance. The said number of clusters as 6 has been used for further processing. **Step 11:** The cluster centers of 6 clusters are as follows: Cluster 1 as 1255, cluster 2 as 3045.7, cluster 3 as 34.6, cluster 4 as 199.9, cluster 5 as 723, cluster 6 as 86.5.

Step 12: The data values based on the network label the data values have been placed in clusters as formed in step 9.

Step 13: From actual data it has been observed that out of 25 normal network level 12 numbers belong to cluster 4, 5 numbers belong to cluster 6, 1 belong to cluster 5, 3 numbers belong to cluster 3 4 numbers belong to cluster 1. Out of 25 back levels 25 belongs to cluster 2. Out of 51 ipsweep levels, 22 belong to cluster 6, 11 numbers belong to 3, 18 numbers belong to cluster 1. Out of 51 nmap levels, 28 numbers belong to cluster 1, 13 numbers belong to cluster 3, 10 numbers belong to cluster 6. Out of 51 smurf levels, 45 numbers belong to cluster 5 and 6 numbers belong to cluster 1. Out of 46 neptune levels, 31 numbers belong to cluster 4 and 15 numbers belong to cluster 1 respectively.

Step 14: Based on the maximum cluster allocation the selected cluster number has been mapped with the network level data types. Therefore, it can be mentioned that cluster 4 is meant for 'normal' type network, cluster 2 for 'back' network type, cluster 6 for 'ipsweep' type, cluster 1 for 'nmap' type, cluster 5 for 'smurf' type and cluster 4 for 'neptune' type.

Step 15: Based on mapping of data items with network type along with cluster number, a confusion matrix has been formed based on certain parameters as furnished in table 5. The parameters used are as follows:

- Accuracy = (TP + TN)/(TP + FP + TN + FN)
- Recall = TP/(TP + FN)
- Precision = TP/(TP + FP)
- Specificity = TN/(FP + TN)
- F-Measure = (2 * precision * recall)/(precision + recall)
- Where TP stands for True Positive, TN stands for True Negative, FP stands for False Positive, and FN stands for False Negative respectively.

Table 5. Confusion matrix

Network Type	Accuracy	Recall	Precision	Specificity	F-measure
Normal	0.7799	0.449	0.279	0.8296	0.3427
Back	1	1	0.48	1	0.6486
ipsweep	0.8069	0.431	0.6875	0.9338	0.529
nmap	0.7118	0.549	0.394	0.758	0.4569
smurf	0.9588	0.882	0.978	0.992	0.9275
neptune	0.858	0.6739	0.7209	0.9167	0.6966

Step 16: In order to improve the performance of the system, deep learning based neural network has been employed on the actual source data to get the estimated data value as computed in step-8.

Step 17: K-means algorithm has been used on the estimated data value based on deep learning neural network as computed in step 16.

Step 18: It has been observed that the number of clusters as 6 gives minimum intra cluster distance as compared to with other cluster numbers. The said number of clusters as 6 has been used for further processing.

Step 19: The cluster centers of 6 clusters are as follows: Cluster 1 as 166.53, cluster 2 as 3020, cluster 3 as 737.39, cluster 4 as 98.21, cluster 5 as 2680, cluster 6 as 236.25.

Step 20: Based on the network label the data values (cluster centers) the estimated data values based on deep learning based neural network have been placed in clusters as formed in step 19.

Step 21: From actual data it has been observed that out of 25 normal network level 12 numbers belong to cluster 6, 11 numbers belong to cluster 4, 1 belong to cluster 3, 1 number belong to cluster 1. Out of 25 back levels 23 belongs to cluster 2, 1 number belong to cluster 4 and 1 belong to cluster 5. Out of 51 ipsweep levels, 51 numbers belong to cluster 4. Out of 51 nmap levels, 26 numbers belong to cluster 3, 25 numbers belong to cluster 4. Out of 51 smurf levels, 26 numbers belong to cluster 3 and 25 numbers belong to cluster 3. Out of 19 neptune levels, 16 numbers belong to cluster 1, 3 numbers belong to cluster 6 respectively.

Step 22: Based on the maximum number of items in cluster allocation, the selected cluster number has been mapped with the network level data types. Therefore it can be mentioned that cluster 6 is meant for 'normal' type network, cluster 2 for 'back' network type, cluster 4 for 'ipsweep' type, cluster 3 for 'nmap' type, cluster 1 for 'smurf' type and cluster 1 for 'neptune' type.

RESULTS

Based on mapping of data items with network type along cluster number, a confusion matrix has been formed based on certain parameters. The confusion matrix is furnished in table 6. The parameters used in confusion matrix are as follows:

- Accuracy = (TP + TN)/(TP + FP + TN + FN)
- Recall = TP/(TP + FN)
- Precision = TP/(TP + FP)
- Specificity = TN/(FP + TN)
- F-Measure = (2 * precision * recall)/(precision + recall)
- Where TP stands for True Positive, TN stands for True Negative, FP stands for False Positive and FN stands for False Negative respectively.

Table 6. Confusion matrix

Network Type	Accuracy	Recall	Precision	Specificity	F-measure
Normal	0.9408	0.75	0.667	0.9607	0.7061
Back	0.9876	1	0.92	0.9855	0.9583
ipsweep	0.811	0.579	1	1	0.733
nmap	0.779	0.565	0.509	0.842	0.5355
smurf	0.8112	0.646	0.608	0.459	0.6264
neptune	0.8196	0.333	0.842	0.9143	0.4773

CONCLUSION

A comparison is made based on the confusion matrix as formed using estimated data based on deep learning based neural network and that of original data (without using deep learning based neural network). A comparative study on the performance of confusion matrix based on two methods has been furnished in table 7.

From table 7, it has been observed that based on five parameters (accuracy, recall, precision, specificity and f-measure) out of 30 cases, deep learning technique is preferred by 18 cases and the model without learning is preferred by 11 cases and in 1 case both the models give same performance. Therefore, it can be concluded that the performance of the model is improved through the application of deep learning based neural network model. Deep learning is a branch of machine learning (ML)

Table 7. Comparative statistics of confusion matrix

Network Type	Accuracy Deep Learn	Accuracy without learning	Recall Deep Learn	Recall without Learn	Precision Deep Learn	Precision without Learn	Specificity Deep Learn	Specificity without learn	F-measure Deep Learn	F-measure without learn
Normal	0.94	0.7799	0.75	0.444	0.667	0.279	0.961	0.8296	0.706	0.3427
Back	0.987	1	1	1	0.92	0.48	0.985	1	0.958	0.6486
ipsweep	0.811	0.8069	0.579	0.431	1	0.6875	1	0.9338	0.733	0.529
nmap	0.779	0.7118	0.565	0.549	0.509	0.394	0.842	0.758	0.5355	0.4569
smurf	0.8112	0.9588	0.646	0.882	0.608	0.978	0.459	0.992	0.6264	0.9275
neptune	0.8196	0.858	0.333	0.6739	0.842	0.7209	0.9143	0.9167	0.4773	0.6966

that follows the functioning of the human brain to find correlations and similar patterns by processing data with a specified logical structure. Neural network based on deep learning uses multiple hidden layers in the neural network as opposed to traditional neural networks that only contain a number of hidden layers. Deep learning algorithms map inputs to already trained data to deliver an accurate output. In deep learning based neural network as well as without deep learning based neural network both training and testing of data are possible. That is the reason of superiority of the proposed model as compared to other models.

In order to know whether the network is hacked by somebody or not, the network parameter values have to be taken. The method of factor analysis has to be applied on the network parameter values to get the cumulative data. Now deep learning based neural network has to be applied on the cumulative value as formed using factor analysis to get the estimated value. Thereafter this estimated value based on deep learning based neural network has to be compared with the cluster center value as formed in step-19 of section 5 named implementation. Based on minimum distance value, it can be decided that the network parameter value which have been collected now, belongs to the characteristic of that cluster. If the cluster belongs to normal category, then it can be mentioned no hacking has been done to the network otherwise there may be a problem in the network data. As advancement of work in future, it can be mentioned that other machine learning algorithms can be applied here for further better performance of the work.

REFERENCES

Ahmad, Z., Shahid Khan, A., Wai Shiang, C., Abdullah, J., & Ahmad, F. (2021). Network intrusion detection system: A systematic study of machine learning and deep learning approaches. *Transactions on Emerging Telecommunications Technologies*, *32*(1), e4150.

Alkahtani, H., & Aldhyani, T. H. (2021). Intrusion detection system to advance internet of things infrastructure-based deep learning algorithms. *Complexity*.

Awad., N. A. (2021). *Enhancing Network Intrusion Detection Model Using Machine Learning Algorithms.* Computers, Materials & Continua Tech Science Press. DOI: doi:10.32604/cmc.2021.014307

Haq, N. F., Onik, A. R., Hridoy, M. A. K., Rafni, M., Shah, F. M., & Farid, D. M. (2015). Application of machine learning approaches in intrusion detection system: A survey. *IJARAI-International Journal of Advanced Research in Artificial Intelligence*, *4*(3), 9–18.

Hidalgo-Espinoza, S., Chamorro-Cupuerán, K., & Chang-Tortoler, O. (2020). *Intrusion Detection in Computer Systems by Using Artificial Neural Networks with Deep Learning Approaches.* AIRCC Publishing Corporation.

Jha, J., & Ragha, L. (2013). Intrusion detection system using support vector machine. *International Journal of Applied Information Systems*, *3*, 25–30.

Kok, S. H., Abdullah, A., Jhanjhi, N. Z., & Supramaniam, M. (2019). A review of intrusion detection system using machine learning approach. *International Journal of Engineering Research & Technology (Ahmedabad)*, *12*(1), 8–15.

Liu, H., & Lang, B. (2019). Machine learning and deep learning methods for intrusion detection systems: A survey. *Applied Sciences, 9*(20), 4396.

Moradi, M., & Zulkernine, M. (2004). A Neural Network Based System for Intrusion Detection and Classification of Attacks, *Proceedings of International Conference on Advances in Intelligent Systems*, 148-04.

Moualla, S., Khorzom, K., & Jafar, A. (2021). Improving the performance of machine learning-based network intrusion detection systems on the UNSW-NB15 dataset. *Computational Intelligence and Neuroscience*.

Othman, S. M., Ba-Alwi, F. M., Alsohybe, N. T., & Al-Hashida, A. Y. (2018). Intrusion detection model using machine learning algorithm on Big Data environment. *Journal of Big Data*, *5*(1), 1–12.

Priyadarsini, P. I., Leela, P. S., & Jyothi, B. (2021). Towards Intelligent Machine Learning Models for Intrusion Detection System. *Turkish Journal of Computer and Mathematics Education*, *12*(5), 643–655.

Shilpashree, S., Lingareddy, S. C., Nayana, G. B., & Sunil, K. G. (2019). Decision Tree: A Machine Learning for Intrusion Detection. *International Journal of Innovative Technology and Exploring Engineering*, *8*, 1126–1130.

Sung, A. H., & Mukkamala, S. (2003). Identifying Important Features for Intrusion Detection Using Support Vector Machines and Neural Networks. *Proceedings of the 2003 Symposium on Applications and the Internet (SAINT'03*.

Thakur, M. R., & Sanyal, S. (2012). *A multi-dimensional approach towards intrusion detection system.* arXiv preprint arXiv:1205.2340.

Vinayakumar, R., Alazab, M., Soman, K. P., Poornachandran, P., Al-Nemrat, A., & Venkatraman, S. (2019). Deep learning approach for intelligent intrusion detection system. *IEEE Access: Practical Innovations, Open Solutions*, *7*, 41525–41550. doi:10.1109/ACCESS.2019.2895334

Chapter 6
Face Detection and Recognition From Distance Based on Deep Learning

Hui Wang
Auckland University of Technology, New Zealand

Wei Qi Yan
Auckland University of Technology, New Zealand

ABSTRACT

Face recognition is an important biometric in video surveillance. However, the conventional algorithms of face recognition are also susceptible to various conditions. The contribution of this chapter is to explore face recognition by using deep learning, including detecting the location of human faces on the given images at various distances and multiple angles. In the distances, the influence of the distance from the camera to a face and the size of the face in the images is explored. There are 500 images collected from various videos as the input and they are applied to train the proposed models. The accuracy of face recognition from the videos excluding training dataset is at 90.18%. The results indicate that this method is able to recognise human faces with partial occlusion and various distances.

INTRODUCTION

With the rapid development of computer vision, artificial intelligence (AI) has become the core of contemporary high-tech, its applications include face detection and recognition. The key issue in face detection and recognition is feature extraction

DOI: 10.4018/978-1-6684-4558-7.ch006

which has been developed rapidly based on computational intelligence (Bonetto et al. 2015; Wang and Srinivasan, 2017). There are many types of applications of face recognition, e.g., gender identification, ages and emotions are the most important characteristics of human faces. The main purpose of this book chapter is to automatically recognize human faces and affirm the class of the objects. This topic is also one of the important research fields in computer vision and deep learning (LeCun et al., 2015).

Face recognition, as a biometric, is a significant components of video surveillance and visual security which has been applied to human identification nowadays. In large shopping malls, face recognition is employed to monitor the passengers and provide users with convenient services. At the entrance of a railway station, airport, bank, supermarket, school or company, face recognition is applied to implement access control, which prevents the entry of aliens and ensures the security of premise (Zhang, et al., 2017). With the development of human face recognition, it has been applied to protect the privacy of users, improve the security of visual data. Face recognition, as a special part of human-computer interaction (Bian et al., 2016) identifies users, serves them with great convenience.

In 1943, McCulloch and Walter (Landahl et al., 1943) proposed that the first artificial neuron model: MP model who connected the basic unit together to understand how human brain produces highly complex patterns. This has made a significant contribution to the development of artificial neural networks. In 1958, Rosenblatt greatly developed the neural network theory and applied it to real problems. In 1986, Rinehart et al. proposed backpropagation algorithm, which is an important method in the neural network to calculate the errors of neurons after data processing (Liu, and Liang, 2005). This algorithm is still the most popular one of the most broadly applied artificial neural networks in artificial intelligence.

With the development of neuroscience, computer science scientists have found that brain signals are transmitted through a complex structure; if time permits, the characteristics are applied to understand digital signals, which led to the emergence of deep learning (LeCun et al., 2015) for the establishment and simulation of human brain for analysis and learning. Convolutional neural networks (CNNs) (Karpathy et al., 2014) have been successfully applied to visual imagery in the past few years. One of the most important factors is the need to provide a large amount of training data. But in face recognition, due to lack of large scale of data sets, a few of experiments were limited.

The contribution of this book chapter is based on deep learning for face recognition, which will be completed in real time. For example, if people are near to the camera, the system will verify the influence of proportion of face to the total size of the given images, the proportion is thought as a major core. The relevant experiments require four parts: 1) Collecting the data set, 2) accepting the command parameters, and 3) defining the neural network model, 4) training and testing model.

This book chapter is organized as follow. Literature review is presented after this introduction section, then the method and final results are demonstrated, the conclusion is drawn at last.

RELATED WORK

Deep Neural Networks (DNNs) have a history of more than 10 years. The DNNs were originated in 1943 when Pitts and McCulloch (McCulloch and Pitts, 1943) created a computer model based on human brain neural network that eventually became a hot topic after a century of development. Neocognitron (Fukushima and Miyake, 1982) was the first artificial neural network that introduced CNNs, where the receptive field of a convolutional unit gave weight vector. In 2006, Hinton (Hinton et al., 2006) presented the concept of a fast-learning algorithm for deep belief net, who presented the deep learning methods and improvement of DNNs training model. However, deep learning remains in theoretical stage till Hinton's team won the championship of ImageNet Large Scale Visual Recognition Challenge (ILSVRC) (Simonyan, 2015) by using AlexNet in 2012, it is an important milestone in the history (Schmidhuber, 2015). The deep learning has aroused widespread concern after the ImageNet award.

There are four reasons (Simonyan, 2015) that why AlexNet succeeded and DNN became one of the most popular topics: 1) Big dataset with millions ImageNet data, 2) assisting with GPU acceleration for model training, 3) the methods of preventing overfitting, e.g., dropout and data augmentation; 4) the development of nonlinear activation function, e.g., ReLU, tan, sigmoid.

The number of images in dataset is an important factor that determines the accuracy of visual object recognition in deep learning. The method of data augmentation is to enhance the training data by using mathematical transformations such as Affine transformation, in order to achieve the purpose of reducing overfitting and improving the accuracy of recognition results. The two distinct forms of data augmentation respectively are to generate image translations and horizontal reflections and to alter the intensities of the RGB channels in training images (Krizhevsky et al., 2012). Both methods are able to convey multiple images from the original one with very few computations; the transformed images do not need to be stored on disk which are generated before model training in deep learning.

Dropout was presented by Hinton (Srivastava et al., 2014) in 2012. The dropout is a neural network unit temporarily discarded from deep learning models in accordance with a probability in the training process of deep learning. It should be noted that the temporarily discarded neuron parameters are merely hidden in this training phase; the essence is to ignore the part of feature classifier, which means that the part of hidden layer nodes tends to zero in each loop of training. This approach can reduce the interaction in feature classifier, thus, effectively diminish the overfitting phenomenon.

Dropout is broadly employed in the field of DNNs (Gal and Ghahramani, 2016), which directly shows the superiority of this method in improving the accuracy of verification results. But the drawbacks of dropout are also noteworthy, which greatly increase the time of data training and the complexity of the nonlinear activation function (Maalej et al., 2016). However, both dropout and data augmentation are effective methods to reduce overfitting.

Multilayer perceptron (MLP) is interpreted as an artificial neural network, which contains input layer, hidden layer, and output layer. The layers are connected by using fully-connected layer in MLP; the simplest MLP can have only one hidden layer. In CNNs, an MLP consisting of multiple fully connected layers with nonlinear activation functions (Lin et al., 2013). We see that images input to the MLP layer (Bengio et al., 2013) in the CNNs are an abstract one from convolution layers which describes that this feature is invariant to variations of the same concept after the feature extraction from convolutional layers.

In MLP, the function is described (Gal and Ghahramani, 2016), if the input vector is x, the output vector is $f(x)$, bias vectors are $b^{(1)}$ and $b^{(2)}$, weight matrices are $W^{(1)}$ and $W^{(2)}$, activation functions are $G(\cdot)$ and $s(\cdot)$, then the matrix notation of MLP is,

$$f(x) = G\left(b^{(2)} + W^{(2)}\left(s\left(b^{(1)} + W^{(1)}x\right)\right)\right). \tag{1}$$

The output vector of MLP is obtained,

$$o(x) = G\left(b^{(2)} + W^{(2)}h(x)\right). \tag{2}$$

In order to train the MLP layer, the DNN model needs to be trained with all the parameters, the set of parameters is $\{W^{(2)}, b^{(2)}, W^{(1)}, b^{(1)}\}$.

METHODOLOGY

In this paper, we collected face images as the training dataset for five classes. The images with different distances, environments with various lighting conditions, human faces with multiple angles were taken as the test dataset, which increases the difficulty of face detection and recognition. Figure 1 shows the dataset.

In order to improve the accuracy of face recognition, the amount of original data was augmented by generating new training dataset using the existing images. In this project, an image is generated 50 images after data augmentation like random cropping and scaling from multiple angles, random cropping is to enrich the face size and information, the position and size of the face have been modified after the randomly cropping. Figure 2 shows an image after randomly cropping, scaling, and rotating.

In deep learning, the use of CNNs to achieve face recognition has attracted broad attention. This chapter refers to the SSD (Liu et al., 2016) architecture for model design so as to improve the speed of face recognition. Firstly, the input image is extracted through a CNN architecture. Then, the model takes advantage of two MLP (Cireşan et al., 2011) structures to implement visual object classification and localization respectively as the input of CNN model. Figure 3 is the diagram of model structure.

At first, if the DNN model is trained by using the input images, it is not an image followed by another, but *N* images will be input in one step (Krizhevsky et al., 2012), *N* is set as batch size. At the beginning of this model, the input images are needed, the dimension of model parameters is 4D. Among them, 360×640 is the size of the image, 3 is the number of colour channels of the image, because the image is with RGB 3-color channels (Wu et al., 2007).

Figure 1. A part of the training dataset

In the following convolutional layers of this model, the dimension represents the size of images that has height *H* and width *W*, channel number is *C*. Then, six convolutional layers were setup in this model. In these six convolutional layers, a 5×5 large convolution kernel was setup in the first convolutional layer to capture a wide range of information and assign a 3×3 small convolution kernel at the next five convolutional layers, which is applied to capture a small range of image information. In each of the six convolutional layers, a 2×2 maximum pooling layer is set for each convolutional layer. The maximum pooling operation means that for each 2×2 small mesh, the maxima of pixel intensity has been taken as the output, which reduces the size of the special name at the same time.

After feature extraction of six convolutional layers, the feature maps of each sample were organized into a vector and further converted to a matrix. By expanding the vectors, dropout operations were added. The dropout operation indicates that at the time of output, the corresponding nodes are randomly deleted. If the dropout is conducted before fully connected layers, overfitting could be prevented effectively.

Then, taken the extracted visual features of CNN as input, two dual-layer MLPs were constructed respectively for the classification and localization of visual object. The dimension of the output of the classified MLP is [*N*, *nClass*], where *nClass* represents the number of classes. In our experiment, *nClass* = 5. Each row of the output represents a classification vector,

$$p = [p_1, \ldots, p_{nClass}], \tag{3}$$

where p_k represents the probability of the *k*-th classification of the input, which is applied to measure the gap between the predicted classification and the actual classification of the sample, cross entropy is generally employed as a loss function. The predicted classification vector of the given input is

$$q = [q_1, \ldots, q_{nClass}]. \tag{4}$$

Figure 2. Images after randomly cropping

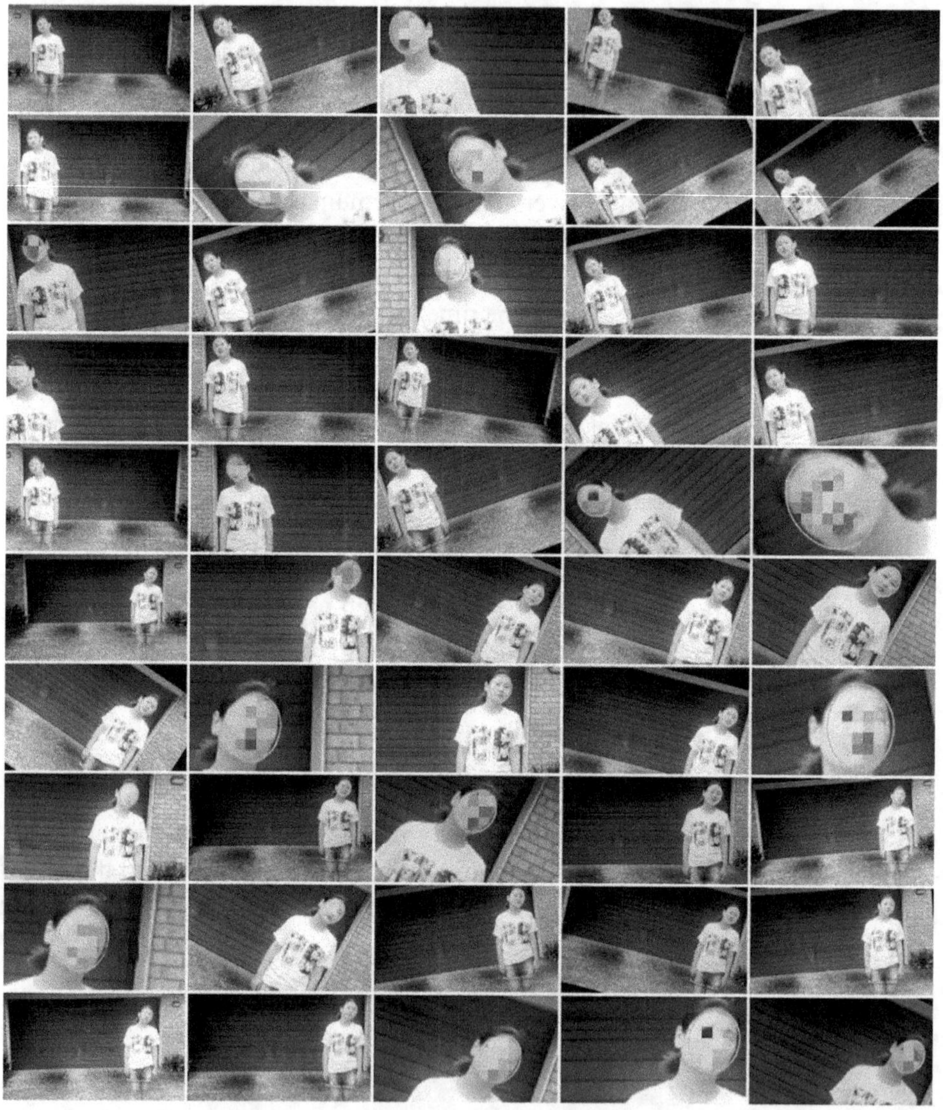

It satisfies that

$$q_k = \begin{cases} 1k = j \\ 0k \neq j \end{cases}. \tag{5}$$

The loss function of classification model is

$$L_{cls} = -\sum_{k=1}^{nClass} q_k \log p_k \tag{6}$$

Because the feature map of location MLP is [N, 5], each row of the output result represents the code of an ellipse shape. Let $\widehat{E}$ be the ellipse position predicted by the model, E be the actual ellipse position of the sample, then the location loss function of model is

$$L_{loc} = \sum_{k=1}^{5} f\left(\widehat{E}_k - E_k\right) \tag{7}$$

The norm of vector $\widehat{E}_k - E_k$ was calculated. The smooth 1-norm of function $f(\bullet)$ is chosen, then

$$f(x) = \begin{cases} |x| - 0.5x < 1 \\ 0.5x^2 x \geq 1 \end{cases} \tag{8}$$

Figure 3. The structure of the proposed model

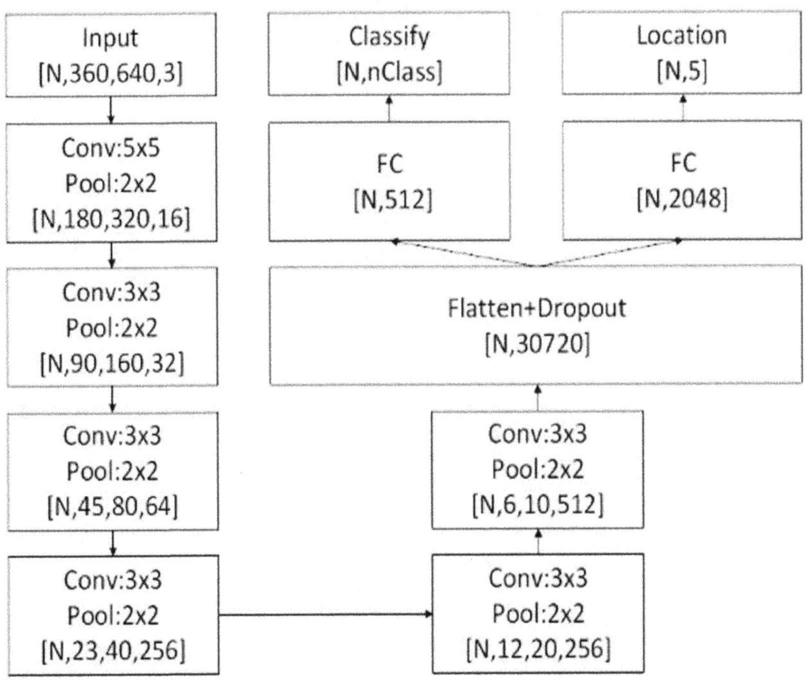

RESULT AND ANALYSIS

Corresponding to the research objectives of this book chapter, three experiments were conducted. In order to complete the task of currency detection, the secondary work embarked on is the stages of research work from data generating, training data and resultant analysis. The experimental implementation can considerably benefit from the basic idea regarding the specific process of currency identification.

According to the model design, the two sets of codes $E_1 = [x_c, y_c, a, b, 180\phi/\pi]$ and E= [x1, x2, y1, y2, b] are taken for model training. By taking weight wÎ{1,10}, a total of four models were trained. Related to 2,5000 training samples, a batch size of 50 was taken with 75 epochs, which requires a total of 30,000 steps. The model was implemented by using TensorFlow and NVIDIA GTX 1070 graphics card for accelerated training, each model training process spent about 4 hours. The training results are shown in Table 1.

Table 1. Training results comparation

Models	Bounding Boxes	Validations
I	$[x_c, y_c, a, b, 180\phi/\pi]$	0.8890
II	$[x_c, y_c, a, b, 180\phi/\pi]$	0.8832
III	$[x_1, x_2, y_1, y_2, b]$	0.8962
IV	$[x_1, x_2, y_1, y_2, b]$	0.9018

Figure 4. The curve of training process

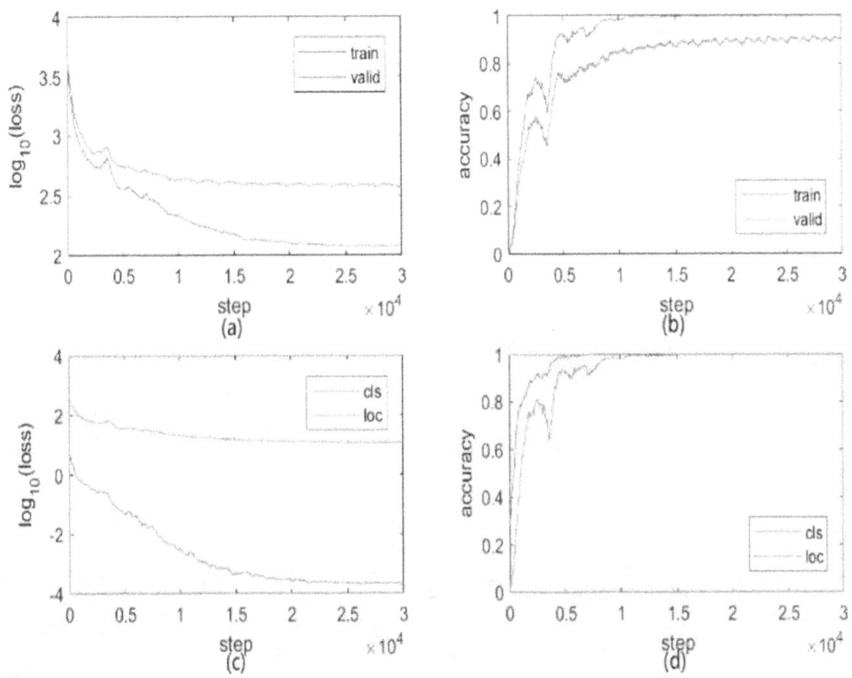

The experimental results show that the accuracy of each model in the training is more than 99.00%, which indicates that the model has been fully trained. The correctness of the model is mainly compared by using the accuracy based on the verification set. Table 1 shows the model IV with elliptic code E2, positioning weight w=10 has the highest accuracy based on the verification set, which reached to 90.18%. In order to further understand the training process of our model, a training curve is shown in Fig. 4.

Figure 4(a) represents the loss function value, which was mainly employed to observe the overfitting of the model. If the loss function on the training set decreases while the loss function on the validation set does not increase, then the model did not appear overfitting. Figure 4(a) shows the model had not apparently overfitting.

Figure 4(b) shows the results to compare the accuracy of the training and verification to observe whether the model has been adequately trained. The model basically converges at about 20,000 steps, the accuracy on the training set is almost 100.00%, which indicates that the model has been adequately trained.

Figure 4(c) shows the comparison of the loss function values located and classified on the training set. The Figure 4(d) displays the accuracy for positioning and classification on the training set. The decrease of the value of the classification loss function is larger than the value of the loss function of localization.

Of course, various sizes of a face will be obtained at different distance. As shown in Figure 5, if a person moves closer to the camera, deep learning algorithms are able to detect the human face with a diversity of sizes in different distance. The size of the face in the image is an important factor that affects the recognition results.

Figure 5. Human face with different sizes

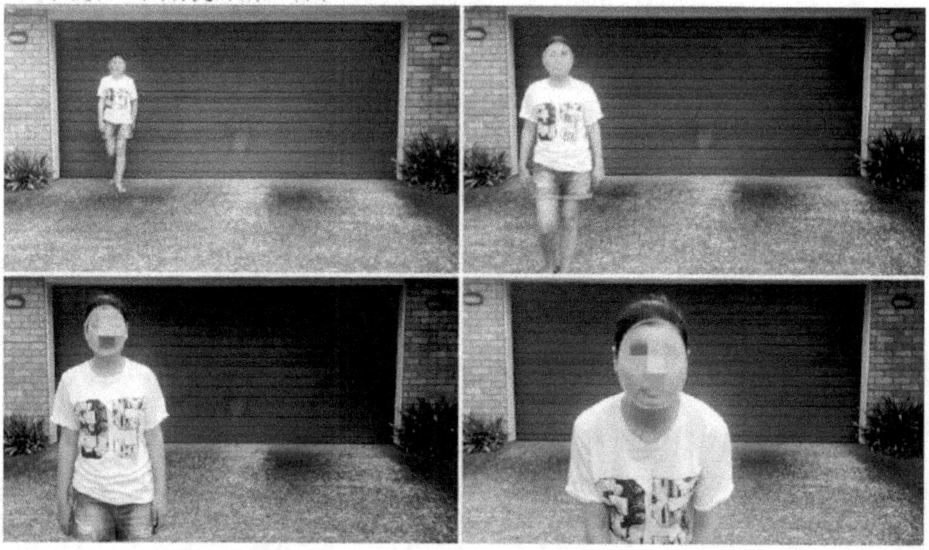

The size of human face is measured by using proportion of the face to the total size of the image. Let the width and height of the image be w and h, respectively; the ellipse shape of a face is denoted as $\{x_c, y_c, a, b, \phi\}$, then the area of the bounding box of the human face is

$$S_F = 4\sqrt{(a\cos\phi)^2 + (b\sin\phi)^2}\sqrt{(a\sin\phi)^2 + (b\cos\phi)^2} \tag{9}$$

Thus, the ratio of the face in the image is obtained by using

$$A = \frac{4}{wh}\sqrt{(a\cos\phi)^2 + (b\sin\phi)^2}\sqrt{(a\sin\phi)^2 + (b\cos\phi)^2} \tag{10}$$

Obviously, if A is larger, it indicates a larger face in the image, people are closer to the camera; otherwise, if A is smaller, it reveals a smaller face is detected in the image, that represents that human face is far from the camera. In order to better understand the influence of proportion of a human face on the accuracy, the accuracy rates and IoUs for different sizes of faces were calculated.

Figure 6. The relationship between face ratio and accuracy

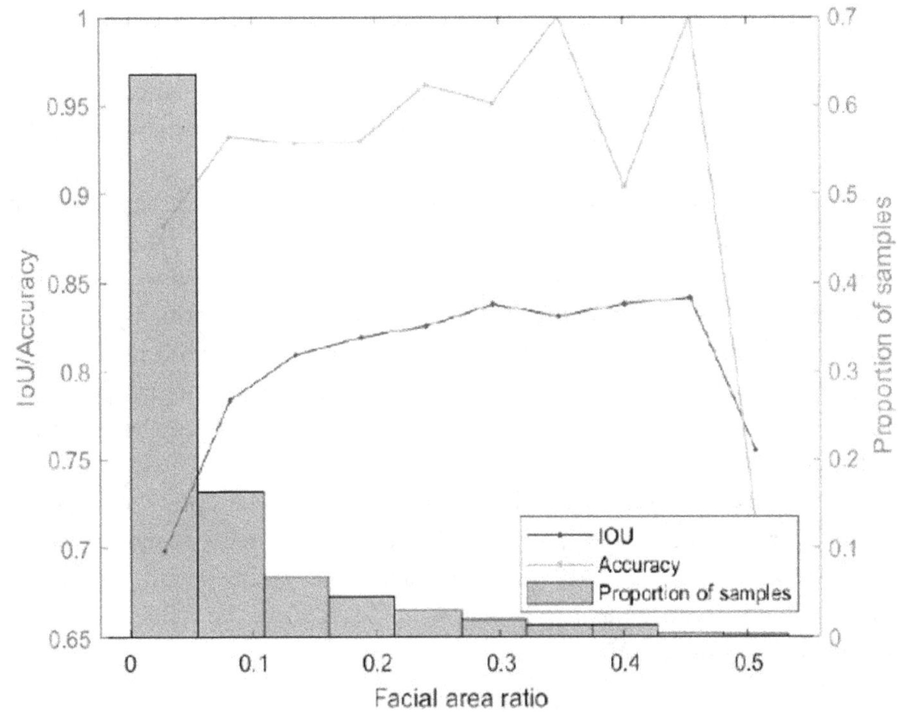

From the histogram, if the proportion of a human face is small, the number of samples is large; if the ratio of faces increases, the number of samples gradually decreases. At the same time, both the accuracy and the IoU are increasing at first and then decrease. The reasons are: (1) If the face occupies a large proportion of the image, it is easily to be recognized and the accuracy is high; (2) The proportion of the face area to the image is large, the number of samples is less. Therefore, the values of accuracy and IoU are around the ratio 0.40, which begins to decline, because there are few samples, the statistical results fluctuate obviously.

CONCLUSION

There are two types of algorithms for detecting human faces from digital images and videos which are conventional machine learning and deep learning. Both algorithms are able to achieve high accuracy in face recognition, but conventional machine learning was not able to make a significant breakthrough based on aging, distance, partial occlusion, facial expression (Feng et al., 2000, Cui, 2014, Cui and Yan, 2016). In this book chapter, the use of ConvNets algorithms is an excellent solution on human face recognition, which greatly improves the efficiency of face recognition. The test videos contain a face with a broad range of distances, the proposed model can still accurately detect the human face. Face detection using deep learning algorithms is beyond the recognition of using conventional machine learning methods.

Deep learning algorithms are effectively applied to solve a variety of external interferences in face recognition, but which requires a bit big dataset and huge training time. It may take much time in image augmentation and model training, even using a powerful GPU. In addition, the face detection algorithm by using deep learning algorithm in this book chapter mainly refers to the SSD model (Liu et al., 2016). There are many other deep learning algorithms that might optimize the neural network model, such as sparse coding, autoencoder, and deep belief network (Arel et al., 2010).

In future, the proposed network model is needed to be optimized based on the existing results (Yan, 2015, 2019, 2021). Firstly, the network model needs to effectively be designed by matching with facial features. Secondly, the training dataset should be reduced as much as possible to improve the training efficiency and availability (Wang, 2018).

REFERENCES

Arel, I., Rose, D. C., & Karnowski, T. P. (2010). Deep machine learning - A new frontier in artificial intelligence research. *IEEE Computational Intelligence*, *5*(4), 13–18. doi:10.1109/MCI.2010.938364

Bengio, Y., Courville, A., & Vincent, P. (2013). Representation learning: A review and new perspectives. *IEEE Transactions on Pattern Analysis and Machine Intelligence*, *35*(8), 1798–1828. doi:10.1109/TPAMI.2013.50 PMID:23787338

Bian, Z. P., Hou, J., Chau, L. P., & Magnenat-Thalmann, N. (2016). Facial position and expression-based human–computer interface for persons with tetraplegia. *IEEE Journal of Biomedical and Health Informatics, 20*(3), 915–924. doi:10.1109/JBHI.2015.2412125 PMID:25775501

Bonetto, M., Carrato, S., Fenu, G., Medvet, E., Mumolo, E., Pellegrino, F. A., & Ramponi, G. (2015). Image processing issues in a social assistive system for the blind. In *International Symposium on Image and Signal Processing and Analysis* (pp. 216-221). 10.1109/ISPA.2015.7306061

Cireşan, D., Meier, U., Masci, J., & Schmidhuber, J. (2011). A committee of neural networks for traffic sign classification. In *International Joint Conference on Neural Networks* (pp. 1918-1921). 10.1109/IJCNN.2011.6033458

Cui, W. (2014). *A Scheme of Human Face Recognition in Complex Environments* [Master's Thesis]. Auckland University of Technology, New Zealand.

Cui, W., & Yan, W. (2016). A scheme for face recognition in complex environments. *International Journal of Digital Crime and Forensics, 8*(1), 26–36. doi:10.4018/IJDCF.2016010102

Feng, G. C., Yuen, P. C., & Dai, D. Q. (2000). Human face recognition using PCA on wavelet subband. *Journal of Electronic Imaging, 9*(2), 226–234. doi:10.1117/1.482742

Fukushima, K., & Miyake, S. (1982). Neocognitron: A self-organizing neural network model for a mechanism of visual pattern recognition. In Competition and Cooperation in Neural Nets (pp. 267-285). Springer. doi:10.1007/978-3-642-46466-9_18

Gal, Y., & Ghahramani, Z. (2016). A theoretically grounded application of dropout in recurrent neural networks. In Advances in Neural Information Processing Systems (pp. 1019-1027). Academic Press.

Hinton, G. E., Osindero, S., & Teh, Y. W. (2006). A fast learning algorithm for deep belief nets. *Neural Computation, 18*(7), 1527–1554. doi:10.1162/neco.2006.18.7.1527 PMID:16764513

Karpathy, A., Toderici, G., Shetty, S., Leung, T., Sukthankar, R., & Fei-Fei, L. (2014). Large-scale video classification with convolutional neural networks. In *IEEE Conference on Computer Vision and Pattern Recognition* (pp. 1725-1732). 10.1109/CVPR.2014.223

Krizhevsky, A., Sutskever, I., & Hinton, G. E. (2012). ImageNet classification with deep convolutional neural networks. In Advances in Neural Information Processing Systems (pp. 1097-1105). Academic Press.

Landahl, H. D., McCulloch, W. S., & Pitts, W. (1943). A statistical consequence of the logical calculus of nervous nets. *Bulletin of Mathematical Biology*, *5*(4), 135–137.

LeCun, Y., Bengio, Y., & Hinton, G. (2015). Deep learning. *Nature*, *521*(7553), 436–444. doi:10.1038/nature14539 PMID:26017442

Lin, M., Chen, Q., & Yan, S. (2013). *Network in network*. arXiv:1312.4400.

Liu, J., & Liang, D. (2005). A survey of FPGA-based hardware implementation of ANNs. In *IEEE International Conference on Neural Networks and Brain* (pp. 915-918). IEEE.

Liu, M., & Yan, W. (2022). *Masked face recognition in real-time using MobileNetV2*. ACM ICCCV.

Liu, W., Anguelov, D., Erhan, D., Szegedy, C., Reed, S., Fu, C. Y., & Berg, A. C. (2016). SSD: Single shot multibox detector. In *European Conference on Computer Vision* (pp. 21-37). Academic Press.

Maalej, R., Tagougui, N., & Kherallah, M. (2016). Online Arabic handwriting recognition with dropout applied in deep recurrent neural networks. In *IAPR Workshop on Document Analysis Systems* (pp. 417-421). 10.1109/DAS.2016.49

McCulloch, W. S., & Pitts, W. (1943). A logical calculus of the ideas immanent in nervous activity. *The Bulletin of Mathematical Biophysics*, *5*(4), 115–133. doi:10.1007/BF02478259

Schmidhuber, J. (2015). Deep learning in neural networks: An overview. *Neural Networks*, *61*, 85–117. doi:10.1016/j.neunet.2014.09.003 PMID:25462637

Srivastava, N., Hinton, G. E., Krizhevsky, A., Sutskever, I., & Salakhutdinov, R. (2014). Dropout: A simple way to prevent neural networks from overfitting. *Journal of Machine Learning Research*, *15*(1), 1929–1958.

Wang, H. (2018). *Real-time Face Detection and Recognition Based on Deep Learning* [Master's Thesis]. Auckland University of technology, New Zealand.

Wang, Z., & Srinivasan, R. S. (2017). A review of artificial intelligence-based building energy use prediction: Contrasting the capabilities of single and ensemble prediction models. *Renewable & Sustainable Energy Reviews*, *75*, 796–808. doi:10.1016/j.rser.2016.10.079

Wu, M. N., Lin, C. C., & Chang, C. C. (2007). Brain tumor detection using color-based k-means clustering segmentation. In *International Conference on Intelligent Information Hiding and Multimedia Signal Processing* (pp. 245-250). 10.1109/IIHMSP.2007.4457697

Yan, W. (2019). *Introduction to Intelligent Surveillance: Surveillance Data Capture, Transmission, and Analytics*. Springer. doi:10.1007/978-3-030-10713-0

Yan, W. (2021). *Computational Methods for Deep Learning: Theoretic, Practice and Applications*. Springer. doi:10.1007/978-3-030-61081-4

Yan, W., & Kankanhalli, M. (2015) Face search in encrypted domain. *Pacific-Rim Symposium on Image and Video Technology*, 775-790.

Zhang, S., Wei, Z., Nie, J., Huang, L., Wang, S., & Li, Z. (2017). A review on human activity recognition using vision-based method. *Journal of Healthcare Engineering, 2017*, 2017. doi:10.1155/2017/3090343 PMID:29065585

ADDITIONAL READING

Gao, X., Nguyen, M., & Yan, W. (2021) Face image inpainting based on generative adversarial network. In *International Conference on Image and Vision Computing New Zealand*. 10.1109/IVCNZ54163.2021.9653347

Kingsbury, B. (2009). Lattice-based optimization of sequence classification criteria for neural-network acoustic modeling. In *IEEE International Conference on Acoustics, Speech and Signal Processing* (pp. 3761-3764). 10.1109/ICASSP.2009.4960445

Kong, T., Yao, A., Chen, Y., & Sun, F. (2016). Hypernet: Towards accurate region proposal generation and joint object detection. In *IEEE Conference on Computer Vision and Pattern Recognition* (pp. 845-853). 10.1109/CVPR.2016.98

Lee, Y., Kim, H., Park, E., Cui, X., & Kim, H. (2017). Wide-Residual-Inception networks for real-time object detection. In *IEEE Intelligent Vehicles Symposium* (pp. 758-764).

Nagi, J., Ducatelle, F., Di Caro, G. A., Cireşan, D., Meier, U., Giusti, A., ... Gambardella, L. M. (2011). Max-pooling convolutional neural networks for vision-based hand gesture recognition. In *IEEE International Conference on Signal and Image Processing Applications* (pp. 342-347). 10.1109/ICSIPA.2011.6144164

Wu, J., Leng, C., Wang, Y., Hu, Q., & Cheng, J. (2016). Quantized convolutional neural networks for mobile devices. In *IEEE Conference on Computer Vision and Pattern Recognition* (pp. 4820-4828). 10.1109/CVPR.2016.521

Chapter 7
Investigation of Deep Fake Images Using Pre-Trained CNN Frameworks

Anitha Ruth J.
https://orcid.org/0000-0003-1900-6173
SRM Institute of Science and Technology, India

Uma R.
https://orcid.org/0000-0002-0053-0162
Sri Sairam Engineering College, India

Vijayalakshmi G. V. Mahesh
B. M. S. Institute of Technology and Management, India

P. Ramkumar
Sri Sairam College of Engineering, India

ABSTRACT

Deep learning technologies, such as neural networks, have tackled complicated issues from large-scale data processing to computer vision and human-level control. Editing photographs with software designed for commercial purposes makes it easy for anyone to manipulate images in order to create fictitious ones. Generative adversarial networks (GANs) are currently being utilised to generate superficially realistic photographs, as opposed to the old methods that were previously used to create phony images. The GANs images are referred to as deep fakes. To the unaided eye, they appear to be real photographs. As a result, it's impossible to spot a phony image produced with GANs. The social network is made less safe as a result of the uploading of these bogus photographs. It is therefore critical that the digital image's legitimacy be detected before it is uploaded. Thus, in this chapter, the authors suggest a few pre-trained deep learning frameworks that may be used to effectively detect deep fake images.

DOI: 10.4018/978-1-6684-4558-7.ch007

INTRODUCTION

Smart phones' rising complexity and the rise of social networks' digital object content have led to an enormous number of new digital object content in recent years. As a result of the widespread use of digital photographs, a proliferation of tools and methods for manipulating image data has occurred. Because these methods were tedious and time-consuming, they had previously been out of the reach of the majority of people. Artificial intelligence-based false picture production is now possible thanks to deep generative models, which allow for the rapid transmission of high-quality tampered media material (Li et al., 2020). In the field of image improvement and manipulation, one of the most promising recent developments has been the use of Generative Adversarial Networks (GANs). Splicing, resampling, and copy moving are all examples of digital image modifications that can be detected using digital image forensics tools and methodologies (Nataraj et al., 2019). Image augmentation and manipulation have been greatly improved by the use of generative adversarial networks (GANs). GANs are made up of two networks, one that generates false pictures and the other that assesses whether an image is real or fake (Chen et al., 2022). Digital picture forensics is devoted to identifying and preventing image forgeries in order to control the circulation of such fabricated material. " According to various estimates, the internet receives over two billion photographs each day. Image forgery detection has made significant progress, but digital video falsification detection is still a challenging problem. Due to the significant deterioration of video frames when they are compressed, many image processing techniques cannot be applied to video. Digital image forensics has had success using deep learning. However, deep learning may be used to fake videos as well (Bonettini et al., 2020). There are inherent picture disparities across the borders that make face editing procedures fundamentally recognizable despite the standard process of blending a changed face into an existing backdrop (Durall et al., 2019). One of the most important issues in today's digital society is the manipulation of visual material. Face expression manipulation and identity manipulation are two of the most common ways of facial manipulation now in use. It is possible to communicate the facial emotions of one person to another in real time using only inexpensive equipment. This is the second type of facial forgery in which a person's face is replaced with an image of another person. However, DeepFakes uses deep learning to conduct face swapping as well. DeepFakes, on the other hand, must be trained for each pair of movies in order to do face swapping in real time. (de Lima et al., 2020). Massive advancements in the area of facial modification have shown a difficult footprint that may be exposed to the specifics of automated video editing techniques in the last few years. Forensic footprints are frequently quite delicate and difficult to detect, which has sparked a lot of interest in the procedures. New artistic possibilities are opened up by facial modification (e.g., movie creation, visual effects). However, criminal individuals may easily create video forgeries by manipulating the facial expressions. Detecting face modification using recent technologies is the focus of this article (Afchar, 2019).

This Chapter is organized as follows, background section gives a brief synopsis of the underlying research, main focus of the Chapter section discusses about the Deep learning frameworks that can be used to detect Deep fake images. solutions and recommendations section provide the results from the application of TENSOR FLOW and KERAS frameworks and the final section with future scope and conclusion.

BACKGROUND

Deepfake detection may outperform existing state-of-the-art approaches. This work approaches generalizable deep fake detection from a straightforward premise: a representation should be susceptible to a variety of different forms of forgery. Synthesising augmented forgeries from a pool of forgery configurations and guaranteeing the model's sensitivity to forgery configurations has been proposed. In this research offers a method for detecting deepfakes that is capable of generalising well to previously encountered contexts. To construct forgeries, a synthesiser and an adversarial training system has been used. The primary restriction of the existing technology is that the synthesizer's augmentation type remains limited (Chen et al., 2022). Face manipulation detection in video sequences that target contemporary facial manipulation techniques is the subject of this article. On two publicly available datasets with over 119,900 videos, is has been demonstrated how various models may be generated from a single base network. The prevalence of videos in our daily lives and in mass communication means that the ability to tell whether or not a video has been altered is more important than ever. The method that has been proposed is based on the family of models and improves upon an ensemble of models trained using the fundamental concepts (Bonettini et al., 2020). Despite the fact that many face-editing algorithms create human-like results, they contain artefacts in particular areas that are difficult to detect. Classic frequency domain analysis is the foundation of the approach, followed by a simple classifier. When trained on just 20 annotated examples, it achieves a flawless classification accuracy of 100%. Using two datasets, including data from multiple GANs, it has been demonstrated that the proposed technique can recognise high and medium resolution deepfake images with 100% accuracy. Low-resolution material is more difficult to recognise since the accessible frequency spectrum is smaller, making it more difficult. With a 91% accuracy rate, it was able to detect low-resolution forgeries of an industry standard (Durall et al., 2019). The fast advancement in the creation and manipulation of synthetic images raises serious concerns about the consequences for society. This research investigates the realism of current image modifications and the difficulty of spotting them in their original form. In addition to a database of over 1:8 million modified photos, the benchmark is accessible to the public. Trained forgery detectors can spot even the most advanced alterations to a person's facial features. A new dataset of films of modified faces has been proposed to train detectors using domain-specific information. This dataset dwarfs all other publicly accessible forensic datasets by an order of magnitude. It has been shown that this dataset and benchmark will serve as a springboard for further investigation (Rossler et al., 2019). Detection approaches for deepfakes rely solely on individual video frames, so they are unable to learn from temporal information. Using the Celeb-DF dataset, a benchmark for the performance of spatiotemporal convolutional algorithms has been established. Modern frame-based detection algorithms were outperformed by the proposed one. AI-generated Deepfakes may be easily detected using action detection methods, which has been explained and assess in detail in this study. Even I3D, which was superior at action. recognition, was no match for R3D in terms of performance. Researchers in the future may benefit from the findings by better understanding how Deepfake can be identified (de Lima, 2019). This research proposes Face X-ray as a new picture format for detecting fraud in face photos. When an image is fake, it shows where the blending line is, and when it's real and is not. Facial X-rays can be taught without the use of any of the current face manipulation methods. There are inherent image inconsistencies across the blending zones in most known face manipulation methods, and a new method to detect face forgeries based on this fact has been suggested. It is now possible to train a face forgery detector using face X-ray instead of the current state-of-the-art face manipulation techniques (Li et al., 2020). Face tampering in videos, including the more current Deepfake and Face2Face approaches, may be detected automatically and effectively using the technology shown in this study. In most cases, image forensics approaches are ineffective. Videos suffer greatly as a result of the compression used. Under real-world internet dispersion conditions, Deepfake detects Deepfake videos with a 98 percent accuracy rate and Face2Face videos with a 95 percent accuracy rate. Detection of phoney faces relies heavily on the eyes and mouth, according to the tests (Afchar et al., 2019). In this paper, pixel co-occurrence matrices and deep learning are combined to present a unique method for detecting GAN-generated bogus images. It is possible to train a Convolutional Neural Network to tell the difference between images created by GAN and those that are real. GAN experiments reveal that the approach is both effective and generalizable, as evidenced by the results (Nataraj et al., 2019). This study is based on deep learning methodologies, here, the author (Almars, 2021) presents an in-depth analysis of deepfake production and detection systems. A full examination of the various technologies and their applications in the identification of deepfakes is also provided. Because it covers the most recent state-of-the-art approaches for discovering deepfakes in social content. Using neural networks, this research (Sai Vamsi et al., 2022) describes how to distinguish between bogus and real videos. In light of the results, it may be determined that the project was effective in its implementation based on the results. a consequence of training the model on the Celeb-DF dataset using ResNet CNN for frame-level feature recognition, screenshots of its performance and predicted outcomes are provided. For comparing video frames, LSTM had an average accuracy of 91% on the comparisons tested.

MAIN FOCUS OF THE CHAPTER

The term "Deepfake" is a combination of the terms "Deep learning" and "fake," and it refers to information created by an artificial neural network, a field of machine learning that is increasingly popular.
The primary points of the Chapter are summarized as follows,

1. The Chapter contributes to discussing many successful Deep learning strategies such as MesoNet, ResNet50 and CNN for dealing with Deepfake images
2. We can detect fabricated face videos by utilising a pre-trained Deep learning techniques at the mesoscopic level of scrutiny.
3. The MESONET, RESNET50 are implemented using TENSOR flow and KERAS framework.
4. The experimental results prove that MESONET framework provides 96% of accuracy in detecting the fake images while using the customized data set.
5. Whereas RESENET50 and CNN provides 94% and 90% accuracy in detecting the fake images while using the Kaggle (2019) dataset.
6. Finally, in comparison to other frameworks, the results show that the MESONET framework is more effective at detecting fake images

The Chapter uses a range of strategies to detect manufactured face movies at the mesoscopic level. Microscopy is not applicable because compressed video has worsened the picture noise to such a degree that microscopic analysis based on image noise is not possible. When an image depicts a person's face features, the human eye has even more difficulty recognising it at a higher semantic level. Deep Neural Network algorithms are used to detect Deep Fake Images efficiently in order to overcome this issue. Deepfake is a video manipulation technique that seeks to replace the face of a targeted individual with the face of another person in a video clip. Pre-trained framework's approach and architecture are discussed in the following paragraphs

MESONET

This network begins with a sequence of four layers of successive convolutions and pooling and is followed by a dense network with one hidden layer. In order to improve generalisation, the convolutional layers employ ReLU activation functions, which introduce nonlinearities, as well as Batch Normalization (Ioffe and Szegedy, 2015), which regularises their output and prevents the vanishing gradient effect. The fully connected layers employ Dropout (He et al., 2015), which regularises their output and improves their robustness. The architecture diagram for MESO-4 is represented in the figure 1 (Gong et al, 2021).

Figure 1. The Architecture of MESO-4

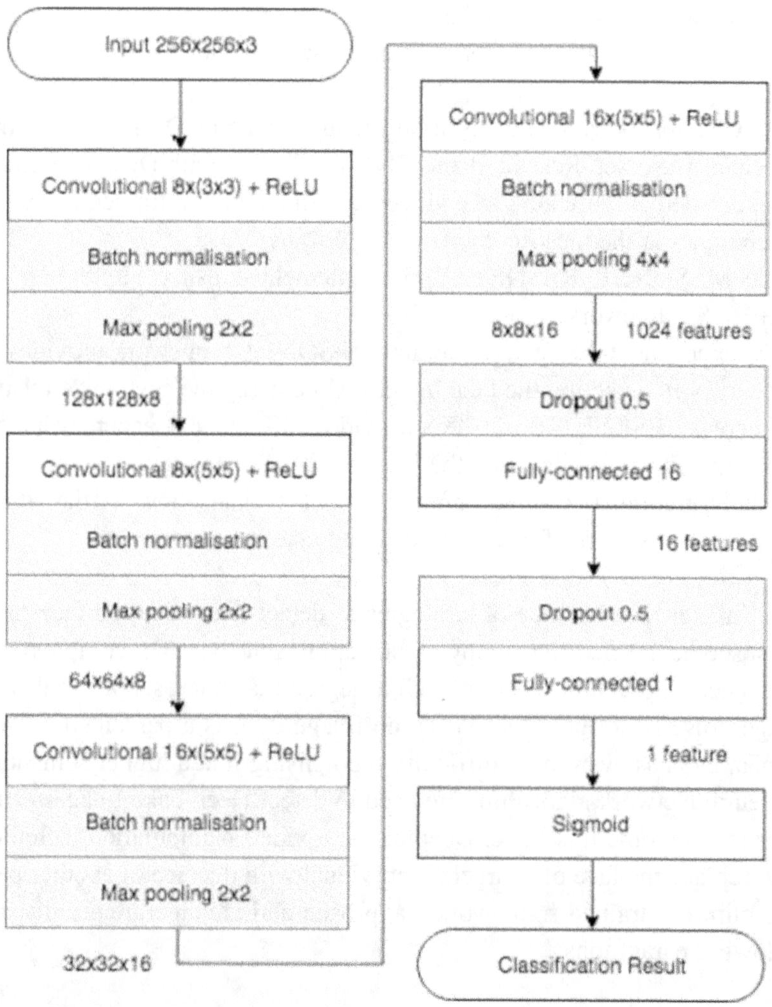

RESNET

In this study we use ResNet model presented by Shaoqing Ren, Kaiming He, Jian Sun, and Xiangyu (He et al., 2015, Goodfellow et al., 2014) is one of the most popular Deep learning models in detecting the Deep fake images. This research uses ResNet to evaluate the performance of deepfake detection because stacking more layers raises the issue of disappearing/exploding gradients while training ultra-deep neural networks Here, ResNet50 is a ResNet version that consists of 48 Convolution layers as well as 1 MaxPool and 1 Average Pool layer is used in detecting the fake images. It is a variant of the ResNet model that is used for image recognition. The following figure 3 shows the architecture of Res Net 50 (Gong et al., 2021, Goodfellow et al., 2014).

Figure 2. Architecture of RESTNET 50

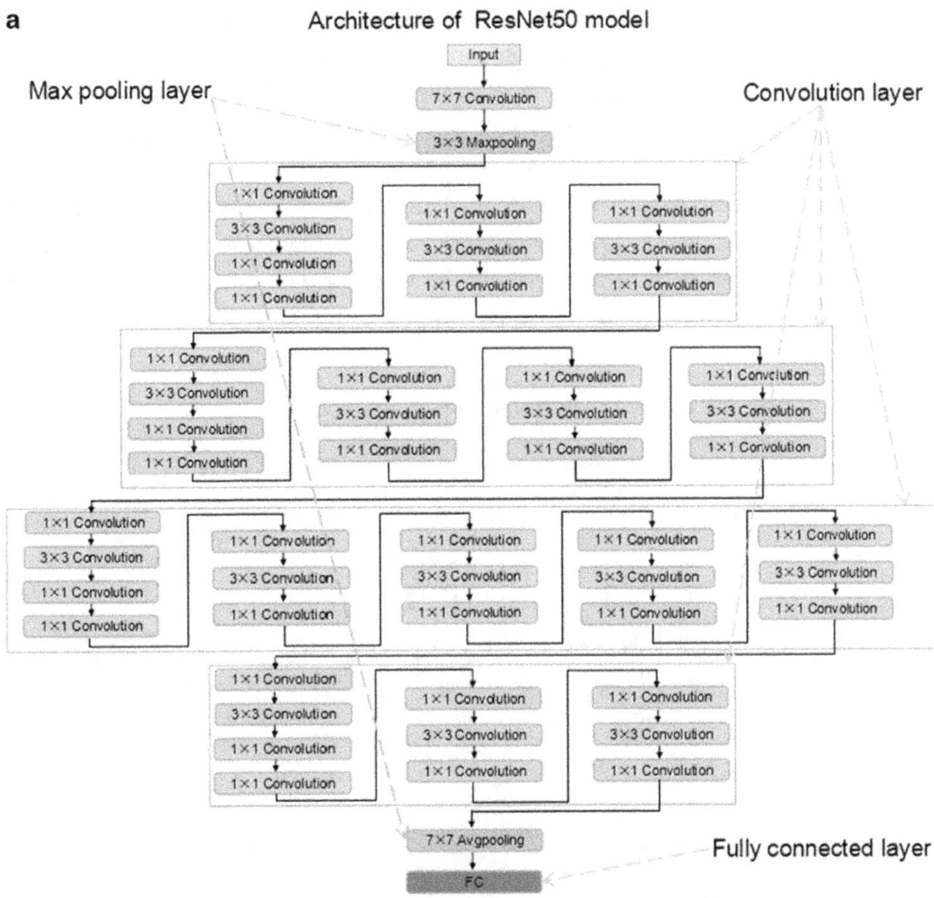

CONVOLUTIONAL NEURAL NETWORK (CNN)

An analysis was done using CNN (Peng et al., 2019) to determine whether or not a face images are authentic or a hoax. To do this experiment data was gathered via Kaggle (2019) and the images for training are around 1450, and images for validation are around 300. A convolutional layer divides a given input into smaller parts, uses a kernel to perform a convolution operation that extracts facial patterns from each part, and finally outputs a feature map. A 3x3 kernel size is being considered for the proposed work. Typically, a pooling layer follows a convolutional layer to reduce complexity by down sampling the convolutional output using a pooling function like average pooling or max pooling, because the generated features from these layers can be quite large. In a CNN, the convolutional and pooling layers serve as the foundation for a classification layer that may include dropout layers as well as fully connected layers. Specifically, a dropout layer serves to prevent neural networks from becoming overfitted. The layer "drops out" a random group of neurons, causing the neural network to ensure that it can deliver proper classifications without relying too much on individual activated neurons, preventing it from in a CNN, the convolutional and pooling layers serve as the foundation for a classification layer that may include dropout layers as well as fully connected layers. Specifically, a dropout layer serves to prevent neural networks from becoming overfitted. The layer "drops out" a random group of neurons, causing the neural network to ensure that it can deliver proper classifications without relying too much on individual activated neurons, preventing it from memorizing the training data completely. Following figure 3 shows the architecture of Convolutional neural network.

Figure 3. Architecture of Convolutional neural network

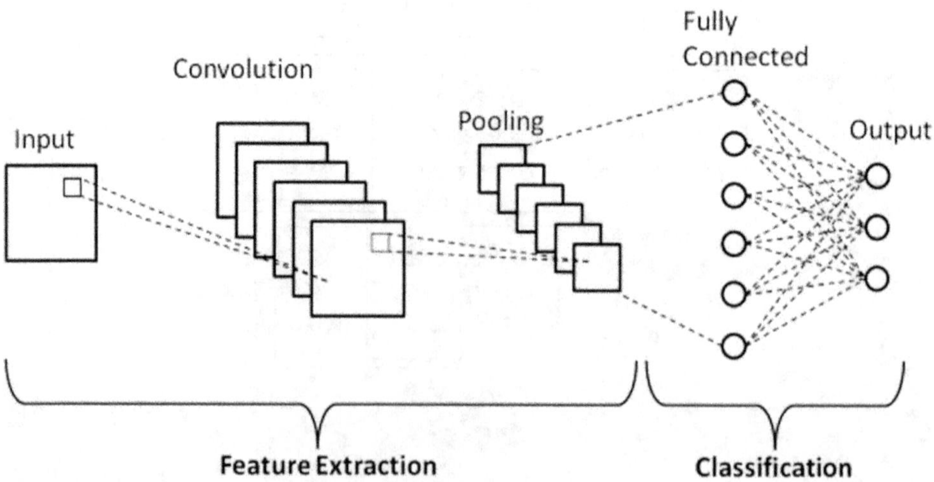

SOLUTIONS AND RECOMMENDATIONS

Pre-trained Deep learning techniques were used in this experiment to improve the accuracy of Deep fake picture detection This work proposed to use MESONET, RESNET50 and CNN for detecting Deep fake images. Both custom data and data from the Kaggle Repository (2019) are used to train the pre-trained Deep Neural Network architectures. The custom data has 100 Deep fake images and 100 Real images for training and testing data. We have 2041 Kaggle Repository files, 960 of which are training false photos and 1081 of which are real photographs for testing. The images are provided as input to the pre-trained framework for training and then predicting. The performance of the model is later tested for validation. Using the performance metrices.

Verification of the proposed procedure is carried out using images from the dataset that have been meticulously altered and of extremely high quality. The images are composites of different faces, separated by the eyes, the nose, the mouth, or the whole of the facial structure are taken as input to the pre-trained models.

In the proposed work training and testing set for pre-trained models are split into three and two sets, respectively. There were two classes of images used throughout the training phase: "0" denoted the REAL image and "1" indicated the FAKE image, with X = "0" as the default. A set of images labelled with classes were fed into the pre-trained models, which generates the classifier models.

Pre-trained models such as MESONET, RESNET50 and CNN were developed by fine-tuning the learning parameters. The models were then tested using characteristics from the testing data set, and the proposed method was evaluated using standard metrics derived from confusion matrix. The following Table 1 shows the real and fake images that were identified by the pretrained models are a variety of computational metrics used to evaluate the pre-trained models' performance, including Accuracy, Specificity/Precision, RECALL, and F1-Score. True Positive (TP), True Negative (TN), and False Positive (FP) and False Negative (FN) images are used in the metrics for evaluation.

Table 1. Real and fake images

Real Images	Fake Images

In this work performance of the pre-trained models is determined by calculating its Accuracy of detecting Fake images from Real images. The following equation determines the Classification accuracy

$$\text{Classification Accuracy} = \frac{(\text{TP} + \text{TN})}{(\text{TP} + \text{TN} + \text{FP} + \text{FN})} \quad (1)$$

The Classification Accuracy of the three pre-trained model is represented in the Table 2 and the graph the figure 4 pictorially represents the performance of each pre- trained models (MESONET, RESNET50 and CNN)

Table 2. Classification accuracy

Model	Accuracy
MesoNet	96%
CNN	90%
ResNet	94%

Figure 4. Accuracy of FAKE IMAGE DETECTION graph of different models

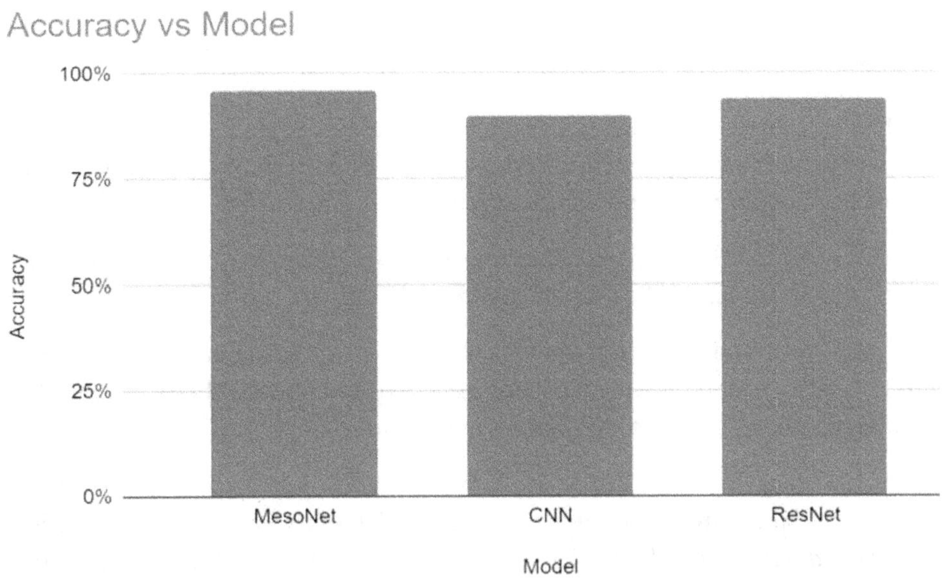

According to the findings, pre-trained models such as MESONET, RESENT50, and CNN do a superior job of distinguishing between fictitious and authentic images.

FUTURE RESEARCH DIRECTIONS

The further performance of Deep fake reduction can be improved by combining RESNET with LSTM and also Computer Vision algorithm can be applied for detection of Deep Fake images.

CONCLUSION

Face alteration in video is now widely acknowledged as a hazard. As a result of our research, we have used three pre-trained network architectures to detect forgeries quickly and cheaply. Deep networks are currently used to extract features in the majority of popular algorithms for detecting fraudulent face videos. In this study the paper highlights that pre-trained model such as MESONET.RESNET50 and CNN can be used in detecting the deep fake images. The experimental results prove that pre-trained models provide high accuracy in detecting the FAKE images from the given dataset.

REFERENCES

Afchar, D., Nozick, V., Yamagishi, J., & Echizen, I. (2018, December). Mesonet: a compact facial video forgery detection network. In 2018 IEEE international workshop on information forensics and security (WIFS) (pp. 1-7). IEEE.

Almars, A. M. (2021). Deepfakes detection techniques using deep learning: A survey. *Journal of Computer and Communications*, *9*(5), 20–35.

Bonettini, N., Cannas, E. D., Mandelli, S., Bondi, L., Bestagini, P., & Tubaro, S. (2021, January). Video face manipulation detection through ensemble of cnns. In *2020 25th international conference on pattern recognition (ICPR)* (pp. 5012-5019). IEEE.

Chen, L., Zhang, Y., Song, Y., Liu, L., & Wang, J. (2022). Self-supervised Learning of Adversarial Example: Towards Good Generalizations for Deepfake Detection. In *Proceedings of the IEEE/CVF Conference on Computer Vision and Pattern Recognition* (pp. 18710-18719). IEEE.

de Lima, O., Franklin, S., Basu, S., Karwoski, B., & George, A. (2020). *Deepfake detection using spatiotemporal convolutional networks.* arXiv preprint arXiv:2006.14749.

Durall, R., Keuper, M., Pfreundt, F. J., & Keuper, J. (2019). *Unmasking deepfakes with simple features.* arXiv preprint arXiv:1911.00686.

Gong, D., Yogan, J. K., Goh, O. S., Ye, Z., & Chi, W. (2021). DeepfakeNet, an efficient deepfake detection method. *International Journal of Advanced Computer Science and Applications*, *12*(6).

Goodfellow, I., Pouget-Abadie, J., Mirza, M., Xu, B., Warde-Farley, D., Ozair, S., ... Bengio, Y. (2014). Generative adversarial nets. *Advances in Neural Information Processing Systems*, 27.

He, K., Zhang, X., Ren, S., & Sun, J. (2016). Deep residual learning for image recognition. In *Proceedings of the IEEE conference on computer vision and pattern recognition* (pp. 770-778). IEEE.

Ioffe, S., & Szegedy, C. (2015, June). Batch normalization: Accelerating deep network training by reducing internal covariate shift. In *International conference on machine learning* (pp. 448-456). PMLR.

Li, L., Bao, J., Zhang, T., Yang, H., Chen, D., Wen, F., & Guo, B. (2020). Face x-ray for more general face forgery detection. In *Proceedings of the IEEE/CVF conference on computer vision and pattern recognition* (pp. 5001-5010). IEEE.

Li, Y., Chang, M. C., & Lyu, S. (2018, December). In ictu oculi: Exposing ai created fake videos by detecting eye blinking. In *2018 IEEE International workshop on information forensics and security (WIFS)* (pp. 1-7). IEEE.

Nataraj, L., Mohammed, T. M., Manjunath, B. S., Chandrasekaran, S., Flenner, A., Bappy, J. H., & Roy-Chowdhury, A. K. (2019). Detecting GAN generated fake images using co-occurrence matrices. *Electronic Imaging*, *2019*(5), 532–1.

Peng, J., Kang, S., Ning, Z., Deng, H., Shen, J., Xu, Y., ... Liu, L. (2020). Residual convolutional neural network for predicting response of transarterial chemoembolization in hepatocellular carcinoma from CT imaging. *European Radiology*, *30*(1), 413–424.

Real and fake face detection. Kaggle. (2019, January 14). Retrieved from https://www.kaggle.com/datasets/ciplab/real-and-fake-face-detection?resource=download

Rossler, A., Cozzolino, D., Verdoliva, L., Riess, C., Thies, J., & Nießner, M. (2019). Faceforensics++: Learning to detect manipulated facial images. In *Proceedings of the IEEE/CVF international conference on computer vision* (pp. 1-11). IEEE.

Vamsi, V. V. V. N. S., Shet, S. S., Reddy, S. S. M., Rose, S. S., Shetty, S. R., Sathvika, S., & Shankar, S. P. (2022). *Deepfake Detection in Digital Media Forensics. Global Transitions Proceedings.*

Chapter 8
Implementation of Machine Learning-Aided Speech Analysis for Speaker Accent Identification Applied to Audio Forensics

Vijayalakshmi G. V. Mahesh
https://orcid.org/0000-0002-1917-7506
B. M. S. Institute of Technology and Management, India

Alex Noel Joseph Raj
https://orcid.org/0000-0003-1505-3159
Shantou University, China

Ruban Nersisson
https://orcid.org/0000-0003-1695-3618
Vellore Institute of Technology, India

ABSTRACT

Accent recognition as a subset of speech recognition is crucial in audio forensics as it provides the authenticity of the speech that can be presented to the judicature as evidence. The challenge here is to design a speaker accent identifying system that can provide significant information to match with the standards of the court of justice. This process requires robust descriptors to represent speech signal with good discrimination ability. This chapter proposes to use Mel Frequency Cepstral Coefficients to identify and represent the human utterances by transforming the frequency from normal scale to Mel scale. The work utilized support vector machine,
DOI: 10.4018/978-1-6684-4558-7.ch008

k nearest neighbors, XG boost, linear discriminant analysis, quadratic discriminant analysis, and decision tree algorithms to recognize the accent of the speaker. The experiment conducted on the accent recognition dataset demonstrated the ability of Mel Frequency Cepstral Coefficients and kNN classifier in identifying and discriminating six accents belonging to different speakers with better accuracy.

INTRODUCTION

With the advancements in Artificial intelligence, signal processing and machine learning algorithms, there is growing demand for speech processing and speech/accent recognition applications in banking sector, tourism industry, marketing, healthcare, law enforcement, forensics, language learning etc., Further the introduction of voice assistants with AI and Internet of Things have transformed speech recognition technology and have changed the way human interact with devices. Speech or accent recognition involves understanding, analyzing the human speech and make the right decision.

Speech processing and speech/accent recognition plays a significant role in audio forensics (AF). AF is a part of forensic science that serves as evidence for investigation as required for law enforcement. This involves (i) Audio/Speech data acquisition, (ii) Analysis, (iii) Interpretation and (iv) Evaluation as major processing steps. The overview of the process is displayed in Fig.1.The acquired data has to be preprocessed to improve its quality by using filters and enhancement techniques. The preprocessing improves the speech intelligibility by removing background noise, distortions and artifacts thus providing authenticity of the evidence. Further it is very important to note the key frequency components and frequency range in the audio/speech signal to observe and gather required information to make it available as evidence.

Digital signal processing algorithms such as Fourier transform, Wavelet transform, and Mel Frequency Cepstral Coefficients serve as a better choice for frequency analysis of the audio signals. This analysis later serves in identifying the suspect based on identifying the speech and accent of the speaker. This chapter emphasizes on applying frequency analysis to extract MFCC features from the speech signals and provide them to the machine learning algorithm and evaluate its output to interpret the result.

Figure 1. Overview of Audio Forensic Process

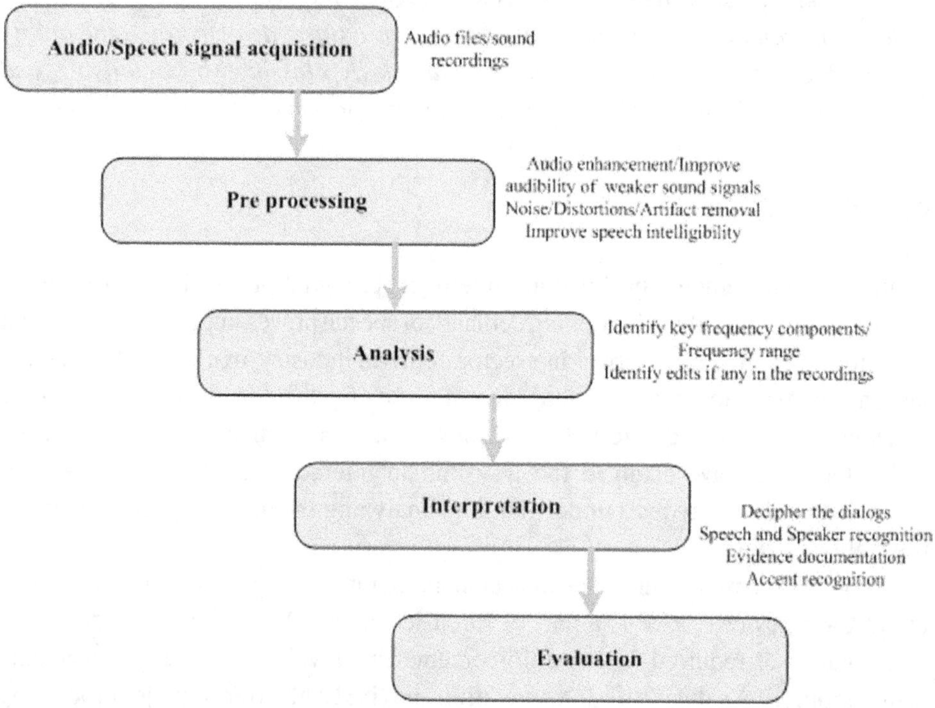

RELATED WORK

A lot of research has been carried out on speech recognition and to identify the accent of the speaker. A critical review on the various methods used for accent-based speech recognition is provided in (Thandil and Basheer, 2020; Bhagath and Das, 2004). Automatic speech recognition framework can be developed based on acoustic phonetic method and pattern recognition (Jahangir et al., 2021).

Acoustic phonetic method explores the acoustic properties of speech signal such as time domain characteristics of the speech that include the fundamental frequency, its duration, mean squared amplitude of the signal or transform domain characteristics such as frequency spectrum to represent and identify the speech. Whereas the pattern recognition (Rabiner, 1992) methods involve extracting the patterns from the speech signal, training the pattern to generate the model and finally adapting the model for speech recognition. Numerous approaches have been developed to extract the patterns or features based on independent component analysis (ICA), principal component analysis (PCA), Liner predictive coding (LPC), zero crossing detection (ZCD), Wavelet transform, Mel Frequency Cepstral coefficient (MFCC), Guassian mixture modeling (GMM), Vector quantization (VQ), Dynamic time warping (DTW), Hidden Markov modeling (HMM) and deep learning architectures (Nassif et al., 2019) to be applied in speech recognition.

The early works on these methods can be traced back to 1975, where Stanford research institute (SRI) (Walker, 1975) developed a system based on acoustic phonetic method to predict the word sequence in an utterance. Later Sperry Univac continuous speech recognition system was presented by (Diller, 1979), where the system considered time variant energy values of assured frequency bands, ratio of energy, the frequency component with highest energy, formants and spectral shape variation between adjacent frames for speech recognition. The system was evaluated, and it overcame the challenges of missed and unrelated phonetic segments. Acoustic phonetic feature-based methodologies were proposed by (Ali et al., 1999) and (Omar and Hasegawa-Johnson, 2002). In (Ali et al., 1999) the system extracts the stop consonants from the speech signal for classification with multi-level decision. The proposed methodology was validated for 300 samples acquired from 30 individuals with six dialects. The performance was measured to be 86% accurate which provided voicing and articulation accuracy of 97% and 90% respectively. (Omar and Hasegawa-Johnson, 2002) emphasized about selecting best descriptors to represent phonological features. A methodology based on maximum mutual information was proposed to select the distinct acoustic features to enhance robustness and also the performance of the speech recognition system.

A method based on phonetic features was put forth by (Siniscalchi et al., 2009) where a set of 22 features: fricative glide liquid stop vowel coronal dental glottal high labial low mid retroflex velar anterior back continuant round tense voiced silence were integrated with features of sound pattern and incorporated log likelihood based decoding scheme for large vocabulary continuous speech recognition system. The experimental results were evident in demonstrating the ability of the methodology in improving the performance of the system. (Ding Jr. et al., 2013) focused on using Dynamic time warping based on supervised machine learning methods: incremental learning and priority rejection learning and unsupervised method: most matching learning. The efficacy of the proposed methods was analyzed and validated using a small vocabulary which demonstrated the better performance of incremental learning. (Vimala and Radha, 2015) presented a Tamil language speaker independent isolated speech recognition system that utilized machine learning algorithms: DTW, GMM, HMM, Multilayer perceptron neural network (MLP), support vector machine (SVM) and Decision tree (DT). The model was assessed with the samples obtained from four different speakers who uttered 10 Tamil digits and 5 names which indicated a highest word recognition accuracy of 100% during training and 97.92% under testing for HMM method.

The approaches were further explored for recognizing the speech across different languages (Widyowaty and Sunyoto, 2020) and also accent recognition/classification.

A method based on analyzing mono-phones and poly-phonemes for distinguishing the languages German, English and Japanese was presented by (Berkling et al., 1994). The system utilized feature selection where the required features were derived from a larger feature space which provided a performance loss as low as 5% and the effectiveness of the system in identifying different languages was significant as it provided an accuracy of 84.1%. (Kannadaguli and Bhat, 2015) compared the performance of phoneme recognition system designed using Guassian mixture modeling and Hidden markov modeling developed for Kannada language. The system extracted Mel frequency Cepstral coefficinents from the 15 Kannada phonemes as features for training and testing the proposed system. The validation of the results indicated better performance of dynamic modeling scheme- Hidden markov with least phoneme error rate.

In (Ge, 2015) the authors have developed a method by integrating phonetics(vowels) with acoustic features to improve the performance of accent recognition system. Here the features after extraction are optimized using principal component analysis and heteroscedastic linear discriminant analysis and provided to mixture model-universal background model-based classifier with normalized perceptual linear predictive features. The method utilized the foreign accented English (FAE) database with 4925 sentences of 23 accents for performance assessment. The simulation results demonstrated an accuracy of 54% which is effective as compared to the state-of-the-art techniques. Abdullah et al. (2019) proposed accent and speaker recognition system using wavelets: Discrete wavelet packet (DWPT), Wavelet packet transform (WPT) and Dual tree complex wavelet packet transform (DT-CWPT). The features extracted from the wavelets are provided to k nearest neighbor (kNN), SVM and Extreme learning (ELM) classifiers for modeling and quantifying the system. The method utilized 10 English digits and Malay words for the experiment. The analysis of the results declared 1n accuracy of 93.54% in identifying the speaker while 95.86% for recognizing the accent for Malay words. A work on recognizing the accent of Telugu language was presented in (Mannepalli et al., 2016) where the authors used MFCC and GMM for feature extraction and classification respectively. The samples of the speech signals for the work were collected from the speakers of coastal Andhra, Rayalaseema and Telangana regions as these is accent variation in these regions. The proposed method was successful as it indicated a performance of 91% accuracy.

As accent recognition plays a important role in the society by helping to identify different people with varying speaking styles has significant applications in the domains of forensics, law enforcement, tourism and travel, customer service (Widyowaty and Sunyoto, 2020) voice controlled applications (Kandhari et al., 2018). An application on Forensic speaker recognition is presented in (Saleem, Subhan, Naseer, Bais, and Imtiaz, 2020). The work used baseline methods such as GMM-Universal background model, i-vector and GMM-SVM with MFCC as the features of the speech signal and Deep learning methods: VGGVox, GMM-Convolutional neural network (CNN), Deep neural network (DNN) with x-vector. The experimental results demonstrated acceptable results with an accuracy of 85.4% for accent recognition with x-vector method. The survey of the Literature identified the use of acoustic phonetic and pattern recognition methods along with various classifier models to identify the speech and the accent of the speaker. The works carried out with different frameworks have demonstrated plausible results in terms of the accuracy of the system.

This chapter is an attempt to use the MFCC features combined with the machine learning algorithms to identify the accent of the speaker. The rest of the chapter is organized as follows. Section 2 presents the methodology adopted for the proposed work. The results are discussed in section 3 and finally section 5 concludes the paper.

METHODOLOGY

The framework for the proposed work to identify the accent of the speaker is displayed in Figure 2. The speech signals with variable accents are preprocessed and Mel frequency cepstral coefficients are extracted which are the attributes representing the speech signals. The attributes are channeled to the classifier models for accent recognition. Further the system is assessed through the metrics: Accuracy, Recall, Precision, Matthew's correlation coefficient, kappa value, F-1 and F-beta score that measure the performance of the system quantitatively.

Speech Dataset

The proposed work considered the accent recognition dataset from UCI machine learning repository (Ma and Fokoué, 2014) with 330 samples of 165 US accents and remaining 165 of non-US accents. The non-US accents included UK, ES (Spanish), FR (France), GE (German) and IT (Italian). The speech signals were collected from 11 male and 11 female speakers. Each voice was assigned 15 words and the duration of the speech is 1 sec. The signals are sampled at a rate 44,100 Hz for processing. The distribution of the samples of six accents are indicated in Figure 3.

Feature Extraction

Features play an important role in deciding the performance of the pattern recognition system. As the objective of the proposed system is to identify the accent of the speaker, the features that represent the content of the speech and the sounds produced are to be extracted from the signal. Mel Frequency Cepstral Coefficients (MFCC) have been proved to be the best descriptors (Ma and Fokoué, 2014)

(Jain, Nathani, Ruban, Raj, Zhuang and Mahesh, 2018) as they (i) understand and represent the utterances of the human and the frequency of the utterances by transforming the normal frequency to Mel scale and (ii) Mel scale models the human auditory system as they identify the sounds. The computation of MFCC includes the following: (a) Preemphasis, (b) Windowing, (c) Mel Frequency warping and (d) Computing the Cepstrum coefficients.

Pre-emphasis is a filtering process where a Finite impulse response filter is used to enhance the energy of the higher frequency components. Before providing the speech signal to the pre-emphasis filter, it is divided into blocks of frames and are processed one after other as the speech signal is quasi stationary in nature. The filtered signal output y[n] for the input frame s[n] is given by,

$$y(i)=s(i)-a\ s(i-1) \text{ for } i=1, 2, 3........M \tag{1}$$

Figure 2. Methodology of Speaker accent recognition

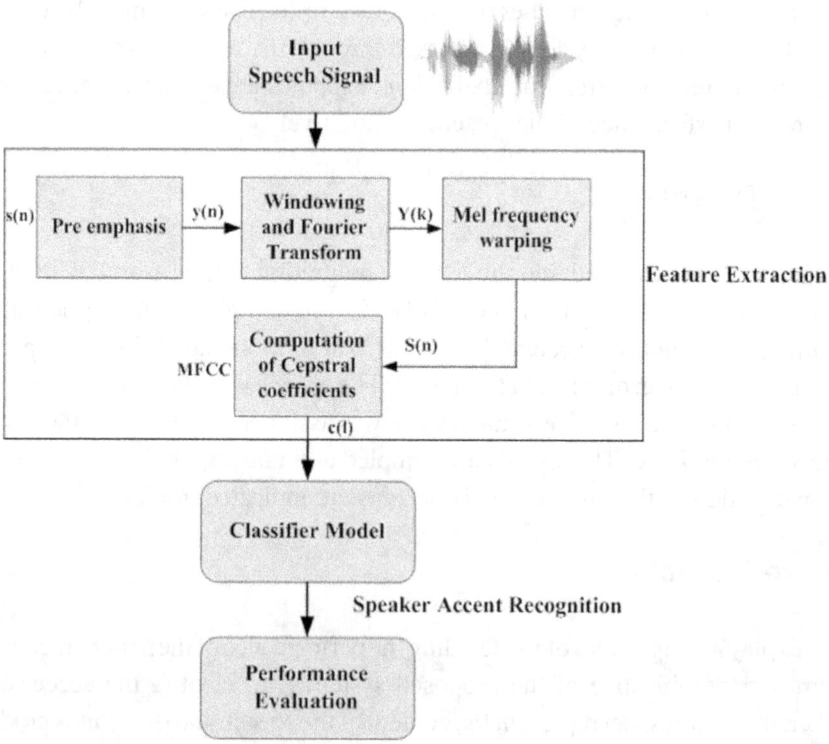

Figure 3. Distribution of the samples of six accents

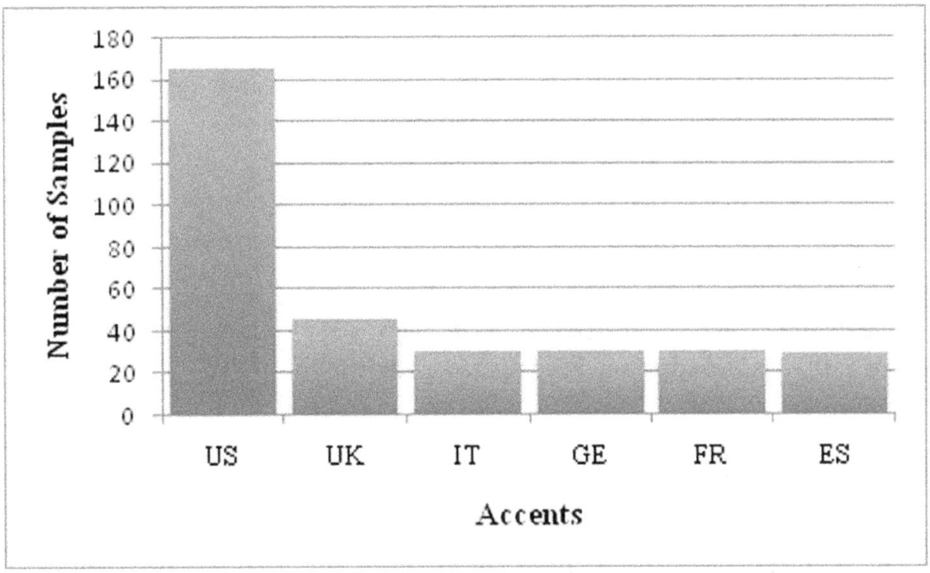

M is the number of samples in each frame and is the factor representing the control factor of the filter.

The filtered signal is transformed into frequency domain using Short term Fourier transform (STFT) with the windowing function. This step enhances the harmonics and reduces the edge effects.

$$Y(k)= \sum_{i=0}^{M-1} s(i)w(i)e^{-j\frac{2\pi ik}{M}} \quad k=0,1,2,......M-1. \tag{2}$$

Here w is the Hamming window function,

$$w(i)=0.54-0.46 \, Cos\left(\frac{2\pi i}{M-1}\right) i=0,1,2,......M-1 \tag{3}$$

Humans are sensitive in perceiving the small changes in the pitch of the voice at lower frequencies as compared to high frequencies. To fine tune this a mapping of frequencies (from Hertz) to Mel scale is required so as to match the features close to human perseverance.

Mel scale is Linear f < 1000 Hz

Mel scale is Logarithmic f >1000 Hz

This process of mapping requires providing the STFT output to Mel filter bank, a set of triangular shaped band pass filters with evenly spaced center frequencies on the frequency axis. The frequency mapping is as indicated,

$$f_M = 2595\log_{10}\left(1+\frac{f}{700}\right) \tag{4}$$

where the frequency f is in Hertz and f_M in Mel scale
From Y[k], the Mel spectrum is computed as shown

$$S(n) = \sum_{k=0}^{M-1} |Y(k)|^2 H(k) \text{ n=0,1,2,3,............N-1;} \tag{5}$$

where N indicates the number of filter banks and

$$H(k) = 1 - \left| \frac{k - \frac{M-1}{2}}{\frac{M-1}{2}} \right| \tag{6}$$

Discrete cosine transform is applied to Mel spectrum to obtain the Cepstral coefficients. Few of the initial coefficient represent signal at large, thus considering only those coefficients as features will be significant truncating the higher order components. 8 to 13 coefficients are widely used excluding the zeroth coefficient as it depicts the average energy with modest information of the speaker. The selected MFCC are expressed as,

$$c(l) = \sum_{n=0}^{N-1} log_{10}(S(n))Cos\left(\frac{\pi l(n-0.5)}{N}\right) \text{ l=0,1,2,..............,L-1} \tag{7}$$

where L is the number of MFCC

The MFCC selected form the features that represent the speech, and they form the basis for identifying the accent of the speaker. Thus, MFCC are provided to the machine learning algorithms for creating the classifier model which is further used for prediction.

One of the requirements of the machine learning algorithms is get the standardized data to learn and create the model. Thus the MLCC features $C=[c(l)\,;_{l=0,1,2,......,L-1}]$were standardized by transforming the data to have a zero mean and standard deviation of one.

$$Cs = \frac{C-\bar{C}}{SD} \tag{8}$$

Here C is the MLCC features; $\bar{C}$ and SD is the mean and standard deviation of the features respectively

The standardized features Cs are next provided to Support vector machine (SVM), k nearest neighbor neighbors (kNN), XG Boost, Linear discriminant analysis (LDA), Quadratic discriminant analysis (QDA) and decision tree (DT) (Duda and Hart, 2006; Chen and Guestrin, 2016; Dougherty, 2012; Larose and Larose, 2014) classifiers for learning and predicting the accent of the speaker.

Machine Learning Algorithms

Discriminant Analysis

The feature set X of an observation can be classified using the decision boundaries obtained by a set of discriminant functions $d_i(X)$, where i indicates the class index. The discriminant function is not unique, and the sample can be classified by finding largest $d_i(X)$.

With prior probabilities $P(c_i)$, the discriminant functions are

$$d_i(X)= -\frac{1}{2}(X-m_i)\sum_i^{-1}(X-m_i)+\ln P(c_i), \tag{9}$$

Where m is the mean value of X and å is the covariance matrix

This gets simplified to $d_i(X)=-\frac{\|X-m_i\|^2}{2\sigma^2}+\ln P(c_i)\,;$ (10)

||.|| is the L2 norm or Euclidean distance

Expansion of the above equation results in

$$d_i(X)=\frac{m_i^{\;T}}{\sigma^2}-\frac{1}{\sigma^2}m_i^T m_i+\ln P(c_i) \tag{11}$$

The second term of equation indicated the threshold of any ith class. For binary classification the decision surfaces are defined by

$$d_i(X) = d_j(X) \text{ with } C^T(X\text{-}X_0) = 0, \tag{12}$$

where $C=m_i\text{-}m_j$ and

$$X_0 = \frac{1}{2}\left(m_i+m_j\right)-\frac{\sigma^2}{\left\|m_i-m_j\right\|^2}.\ln P(c_i).\left(m_i-m_j\right) \tag{13}$$

If P(ci) are equal for both the classes, then the decision is provided by measuring the Euclidean distance between the feature vector of the given sample and the centroids of each class $||X\text{-}m_i||$ and assign X to the class pertaining to the shorter distance.

k Nearest Neighbors (kNN)

The algorithm is considered to be a lazy learning algorithm but very simple to implement. For binary classification with classes c1 and c2, the algorithm categorizes the given observation or sample as c1 or c2 based on its nearest neighbor's 'k'. The neighbors are found using the majority vote rule on the distances between the query and the points in the training set. The distance between the query and the training points can be determined using various distance metrics. The most widely used is the Euclidean distance provided in equation,

$$D_{Euc}=\sqrt{\sum_{i=1}^{M}\left(X_i-X_q\right)^2} \tag{14}$$

where,

X_i is the ith training sample from a set of M samples
X_q is the query sample

Choosing a smaller value of k may lead the model into overfittining while a larger value of k indicates smooth decision boundary.

Support Vector Machine (SVM)

SVM is basically a binary classifier that classifies the sample by finding the optimal separating hyperplane from a set of hyperplanes by maximizing the margin. The hyperplane is represented as

$W^TX+b=0$ where W and b are parameters of the classifier model

The distance between a training sample X_i and the hyperplane is

$$d=\frac{W^T X+b}{\|W\|} \tag{15}$$

The samples closer to the hyperplane are the support vectors that influence the orientation and position of it. Select the hyperplane for classification where the distance between the support vectors and hyperplane is highest .

For non linear classification, the feature space has to be projected on to higher dimensional space using kernel trick $K(X_i, X_j)$ where the data can be classified. The widely used kernel functions are

1. Tan Sigmoid kernel : $K_{sigmoid}(X_i, X_j) = \tanh(k\, X_i.X_j + c)$
2. Polynomial kernel of degree *r* : $K_{poly}(X_i, X_j) = (X_i.X_j + 1)^r$
3. Gaussian radial basis kernel function: $K_{rbf}(X_i, X_j) = \exp(-\|X_i - X_j\|^2 / 2\sigma^2)$

Decision Tree (DT)

Classification using tree involves construction of decision tree from root node moving downwards terminating in leaf nodes. The tree has decision nodes where the attributes of the samples are tested to get the outcome that results in a branch. This branch based on the result may lead to another decision node or end up in leaf node. Classification and Regression tree (CART) is one of the important algorithm used in constructing the decision trees.

CART algorithm constructs the decision tree by performing an exhaustive search on all the available variables and all splitting values for each decision node and selects an optimal split based on the following criteria. The goodness measure $\phi(s|n)$ of an observation split s at node n is given by

$$\varnothing(s|n) = 2P_L P_R \sum_{k=1}^{N} | P(k \mid n_L) - P(k|n_R) \tag{16}$$

where,
n_L left child node at node n
n_R right child node at node n

P_L is the ration of $\dfrac{\text{Number of samples at } n_L}{\text{Number of samples in training dataset}}$

P_R is the ratio of $\dfrac{\text{Number of samples at } n_R}{\text{Number of samples in training dataset}}$

$P(k|n_R)$ is the ratio of $\dfrac{\text{Number of samples of class k at } n_L}{\text{Number of samples at node n}}$

The split that maximizes the measure $\phi(s|n)$ over all possible splits at node n is the optimal split

XG Boost

XG Boost expands to Extreme gradient boosting, an ensemble machine learning algorithm that has proved to be successful in classification tasks in terms of its speed and performance. The factor that contributes for its remarkable performance is the algorithm's scalability. It combines the outcomes of Decision trees as base learners to make a final decision on prediction. XG Boost algorithm is trained in an additive manner. During the training process, at every time step 'r' the algorithm grows a tree to minimize the error of the current model. For the data with feature vector X_j and class label l_j with the regularization parameter α, the objective function of the algorithm is expressed as,

$$S^r = \sum_{j=1}^{N} s(l_j, l_j^{r-1} + f_r(X_j)) + \alpha(f_r) \tag{17}$$

where,
N Number of samples

l loss function that measures the difference between the actual and predicted class label

l_j j^{th} predicted label

f_r is the new tree added to minimize the objective function and for classifying the sample

RESULTS AND DISCUSSION

The objective of the work was to identify and classify US and five non-US accents. Thus, a framework incorporating the MFCC features, and machine learning algorithms is proposed. The experiment on recognizing the English accent of the speaker was conducted on the accent recognition dataset of 330 speech samples with six speaking styles that include US, UK, ES (Spanish), FR (France), GE (German) and IT (Italian). For validating the proposed work, the dataset was fractionated into two sets of training and testing in the ratio of 80:20. The features of the training set are labeled with six accent categories A= {'US', 'UK', 'ES', 'FR', 'GE', 'IT'} = {a_i; i=1,2,...6}. The labeled training set is given to the algorithms to generate the classifier model which is the function of C and A.

During the training process, the learnable parameters are varied to reach the performance goal. The SVM classifier was trained using linear kernel with c=1 for which the model provides the better results. With kNN algorithm, the number of neighbors were gradually varied from 3 to 10 with an incremental step of 1. The classifier was able to learn with 10 neighbors using Euclidean distance to demonstrate good performance on the training and also on the testing data. Further for XG boost, one of the boosting algorithms with gradient boosting the proposed work considered 100 estimators. The learning rate selected was 0.1. Likewise, minimum samples leaf and minimum samples split for decision tree of 1 and 2 were selected for training. Once the algorithms were trained, the classifier models were generated.

The classifier model is then used to predict the class label a_q of the new speech signal C_q presented to it; a_q=f(C_q, C, a_i, learnable parameters of machine learning algorithm) such that $a_q \in A$.

To assess the performance of the system, the quantitative parameters are derived based on the number of True positives, True negatives, False positives and False negatives from the Confusion matrix (Han et al., 2011). The details of the elements of the matrix and computation of quantitative measures are as presented below considering the binary classification of US and Non-US accents,
The entries of the confusion matrix are,

True Positive: A speech sample of the US accent is predicted as US

True Negative: Actual Non-US sample predicted as non-US
False Positive: Non-US sample predicted as US accent
False Negative: Sample from US accent is predicted as non-US accent

Table 1. Confusion matrix

		Predicted Accent	
	Accent	**US**	**Non US**
Actual Accent	US	True Positive(TP)	False Negative(FN)
	Non US	False Positive(FP)	True Negative(TN)

The parameters derived from confusion matrix include,

a. Accuracy= (TP+TN)/(TP+TN+FP+FN) (18)

b. Recall= TP/(TP+FN) (19)

c. Precision= TP/(TP+FP) (20)

d. Mathew Correlation Coefficient(MCC)= (TP × TN - FP × FN)/Z (21)

where, $Z = \sqrt{((TP+FP)\times(TP+FN)\times(TN+FP)\times(TN+FN))}$

e. Kappa= $(P_p - P_t)/(1-P_t)$ (22)

with P_p= Accuracy(ACC)

$P_t=((TP+FN)\times(TP+FP)+(FP+TN)\times(FN+TN))/(TP+TN+FP+FN)^2$

Here the subscript p indicates the predicted class whereas t indicates the target class

f. F1 score = (2 × Precision × Recall) /(Precision + Recall) (23)

The performance measures attained after validating the classifiers are illustrated in Figure 4A., 4B., and 4C.

The measures Precision, Recall and Accuracy are displayed in Figure 4A. The plot indicates that the QDA, XG Boost and kNN classifiers have performed well and have provided the measures greater than 80%. Further the detailed observation reveals the best presentation of kNN classifier with an Accuracy of 89.4%. For any classification problem measuring Accuracy is not just enough to decide the goodness of the model. So, it is also important to observe Precision and Recall. Precision

Figure 4a. Plot of the metrics Precision, Recall and Accuracy

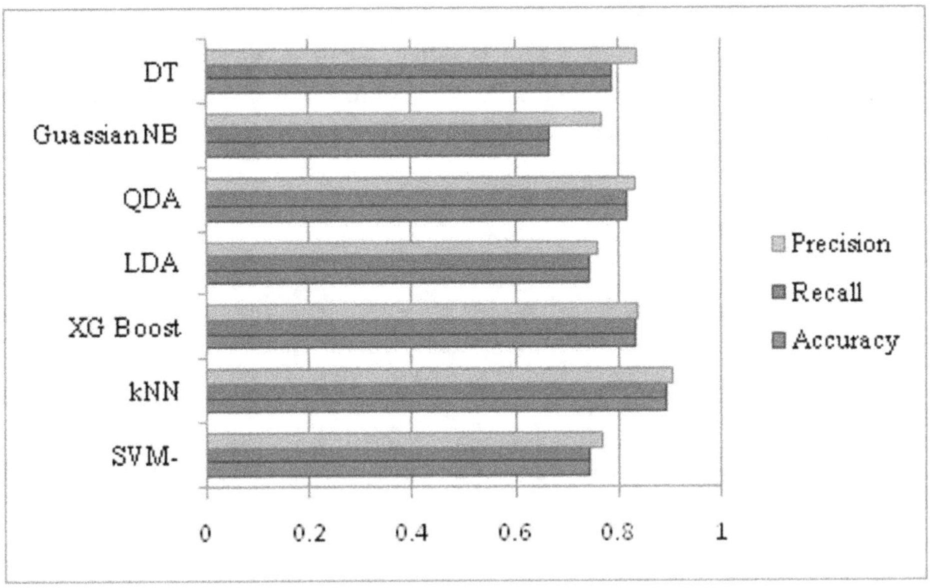

indicates how close are the predicted accents to each other belonging to a certain class. For the kNN classifier the Precision was found to be 90.6%, thus it provides very few False positives with a rate of 9.4%. Recall specifies the sensitivity of the model which is 89.4%.

The models were analyzed further using MCC, Kappa value and F1-score. Figures 4B and 4C presents the same. F1-score is the harmonic mean or weighted average of Precision and Recall. F1-score is important to be considered for investigating the results of the presented work for the following reasons: (i) The score is best suited to assess the data with imbalanced data. The accent dataset considered for validating the present work is not balanced as there is uneven distribution of samples belonging to six classes. As observed in Figure 4. 50% of the samples are in class 1 and the remaining samples are distributed between other five classes. (ii) To efficiently compare the performance of different classifier models. From the results obtained

(Figure 4A) it is noticed that the models have exhibited higher Precision as compared to Recall. So, it becomes obvious to prefer an alternate metric that combines these scores and present better analysis.

From the plot of F1-score displayed in Figure 4B for all the classifiers, a score of 0.8969 is observed from kNN classifier. This score is towards the higher margin of the range of F1-score [0 1] indicating the ability of the classifier in discriminating the accents of the speakers.

MCC and Kappa values also play a significant role in deciding the efficacy of a classifier. They indicate the concurrence between the actual accent and the predicted accent of the speakers by the classifier model. A value equal to 1 indicates absolute agreement and a value less than zero(negative) signifies disparity between them. Though kNN, XG Boost, QDA and DT models were able to generate the scores with an agreement level of greater than 70%, while kNN was its best showing notable

Figure 4b. Plot of F1-score

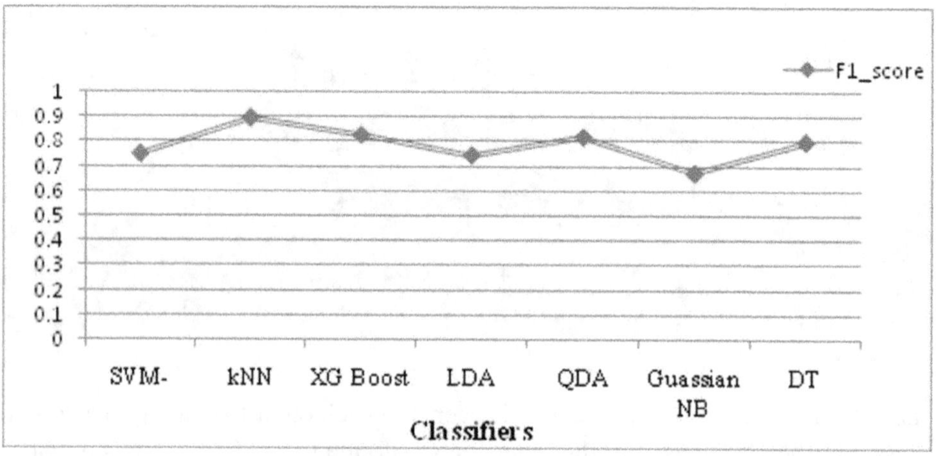

performance with kappa value of 0.8433 and MCC=0.8454. Thus, out of seven classifier models created training the SVM, kNN, XG Boost, LDA, QDA and DT algorithms and a careful quantitative analysis of all the performance metrics, kNN was noticeable in identifying and categorizing the accent of the speaker.

CONCLUSION

This chapter presents a pattern recognition-based framework with MFCC features to identify and classify the accent of the speaker, a role in audio forensics. The

Figure 4c. Plot of the metrics MCC and Kappa value

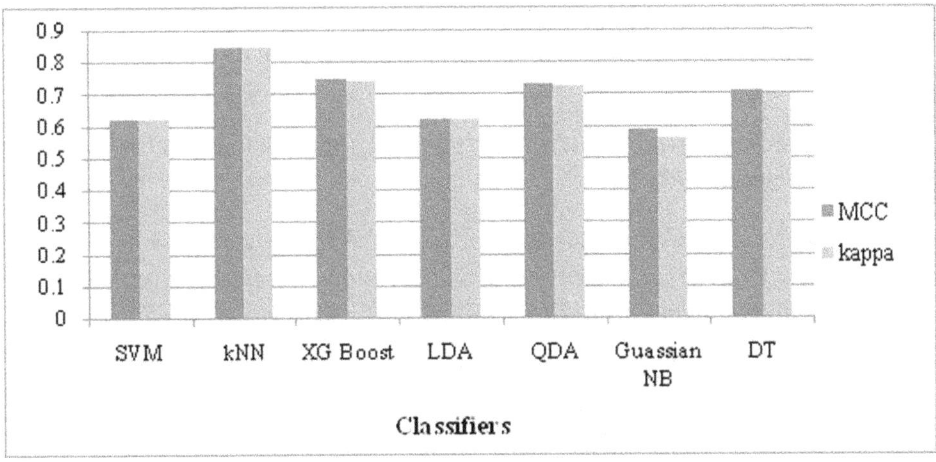

work was conducted on the accent recognition dataset with 330 speech samples belonging to US accent and five non-US accents. From the speech samples MFCC based features were extracted which are crucial in identifying the accent. The MFCC features were provided to the supervised machine learning algorithms: SVM, kNN, XG Boost, LDA, QDA and DT to observe, understand and establish the relationship between the features and accent categories. The classifier models were assessed using important quantitative parameters (Accuracy, Precision, Recall, MCC, Kappa and F1-score) for performance measurement. The analysis of experimental results using the metrics mentioned demonstrated the better performance of the kNN classifier in discriminating the accents of different speakers.

REFERENCES

Abdullah, R., Muthusamy, H., Vijean, V., Abdullah, Z., & Kassim, F. N. C. (2019). Real and Complex Wavelet Transform Approaches for Malaysian Speaker and Accent Recognition. *Pertanika Journal of Science & Technology*, *27*(2).

Ali, A. M. A., Spiegel, J. V., & Mueller, P. (1999, August). Automatic detection and classification of stop consonants using an acoustic-phonetic feature-based system. In *XIVth International Congress of Phonetic Sciences* (pp. 1709-1712). Academic Press.

Berkling, K. M., Arai, T., & Barnard, E. (1994, April). Analysis of phoneme-based features for language identification. In *Proceedings of ICASSP'94. IEEE International Conference on Acoustics, Speech and Signal Processing* (Vol. 1, pp. I-289). IEEE. 10.1109/ICASSP.1994.389298

Bhagath, P., & Das, P. K. (2004). Acoustic phonetic approach for speech recognition: A review. *Language, 77*, 93.

Chen, T., & Guestrin, C. (2016, August). Xgboost: A scalable tree boosting system. In *Proceedings of the 22nd acm sigkdd international conference on knowledge discovery and data mining* (pp. 785-794). 10.1145/2939672.2939785

Diller, T. (1979, April). Phonetic word verification. In *ICASSP'79. IEEE International Conference on Acoustics, Speech, and Signal Processing* (*Vol. 4*, pp. 256-261). IEEE. 10.1109/ICASSP.1979.1170731

Ding, I. Jr, Yen, C. T., & Hsu, Y. M. (2013). Developments of machine learning schemes for dynamic time-wrapping-based speech recognition. *Mathematical Problems in Engineering, 2013*, 2013. doi:10.1155/2013/542680

Dougherty, G. (2012). *Pattern recognition and classification: An introduction.* Springer Science & Business Media.

Duda, R. O., & Hart, P. E. (2006). *Pattern classification.* John Wiley & Sons.

Ge, Z. (2015, October). Improved accent classification combining phonetic vowels with acoustic features. In *2015 8th International Congress on Image and Signal Processing (CISP)* (pp. 1204-1209). IEEE. 10.1109/CISP.2015.7408064

Han, J., Pei, J., & Kamber, M. (2011). *Data mining: concepts and techniques*. Elsevier.

Jahangir, R., Teh, Y. W., Nweke, H. F., Mujtaba, G., Al-Garadi, M. A., & Ali, I. (2021). Speaker identification through artificial intelligence techniques: A comprehensive review and research challenges. *Expert Systems with Applications, 171*, 114591. doi:10.1016/j.eswa.2021.114591

Jain, U., Nathani, K., Ruban, N., Raj, A. N. J., Zhuang, Z., & Mahesh, V. G. (2018, October). Cubic SVM classifier based feature extraction and emotion detection from speech signals. In *2018 International Conference on Sensor Networks and Signal Processing (SNSP)* (pp. 386-391). IEEE. 10.1109/SNSP.2018.00081

Kandhari, M. S., Zulkemine, F., & Isah, H. (2018, November). A Voice Controlled E-Commerce Web Application. In *2018 IEEE 9th Annual Information Technology, Electronics and Mobile Communication Conference (IEMCON)* (pp. 118-124). IEEE.

Kannadaguli, P., & Bhat, V. (2015, March). A comparison of Gaussian Mixture Modeling (GMM) and Hidden Markov Modeling (HMM) based approaches for Automatic Phoneme Recognition in Kannada. In *2015 International Conference on Signal Processing and Communication (ICSC)* (pp. 257-260). IEEE. 10.1109/ICSPCom.2015.7150658

Larose, D. T., & Larose, C. D. (2014). *Discovering knowledge in data: an introduction to data mining* (Vol. 4). John Wiley & Sons.

Ma, Z. C., & Fokoué, E. (2014). A Comparison of Classifiers in Performing Speaker Accent Recogni- tion Using MFCCs. *Open Journal of Statistics*, *4*(04), 258–266. doi:10.4236/ojs.2014.44025

Mannepalli, K., Sastry, P. N., & Suman, M. (2016). MFCC-GMM based accent recognition system for Telugu speech signals. *International Journal of Speech Technology*, *19*(1), 87–93. doi:10.100710772-015-9328-y

Nassif, A. B., Shahin, I., Attili, I., Azzeh, M., & Shaalan, K. (2019). Speech recognition using deep neural networks: A systematic review. *IEEE Access: Practical Innovations, Open Solutions*, *7*, 19143–19165. doi:10.1109/ACCESS.2019.2896880

Omar, M. K., & Hasegawa-Johnson, M. (2002, May). Maximum mutual information based acoustic-features representation of phonological features for speech recognition. In *2002 IEEE International Conference on Acoustics, Speech, and Signal Processing* (Vol. 1, pp. I-81). IEEE.

Rabiner, L. R. (1992). Speech recognition based on pattern recognition approaches. In *Digital Speech Processing* (pp. 111–126). Springer. doi:10.1007/978-1-4757-2148-5_5

Saleem, S., Subhan, F., Naseer, N., Bais, A., & Imtiaz, A. (2020). Forensic speaker recognition: A new method based on extracting accent and language information from short utterances. *Forensic Science International: Digital Investigation*, *34*, 300982.

Siniscalchi, S. M., Svendsen, T., & Lee, C. H. (2009, April). A phonetic feature based lattice rescoring approach to LVCSR. In *2009 IEEE International Conference on Acoustics, Speech and Signal Processing* (pp. 3865-3868). IEEE. 10.1109/ICASSP.2009.4960471

Thandil, R. K., & Basheer, K. M. (2020). Accent based speech recognition: A critical overview. *Malaya Journal of Matematik*, *8*(4), 1743-1750.

Vimala, C., & Radha, V. (2015). Isolated speech recognition system for Tamil language using statistical pattern matching and machine learning techniques. *Journal of Engineering Science and Technology*, *10*(5), 617–632.

Walker, D. (1975). The SRI speech understanding system. *IEEE Transactions on Acoustics, Speech, and Signal Processing*, *23*(5), 397–416. doi:10.1109/TASSP.1975.1162726

Widyowaty, D. S., & Sunyoto, A. (2020, November). Accent Recognition by Native Language Using Mel-Frequency Cepstral Coefficient and K-Nearest Neighbor. In *2020 3rd International Conference on Information and Communications Technology (ICOIACT)* (pp. 314-318). IEEE. 10.1109/ICOIACT50329.2020.9332026

Chapter 9
Medical Image Encryption Using Distance-Based Biokey Generation

Vijayarajan Rajangam
Centre for Healthcare Advancement, Innovation and Research, Vellore Institute of Technology, Chennai, India

Shani S. Kumar
School of Electronics Engineering, Vellore Institute of Technology, Chennai, India

Sathiya Narayanan
Center for Advanced Data Science, Vellore Institute of Technology, Chennai, India

Sangeetha N.
School of Computer Science Engineering, Vellore Institute of Technology, Chennai, India

Avudaiammal R.
Department of ECE, St. Joseph's College of Engineering, Chennai, India

ABSTRACT

As the internet of things and cloud computing create new technological revolutions in the field of healthcare, the issues such as security, privacy, authentication, the integrity of patient data, and medical images become sensitive. This chapter proposes a cryptographic technique for the secure storage of medical images based on biometric key generation. Cryptographic algorithms can be used to enhance the security of cloud storage systems. The proposed biometric-based encryption scheme takes the advantage of biometric features of the fingerprint and iris of the user to meet the desired security characteristics. A 256-bit bio-key is generated based on

DOI: 10.4018/978-1-6684-4558-7.ch009

the distance between the fingerprint features and used in the advanced encryption standard (AES) for image encryption. The experiments conducted on the set of medical images also prove the effectiveness and security aspects of the proposed biometric key-based image encryption. The encryption method is also tested on the set of medical images and compared with other encryption schemes.

INTRODUCTION

Security of medical data and diagnostic images is drawing more attention in the present world. As healthcare evolves by making use of cloud computing and the Internet of Things (IoT), health institutions use third-party servers to store medical data. Guaranteeing the security, privacy, and integrity of these medical data becomes troublesome and is a challenge. Various security algorithms have been investigated over the decades to protect the users' documents and multimedia contents. When the user wants to store the data on the desktop, laptop, and personalized digital gadgets, there is a login protection mechanism that restricts malicious users to access the data (Panchal et al., 2019). The data can also be protected using file passwords, folder locking, and directory locking methods. The documents can also be protected using security certificates but to be provided and installed by third-party vendors. On the other hand, the encryption algorithms contribute to protecting the documents from malicious access. Personalized documents and multimedia contents of the user are encrypted using encryption algorithms. The key for the encryption algorithms can be generated from various key generation strategies. In this paper, the features of the biometrics traits are used for bio-key generation. The feature selection for bio-key generation is performed using different strategies.

Biometric authentication recognizes a user based on unique physiological attributes (Shaheed et al., 2021). The biometric traits in the form of images and signals, captured using imaging modalities and sensors, deliver various biometric features of the user. The extracted features from the biometrics such as fingerprint, iris, ear, face, and other physiological signals are widely used for user authentication. The above-said biometrics are also be used for key generation to the encryption algorithms. Hence, biometric-based cryptography takes the advantage of biometric-based user authentication and subsequent key generation from the biometric templates. The processing steps ensure two levels of authentication and key generation for encryption and decryption.

Compared to the conventional cryptosystems that use token keys or knowledge keys, a bio-cryptosystem offers a non-repudiable, flexible, and reliable method of security and authentication. The traditional authentication systems have the risk of users forgetting or losing the credentials, while the bio-cryptosystems need not require the user to keep track of any credentials. The security system proposed in this paper makes use of biometrics such as iris and fingerprints for authentication and encryption. A unique key-generation scheme based on distances between minutiae points is applied in this work. Encryption of medical images is done using symmetric key cryptography which enhances faster computation and requires less memory footprint. The robustness of the proposed algorithm is also increased by pixel scrambling. The scrambled version of the plain image at a particular iteration step is selected for encryption using a 256-bit bio-key derived from the fingerprint and iris features of the user. First, the user is authenticated by iris features. The second level of authentication is carried out from fingerprint features. After authentication, the distance between each minutia point with all other minutiae points is evaluated. The distance values are used to decide the bits of the key. The maximum distance decides the length of the key. A key length of 256 bits is obtained by zero padding. A similar bio-key is needed for decryption. Hence, the user needs to execute biometric authentication, bio-key-based decryption, and inverse pixel scrambling to get back the plain image. The performance of the proposed method is also compared with some of the existing image encryption methods.

The paper proceeds as follows. Related works are summarized in section II. The methodology is described in section III. Dataset details and results are presented in section IV which is followed by a conclusion in section V.

Background

Bian et al. (2020) introduced an authentication protocol based on two factors. Physically Unclonable Functions (PUFs) and fingerprint biometrics were the two factors that served the purpose. The proposed scheme did not require any password, instead used the unique features of the PUFs to enhance the robustness of the system. The key agreement scheme was based on mutual authentication and the system was capable of withstanding various security attacks. Zhang et al. (2015) proposed a method of securing the storage and transmission of medical images using encryption and compression. The system had a compressive sensing phase where the plain images were compressed and encrypted. Chaotic Chebyshev mapping was performed to generate the measurement matrix. Chaos-based permutation-diffusion improved the measure of security in the next phase where the quantized measurements were encrypted.

A technique of encrypting and watermarking medical images was proposed by Kester et al. (2015). The experiment was able to fully recover and reverse the encrypted images. Access to the system was based on client authentication. Symmetric encryption technique was employed, and watermarking was based on the spatial domain. The entropy and mean for the plain images before and after the encryption remained the same. Saranya and Prabhu (2016) proposed a mechanism for securing medical image storage and transmission. The paper suggested extracting the features of the user's face using an automated face recognition system. A database was maintained for storing the extracted features and made use of a virtual neural network to identify any intruders. The encryption scheme employed was the RSA algorithm. Jagadeesan et al. (2010) proposed an integration method of iris and fingerprint biometric features for the cryptographic key generation. The extracted features from the fingerprint and iris were fused to form a multi-biometric template and generated a 256-bit key for encryption. Security of the system improved with the complexity in factoring larger numbers. The system could provide authentication and security for the users.

A watermarking scheme for medical images based on the key generated from biometrics is proposed by Badgi et al. (2020). Iris images from patients were used for generating the biometric keys. Magnetic resonance imaging (MRI) of patients and the electronic health records (EHR) were the inputs for encryption. The MRI images were encrypted using the SHA-256 algorithm whereas the EHR was encrypted using the ECC algorithm using the biometric key. Information from both inputs was concatenated after encryption and bit streams were compressed using an arithmetic encoding algorithm. The reversible watermarking proposed by the authors was efficient and could sustain the image quality despite various attacks. Wang et al. (2021) proposed an asymmetric encryption scheme for medical image transmission. Iris was used for encrypting the medical images, which provided enhanced security. Two spiral phase masks (SPM) generated from the iris performed the encryption. The result was a robust and feasible encryption scheme that could defend against occlusion attacks. Information entropy and correlation were also the added advantages.

Vijayarajan et al. (2019) proposed a biometric key-based image cryptosystem in which the coordinates of the minutiae points were used for generating a bio-key. The coordinates of the minutiae points of the fingerprint templates were arranged like a look-up table in the fingerprint template database. The Cartesian coordinates of all the minutiae points were arranged in the look-up table with an index for all the coordinates. The passcode, entered by the user, represents the index of the minutiae points to derive the bio-key from the coordinates. The same procedure is repeated for decryption. In this method, the coordinates of the minutiae points were affected by spatial distortion. In this chapter, the proposed encryption algorithm employs two levels of authentication and generates the bio-key using the distance between the minutiae points of the fingerprint. The key points of the five encryption methods are presented in Table 1.

Table 1. Review of encryption methods for medical images

S.No.	Paper	Description
1.	Bian et al. (2020)	• Authentication protocol based on unclonable functions and fingerprint biometrics. • Password not required. • Unique features are used for authentication • The key agreement scheme is based on mutual authentication
2.	Zhang et al. (2015)	• Uses encryption and compression for secured storage and transmission of medical images • Uses compressive sensing to compress and encrypt plain images • Chaotic-based Chebyshev mapping was performed to generate the measurement mapping
3.	Saranya & Prabhu (2016)	• RSA algorithm is used for encrypting medical images • The features extracted from the user's face are used for recognition • A neural network is used to identify any intruders
4.	Jagadeesan et al. (2010)	• Cryptographic key is generated by iris and fingerprint features • The features are fused to generate a multi-biometric template • Complexity of the system is increased by factoring large numbers
5.	Wang et al. (2021)	• Asymmetric key is used for the encryption of medical images • Iris features are used for encryption • This is method can defend against occlusion attacks

PROPOSED METHODOLOGY

The proposed methodology involves the following steps. The first step is the authentication of the user using the iris features. The next level of authentication is via fingerprint features. Based on the minutiae points on the fingerprint, a key is generated, and the images are encrypted. In the second step, one of the scrambled images is selected from the nth iteration of Arnold transform. It is well known that Arnold transforms exhibits periodic property that delivers an original image after a specific number of iterations. The bio-key generated from the fingerprint features is used to encrypt the plain image which is selected from the pixel scrambling algorithm.

Iris Authentication

Iris-based recognition and authentication can be considered one of the accurate methods for identifying a person due to the extremely unique characteristics of the iris biometric. Doughman's approach has been tested over millions of images without producing any false results and allows exhaustive search in large datasets. Iris has the advantage of unique pattern variability in every person. Iris, being an internal organ of the eye, remains protected and stable. The biometric template generated from the iris can be efficiently used to recognize authenticated users and imposters since any usage of glasses or lenses or eye surgery will not create any changes in the characteristics of the iris.

Dataset for Iris Images

The Multimedia University Iris Database- version-1((MMU) is used for iris recognition. The dataset includes 450 images in total from 46 individuals. Five images of each left and right eye were included in the dataset. The images were captured using an iris scanning sensor- LG IrisAccess 2200 and the range of capture is about 7-25 cm (Alrifaee, 2020).

Preprocessing

The iris image acquired may have artifacts like eyelashes, eyelids, reflection, etc. Also, the distance between the eye and the camera, and the brightness of the ambiance under which the image was captured do have an impact on the eye image. Hence preprocessing is carried out to process the original image. Localization of the iris image is done for successful recognition in which both the boundaries - inner and outer, are identified and located. The center diameter of the iris and the pupil area is detected using integro-differential operators. This is given by

$$\max\left(r, x_o, y_o\right)\left|G_\sigma \frac{\partial}{\partial r}\int \frac{I(x,y)}{2\pi r}ds\right| \tag{1}$$

where I(x,y) is the pixel intensity of the eye image at the coordinates x and y, r denotes the radius of the circular regions, σ is the standard deviation of Gaussian distribution, (x0, y0) is the assumed center coordinates of the iris, ‘s’ is the contour of the circle and $G\sigma_{(r)}$ is the smoothing function of scale σ (Daugman, 2009). The pupillary boundary, as well as the outer (limbus) boundary of the iris, can be found using equation (1). Once the iterative search for finding these boundaries reaches the precision of a single pixel, then curvilinear edges are detected to localize the boundaries of both upper and lower eyelids.

Gaussian smoothing, which is a two-dimensional convolution operation, is performed next to smoothen the eye image and thereby remove the noises. Canny edge detector is used for segmenting the iris images and locating the boundaries. This algorithm produces a low error rate and optimally localizes the edge points. This involves smoothing the image and marking the edges by finding gradients (Daugman, 2009).

Iris texture is transformed from Cartesian to polar coordinates in the step of normalization. The method used is Daugman's rubber sheet model technique. This is employed to cope with the issue of distance variation while capturing the eye image.

Feature Extraction and Iris Code Generation

Feature extraction involves capturing unique information from the normalized image of the iris. 1D-log Gabor filters are applied for iris feature extraction and analyzing the orientation of the texture. Iris textures are analyzed both horizontally and vertically and all the details are combined (Fasna et al., 2016).

Iris Matching using Hamming Distance

Once the iris codes are stored in the template database, the authorization stage compares the current code with those in the database to find a match. Hamming distance, which is a measure of similar bits in two-bit patterns, is used for taking a decision. This is found by doing the EXOR function to the corresponding bit strings with a threshold of 0.2 (Gite and Mahendar, 2011). If the hamming distance between two iris templates is less than 0.2, the templates are identified as that of the same person. Otherwise, the iris template is not of the same person and hence declared as unauthorized. After ensuring the identity of the user, the second level of authentication and subsequent key generation is implemented using fingerprint features.

Figure 1. Block diagram of iris enrollment and authorization stages

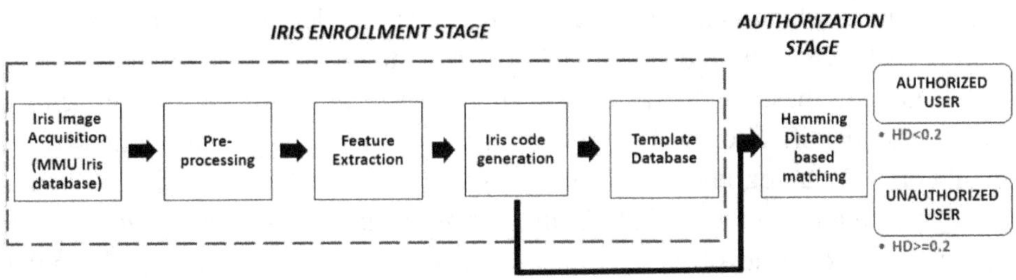

Figure 2. Iris images 'aevall.bmp' and 'bryanll.bmp', respectively from MMU Iris Database. Both irises are of the left eye. Hamming distance is found to be 0.20111, indicating that the irises do not match.

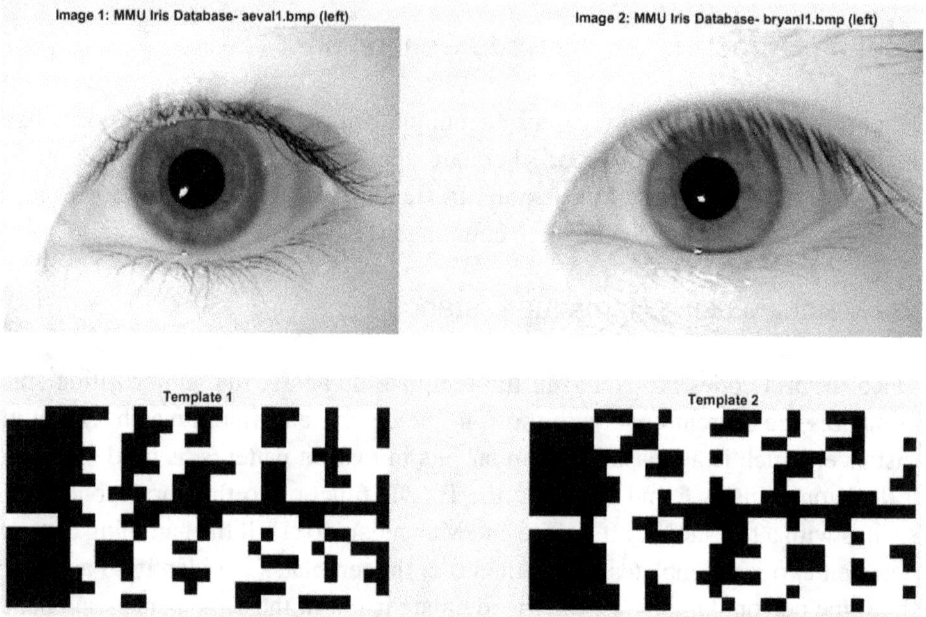

HAMMING DISTANCE = 0.20111, IRISES DO NOT MATCH

Fingerprint Authentication

A fingerprint, which is a unique feature in human, is defined by certain lines or valleys that create a unique pattern. Minutiae extraction plays an important role in recognizing these unique features from the fingerprint and is an approach for fingerprint identification. A fingerprint sensor could be easily incorporated with a mouse or keyboard or other peripherals, making it easy to use. Experimental results are carried out using the FVC2002 fingerprint image database. The algorithm for minutiae extraction involves the following steps: (i) Pre-processing, (ii) Minutiae extraction, and (iii) post-processing.

Preprocessing

Image enhancement of the fingerprint is done as a preprocessing step to obtain a clear image. The contrast between the valleys and ridges is increased during this process. The fingerprint image is divided into small blocks of spatial resolution with 32×32 pixels and the Fourier transform is applied to obtain the enhanced fingerprint image. The next step involves ridge segmentation to normalize the fingerprint image and also segment the ridge areas. A masked image is obtained with normalized intensity values. Ridge orientation is performed to evaluate the orientation of the ridges in the fingerprint. Ridge frequency, which is the frequency/count of the ridges, is calculated. Using oriented filters, the fingerprint image is enhanced to obtain a binary image. The next step is to extract the Region of Interest (ROI). Areas of the fingerprint without efficient ridges are discarded in this step as they contribute to noise. The boundary of the remaining area is traced to get the ROI. Morphological operations are performed on the image to have a uniform thickness of ridges of about one pixel and a thinned image is obtained (Dharmendra Kumar et al., 2012).

Minutiae Extraction

Minutiae extraction is performed by marking the minutiae points using the concept of Crossing Numbers (CNs) (Sudiro et al. 2007; Sudiro and Yuwono 2012). The intensity difference between the neighbouring pixels is halved to find the crossing number (Raghavan and John Singh, 2022). According to the values of this CN, bifurcation, termination, and normal ridge are identified. CN is 1 for termination, 2 for normal ridge and 3 for bifurcation (Nachar et al. 2020; Deshpande et al. 2022). All the minutiae points in the fingerprint are labeled with a unique id.

Minutiae Post-Processing

The post-processing of minutiae involves the removal of false minutiae points as they impact the accuracy of matching. False minutiae points are removed by morphological processing. The defects such as breakage and cross-connection are spurious minutiae points. Post-processing deals with the removal of false minutiae before fingerprint matching. If the average inter ridge distance is greater than a bifurcation and termination minutiae, then it is classified as a false minutia. The multiple bifurcations on the consecutive ridges with a distance less than the inter ridge distance can be removed. Two termination minutiae with minute variation in orientation and the ridge distance less than the inter ridge distance are also removed from the observed minutiae points (Surajkanta and Pal 2021). The processed images from the template database during enrollment, against which at later stage, authorization is verified.

Matching Stage

The matching algorithm is alignment-based to check if the fingerprint is from an authorized user. If the similarity measure is greater than or equal to 0.48, then the fingerprints are considered matching, else they are non-matching (Aju et al., 2018).

Figure 3. Block diagram of fingerprint enrollment and authorization stages

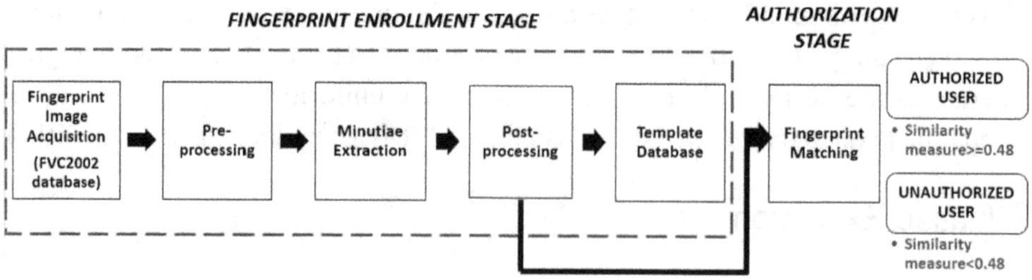

Figure 4. (a) Fingerprint images '101_1.tif' and '103_1.tif' respectively from FVC2002 with minutiae points. (b) A similarity measure of both the fingerprints with '103_2. tif' is shown below. The similarity score of 0.2176 indicates fingerprints do not match. The similarity score of 0.89709 indicates a fingerprint match.

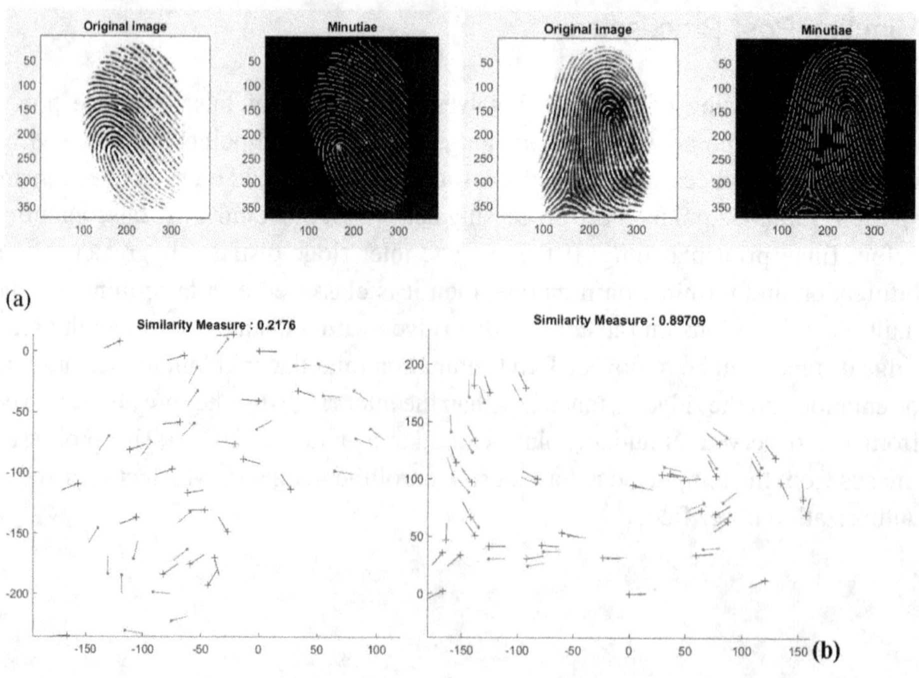

Secret Passcode

Once the two levels of authentication are cleared, then the user may optionally enter a passcode. The passcode is a secret key of fewer digits (Nyarko-Boateng et al., 2017). The stage is included to make sure that any other authenticated person would be able to decrypt the images encrypted by another person, in his/her absence. Once the secret key has been entered, then the corresponding feature vector will be selected from the template database, thereby decrypting the images.

Key Generation

Feature extraction algorithm on the fingerprint gives unique features to the fingerprint. The minutiae point hence identified are represented as (x_i, y_i, Θ_i), where (x_i, y_i) are the coordinates and Θ_i is the angle of alignment. If the total number of minutiae points detected from the fingerprint is n, then the steps for key generation from these points are described below:

1. 1. The Euclidean distances between all the minutiae points are computed. The method follows the approach of Delaunay triangulation. These distance values are stored in a matrix D.

$$d_{i,j} = \sqrt{\left(x_i - x_j\right)^2 - \left(y_i - y_j\right)^2} \tag{2}$$

2. 2. The values in matrix D are sorted and the unique distance values are stored in a vector A_1.

$a_1 < a_2 < a_3 < a_4 \ldots\ldots < a_m$, where m is the number of unique distances in the vector.

3. 3. These unique values are then copied to another vector A_2, such that the value a_m will be placed at a position where the index value equals a_m.

$A_2[a_m] = a_m$

4. The positions occupied are replaced with binary 1's and the vacant positions are filled with zeroes.

```
if (A2[am] ≠ 0) then
      A2[am] = 1
else
      A2[am] = 0
```

The size of the key depends upon the maximum value of the distance between the minutiae points. The rest of the positions can be padded with zeroes to obtain the conventional length of key required for encryption.

Figure 5. Distance between minutiae points

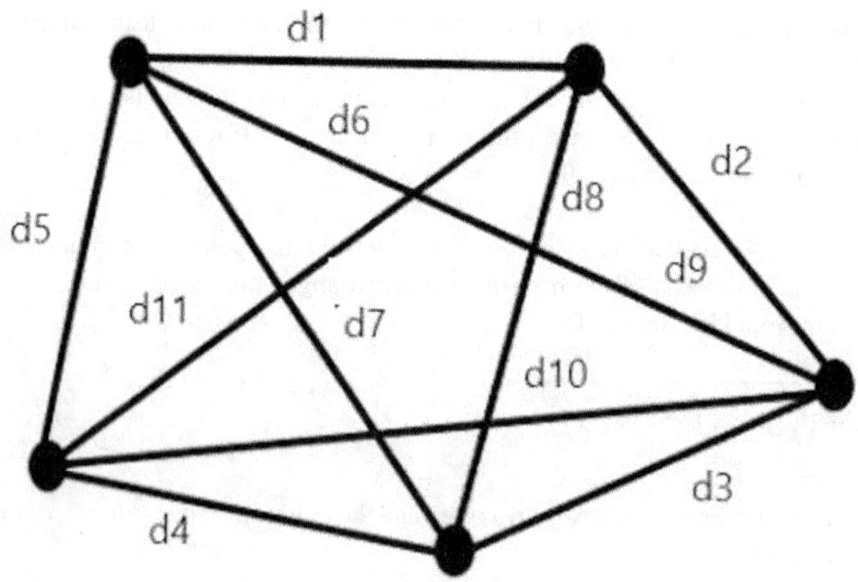

Figure 6. Distance matrix

	1	2	3	4	5
1	0	21	34	28	40
2	21	0	13	20	24
3	34	13	0	16	26
4	28	20	16	0	32
5	40	24	29	32	0

Figure 7. Key generation from the minutiae points

Index	0	1	2	3	4	5	6	7	8	9	10	11	12	13	14	15	16	17	18	19	20
Distance	0													13			16				20
Key	1	0	0	0	0	0	0	0	0	0	0	0	0	1	0	0	1	0	0	0	1

Index	21	22	23	24	25	26	27	28	29	30	31	32	33	34	35	36	37	38	39	40
Distance	21			24		26		28	29			32		34						40
Key	1	0	0	1	0	1	0	1	1	0	0	1	0	1	0	0	0	0	0	1

Bio-Key-Based Encryption and Decryption

AES algorithm is based on a symmetric key, which means that the same key has to be used for encryption as well as decryption (Nyarko-Boateng et al., 2017). The key size in AES could be 128, 192, or 256 bits. This key is used for encrypting a block of 128 bits. The key size is an important factor in AES as it determines the level of security.

The encryption process in AES is implemented as follows:

1. Byte substitution
2. Shift rows
3. Mix columns
4. Add round key

The key size determines the number of rounds in AES. The rounds used can be 10, 12, or 14 for AES-128, AES-192, and AES-256 respectively. The key generated from the fingerprint input is expanded by the key expansion method. Each round undergoes the above-mentioned stages except the last round, which excludes the mix columns operation. The image blocks are processed parallel in each round.

The decryption process, which is an inverse of the encryption, reconstructs the plain image from the cipher image. Decryption is implemented as follows:

1. Inverse shift row
2. Inverse byte substitution
3. Add round key
4. Inverse matrix columns

Figure 8. Encryption and decryption scheme based on AES. For AES-128, a cipher key of 128 bits is considered and the corresponding number of rounds is 10. The pixel values of the plain image(256x256) of 128 bits are divided into a 4x4 matrix called a state. Each round has three sub-rounds called substitute bytes, shift rows, mix columns and add round key, except the last round. Decryption follows a reverse process.

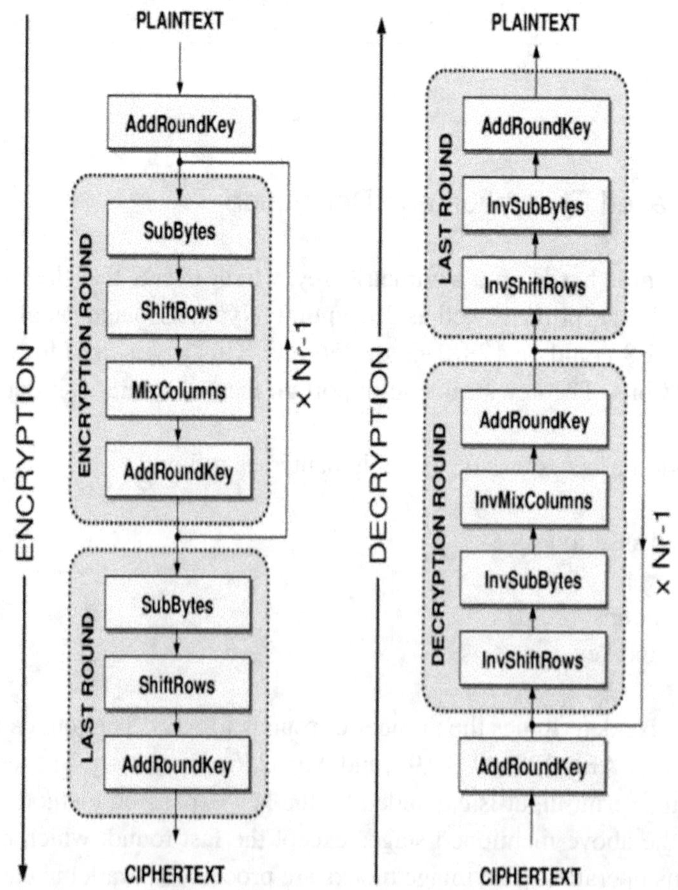

The overall structure of the AES scheme (Nyarko-Boateng et al., 2017) is shown in Figure 8.

EXPERIMENTS AND RESULT ANALYSIS

The proposed two-level authentication and key generation for the encryption of images are experimented with two sets of images. The first set of images is x-ray and ultrasound images, and the second set has CT-MRI images. The section describes the experimental setup, results, and performance analysis. The experiments were performed on a personal computer with AMD Ryzen 5 3500U CPU at 2.10 GHz. The tool used for the entire setup is MATLAB R2020b.

Performance Measures

The performance of the proposed cryptosystem is analyzed by information entropy, correlation coefficient, number of pixels change rate (NPCR), and unified average change intensity (UACI). The metrics are discussed below.

Information Entropy Analysis

Entropy is the measure of the randomness in the image. A high degree of randomness is expected that makes the subjective analysis of the encrypted images difficult. Shannon's entropy for the information sources is given as

$$H(s) = -\sum_{i=0}^{2^n-1} P(s_i)\log_2\left[P(s_i)\right] \tag{3}$$

Where, $P(s_i)$ denotes the probability of occurrence of symbol s_i and 2^n denotes the number of states possible (Liu et al., 2020).

Correlation Analysis

A good encryption scheme should be able to construct the cipher images with an ideal correlation of value zero. Whereas the decrypted image should have an ideal correlation value of ± 1. The correlation coefficients are given by

$$r_{(x,y)} = \frac{E\left(\left(x-E(x)\right).\left(y-E(y)\right)\right)}{\sqrt{D(x)D(y)}} \tag{4}$$

$$E(x) = \frac{1}{N}\sum_{i=1}^{N} x_i \tag{5}$$

$$D(x) = \frac{1}{N}\sum_{i=1}^{N}\left(x_i - E(x)\right)^2 \tag{6}$$

where N denotes the total number of pixels, x and y is the gray value of adjacent pixels, E(x) is the expectation of x, and D(x) denotes the variance of x. Table 2 compares the correlation values of plain images and cipher images.

Differential Attack

To measure the robustness and resistance to attack of the encryption algorithm, NPCR and UACI can be used. NPCR involves slightly modifying the plain image and encrypting it to obtain a new cipher image while performing decryption with the original cipher image. If such a change has a great impact on the encrypted image, then the encryption scheme is resistive to the differential attack. UACI gives the difference in the average intensities of the plain image and the recovered or decrypted image (Saraswathi & Balasubramaniam, 2010).

$$NPCR = \frac{1}{M \times N}\sum_{i=0}^{M-1}\sum_{j=0}^{N-1} D(i,j) \times 100\% \tag{7}$$

$$UACI = \frac{1}{M \times N}\sum_{i=0}^{M-1}\sum_{j=0}^{N-1} \frac{C(i,j) - C'(i,j)}{255} \tag{8}$$

Where D(i,j) is the decrypted image. C(i,j) is the plain image, and C'(i,j) is the encrypted image. M and N are the number of rows and columns in the image. The values of NPCR and UACI for each image are presented in Table 2.

Experiments and Analysis

The performance of the proposed bio-cryptosystem is verified by the experiments with grayscale medical images. Few of the iris images from the MMU Iris dataset and fingerprint images from the FVC2002 dataset were selected, processed, and extracted for creating the template database. Recognition and authentication based on the extracted features were performed and the bio-key was generated using the key-generation scheme.

The input images were resized to a spatial resolution of 256×256. The bio-key was then used to encrypt the images using the AES encryption algorithm. To decrypt the images, the user needs to repeat the same steps. The user must first provide the iris and fingerprint inputs for self-authentication. The key for decryption would then be generated, which is similar to the one used for encryption.

Four medical images are encrypted using randomly selected fingerprint images from the FVC2002 database. A key length of 256 bits is used.

To summarize, below are the complete steps involved in the proposed work:

1. The user needs to ensure authentication by iris recognition.
2. Provide the fingerprint as the next level of authentication.
3. Once the system identifies the user as authorized, a secret key is constructed from the fingerprint. Users may also enter the passcode for selecting the feature vectors from the database.
4. The bio-key thus formed is used for the cryptosystem in encrypting and decrypting the medical images.

Figure 9. Bio-cryptosystem using AES encryption

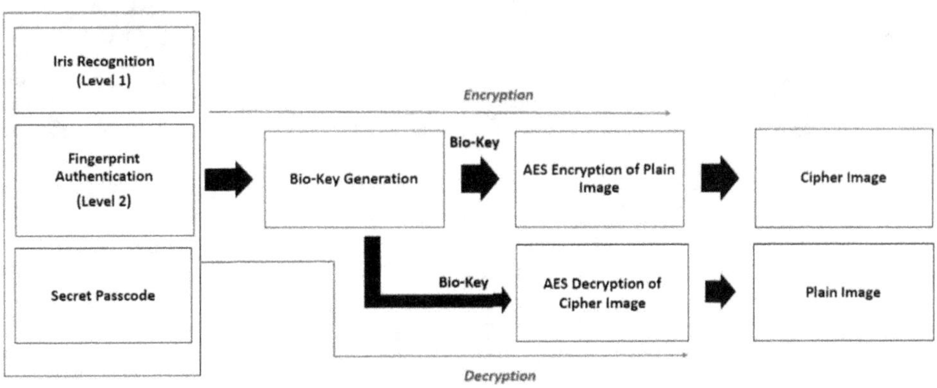

Histogram Analysis

Histograms of cipher images indicate the quality of encryption. A good encryption scheme produces a histogram that is uniformly distributed. Column (d) of Figure 10 shows the uniformly distributed histogram of cipher images. These are different from the plain images as shown in column (b). This indicates that the encryption was successful in hiding the redundant information in the plain image.

Figure 10. (a) Plain image input (b) Histogram of the plain image (c) Encrypted/ cipher image (d) Histogram of cipher image (e) Decrypted image

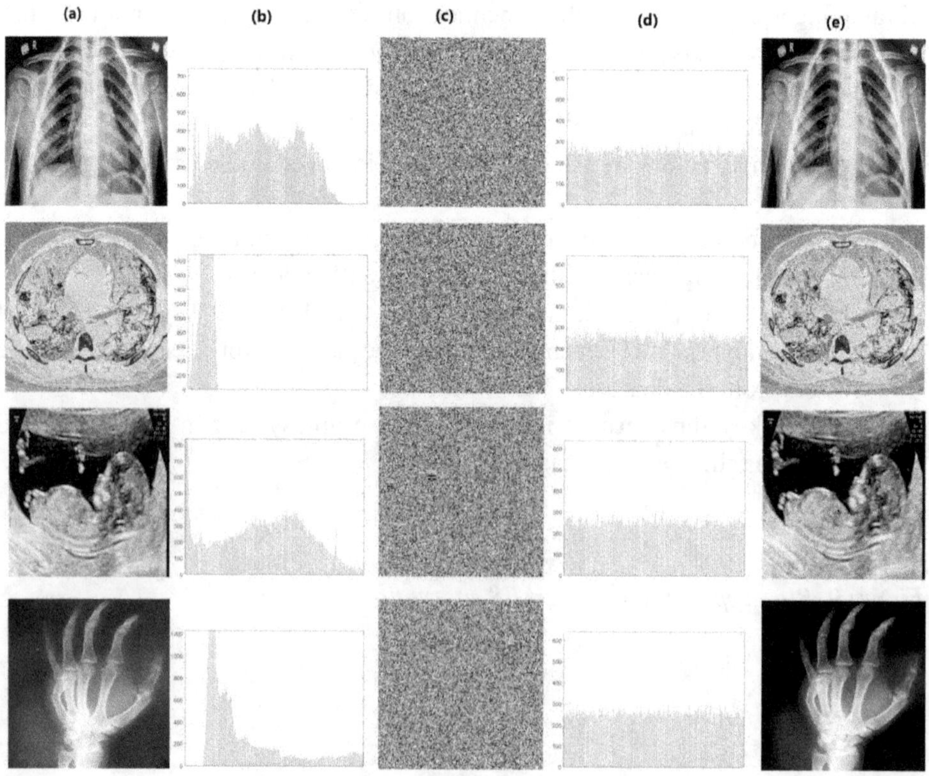

Table 2. Analysis of cryptosystem

Image	Correlation of plain images	Correlation of cipher images	Entropy of plain images	Entropy of cipher images	NPCR	UACI
Image 1	0.9819	0.0033	7.6301	7.9971	99.5926	20.0709
Image 2	0.7115	-0.0045	5.0396	7.9971	99.6140	40.2128
Image 3	0.9664	0.0103	7.6877	7.9968	99.5743	20.9710
Image 4	0.9906	-0.0003	6.9040	7.9972	99.5819	25.9839

Bio Cryptosystem for CT-MRI Images

The proposed bio-key-based algorithm is tested on CT-MRI images with a dark background. The first experiment is conducted on the images using bio-key-based AES.

The background of the images has its impact on AES encryption. It could be observed that the foreground details can be differentiated in the encrypted image. There is an information leak from the plain image due to the background. In the second experiment, pixel scrambling using Arnold transform is tested on the plain images. It could be observed from the encrypted images that the texture pattern is exhibited in pixel scrambling which may lead to the information of the encryption algorithm. If the encrypted image is subjected to Arnold transform with a certain number of iterations, the plain image is obtained. The bottlenecks in AES and Arnold transform are avoided by combining both. First, the plain image is scrambled using Arnold transform. Here the scrambled image is selected at a particular iteration. This scrambled image selection offers one level of security to encryption. The scrambled image is again encrypted using the bio-key generated by the iris and fingerprint features of the user. A 256-bit bio-key is generated from the biometrics for AES encryption. Another encryption algorithm, considered for comparison is a hyperchaotic system using the Fibonacci matrix. In this encryption, the plain image is scrambled using numbers using six dimensions hyperchaotic system followed by an image permutation and Fibonacci matrix. A lightweight encryption algorithm known as a secure IoT algorithm (SIT) is tested on the input images using a 64-bit key. It could be observed that the information leak is present in the encrypted images.

The four metrics, presented in Table 2, are evaluated for the encrypted CT-MRI images and the other three encryption algorithms. The values are plotted in Figure 12. It could be observed that the proposed bio-key-based ATAES algorithm delivers the entropy close to eight to all the input images. The Red line in the boxplot represents the mean value of the metrics. The minimum and maximum values are also presented in the boxplot for the four metrics. AES without AT delivers entropies ranging from

Figure 11. (a) CT-MRI plain images, encrypted images using AES with bio-key, AT, ATAES, HCS, and SIT, and decrypted images

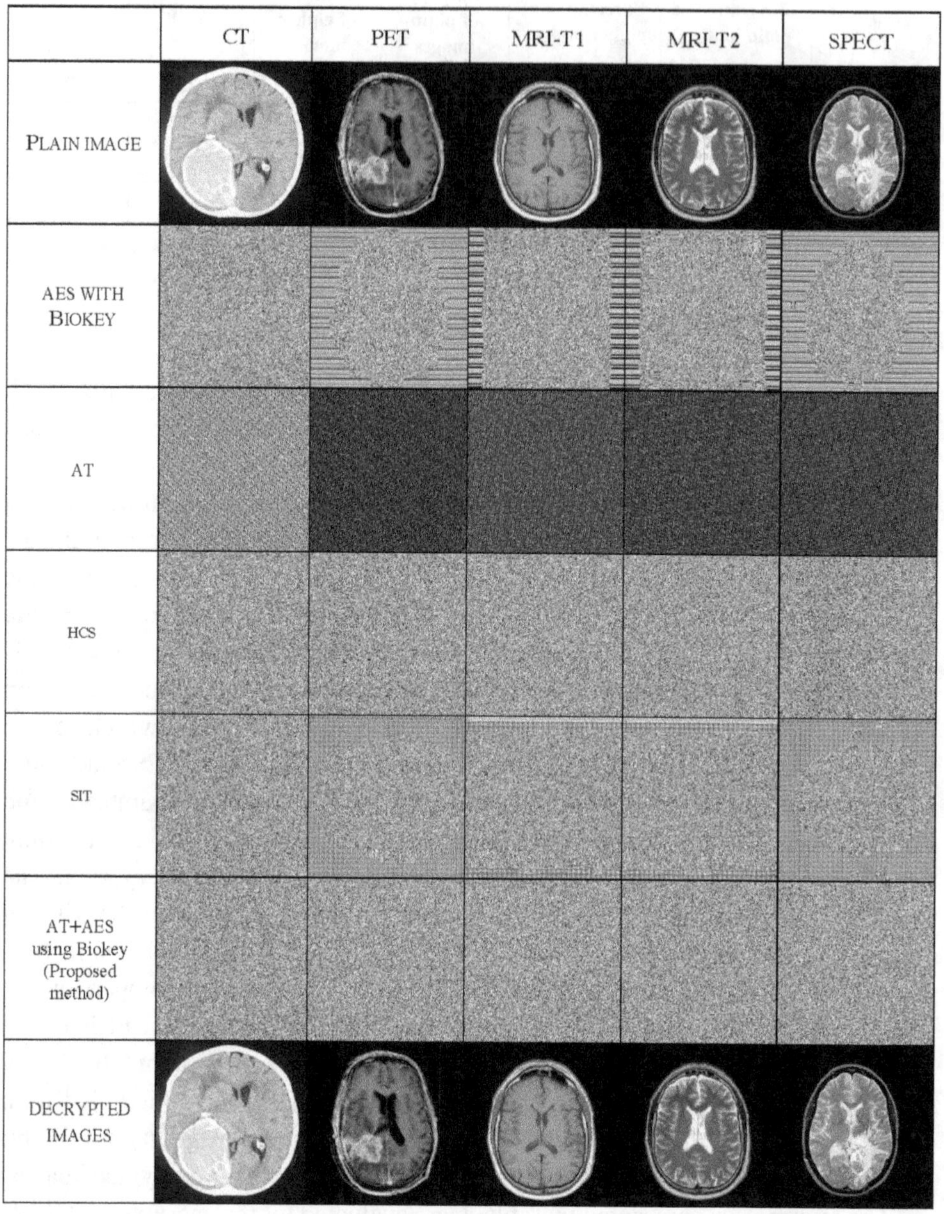

Figure 12. Performance metrics for CT-MRI images

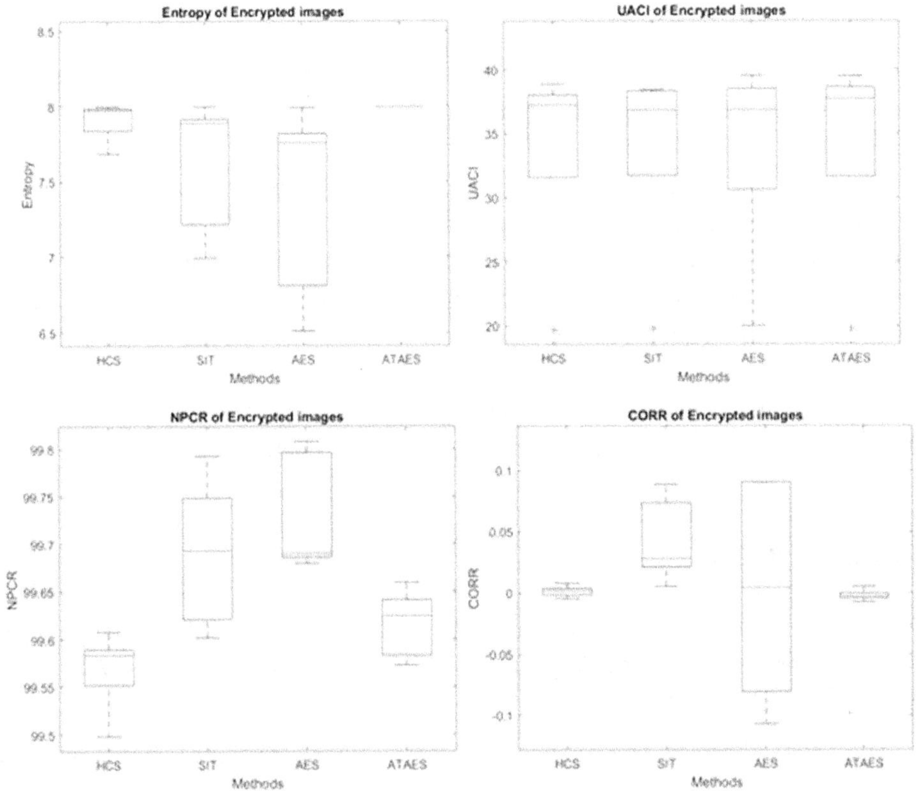

6.4 to 7.9. HCS performs close to the proposed method, but the values are from 7.7 to 7.9. Entropy values very close to eight describe the maximum randomness achieved by the encryption algorithm. The proposed method achieves a high degree of randomness in all the five images taken for experimentation. A similar performance could be observed from the Pearson correlation coefficient. The values close to zero represent no correlation among the neighboring pixels. The proposed method achieves a correlation coefficient very close to zero for almost all the input images. AES without AT performs vice-versa. NPCR value of close to a hundred reveals the robustness of the encryption method against differential attacks. For this metric, the proposed method performs moderately well compared to the remaining methods. The values are in the range of 99.58 to 99.65. Similar performance is repeated by the proposed method for UACI also.

CONCLUSION

The paper focused on securing the medical images while being stored on the cloud platforms or third-party servers by the hospitals. The proposed approach enrolls and authorizes a user to use the iris and fingerprint biometrics. The symmetric key generated from the fingerprint was used to encrypt the images before storing them in the cloud. The experimental results suggest that the encryption scheme used is capable of successfully resisting the differential and statistical attacks and provides satisfactory performance. The work could be scalable for the security requirements and implemented using other biometric features. Future work aims at incorporating deep learning for identifying the features from huge datasets of images. Convolutional neural network can be used to build a system that extracts features from the iris and fingerprints, thereby replacing the traditional biometric feature extraction techniques. Also, incorporating chaotic-based schemes with AES could be efficient.

REFERENCES

Aju, O. G., Orimoloye, S. M., & Omomule, T. G. (2018). An Enhanced Minitiae-based Fingerprint Matching Algorithm. *International Journal of Computers and Applications*, *975*, 8887.

Alrifaee, M. M. (2020). *A short survey of iris images databases.* Available at SSRN 3616735.

Badgi, P., Ravishankar, K., & Neha, K. S. (2020). Multilevel Image Encryption and Decryption Based On Biometric Approach. *International Journal of Progressive Research in Science and Engineering*, *1*(5), 79–84.

Bian, W., Gope, P., Cheng, Y., & Li, Q. (2020). Bio-AKA: An efficient fingerprint based two factor user authentication and key agreement scheme. *Future Generation Computer Systems*, *109*, 45–55.

Daugman, J. (2009). How iris recognition works. In *The essential guide to image processing* (pp. 715–739). Academic Press.

Deshpande, U. U., Malemath, V. S., Patil, S. M., & Chaugule, S. V. (2020). Automatic latent fingerprint identification system using scale and rotation invariant minutiae features. *International Journal of Information Technology*, 1-15.

Fasna, K. K., Athira, P., & Remya Krishna, J. S. (2016). A review on iris feature extraction methods. *International Journal of Engineering Research and General Science*, *4*(2), 663–667.

Gite, H. R., & Mahendar, C. N. (2011). Iris code generation and recognition. *International Journal of Machine Intelligence*, *3*(3), 103–107. doi:10.9735/0975-2927.3.3.103-107

Jagadeesan, A., Thillaikkarasi, T., & Duraiswamy, K. (2010). Cryptographic key generation from multiple biometrics*: Fusing minutiae with iris feature. International Journal of Computers and Applications*, *2*(6), 16–26. doi:10.5120/673-946

Kester, Q. A., Nana, L., Pascu, A. C., Gire, S., Eghan, J. M., & Quaynor, N. N. (2015). A cryptographic technique for security of medical images in health information systems. *Procedia Computer Science*, *58*, 538–543.

Kumar, R. D., Karthikeyan, K., & Ramakrishna, T. (2012). Finger Print Image Enhancement Using FFT For Minutia Matching With Binarization. *International Journal of Engineering Research & Technology (Ahmedabad)*, *1*(8), 1–6.

Liu, Y., Jiang, Z., Xu, X., Zhang, F., & Xu, J. (2020). Optical image encryption algorithm based on hyper-chaos and public-key cryptography. *Optics & Laser Technology*, *127*, 106171.

Nachar, R., Inaty, E., Bonnin, P. J., & Alayli, Y. (2020). Hybrid minutiae and edge corners feature points for increased fingerprint recognition performance. *Pattern Analysis & Applications*, *23*(1), 213–224.

Nyarko-Boateng, O., Asante, M., & Nti, I. K. (2017). Implementation of advanced encryption standard algorithm with key length of 256 bits for preventing data loss in an organization. *International Journal of Science and Engineering Applications*, *6*(03), 88–94.

Panchal, G., Samanta, D., & Barman, S. (2019). Biometric-based cryptography for digital content protection without any key storage. *Multimedia Tools and Applications*, *78*(19), 26979–27000.

Raghavan, R., & John Singh, K. (2022). An enhanced and hybrid fingerprint minutiae feature extraction method for identifying and authenticating the patient's noisy fingerprint. *International Journal of System Assurance Engineering and Management*, 1-14.

Saranya, R., & Prabhu, S. (2016). Image encryption using RSA algorithm with biometric recognition. *Int. J. Adv. Trends Comput. Sci. Eng.*, *5*(11), 19149–19154.

Saraswathi, K., & Balasubramaniam, R. (2010). Biocryptosystems for authentication and network security-a survey. *Global Journal of Computer Science and Technology*, *10*, 12–16.

Shaheed, K., Mao, A., Qureshi, I., Kumar, M., Abbas, Q., Ullah, I., & Zhang, X. (2021). A systematic review on physiological-based biometric recognition systems: Current and future trends. *Archives of Computational Methods in Engineering*, *28*(7), 4917–4960.

Sudiro, S. A., Paindavoine, M., & Kusuma, T. M. (2007, June). Simple fingerprint minutiae extraction algorithm using crossing number on valley structure. In *2007 IEEE Workshop on Automatic Identification Advanced Technologies* (pp. 41-44). IEEE.

Sudiro, S. A., & Yuwono, R. T. (2012). Adaptable fingerprint minutiae extraction algorithm based-on crossing number method for hardware implementation using FPGA device. *International Journal of Computer Science, Engineering and Information Technology, 2*(3).

Surajkanta, Y., & Pal, S. (2021). A Digital Geometry-Based Fingerprint Matching Technique. *Arabian Journal for Science and Engineering*, *46*(4), 4073–4086.

Vijayarajan, R., Gnanasivam, P., & Avudaiammal, R. (2019). Bio-key based AES for personalized image cryptography. *The Computer Journal*, *62*(11), 1695–1705.

Wang, X., Zhu, Z., Wang, F., Ni, R., Wang, J., & Hu, Y. (2021). Medical image encryption based on biometric keys and lower–upper decomposition with partial pivoting. *Applied Optics*, *60*(1), 24–32.

Zhang, L. B., Zhu, Z. L., Yang, B. Q., Liu, W. Y., Zhu, H. F., & Zou, M. Y. (2015). Medical image encryption and compression scheme using compressive sensing and pixel swapping based permutation approach. *Mathematical Problems in Engineering*.

Chapter 10
Deep Learning-Based Automatic Student Authentication

Sheetalrani R Kawale
Karnataka State Akkamahadevi Women's University, Vijayapura, India

Namitha A. R.
BGS Institute of Technology, Adichunchanagiri University, India

Swetha K. R.
BGS Institute of Technology, Adichunchanagiri University, India

Dankan Gowda V.
B. M. S. Institute of Technology and Management, India

Swathi Pai M.
https://orcid.org/0000-0003-1847-8267
Presidency University, India

ABSTRACT

Classroom management relies heavily on the ability to keep track of student attendance. Attendance checks by calling names or handing out a sign-in sheet are time-consuming and vulnerable to fraud, especially the latter. Data science and image processing are the focus of this regarding counting the number of people present at a gathering for various objectives, such as determining a person's duty status, determining a person's physical presence in a classroom, determining a person's security clearance to enter a meeting hall, etc. It takes a lot of time and effort to maintain a database for future use when generating attendance records using the standard technique. With the help of the latest technology, attendance can be entered automatically. It is a frequently used face recognition technique that generates a binary code for each cell and compares it to the reference image. With the use of deep learning, this LBP method has been reworked in order to automate attendance generation.

DOI: 10.4018/978-1-6684-4558-7.ch010

INTRODUCTION

Humans have a certain amount of time in which to fulfill their goals. Spending time on mindless, mindless physical labour is a waste of time and a distraction from more important matters. Using Deep Neural Networks to solve the mass surveillance issue, offer an automation-based strategy to avoid such pointless effort, focusing primarily on the sub problem of enhancing teacher efficiency by automating the attendance taking process (Girshick et al., 2014). Intensely complex neural networks Using Deep Learning frameworks for face detection and recognition, this chapter proposes ways to lessen the burden on teachers by delivering fast and accurate results while also overcoming existing method shortcomings like multiclass identification problems, multiple appearances of the same person, illumination variance, and occlusion (Ren et al., 2015). Using deep learning, data is routed through several layers of non-linear mappings before the computer can construct a representation for it. Finally, Deep Learning Models are nothing but a function approximator capable of learning each and every function that depends on the input dataset. In the end, An extensive variety of subjects is included under the umbrella term "deep learning," which includes anything from supervised regression models to reinforcement learning-based AI. In Deep Learning, the problem of face detection and recognition is extremely challenging and contentious (Redmon et al., 2016). Face recognition on a broad scale has proven difficult due to a scarcity of properly labelled training data. Current state-of-the-art methods have been pushed aside by Nvidia Graphics cards, which can perform matrix operations very quickly. For a long time, Image and Vision Computing was dominated by non-deep learning algorithms as Viola Jones (Viola and Jones, 2004). Clustering and HOG, but noise in the data, such as occlusion and luminance variation, has greatly hindered these methods. Before Deep Learning, only Feature Engineering, Data Preprocessing (Zhu et al., 2006), Output Parsing, and KDD Tree Structures could provide an acceptable result in face recognition. RCNN, Faster and Faster RCNN, Overfeat, and Yolo can now operate in near-real time on commercial workstations because of the improved processing capability. The application of Deep Learning techniques for image and vision computing skyrocketed with the invention of Convolutional Neural Networks (Ding et al., 2014). For example, in Deep Learning, the use of data augmentation procedures during training may ensure that the model is invariant to noise and has a good generalizability so that it can overcome challenges with noise and erroneous predictions caused by things like occlusion.

There are two parts to a Face Recognition challenge in general: detecting a face in the picture and accurately classifying the image (Krizhevsky et al., 2012). To put it another way, we're dealing with an issue with the detection and classification of objects. How can an object detection framework be described? First, the neural network must be able to locate the item to be identified in an image, and secondly, it must be able to predict with high certainty that this object belongs to a certain class. There are a variety of ways to solve the issue, but the two most common are branch networks and a single network. Multiple Neural Network topologies are used in Branch Networks to conduct the many subtasks necessary to complete the pen-ultimate task, as the name indicates In nature, the branching sub-networks are decoupled, and each of them has been taught to mimic a unique function (Liu et al., 2016). Subnetworks that focus on the issue of region proposal are used in object detection networks. This means that the network is trying to learn which area in the picture is most likely to contain an item of interest. Classification of the observed item is taught to the second branching sub-network. The proposal of (Lowe, 2004) R-CNN with deep learning features a rich hierarchical feature set for accurate object detection and semantic segmentation. Region extraction is the initial phase of R-CNN, which may be done using approaches like objectness and selective search, limited parametricmin cuts, and so on. Selective search has been utilised to obtain region ideas for all of the experiment's goals.

To identify and classify objections, (He et al., 2016) suggested Alex net as a feature extraction method. SVMs (Support Vector Machines) are used to further categorise the information received from the regions (SVM). Using Convolutional Neural Networks, the R-CNN model uses a low-dimensional space to extract characteristics from the data, similar to the pyramid representation strategy used by the Bag of Words model in NLP. (Lin and Maji, 2016). proposed employing deep CNNs for ImageNet classification. In a class-specific collection of SVMs, the mod offers a score for each class using information from a convolutional neural network (CNN). According to the NMS algorithm, regions that have lower scores than those with better scores are filtered out of data sets. Models that beat existing best-practices for object recognition are the product of several key breakthroughs in these single network models. Real-time item recognition in model designs is another benefit of the advancements. Topologies such as YOLO, YOLO 9000, and Single Shot MultiBox Detector are common. YOLO is a Unified system with real-time object detection, as suggested by (Yang et al., 2016). The YOLO is lowered from 448 to 416 while in detection mode for the input size. For huge objects, it is best to anticipate the centre rather than four coordinates, since it tends to take up a considerable amount of space. To counter that, it makes a larger number of forecasts, but those predictions are less accurate. YOLO9000 was suggested by (Athanesious et al., 2019) for improved, quicker, and stronger detection of objects. The traditional YOLO model has been updated with the YOLO9000. Overfitting and speedier convergence are both addressed by the new YOLO9000, which replaces the dropout layer with Batch-Normalization. In addition, the anchor centre must be initialised.

Using a Single Shot MultiBox Detector Model, Liu et al. suggested an objection detection approach (SSD). To create feature maps in the SSD model, this approach uses a base network and an auxiliary network. These feature maps are used by the auxiliary network to forecast the bounding boxes. Addition of convolutional feature layers allows for prediction at different scales, making this an auxiliary element of the network. In order to forecast class scores or offsets, the SSD network utilises an additional feature layer of size MN and p channels by applying a kernel of size 33p to each feature map location. For object recognition, Scalar Invariant Feature Transformation (SIFT) was introduced by (Bae et al., 2015). It is possible to locate candidate matching features by using euclidean distance-based feature matching. There is a temporal cost to this approach, though. For picture recognition, he and his colleagues suggested deep residual learning (Diwaker et al., 2018). Training hundreds or thousands of layers is achievable using ResNet. Since a consequence of the stacking layers employed in ResNet, network speed is unaffected, as it is merely a stacking of identity mappings. The deeper model should not have a learning error, as this says. It is also difficult to achieve convergence to an almost optimum solution using region proposal-based decoupled systems (Jogiji et al., 2017). This research presents a single network-based deep learning strategy for automated attendance systems in order to address the branch network issue. Different object recognition at multiple periods, with illumination changes and partial occlusion are all handled by the proposed DPAAS method, which yields rapid and accurate results.

PROPOSED DAAS

Deep Learning-based Automated Attendance System (DPAAS) is designed to reliably identify faces in a variety of situations. Multiple challenges with non-trivial solutions must be addressed by the DPAAS approach offered. First, the proposed DPAAS uses face detection algorithms to identify people in a picture, and then the algorithms identify the person's label based on their facial features. Face detection is handled using a Neural Network called the single shot multi-box detector, while face recognition is handled by a VGG network. The SSD model's feature maps are generated using the SSD model's base network (Ahmedi et al., 2015). The bounding boxes are predicted by the auxiliary network using feature maps. Addition of convolutional feature layers allows for prediction at different scales, making this an auxiliary element of the network. SSD network applies a kernel of size 33p to a feature layer with a size of mn and p channels, which is used to forecast the class score or to compute offsets based on box position in relation to the location of each feature map (Krishnan et al., 2016). Every feature map cell has a set of default boxes, which act as a kind of convolutional tile for the cell. As a result, the box's location in relation to the cell is altered. Titled default boxes are also intended to be sensitive to specified scale for accurate feature mapping studies. When it comes to aspect ratio, a similar technique is used, with the aspect ratios being '1, 2, 3, 12, 13'. As a result, each feature map cell now contains six standard boxes by default, one for each of the objects with an aspect ratio of 1. Features maps from multiple layers are used to achieve scalar invariance since they include both low-level layer information for handling tiny pictures and large-scale context information.

$$DPL(x,l,c,p)=\frac{1}{N}\left(DPL_{conf}(x,c)+\propto DPL_{loc}(x,l,g)\right) \tag{1}$$

$$DPL_{loc}(x,l,g)=\in^{N}_{mc(cx,cy,k,l)}\in x_{y} smooth_{Li}\left(l_i^m-g_i^m\right) \tag{2}$$

$$c_i^p=exp\left(c_i^p\right)/\in_p exp\left(c_i^p\right) \tag{3}$$

There is an overall loss function called DPL, a localization loss called DPLconf, a confidence loss known as DPLloc and a weight term set to 1. The predicted and ground truth boxes, respectively, are denoted by l and g. The default bounding box's weight (w) and height (h) are located at cx and cy (h). Confidences of many classes are c.

The pre-installed boxes come in a variety of sizes, aspect ratios, and placements. Ground truth is assigned to a certain default box space for training purposes. When comparing the default box to the ground truth, the jaccard overlap is 0.5. If there is an overlap in the network's training issue, it can anticipate high scores. There are N default boxes for each category, and the word xp ij signifies the matching between the ith default box and the jth ground truth box of that category (Shengli et al., 2015). Confidence losses are SoftMax, and the localization losses are referred to as SmoothL1 losses. SSD was chosen over YOLO9000 because of SSD's superior object identification performance in the AP (Average Precision) - 50 scores of the MS COCO dataset when compared to YOLO9000. SSD is a better choice for object detection than YOLO and branching networks since it is quicker and more resilient. Faces are the sole things of interest in a Face Detection scenario. Faces may be utilised as positive examples for parameter optimization, while other objects can be used as background and exploited in methods such as Negative Hard Mining to increase the generalizability of the Face Detection model. The time it takes the network to process each video frame collected by the camera is referred to as the inference time.

To get a sense of the average inference, it can be seen that it's around 0.035 seconds, although this might vary depending on how much detail is collected in each frame. By employing two branch networks, one to determine the chance that an interesting item is present in the area using the softmax regression approach (Konatham et al., 2016) and another to determine the bounding box coordinates, these feature vectors may be processed from a series of fully connected layers. The ROI pooling layer's ability to be readily seen is one of its most significant advantages. The object proposal is transformed into H*W-sized feature vectors using the ROI pooling layer. There is no correlation between the (row, column, height, width) coordinates of a ROI and the H and W hyperparameters. Because of this, it is necessary to split up the ROI into smaller h/H * w/W sections in order to maximise the ROI pool's size in H*W. Prior to fine tuning, a small batch of N pictures is sampled using the Fast R-CNN and then an R/N ROI is sampled. It may take longer for the model to come to a conclusion if N is kept modest, since the calculations are split among the RoI's from the same picture. Each picture contains a random sample of R/N ROIs that are evenly distributed across all images, but only those with an IOU score of at least 50% are utilised for parameter tuning. Hard Mining is a method for choosing ROIs with an IoU score greater than 50% for parameter tuning. Using both sibling branches, fast R-CNN makes advantage of multiple Taskloss. This multi-tasking loss is shown in Equation 4. Translations and log-space width and height changes are represented by four coordinates for each class (tw,th): [x (x), y (y), width (w), and height (h). When DPLcls is more than 1, just the loss for non-background classes is calculated in the multitask loss equation, as illustrated in the figure. [u >= 1] denotes precisely that. As shown in Eqn 5, p represents the projected probability, u the ground truth label, and tu the offset for each of the four X,Y and W H coordinates from v respectively. In eqn 6, for example, DPLloc represents the loss of localization, whereas ti and vi represent the offsets from the actual x, y, w, and h coordinates. See Fig. 1 for an illustration of how the Automatic Attendance System uses deep learning.

$$DPL\left(p,u,t^{u},v\right)=DPL_{cls}\left(p,u\right)+\text{»}\left[\mathrm{u}\geq 1\right]\mathrm{DP}L_{loc\left(t^{u},v\right)} \tag{4}$$

$$Smooth_{Li}(x) = 0.5x^2,\ \text{if } |x|<1 \tag{5}$$

$$Smooth_{li}(x) = |x| - 0.5\ \text{otherwise} \tag{6}$$

Figure 1. Automated Attendance System with Complete Workflow Based on Deep Learning

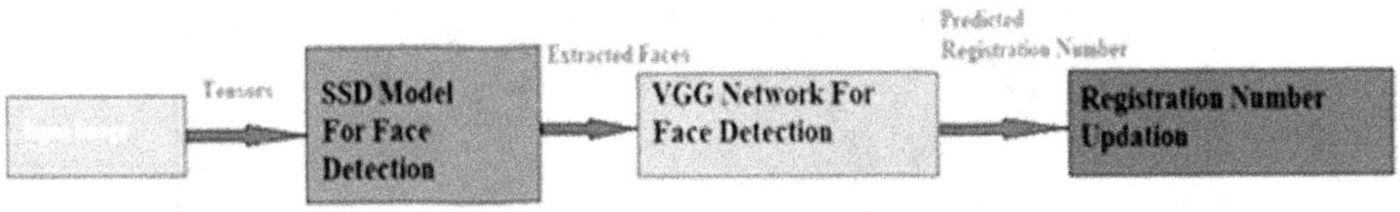

To speed up computing, this model takes an image as an input and transforms it into a tensor, a suitable format for matrix operations. An additional batch of photos is added to the image-to-tensor conversion process in order to speed things up even further. A tensor for the input tensor of the SSD model is then provided. X,Y,W,H values are compared to the ground truth values and the difference between these values is used to update weights. ' When the validation loss of the network stays constant across several epochs or reaches a target value, the network training operation is complete. For example, if you look at the SSD model's inference version, you'll see that it predicts all possible class probabilities in a picture, and those probabilities will be used to determine whether or not the detected area is a face. The captured video frames are then cropped to remove the subject's face using these coordinates. The VGG network is then fed with the retrieved pictures. The input picture is subjected to a variety of changes throughout the pipeline, including rotation, scaling, and flipping. The number of pictures available for training the network grows exponentially as a result of these modifications, enhancing the network's generalizability (Kar et al., 2012). After the picture has been processed, it is transformed to a tensor and then batched with the rest of the photos, much like an SSD. These tensors are sent to the VGG network for the purpose of network training. Ground truth class labels are compared to the network's predicted outcomes. The difference in entropy between the expected and actual labels is known as cross entropy loss. The face can be predicted after the VGG network has been trained. The database is then updated with the new face's registration number.

SYSTEM ARCHITECTURE

There are three major stages to this system. Image Capture, Face Detection, and Recognition are all part of it. In the pseudocode illustrated in Figure 2, the whole procedure is presented.

Figure 2. System architecture pseudocode

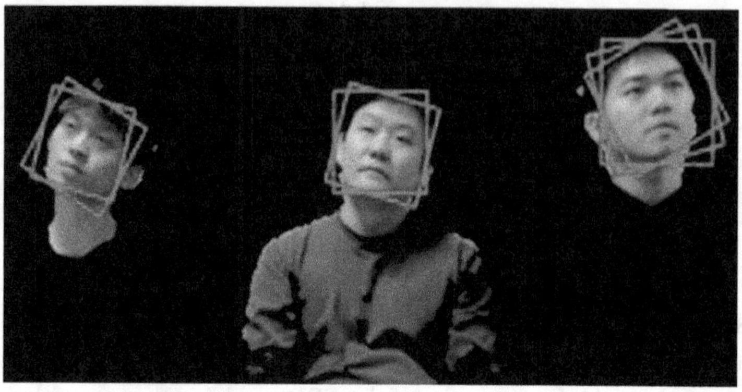

There is a need for a classroom with three rotating cameras, two in each corner and one in the middle in front. Figure 3 shows (as an example). Three spinning cameras would allow us to see the whole classroom from every angle. Figure 4 depicts what the scene might look like.

Figure 3. Classroom setup

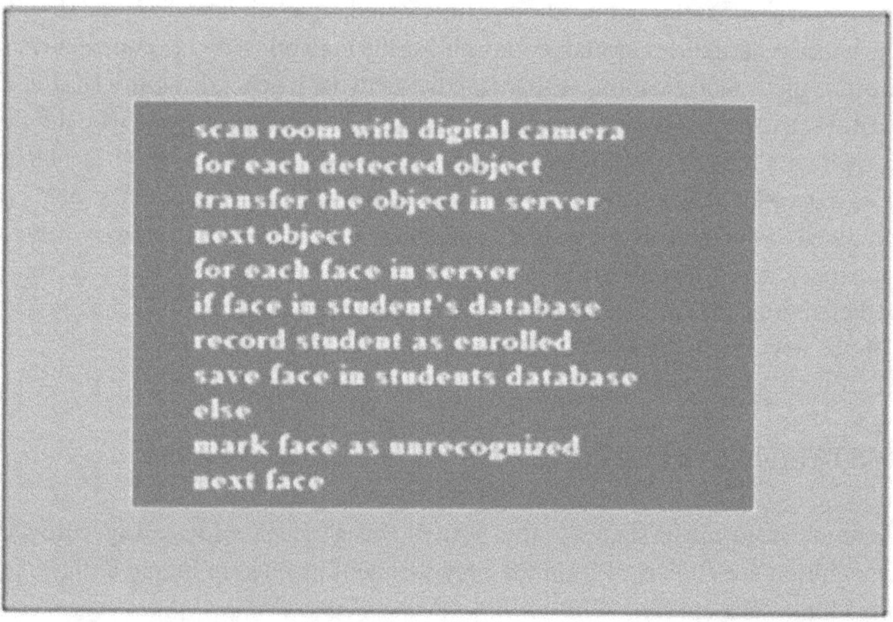

Figure 4. A classroom with students

For an alternate method, a camera might be placed in front of a door. When it comes to face recognition, the system would have to perform less work, but it would take a lot longer to identify and save the face. If you want a flawless attendance system (Kar et al., 2012), you should put the camera in front of the class. A classroom must have a computer system connected to three classroom cameras and an active internet connection in order to meet the system's requirements (Wagh et al., 2015). To keep track of the whole university's attendance, each classroom system would be linked to a single server.

"Develop candidate architecture models and views" or "System Architecture Definition" may include a job called "Physical Architecture Model Development" (see System Architecture article). When designing a physical solution, you may use this tool to build precise visual representations of how the solution will operate in combination with the logical architectural model, as well as satisfying and balancing the numerous requirements of the system under consideration. The identification of concrete physical elements that can support the functional, behavioural, and temporal characteristics of the system, as well as the expected properties of the system deduced from non-functional system requirements (e.g., the constraint of replacement of obsolescence and/or continued product support), is required following the definition of a logical architecture model. When numerous systems are developed to the same physical architecture model, physical interface standards may be one of the key drivers of the physical architecture model. This is particularly true when several systems are created to the same physical architecture model. There's always a potential that high-level interface standards will be codified in some form or another. Standards may also be defined during the building of the physical architectural model, and they can be critical enablers for the achievement of desired engineering goals such as system families, the introduction of new technology, interoperability, and the use of "open systems." Consider the development of contemporary television, audio, and computer systems, which have all benefited from the use of interface standards. There are several examples of this kind of design, ranging from nuts and bolts to plumbing to electrical installations to rail gauges to TCP/IP to IT systems and software to modular defense systems, and there are many more.

Figure 5. Physical system architecture

DETAIL WORKING

Image Capturing

Python was used to create a desktop-based camera programme for capturing images. We'll extract the face from each picture since we have three cameras in the classroom. A person's identity would be compromised if two portraits of the same person were seen together. Use the conventional CV2 (Computer Vision) library in Python (Turk and Pentland, 1991) to capture the picture.

Images are taken every 25 minutes until all of the faces have been removed or the timer is activated to cease taking pictures. This is a good example of how a camera continues capturing pictures until a face is detected, for example.

Face Detection

Multi-Task Cascaded Convolutional Networks

In an unconstrained context, face identification and alignment are difficult because of the wide range of postures, illuminations, and occlusions. Research shows that today's deep learning techniques can handle these issues. A deep cascaded multi-task framework that utilises the intrinsic connection between detection and alignment is proposed in this research. For face and landmark location prediction, we use a cascaded architecture with three levels of carefully built deep convolutional networks. An online hard sample mining approach that boosts performance even more is proposed in this chapter. Face identification and face alignment are two of the most difficult tasks in computer vision, and our approach outperforms the current state-of-the-art solutions on these hard benchmarks. Our method also maintains real-time speed while achieving greater accuracy.

Figure 6. Face Detection using MTCCN

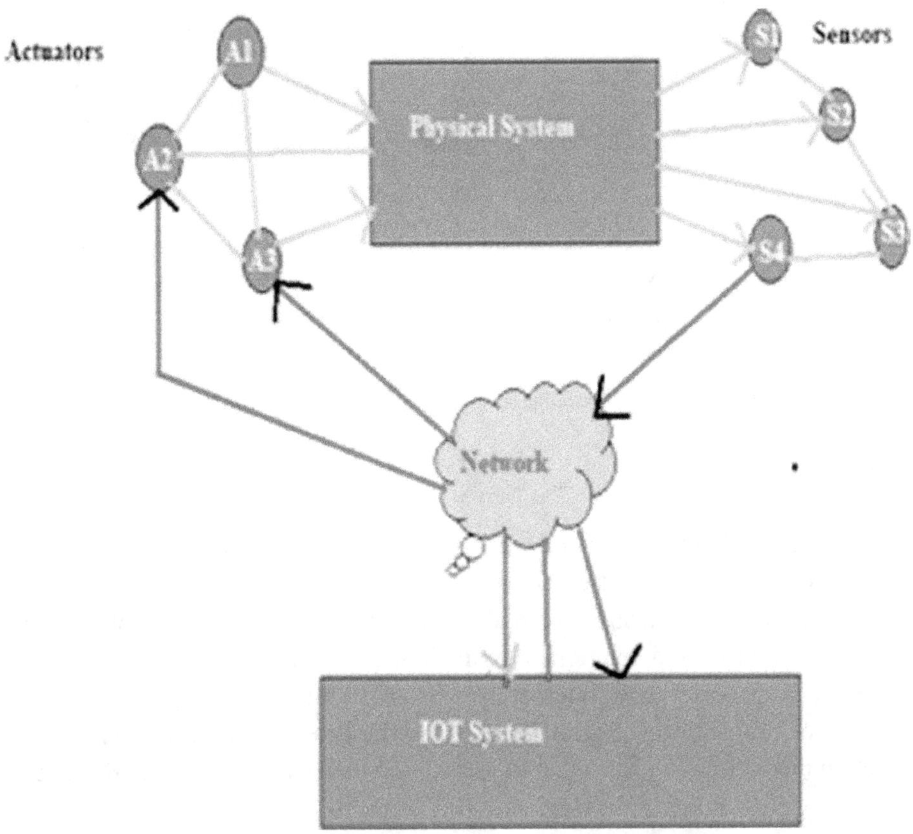

Mobile Net

MobileNets are small, low-power versions that may be customised to fit the needs of a wide range of applications. Like any other large-scale model, such as Inception, they may be developed for embedding, segmentation, classification, and detection. TensorFlow Mobile can be utilised efficiently with MobileNets.
In terms of performance, MobileNets may compete with more well-known models.

Figure 7. Multiple Faces being Detected

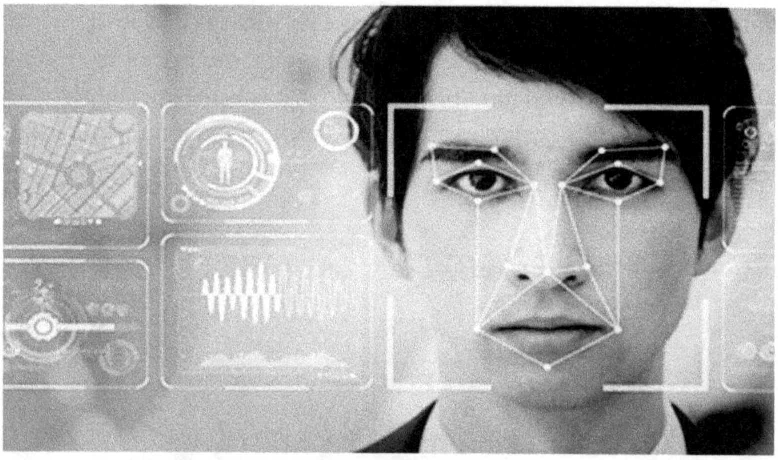

A pre-processed face may be sent into the identification phase of a face detection system employing CNN architecture to get a ROI for the detection phase. The computational part of transfer learning is reduced.

Face Recognition

Eigen Face

This programme is server-based since it requires a lot of computing power. The job of detecting a face is one of object detection, with the face serving as the object of interest. Face identification methods may be affected by a variety of variables, including scale, location, rotation, illumination, and so on. When trying to recognise a face, the same issues exist, but there are also a few more challenges to overcome, as we'll see momentarily. Facial features may be detected using a variety of face detection methods, as well as other objects. Used the HAAR classifier (Krishnan et al., 2016) for face identification in our system since most students face the camera frontally. Intel's Open CV library is used to build this classifier.

Eigenface technique is utilised in Open CV (Kar et al., 2012) library. The PCA (Principle of Component Analysis) (Patil et al., 2014) technique to facial identification using Eigenface is the most frequent and extensively utilised. Here the face is reduced to just the most basic characteristics: the eigenface, which is also the most important part of any learning or training data set. Finally, a person's face is recognised by projecting the picture into the eigenface vector subspace and classifying it based on the individual's location in eigenface. Over other algorithms, eigenface has the benefit of being easy to learn and quick to implement, as well as being unaffected by minor changes in the facial structure.

Figure 8. Eigen Face

To recognise a face, one must be able to identify it from a database of faces. When a student enrols, our institution collects photos, which are currently saved in a database and used to train a model.

Deep Metric Learning

Davis King (Schroff et al., 2015) pre-trained 128 embeddings on a collection of 3 million photos in the wild LFW dataset. According to Schroff and Kalenichenko, it instead generated 128 encoded embeddings that were optimised depending on the loss of triplets.

When it comes to computer vision challenges, models based on deep neural networks are the go-to solutions. In order to get excellent outcomes in computer vision tasks, learning invariant and discriminative features from data is a need. The capacity of deep learning approaches to learn hierarchical feature representations by creating high-level features from low-level ones has been shown to be extremely useful for feature learning.

Figure 9. Triplet Loss

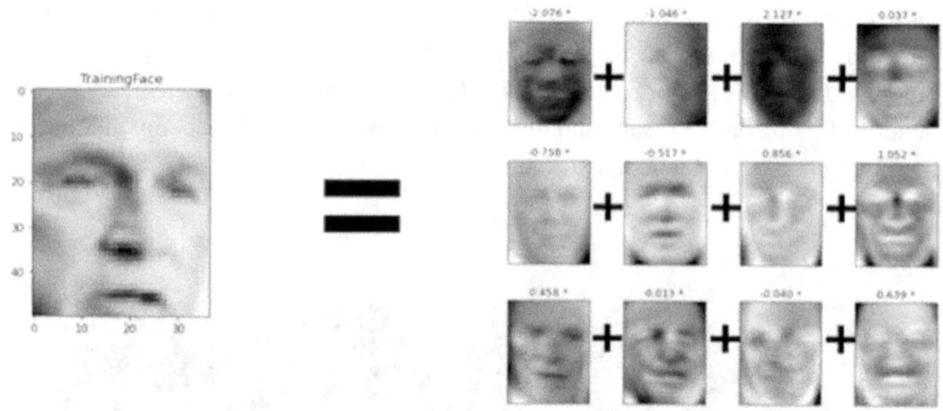

RESULT AND ANALYSIS

Automated optimization of entity markings may be achieved using this method. Due to the lack of external influences like shadows, dust, etc., this procedure will be completed in the shortest period of time possible. Our model can predict with ease in parameter tweaking and less compute for training thanks to the application of supervised deep learning and transfer learning approaches. The trade-off between bias and variance will diminish with time as the number of samples or input increases. Afterwards, we will train the picture to identify if it is a live thing or a photograph.

Figure 10. Multiple Face Being Detected

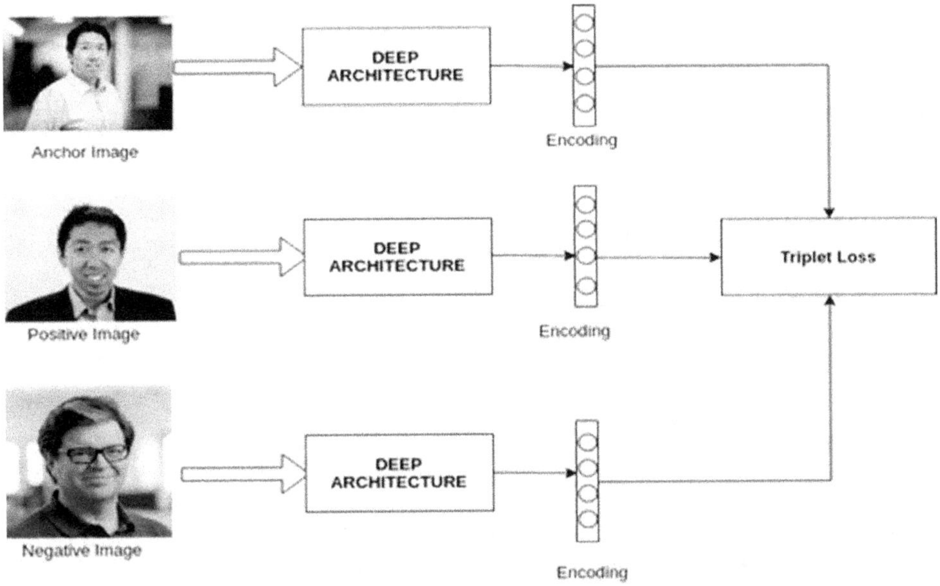

CONCLUSION

Single Shot MultiBox detector neural network model is used to extract the confident area exhibiting the traits of a human face in the unique DPAAS framework, which can be characterised as a deep learning-based automatic attendance system The ResNet base network captures these face traits. The VGG network may then utilise these face areas as inputs. It is a neural network again, but this time it is used to classify rather than detect or extract features. Using the unique registration number, the VGG network can identify the individual from the captured photos. Using this registration number, the attendance of the discovered candidates may be updated. Using a Movidius Neural Compute Stick, a complete pipeline from face detection through identification is completed. It is possible that in the future this work may be relevant in a broader range of use cases, especially when workstation-class PCs and servers are not readily accessible.

One of the most important tools in a business is an automated attendance system. Time-consuming and requiring some kind of human involvement, most of today's systems are. Face-recognition is a key component of our strategy to solving the difficulties. Even with this approach, it is not possible to identify every student in the class, and there is still much room for improvement in terms of calculation speed and precision. Because our system is built in a modular fashion, may make incremental improvements until get a level of accuracy we're satisfied with. The lack of a security module in our system, which is one of the most critical areas for development in the next phase, is a major drawback. No one should ever be able to utilize any images that save on our systems for live monitoring since it is based on real-time data, and data security is a top priority for us. When it comes to upgrading the system, have space for development regardless of whether it is a face or a 2D image.

ACKNOWLEDGMENT

We would like to acknowledge the support given by BMS Institute of Technology and Management, Bangalore, India.

REFERENCES

Ahmedi, A., & Nandyal, S. (2015). An automatic attendance system using image processing. *International Journal of Engineering Science*, *4*(11), 1–8.

Athanesious, J. J., Chakkaravarthy, S. S., Vasuhi, S., & Vaidehi, V. (2019). Trajectory based abnormal event detection in video traffic surveillance using general potential data field with spectral clustering. *Multimedia Tools and Applications*, *78*(14), 19877–19903.

Bae, M. Y., & Cho, D. J. (2015). Design and implementation of automatic attendance check system using BLE beacon. *International Journal of Multimedia and Ubiquitous Engineering*, *10*(10), 177–186.

Ding, W., Wang, R., Mao, F., & Taylor, G. (2014). *Theano-based large-scale visual recognition with multiple gpus.* arXiv preprint arXiv*:1412.2302*.

Diwaker, C., Tomar, P., Poonia, R. C., & Singh, V. (2018). Prediction of Software Reliability using Bio Inspired Soft Computing Techniques. *Journal of Medical Systems*, *42*(5), 93–100.

Girshick, R., Donahue, J., Darrell, T., & Malik, J. (2014). Rich feature hierarchies for accurate object detection and semantic segmentation. *Proceedings of the IEEE conference on computer vision and pattern recognition*, 580-58. 10.1109/CVPR.2014.81

He, K., Zhang, X., Ren, S., & Sun, J. (2016). Deep residual learning for image recognition. *Proceedings of the IEEE Conference on Computer Vision and Pattern Recognition*, 770-778.

Jogiji, A., & Ghate, P. (2017). WSN Based Automatic Attendance Monitoring System. *International Journal of Computer & Mathematical Sciences*, *6*(8).

Kar, N., Debbarma, M.K., Saha, A., & Pal, D.R. (2012). Study of implementing automated attendance system using face recognition technique. *International Journal of Computer and Communication Engineering*, *1*(2), 100-114.

Konatham, S., Chalasani, B. S., Kulkarni, N., & El Taeib, T. (2016, April). Attendance generating system using RFID and GSM. *Systems, Applications and Technology Conference (LISAT), 2016 IEEE Long Island*, 1-3.

Krishnan, R. R., Renuka, R., Swetha, C., & Ramakrishnan, R. (2016). Effective automatic attendance marking system using face recognition with RFID. *IJSRST*, *2920*, 158–162.

Krizhevsky, A., Sutskever, I., & Hinton, G. E. (2012). Imagenet classification with deep convolutional neural networks. *Advances in Neural Information Processing Systems*, 1097–1105.

Lin, T. Y., & Maji, S. (2016). Visualizing and understanding deep texture representations. *Proceedings of the IEEE Conference on Computer Vision and Pattern Recognition*, 2791-2799.

Liu, W., Anguelov, D., Erhan, D., Szegedy, C., Reed, S., Fu, C. Y., & Berg, A. C. (2016). October. Ssd: Single shot multibox detector. *European Conference on Computer Vision*, 21-37.

Lowe, D. G. (2004). Distinctive image features from scale-invariant keypoints. *International Journal of Computer Vision*, *60*(2), 91–110.

Redmon, J., Divvala, S., Girshick, R., & Farhadi, A. (2016). You only look once: Unified, real-time object detection. *Proceedings of the IEEE conference on computer vision and pattern recognition*, 779-788. 10.1109/CVPR.2016.91

Ren, S., He, K., Girshick, R., & Sun, J. (2015). Faster r-cnn: Towards real-time object detection with region proposal networks. *Advances in Neural Information Processing Systems*, 91–99.

Shengli, K., Jun, Z., Guang, S., Chunhong, W., Wenpei, Z., & Tao, L. (2015). The Design and Implementation of the Attendance Management System based on Radio Frequency Identification Technology. *International Conference on Electronic Science and Automation Control.*

Viola, P., & Jones, M. J. (2004). Robust real-time face detection. *International Journal of Computer Vision*, *57*(2), 137–154. doi:10.1023/B:VISI.0000013087.49260.fb

Yang, S., Luo, P., Loy, C. C., & Tang, X. (2016). Wider face: A face detection benchmark. *Proceedings of the IEEE Conference on Computer Vision and Pattern Recognition*, 5525-5533.

Zhu, Q., Yeh, M. C., Cheng, K. T., & Avidan, S. (2006). Fast human detection using a cascade of histograms of oriented gradients. *2006 IEEE Computer Society Conference on Computer Vision and Pattern Recognition (CVPR'06)*, 2, 1491-1498.

Compilation of References

Abdullah, R., Muthusamy, H., Vijean, V., Abdullah, Z., & Kassim, F. N. C. (2019). Real and Complex Wavelet Transform Approaches for Malaysian Speaker and Accent Recognition. *Pertanika Journal of Science & Technology, 27*(2).

Abdulnabi, A. H., Wang, G., Lu, J., & Jia, K. (2015). Multi-task CNN model for attribute prediction. *IEEE Transactions on Multimedia, 17*(11), 1949–1959.

Afchar, D., Nozick, V., Yamagishi, J., & Echizen, I. (2018, December). Mesonet: a compact facial video forgery detection network. In 2018 IEEE international workshop on information forensics and security (WIFS) (pp. 1-7). IEEE.

Agarwal, S., Fan, W., & Farid, H. (2018). A diverse large-scale dataset for evaluating rebroadcast attacks. In *Proceedings of the 2018 IEEE International Conference on Acoustics, Speech and Signal Processing (ICASSP)* (pp.1997–2001). IEEE.

Ahmad, Z., Shahid Khan, A., Wai Shiang, C., Abdullah, J., & Ahmad, F. (2021). Network intrusion detection system: A systematic study of machine learning and deep learning approaches. *Transactions on Emerging Telecommunications Technologies, 32*(1), e4150.

Ahmedi, A., & Nandyal, S. (2015). An automatic attendance system using image processing. *International Journal of Engineering Science, 4*(11), 1–8.

Aju, O. G., Orimoloye, S. M., & Omomule, T. G. (2018). An Enhanced Minitiae-based Fingerprint Matching Algorithm. *International Journal of Computers and Applications, 975*, 8887.

Akbulut, Y., & Dönmez, O. (2018). Predictors of digital piracy among Turkish undergraduate students. *Telematics and Informatics, 35*(5), 1324–1334. doi:10.1016/j.tele.2018.03.004

Akhtar, N., & Mian, A. (2018). Threat of adversarial attacks on deep learning in computer vision: A survey. *IEEE Access: Practical Innovations, Open Solutions, 6*, 14410–14430.

Al Majeed, S. M. S., Askar, S. K., & Fleury, M. (2014, March). H. 265 Codec over 4G Networks for Telemedicine System Application. In *2014 UKSim-AMSS 16th International Conference on Computer Modelling and Simulation* (pp. 292-297). IEEE. doi:10.1109/ICSSIT48917.2020.9214114

Albawi, S., Mohammed, T. A., & Al-Zawi, S. (2017, August). Understanding of a convolutional neural network. In 2017 international conference on engineering and technology (ICET) (pp. 1-6). IEEE.

Al-Garadi, M. A., Mohamed, A., Al-Ali, A. K., Du, X., Ali, I., & Guizani, M. (2020). A survey of machine and deep learning methods for internet of things (IoT) security. *IEEE Communications Surveys and Tutorials*, *22*(3), 1646–1685. doi:10.1109/COMST.2020.2988293

Ali, A. M. A., Spiegel, J. V., & Mueller, P. (1999, August). Automatic detection and classification of stop consonants using an acoustic-phonetic feature-based system. In *XIVth International Congress of Phonetic Sciences* (pp. 1709-1712). Academic Press.

Alkahtani, H., & Aldhyani, T. H. (2021). Intrusion detection system to advance internet of things infrastructure-based deep learning algorithms. *Complexity*.

Almars, A. M. (2021). Deepfakes detection techniques using deep learning: A survey. *Journal of Computer and Communications*, *9*(5), 20–35.

Alrifaee, M. M. (2020). *A short survey of iris images databases.* Available at SSRN 3616735.

Al-Rubaie, M., & Chang, J. M. (2016). Reconstruction attacks against mobile-based continuous authentication systems in the cloud. *IEEE Transactions on Information Forensics and Security*, *11*(12), 2648–2663. doi:10.1109/TIFS.2016.2594132

Al-Rubaie, M., & Chang, J. M. (2019). Privacy-preserving machine learning: Threats and solutions. *IEEE Security and Privacy*, *17*(2), 49–58. doi:10.1109/MSEC.2018.2888775

Amerini, I., Uricchio, T., & Caldelli, R. (2017). Tracing images back to their social network of origin: A cnn-based approach, In *Proceedings of the 2017 IEEE Workshop on Information Forensics and Security (WIFS)* (pp. 1–6). IEEE.

Aminanto, R., Choi, H. C., Tanuwidjaja, P. D., & Yoo, K. (2017). Deep abstraction and weighted feature selection for Wi-Fi impersonation detection. *IEEE Trans. Inf. Forensics Secur.*, *13*(3), 621–636.

Aneja, S., Aneja, N., & Islam, M. S. (2018, November). IoT device fingerprint using deep learning. In 2018 IEEE international conference on internet of things and intelligence system (IOTAIS) (pp. 174-179). IEEE.

Anthi, E., Williams, L., Słowińska, M., Theodorakopoulos, G., & Burnap, P. (2019). A supervised intrusion detection system for smart home IoT devices. *IEEE Internet of Things Journal*, *6*(5), 9042–9053. doi:10.1109/JIOT.2019.2926365

Anwar, F., & Anwar, Z. (2011, December). *Digital forensics for eucalyptus. In 2011 Frontiers of Information Technology*. IEEE.

Arel, I., Rose, D. C., & Karnowski, T. P. (2010). Deep machine learning - A new frontier in artificial intelligence research. *IEEE Computational Intelligence*, *5*(4), 13–18. doi:10.1109/MCI.2010.938364

Arjovsky, M., Chintala, S., & Bottou, L. (2017). Wasserstein Generative Adversarial Networks. In *Proceedings of the International Conference on Machine Learning* (pp. 214–223). Academic Press.

Askar, S., Zervas, G., Hunter, D. K., & Simeonidou, D. (2011). Service differentiation for video applications over OBS networks. *16th European Conference on Networks and Optical Communications*, 200-203.

Athanesious, J. J., Chakkaravarthy, S. S., Vasuhi, S., & Vaidehi, V. (2019). Trajectory based abnormal event detection in video traffic surveillance using general potential data field with spectral clustering. *Multimedia Tools and Applications*, *78*(14), 19877–19903.

Awad., N. A. (2021). *Enhancing Network Intrusion Detection Model Using Machine Learning Algorithms.* Computers, Materials & Continua Tech Science Press. Doi:10.32604/cmc.2021.014307

Azmoodeh, A., Dehghantanha, A., & Choo, K. K. R. (2018). Robust malware detection for internet of (battlefield) things devices using deep eigenspace learning. *IEEE Transactions on Sustainable Computing, 4*(1), 88-95.

Badgi, P., Ravishankar, K., & Neha, K. S. (2020). Multilevel Image Encryption and Decryption Based On Biometric Approach. *International Journal of Progressive Research in Science and Engineering*, *1*(5), 79–84.

Bae, M. Y., & Cho, D. J. (2015). Design and implementation of automatic attendance check system using BLE beacon. *International Journal of Multimedia and Ubiquitous Engineering*, *10*(10), 177–186.

Bai, L., Yao, L., Kanhere, S. S., Wang, X., & Yang, Z. (2018, October). Automatic device classification from network traffic streams of internet of things. In *2018 IEEE 43rd conference on local computer networks (LCN)* (pp. 1-9). IEEE.

Barni, M., Stamm, M. C., & Tondi, B. (2018). Adversarial Multimedia Forensics: Overview and Challenges Ahead. In *Proceedings of the 26th European Signal Processing Conference (EUSIPCO)*. IEEE.

Baroffio, L., Bondi, L., Bestagini, P., & Tubaro, S. (2016). *Camera identification with deep convolutional networks.* arXiv preprint arXiv:1603.01068, 460.

Bassey, J., Adesina, D., Li, X., Qian, L., Aved, A., & Kroecker, T. (2019, June). Intrusion detection for IoT devices based on RF fingerprinting using deep learning. In *2019 Fourth International Conference on Fog and mobile edge computing (FMEC)* (pp. 98-104). IEEE. doi:10.1109/WiMOB.2019.8923325

Bayar, B., & Stamm, M. C. (2016). A deep learning approach to universal image manipulation detection using a new convolutional layer. In *Proceedings of the 4th ACM Workshop on Information Hiding and Multimedia Security* (pp. 5–10). ACM.

Bayar, B., & Stamm, M. C. (2017). Augmented convolutional feature maps for robust cnn-based camera model identification. In *Proceedings of the 2017 IEEE International Conference on Image Processing (ICIP)* (pp. 4098–4102). IEEE.

Bayar, B., & Stamm, M. C. (2018). Constrained convolutional neural networks: A new approach towards general purpose image manipulation detection. *IEEE Transactions on Information Forensics and Security*, *13*(11), 2691–2706.

Bayar, B., & Stamm, M. C. (2018). Towards open set camera model identification using a deep learning framework. *2018 IEEE International Conference on Acoustics, Speech and Signal Processing (ICASSP)*, 2007–2011.

Bengio, Y., Courville, A., & Vincent, P. (2013). Representation learning: A review and new perspectives. *IEEE Transactions on Pattern Analysis and Machine Intelligence*, *35*(8), 1798–1828. doi:10.1109/TPAMI.2013.50 PMID:23787338

Bengio, Y., Lamblin, P., Popovici, D., & Larochelle, H. (2007). Greedy layer-wise training of deep networks. In *Advances in Neural Information Processing Systems* (pp. 153–160). MIT Press.

Beridze, I., & Butcher, J. (2019). When seeing is no longer believing. *Nature Machine Intelligence*, *1*(8), 332–334.

Berkling, K. M., Arai, T., & Barnard, E. (1994, April). Analysis of phoneme-based features for language identification. In *Proceedings of ICASSP'94. IEEE International Conference on Acoustics, Speech and Signal Processing* (Vol. 1, pp. I-289). IEEE. 10.1109/ICASSP.1994.389298

Bestagini, M. C. S. P. (2018). *IEEE signal processing cup 2018 database-forensic camera model identification.* doi, 10, H2XM2P.

Bhagath, P., & Das, P. K. (2004). Acoustic phonetic approach for speech recognition: A review. *Language*, *77*, 93.

Bian, W., Gope, P., Cheng, Y., & Li, Q. (2020). Bio-AKA: An efficient fingerprint based two factor user authentication and key agreement scheme. *Future Generation Computer Systems*, *109*, 45–55.

Bian, Z. P., Hou, J., Chau, L. P., & Magnenat-Thalmann, N. (2016). Facial position and expression-based human–computer interface for persons with tetraplegia. *IEEE Journal of Biomedical and Health Informatics*, *20*(3), 915–924. doi:10.1109/JBHI.2015.2412125 PMID:25775501

Biggs, S., & Vidalis, S. (2009, November). Cloud computing: The impact on digital forensic investigations. In *2009 International Conference for Internet Technology and Secured Transactions (ICITST)* (pp. 1-6). IEEE.

Bin, K., Luo, S., Zhang, X., Lin, J., & Tong, X. (2020). Compressive data gathering with generative adversarial networks for wireless geophone networks. *IEEE Geoscience and Remote Sensing Letters*, *18*(3), 558–562.

Bondi, L., Baroffio, L., Güera, D., Bestagini, P., Delp, E. J., & Tubaro, S. (2016). First steps toward camera model identification with convolutional neural networks. *IEEE Signal Processing Letters*, *24*(3), 259–263.

Bondi, L., Güera, D., Baroffio, L., Bestagini, P., Delp, E. J., & Tubaro, S. (2017). A preliminary study on convolutional neural networks for camera model identification. *Electronic Imaging, 2017*(7), 67–76.

Bonettini, N., Cannas, E. D., Mandelli, S., Bondi, L., Bestagini, P., & Tubaro, S. (2021, January). Video face manipulation detection through ensemble of cnns. In *2020 25th international conference on pattern recognition (ICPR)* (pp. 5012-5019). IEEE.

Bonetto, M., Carrato, S., Fenu, G., Medvet, E., Mumolo, E., Pellegrino, F. A., & Ramponi, G. (2015). Image processing issues in a social assistive system for the blind. In *International Symposium on Image and Signal Processing and Analysis* (pp. 216-221). 10.1109/ISPA.2015.7306061

Boulkenafet, Z., Jukka, K., & Abdenour, H. (2016). Face spoofing detection using colour texture analysis. *IEEE Transactions on Information Forensics and Security, 2016*(11), 1818–1830.

Brown, M. E., Treviño, L. K., & Harrison, D. A. (2005). Ethical leadership: A social learning perspective for construct development and testing. *Organizational Behavior and Human Decision Processes, 97*(2), 117–134. doi:10.1016/j.obhdp.2005.03.002

Caldelli, R., Amerini, I., & Li, C. T. (2018). PRNU-based Image Classification of Origin Social Network with CNN. In *Proceedings of the 2018 26th European Signal Processing Conference (EUSIPCO)* (pp. 1357–1361). Academic Press.

Caldelli, R., Becarelli, R., & Amerini, I. (2017). Image origin classification based on social network provenance. *IEEE Transactions on Information Forensics and Security, 2017*(12), 1299–1308.

Cao, H., & Kot, A. C. (2010). Identification of recaptured photographs on LCD screens. In *Proceedings of the 2010 IEEE International Conference on Acoustics, Speech and Signal Processing* (pp.1790–1793). IEEE.

Cao, Y. J., Jia, L. L., Chen, Y. X., Lin, N., Yang, C., Zhang, B., ... Dai, H. H. (2018). Recent advances of generative adversarial networks in computer vision. *IEEE Access: Practical Innovations, Open Solutions, 7*, 14985–15006.

Carlini, N., & Wagner, D. (2017). Adversarial examples are not easily detected: Bypassing ten detection methods. In *Proceedings of the 10th ACM Workshop on Artificial Intelligence and Security*. ACM.

Carrara, F., Falchi, F., Caldelli, R., Amato, G., & Becarelli, R. (2019). Adversarial image detection in deep neural networks. *Multimedia Tools and Applications, 78*, 2815–2835.

Carrara, F., Falchi, F., Caldelli, R., Amato, G., Fumarola, R., & Becarelli, R. (2017). Detecting adversarial example attacks to deep neural networks. In *Proceedings of the 15th International Workshop on Content-Based Multimedia Indexing*. ACM.

Chae, D. K., Ha, J., Kim, S. W., Kang, B., & Im, E. G. (2013, October). Software plagiarism detection: a graph-based approach. In *Proceedings of the 22nd ACM international conference on Information & Knowledge Management* (pp. 1577-1580). 10.1145/2505515.2507848

Chaturvedi, A., Awasthi, A., & Shanker, S. (2020). Cyber Forensic -A Literature Review. Trinity Journal of Management, IT & Media, *10*(1).

Chen, C., McCloskey, S., & Yu, J. (2018). Focus Manipulation Detection via Photometric Histogram Analysis. In *Proceedings of the IEEE Conference on Computer Vision and Pattern Recognition* (pp. 1674–1682). IEEE.

Chen, C., Zhao, X., & Stamm, M. C. (2018). Mislgan: An Anti-Forensic Camera Model Falsification Framework Using a Generative Adversarial Network. In *Proceedings of the 2018 25th IEEE International Conference on Image Processing (ICIP)* (pp. 535–539). IEEE.

Chen, L., Zhang, Y., Song, Y., Liu, L., & Wang, J. (2022). Self-supervised Learning of Adversarial Example: Towards Good Generalizations for Deepfake Detection. In *Proceedings of the IEEE/CVF Conference on Computer Vision and Pattern Recognition* (pp. 18710-18719). IEEE.

Chen, S., & Wang, Y. (2014). *Convolutional Neural Network and Convex Optimization*. Department of Electrical and Computer Engineering University of California SanDiego.

Chen, T., & Guestrin, C. (2016, August). Xgboost: A scalable tree boosting system. In *Proceedings of the 22nd acm sigkdd international conference on knowledge discovery and data mining* (pp. 785-794). 10.1145/2939672.2939785

Chen, Y., Huang, Y., & Ding, X. (2017). Camera model identification with residual neural network. In *Proceedings of the 2017 IEEE International Conference on Image Processing (ICIP)* (pp. 4337–4341). IEEE.

Choi, H. Y., Jang, H. U., Son, J., Kim, D., & Lee, H. K. (2017). Content Recapture Detection Based on Convolutional Neural Networks. In *International Conference on Information Science and Applications*. Springer.

Chollet, F. (2017). Xception: Deep learning with depth wise separable convolutions. In *Proceedings of the IEEE conference on computer vision and pattern recognition* (pp. 1251–1258). IEEE.

Chopra, S., Hadsell, R., & LeCun, Y. (2005). Learning a Similarity Metric Discriminatively, with Application to Face Verification. In *Proceedings of the 2005 IEEE Computer Society Conference on Computer Vision and Pattern Recognition (CVPR'05)*. IEEE Computer Society.

Cireşan, D., Meier, U., Masci, J., & Schmidhuber, J. (2011). A committee of neural networks for traffic sign classification. In *International Joint Conference on Neural Networks* (pp. 1918-1921). 10.1109/IJCNN.2011.6033458

Cozzolino, D., Poggi, G., & Verdoliva, L. (2017). Recasting residual-based local descriptors as convolutional neural networks: An application to image forgery detection. In *Proceedings of the 5th ACM Workshop on Information Hiding and Multimedia Security* (pp. 159–164). ACM.

Cui, W. (2014). *A Scheme of Human Face Recognition in Complex Environments* [Master's Thesis]. Auckland University of Technology, New Zealand.

Cui, Q., McIntosh, S., & Sun, H. (2018). Identifying materials of photographic images and photorealistic computer generated graphics based on deep CNNs. *Comput. Mater. Contin., 55*, 229–241.

Cui, W., & Yan, W. (2016). A scheme for face recognition in complex environments. *International Journal of Digital Crime and Forensics, 8*(1), 26–36. doi:10.4018/IJDCF.2016010102

Daugman, J. (2009). How iris recognition works. In *The essential guide to image processing* (pp. 715–739). Academic Press.

de Lima, O., Franklin, S., Basu, S., Karwoski, B., & George, A. (2020). *Deepfake detection using spatiotemporal convolutional networks.* arXiv preprint arXiv:2006.14749.

De Marsico, M., Nappi, M., Riccio, D., & Wechsler, H. (2015). Mobile iris challenge evaluation (MICHE)-I, biometric iris dataset and protocols. *Pattern Recognition Letters, 2015*(57), 17–23.

De Rezende, E. R., Ruppert, G. C., Theóphilo, A., Tokuda, E. K., & Carvalho, T. (2018). Exposing computer generated images by using deep convolutional neural networks. *Signal Processing Image Communication, 2018*(66), 113–126.

Deshpande, U. U., Malemath, V. S., Patil, S. M., & Chaugule, S. V. (2020). Automatic latent fingerprint identification system using scale and rotation invariant minutiae features. *International Journal of Information Technology*, 1-15.

Di Francesco, A., Arosio, B., Falconi, A., Di Bonaventura, M. V. M., Karimi, M., Mari, D., ... D'Addario, C. (2015). Global changes in DNA methylation in Alzheimer's disease peripheral blood mononuclear cells. *Brain, Behavior, and Immunity, 45*, 139–144. doi:10.1016/j.bbi.2014.11.002 PMID:25452147

Diller, T. (1979, April). Phonetic word verification. In *ICASSP'79. IEEE International Conference on Acoustics, Speech, and Signal Processing* (*Vol. 4*, pp. 256-261). IEEE. 10.1109/ICASSP.1979.1170731

Ding, W., Wang, R., Mao, F., & Taylor, G. (2014). *Theano-based large-scale visual recognition with multiple gpus.* arXiv preprint arXiv*:1412.2302.*

Ding, X., Chen, Y., Tang, Z., & Huang, Y. (2019). Camera Identification based on Domain Knowledge-driven Deep Multi-task Learning. *IEEE Access, 7*, 25878–25890.

Ding, I. Jr, Yen, C. T., & Hsu, Y. M. (2013). Developments of machine learning schemes for dynamic time-wrapping-based speech recognition. *Mathematical Problems in Engineering, 2013*, 2013. doi:10.1155/2013/542680

Diwaker, C., Tomar, P., Poonia, R. C., & Singh, V. (2018). Prediction of Software Reliability using Bio Inspired Soft Computing Techniques. *Journal of Medical Systems, 42*(5), 93–100.

Dougherty, G. (2012). *Pattern recognition and classification: An introduction.* Springer Science & Business Media.

Duda, R. O., & Hart, P. E. (2006). *Pattern classification*. John Wiley & Sons.

Du, M., Liu, N., Song, Q., & Hu, X. (2018, July). Towards explanation of dnn-based prediction with guided feature inversion. In *Proceedings of the 24th ACM SIGKDD International Conference on Knowledge Discovery & Data Mining* (pp. 1358-1367). 10.1145/3219819.3220099

Durall, R., Keuper, M., Pfreundt, F. J., & Keuper, J. (2019). *Unmasking deepfakes with simple features*. arXiv preprint arXiv:1911.00686.

Dykstra, J., & Sherman, A. T. (2011). *Understanding issues in cloud forensics: Two hypothetical case studies*. UMBC Computer Science and Electrical Engineering Department.

Dykstra, J., & Sherman, A. T. (2012). Acquiring forensic evidence from infrastructure-as-a-service cloud computing: Exploring and evaluating tools, trust, and techniques. *Digital Investigation*, *9*, S90–S98.

Dykstra, J., & Sherman, A. T. (2013). Design and implementation of FROST: Digital forensic tools for the OpenStack cloud computing platform. *Digital Investigation*, *10*, S87–S95.

Elrawy, M. F., Awad, A. I., & Hamed, H. F. (2018). Intrusion detection systems for IoT-based smart environments: A survey. *Journal of Cloud Computing*, *7*(1), 1–20.

Fan, W., Agarwal, S., & Farid, H. (2018). Rebroadcast Attacks: Defenses, Reattacks, and Redefenses. In *Proceedings of the 2018 26th European Signal Processing Conference (EUSIPCO)* (pp. 942–946). Academic Press.

Farid, H. (2006). Digital doctoring: How to tell the real from the fake. *Significance*, *3*(4), 162–166.

Fasna, K. K., Athira, P., & Remya Krishna, J. S. (2016). A review on iris feature extraction methods. *International Journal of Engineering Research and General Science*, *4*(2), 663–667.

Federici, C. (2014). Cloud data imager: A unified answer to remote acquisition of cloud storage areas. *Digital Investigation*, *11*(1), 30–42.

Felzenszwalb, P., Girshick, R., Mcallester, D. A., & Ramanan, D. (2010). *IEEE Transactions on Pattern Analysis and Machine Intelligence*. Institute of Electrical and Electronics Engineers. doi:10.1109/TPAMI.2009.167

Feng, G. C., Yuen, P. C., & Dai, D. Q. (2000). Human face recognition using PCA on wavelet subband. *Journal of Electronic Imaging*, *9*(2), 226–234. doi:10.1117/1.482742

Ferreira, A., Chen, H., Li, B., & Huang, J. (2018). An Inception-Based Data-Driven Ensemble Approach to Camera Model Identification. In *Proceedings of the 2018 IEEE International Workshop on Information Forensics and Security (WIFS)* (pp. 1–7). IEEE.

Fiterman, E. M., & Durick, J. D. (2019). Ghost in the machine: Forensic evidence collection in the virtual environment. *Digital Forensics Magazine*, *2*, 73–77.

Forensic Yard. (2022). *7 Basic Laws and Principles of Forensic Science*. Retrieved from https://forensicyard.com/laws-and-principles-of-forensic-science/

Freire-Obregón, D., Narducci, F., Barra, S., & Castrillón-Santana, M. (2019). Deep learning for source camera identification on mobile devices. *Pattern Recognition Letters*, *126*, 86–91.

Fridrich, J., & Kodovsky, J. (2012). Rich models for steganalysis of digital images. *IEEE Transactions on Information Forensics and Security*, *2012*(7), 868–882.

Fukushima, K., & Miyake, S. (1982). Neocognitron: A self-organizing neural network model for a mechanism of visual pattern recognition. In Competition and Cooperation in Neural Nets (pp. 267-285). Springer. doi:10.1007/978-3-642-46466-9_18

Gal, Y., & Ghahramani, Z. (2016). A theoretically grounded application of dropout in recurrent neural networks. In Advances in Neural Information Processing Systems (pp. 1019-1027). Academic Press.

Gao, H., Huang, W., & Duan, Y. (2021). The cloud-edge-based dynamic reconfiguration to service workflow for mobile ecommerce environments: A QoS prediction perspective. *ACM Transactions on Internet Technology*, *21*(1), 1–23. doi:10.1145/3391198

Gao, H., Kuang, L., Yin, Y., Guo, B., & Dou, K. (2020). Mining consuming behaviors with temporal evolution for personalized recommendation in mobile marketing apps. *Mobile Networks and Applications*, *25*(4), 1233–1248. doi:10.100711036-020-01535-1

Gao, H., Liu, C., Li, Y., & Yang, X. (2020). V2VR: Reliable hybrid-network-oriented V2V data transmission and routing considering RSUs and connectivity probability. *IEEE Transactions on Intelligent Transportation Systems*, *22*(6), 3533–3546. doi:10.1109/TITS.2020.2983835

Gao, X., Qiu, B., Shen, J., Ng, T. T., & Shi, Y. Q. (2010). A smart phone image database for single image recapture detection. In *International Workshop on Digital Watermarking*. Springer.

Ge, Z. (2015, October). Improved accent classification combining phonetic vowels with acoustic features. In *2015 8th International Congress on Image and Signal Processing (CISP)* (pp. 1204-1209). IEEE. 10.1109/CISP.2015.7408064

Girshick, R., Donahue, J., Darrell, T., & Malik, J. (2014). Rich feature hierarchies for accurate object detection and semantic segmentation. In *Proceedings of the IEEE conference on computer vision and pattern recognition* (pp. 580-587). 10.1109/CVPR.2014.81

Gite, H. R., & Mahendar, C. N. (2011). Iris code generation and recognition. *International Journal of Machine Intelligence*, *3*(3), 103–107. doi:10.9735/0975-2927.3.3.103-107

Giudice, O., Paratore, A., Moltisanti, M., & Battiato, S. (2017). A classification engine for image ballistics of social data. In *International Conference on Image Analysis and Processing*. Springer.

Gloe, T., & Böhme, R. (2010). The Dresden Image Database for benchmarking digital image forensics. In *Proceedings of the 2010 ACM Symposium on Applied Computing* (pp. 1584–1590). ACM.

Gong, D., Yogan, J. K., Goh, O. S., Ye, Z., & Chi, W. (2021). DeepfakeNet, an efficient deepfake detection method. *International Journal of Advanced Computer Science and Applications*, *12*(6).

Goodfellow, I. J., Shlens, J., & Szegedy, C. (2014). *Explaining and Harnessing Adversarial Examples*. arXiv 2014, arXiv:1412.6572.

Goodfellow, I., Bengio, Y., & Courville, A. (2016). *Adaptive Computation and Machine Learning series, Deep Learning*. MIT Press.

Goodfellow, I., Pouget-Abadie, J., Mirza, M., Xu, B., Warde-Farley, D., Ozair, S., ... Bengio, Y. (2014). Generative adversarial nets. *Advances in Neural Information Processing Systems*, 27.

Grispos, G., Storer, T., & Glisson, W. B. (2012). Calm before the storm: The challenges of cloud computing in digital forensics. *International Journal of Digital Crime and Forensics*, *4*(2), 28–48.

Guan, H., Kozak, M., Robertson, E., Lee, Y., Yates, A. N., Delgado, A., . . . Fiscus, J. (2019, January). MFC datasets: Large-scale benchmark datasets for media forensic challenge evaluation. In 2019 IEEE Winter Applications of Computer Vision Workshops (WACVW) (pp. 63-72). IEEE.

Güera, D., Wang, Y., Bondi, L., Bestagini, P., Tubaro, S., & Delp, E. J. (2017). A counter-forensic method for cnn-based camera model identification. In *Proceedings of the 2017 IEEE Conference on Computer Vision and Pattern Recognition Workshops (CVPRW)* (pp. 1840–1847). IEEE.

Güera, D., Zhu, F., Yarlagadda, S. K., Tubaro, S., Bestagini, P., & Delp, E. J. (2018). Reliability map estimation for CNN-based camera model attribution. In *Proceedings of the 2018 IEEE Winter Conference on Applications of Computer Vision (WACV)* (pp. 964–973). IEEE.

Gu, J., Wang, Z., Kuen, J., Ma, L., Shahroudy, A., Shuai, B., ... Chen, T. (2018). Recent advances in convolutional neural networks. *Pattern Recognition*, *77*, 354–377.

Gulrajani, I., Ahmed, F., Arjovsky, M., Dumoulin, V., & Courville, A. C. (2017). Improved Training of wasserstein GANs. *Proceedings of the 31st International Conference on Neural Information Processing Systems*.

Hajiheidari, S., Wakil, K., Badri, M., & Navimipour, N. J. (2019). Intrusion detection systems in the Internet of things: A comprehensive investigation. *Computer Networks*, *160*, 165–191. doi:10.1016/j.comnet.2019.05.014

Han, J., Pei, J., & Kamber, M. (2011). *Data mining: concepts and techniques*. Elsevier.

Han, Z., Francesca, C., Nikolic, K., Mirza, K., & Toumazou, C. (2021, May). Signal identification of DNA amplification curves in custom-PCR platforms. In *2021 IEEE International Symposium on Circuits and Systems (ISCAS)* (pp. 1-5). IEEE.

Haodong, L., Han, C., Bin, L., & Shunquan, T. (2018). Can Forensic Detectors Identify GAN Generated Images? In *Proceedings of the APSIPA Annual Summit and Conference 2018* (pp. 722–727). Academic Press.

Hao, W., Bie, R., Guo, J., Meng, X., & Wang, S. (2018). Optimized CNN based image recognition through target region selection. *Optik (Stuttgart)*, *156*, 772–777. doi:10.1016/j.ijleo.2017.11.153

Haq, N. F., Onik, A. R., Hridoy, M. A. K., Rafni, M., Shah, F. M., & Farid, D. M. (2015). Application of machine learning approaches in intrusion detection system: A survey. *IJARAI-International Journal of Advanced Research in Artificial Intelligence*, *4*(3), 9–18.

Hasegawa, K., Yanagisawa, M., & Togawa, N. (2017, July). Hardware Trojans classification for gate-level netlists using multi-layer neural networks. In *2017 IEEE 23rd International Symposium on On-Line Testing and Robust System Design (IOLTS)* (pp. 227-232). IEEE. 10.1109/IOLTS.2017.8046227

He, M. (2018). Distinguish computer generated and digital images: A CNN solution. Concurrency Comput. Pract. Exp., 31(12).

Heck, J. C., & Salem, F. M. (2017, August). Simplified minimal gated unit variations for recurrent neural networks. In *2017 IEEE 60th International Midwest Symposium on Circuits and Systems (MWSCAS)* (pp. 1593-1596). IEEE.

He, K., Zhang, X., Ren, S., & Sun, J. (2016). Deep residual learning for image recognition. In *Proceedings of the IEEE conference on computer vision and pattern recognition* (pp. 770–778). IEEE.

He, K., Zhang, X., Ren, S., & Sun, J. (2016). Deep residual learning for image recognition. *Proceedings of the IEEE Conference on Computer Vision and Pattern Recognition*, 770-778.

Hemdan, E. E. D., & Manjaiah, D. H. (2015). Exploring digital forensic investigation issues for cyber crimes in cloud computing environment. *Proceeding of 1st International Conference on Computer Communication and Networks (i3CN).*

He, P., Jiang, X., Sun, T., & Li, H. (2018). Computer graphics identification combining convolutional and recurrent neural networks. *IEEE Signal Processing Letters*, *25*(9), 1369–1373.

Hidalgo-Espinoza, S., Chamorro-Cupuerán, K., & Chang-Tortoler, O. (2020). *Intrusion Detection in Computer Systems by Using Artificial Neural Networks with Deep Learning Approaches.* AIRCC Publishing Corporation.

Hinton, G. (2011). Boltzmann Machines. In C. Sammut & G. I. Webb (Eds.), Encyclopedia of Machine Learning. Springer. https://doi.org/10.1007/978-0-387-30164-8_83.

Hinton, G. E., Osindero, S., & Teh, Y. W. (2006). A fast learning algorithm for deep belief nets. *Neural Computation*, *18*(7), 1527–1554.

Hori, T., Chen, Z., Erdogan, H., Hershey, J. R., Le Roux, J., Mitra, V., & Watanabe, S. (2017). Multi-microphone speech recognition integrating beamforming, robust feature extraction, and advanced DNN/RNN backend. *Computer Speech & Language*, *46*, 401–418. doi:10.1016/j.csl.2017.01.013

Hou, X., Shen, L., Ke, S., & Qiu, G. (2017). Deep Feature Consistent Variational Autoencoder. *Proceedings of the 2017 IEEE Winter Conference on Applications of Computer Vision (WACV).*

Huang, G. B., Mattar, M., Berg, T., & Learned-Miller, E. (2008). Labeled faces in the wild: A database for studying face recognition in unconstrained environments. *Proceedings of the Workshop on faces in 'Real-Life' Images: Detection, alignment, and recognition.*

Huang, G., Liu, Z., Van Der Maaten, L., & Weinberger, K. Q. (2017). Densely connected convolutional networks, In *Proceedings of the IEEE conference on computer vision and pattern recognition* (pp. 4700–4708). IEEE.

Huang, N., He, J., Zhu, N., Xuan, X., Liu, G., & Chang, C. (2018). Identification of the source camera of images based on convolutional neural network. *Digital Investigation*, *26*, 72–80.

Imran, S., Khan, M. U. G., Idrees, M., Muneer, I., & Iqbal, M. M. (2018). An enhanced framework for extrinsic plagiarism avoidance for research article. *Technical Journal*, *23*(01), 84–92.

Ioffe, S., & Szegedy, C. (2015, June). Batch normalization: Accelerating deep network training by reducing internal covariate shift. In *International conference on machine learning* (pp. 448-456). PMLR.

Isono, T., Yamakura, M., Shimaya, S., Kawamoto, I., Tsuboi, N., Mineo, M., ... Hirai, H. (2020, November). A 12.1 TOPS/W Mixed-precision Quantized Deep Convolutional Neural Network Accelerator for Low Power on Edge/Endpoint Device. In *2020 IEEE Asian Solid-State Circuits Conference (A-SSCC)* (pp. 1-4). IEEE.

Jabbar, S., Malik, K. R., Ahmad, M., Aldabbas, O., Asif, M., Khalid, S., Han, K., & Ahmed, S. H. (2018). A methodology of real-time data fusion for localized big data analytics. *IEEE Access: Practical Innovations, Open Solutions*, *6*, 24510–24520. doi:10.1109/ACCESS.2018.2820176

Jagadeesan, A., Thillaikkarasi, T., & Duraiswamy, K. (2010). Cryptographic key generation from multiple biometrics*: Fusing minutiae with iris feature. International Journal of Computers and Applications*, *2*(6), 16–26. doi:10.5120/673-946

Jahangir, R., Teh, Y. W., Nweke, H. F., Mujtaba, G., Al-Garadi, M. A., & Ali, I. (2021). Speaker identification through artificial intelligence techniques: A comprehensive review and research challenges. *Expert Systems with Applications*, *171*, 114591. doi:10.1016/j.eswa.2021.114591

Jain, U., Nathani, K., Ruban, N., Raj, A. N. J., Zhuang, Z., & Mahesh, V. G. (2018, October). Cubic SVM classifier based feature extraction and emotion detection from speech signals. In *2018 International Conference on Sensor Networks and Signal Processing (SNSP)* (pp. 386-391). IEEE. 10.1109/SNSP.2018.00081

Jha, J., & Ragha, L. (2013). Intrusion detection system using support vector machine. *International Journal of Applied Information Systems*, *3*, 25–30.

Jie, H., Li, S., Albanie, S., Gang, S., & Wu, E. (2017). *Squeeze-and-Excitation Networks*. arXiv: 1709.01507.

Jin, L., Zhang, Y., Tan, W., & Liu, W. (2010). Effect of different treatment rapeseeds on activity of cellulose enzyme in sheep. *The Journal of Northeast Agricultural University*, *17*(1), 57–61.

Jogiji, A., & Ghate, P. (2017). WSN Based Automatic Attendance Monitoring System. *International Journal of Computer & Mathematical Sciences*, *6*(8).

Joseph, R. M., Sun, J. S., Tam, E., & Carlson, J. R. (2017). A receptor and neuron that activate a circuit limiting sucrose consumption. *eLife*, *6*, e24992. doi:10.7554/eLife.24992 PMID:28332980

Joyia, G. J., Liaqat, R. M., Farooq, A., & Rehman, S. (2017). Internet of medical things (IoMT): Applications, benefits and future challenges in healthcare domain. *Journal of Communication*, *12*(4), 240–247.

Kamal, U., Rafi, A. M., Hoque, R., Das, S., Abrar, A., & Hasan, M. (2018). *Application of DenseNet in Camera Model Identification and Post-processing Detection*. arXiv 2018. arXiv preprint arXiv:1809.00576.

Kandhari, M. S., Zulkemine, F., & Isah, H. (2018, November). A Voice Controlled E-Commerce Web Application. In *2018 IEEE 9th Annual Information Technology, Electronics and Mobile Communication Conference (IEMCON)* (pp. 118-124). IEEE.

Kannadaguli, P., & Bhat, V. (2015, March). A comparison of Gaussian Mixture Modeling (GMM) and Hidden Markov Modeling (HMM) based approaches for Automatic Phoneme Recognition in Kannada. In *2015 International Conference on Signal Processing and Communication (ICSC)* (pp. 257-260). IEEE. 10.1109/ICSPCom.2015.7150658

Kar, N., Debbarma, M.K., Saha, A., & Pal, D.R. (2012). Study of implementing automated attendance system using face recognition technique. *International Journal of Computer and Communication Engineering*, *1*(2), 100-114.

Karbab, E. B., Debbabi, M., Derhab, A., & Mouheb, D. (2017). *Android malware detection using deep learning on API method sequences*. arXiv preprint arXiv:1712.08996.

Karpathy, A., Toderici, G., Shetty, S., Leung, T., Sukthankar, R., & Fei-Fei, L. (2014). Large-scale video classification with convolutional neural networks. In *IEEE Conference on Computer Vision and Pattern Recognition* (pp. 1725-1732). 10.1109/CVPR.2014.223

Karras, T., Aila, T., Laine, S., & Lehtinen, J. (2017). *Progressive growing of gans for improved quality, stability, and variation.* arXiv 2017, arXiv:1710.10196.

Kester, Q. A., Nana, L., Pascu, A. C., Gire, S., Eghan, J. M., & Quaynor, N. N. (2015). A cryptographic technique for security of medical images in health information systems. *Procedia Computer Science*, *58*, 538–543.

Khan, A., Sohail, A., Zahoora, U., & Qureshi, A. S. (2019). *A Survey of the Recent Architectures of Deep Convolutional Neural Networks*. arXiv 2019, arXiv:1901.06032.

KishorP.BholaneP. (2006). Forensic Accounting: A Brief Overview. *Journal of Business Issues*. http://ssrn.com/abstract=1642100

Kok, S. H., Abdullah, A., Jhanjhi, N. Z., & Supramaniam, M. (2019). A review of intrusion detection system using machine learning approach. *International Journal of Engineering Research & Technology (Ahmedabad)*, *12*(1), 8–15.

Konatham, S., Chalasani, B. S., Kulkarni, N., & El Taeib, T. (2016, April). Attendance generating system using RFID and GSM. *Systems, Applications and Technology Conference (LISAT), 2016 IEEE Long Island*, 1-3.

Krautheim, F. J., Phatak, D. S., & Sherman, A. T. (2010, June). Introducing the trusted virtual environment module: a new mechanism for rooting trust in cloud computing. In *International conference on trust and trustworthy computing* (pp. 211-227). Springer. 10.1007/978-3-642-13869-0_14

Krishnan, R. R., Renuka, R., Swetha, C., & Ramakrishnan, R. (2016). Effective automatic attendance marking system using face recognition with RFID. *IJSRST*, *2920*, 158–162.

Krizhevsky, A., Sutskever, I., & Hinton, G. E. (2012). ImageNet classification with deep convolutional neural networks. In Advances in Neural Information Processing Systems (pp. 1097-1105). Academic Press.

Krizhevsky, A., Sutskever, I., & Hinton, G. E. (2012). *Advances in Neural Information Processing Systems*. MIT Press.

Krizhevsky, A., Sutskever, I., & Hinton, G. E. (2012). Imagenet classification with deep convolutional neural networks. *Advances in Neural Information Processing Systems*, 1097–1105.

Kumar, R. D., Karthikeyan, K., & Ramakrishna, T. (2012). Finger Print Image Enhancement Using FFT For Minutia Matching With Binarization. *International Journal of Engineering Research & Technology (Ahmedabad)*, *1*(8), 1–6.

Kurakin, A., Goodfellow, I., & Bengio, S. (2016). *Adversarial Machine Learning at Scale*. arXiv 2016, arXiv:1611.01236.

Kurakin, A., Goodfellow, I., Bengio, S., Dong, Y., Liao, F., Liang, M., Pang, T., Zhu, J., Hu, X., & Xie, C. (2018). Adversarial attacks and defences competition. In *The NIPS'17 Competition: Building Intelligent Systems* (pp. 195–231). Springer.

Kuzin, A., Fattakhov, A., Kibardin, I., Iglovikov, V. I., & Dautov, R. (2018, December). Camera model identification using convolutional neural networks. In *2018 IEEE International Conference on Big Data (Big Data)* (pp. 3107-3110). IEEE.

Landahl, H. D., McCulloch, W. S., & Pitts, W. (1943). A statistical consequence of the logical calculus of nervous nets. *Bulletin of Mathematical Biology*, *5*(4), 135–137.

Larose, D. T., & Larose, C. D. (2014). *Discovering knowledge in data: an introduction to data mining* (Vol. 4). John Wiley & Sons.

LeCun, Y., Bengio, Y., & Hinton, G. (2015). Deep learning. *Nature*, *521*(7553), 436–444. doi:10.1038/nature14539 PMID:26017442

LeCun, Y., Bengio, Y., & Hinton, G. (2015). Deep Learning. *Nature, 521*, 436–444.

Li, H., Li, B., Tan, S., & Huang, J. (2018). *Detection of deep network generated images using disparities in color components.* arXiv 2018, arXiv:1808.07276.

Li, Y., Chang, M. C., & Lyu, S. (2018, December). In ictu oculi: Exposing ai created fake videos by detecting eye blinking. In *2018 IEEE International workshop on information forensics and security (WIFS)* (pp. 1-7). IEEE.

Li, H., Wang, S., & Kot, A. C. (2017). Image recapture detection with convolutional and recurrent neural networks. *Electronic Imaging, 2017*(7), 87–91.

Li, L., Bao, J., Zhang, T., Yang, H., Chen, D., Wen, F., & Guo, B. (2020). Face x-ray for more general face forgery detection. In *Proceedings of the IEEE/CVF conference on computer vision and pattern recognition* (pp. 5001-5010). IEEE.

Lin, M., Chen, Q., & Yan, S. (2013). *Network in network.* arXiv:1312.4400.

Lin, T. Y., & Maji, S. (2016). Visualizing and understanding deep texture representations. *Proceedings of the IEEE Conference on Computer Vision and Pattern Recognition*, 2791-2799.

Li, R., Ni, R., & Zhao, Y. (2015). An effective detection method based on physical traits of recaptured images on LCD screens. In *International Workshop on Digital Watermarking*. Springer.

Liu, H., & Lang, B. (2019). Machine learning and deep learning methods for intrusion detection systems: A survey. *Applied Sciences, 9*(20), 4396.

Liu, W., Anguelov, D., Erhan, D., Szegedy, C., Reed, S., Fu, C. Y., & Berg, A. C. (2016). October. Ssd: Single shot multibox detector. *European Conference on Computer Vision*, 21-37.

Liu, W., Anguelov, D., Erhan, D., Szegedy, C., Reed, S., Fu, C. Y., & Berg, A. C. (2016). SSD: Single shot multibox detector. In *European Conference on Computer Vision* (pp. 21-37). Academic Press.

Liu, J., & Liang, D. (2005). A survey of FPGA-based hardware implementation of ANNs. In *IEEE International Conference on Neural Networks and Brain* (pp. 915-918). IEEE.

Liu, M., & Yan, W. (2022). *Masked face recognition in real-time using MobileNetV2*. ACM ICCCV.

Liu, Y., Jiang, Z., Xu, X., Zhang, F., & Xu, J. (2020). Optical image encryption algorithm based on hyper-chaos and public-key cryptography. *Optics & Laser Technology, 127*, 106171.

Liu, Z., Luo, P., Wang, X., & Tang, X. (2015). Deep learning face attributes in the wild. In *Proceedings of the IEEE international conference on computer vision* (pp. 3730–3738). IEEE.

Li, X., Xiao, F., Li, L., Shen, J., & Qian, F. (2018, June). Detection Method of Hardware Trojan Based on Wavelet Noise Reduction and Neural Network. In *International Conference on Cloud Computing and Security* (pp. 256-265). Springer. 10.1007/978-3-030-00018-9_23

Lowe, D. G. (2004). Distinctive image features from scale-invariant keypoints. *International Journal of Computer Vision*, *60*(2), 91–110.

Maalej, R., Tagougui, N., & Kherallah, M. (2016). Online Arabic handwriting recognition with dropout applied in deep recurrent neural networks. In *IAPR Workshop on Document Analysis Systems* (pp. 417-421). 10.1109/DAS.2016.49

Madry, A., Makelov, A., Schmidt, L., Tsipras, D., & Vladu, A. (2017). *Towards deep learning models resistant to adversarial attacks.* arXiv 2017, arXiv:1706.06083.

Mannepalli, K., Sastry, P. N., & Suman, M. (2016). MFCC-GMM based accent recognition system for Telugu speech signals. *International Journal of Speech Technology*, *19*(1), 87–93. doi:10.100710772-015-9328-y

Marra, F., Gragnaniello, D., Verdoliva, L., & Poggi, G. (2018). *Do GANs leave artificial fingerprints?* arXiv 2018, arXiv:1812.11842.

Marra, F., Gragnaniello, D., & Cozzolino, D. (2018). Verdoliva, L. Detection of GAN-generated fake images over social networks. In *Proceedings of the 2018 IEEE Conference on Multimedia Information Processing and Retrieval (MIPR)* (pp. 384–389). IEEE.

Marra, F., Gragnaniello, D., & Verdoliva, L. (2018). On the vulnerability of deep learning to adversarial attacks for camera model identification. *Signal Processing Image Communication*, *65*, 240–248.

Mayer, O., & Stamm, M. C. (2018). Learned forensic source similarity for unknown camera models. In *Proceedings of the 2018 IEEE International Conference on Acoustics, Speech and Signal Processing (ICASSP)* (pp. 2012–2016). IEEE.

Ma, Z. C., & Fokoué, E. (2014). A Comparison of Classifiers in Performing Speaker Accent Recognition Using MFCCs. *Open Journal of Statistics*, *4*(04), 258–266. doi:10.4236/ojs.2014.44025

McCloskey, S., & Albright, M. (2018). *Detecting GAN-generated Imagery using Color Cues.* arXiv 2018, arXiv:1812.08247.

McCulloch, W. S., & Pitts, W. (1943). A logical calculus of the ideas immanent in nervous activity. *The Bulletin of Mathematical Biophysics*, *5*(4), 115–133. doi:10.1007/BF02478259

McDermott, C. D., Majdani, F., & Petrovski, A. V. (2018, July). Botnet detection in the internet of things using deep learning approaches. In 2018 international joint conference on neural networks (IJCNN) (pp. 1-8). IEEE. doi:10.1109/IJCNN.2018.8489489

Meena, D., & Gupta, H. (2013). Digital crime investigation using various logs and fuzzy rules: A review. *International Journal of Advanced Research in Computer and Communication Engineering*, *2*(4).

Meidan, Y., Bohadana, M., Mathov, Y., Mirsky, Y., Shabtai, A., Breitenbacher, D., & Elovici, Y. (2018). N-baiot—Network-based detection of iot botnet attacks using deep autoencoders. *IEEE Pervasive Computing*, *17*(3), 12–22. doi:10.1109/MPRV.2018.03367731

Meidan, Y., Bohadana, M., Shabtai, A., Guarnizo, J. D., Ochoa, M., Tippenhauer, N. O., & Elovici, Y. (2017, April). ProfilIoT: a machine learning approach for IoT device identification based on network traffic analysis. In *Proceedings of the symposium on applied computing* (pp. 506-509). 10.1145/3019612.3019878

Miettinen, M., Marchal, S., Hafeez, I., Asokan, N., Sadeghi, A. R., & Tarkoma, S. (2017, June). Iot sentinel: Automated device-type identification for security enforcement in iot. In *2017 IEEE 37th International Conference on Distributed Computing Systems (ICDCS)* (pp. 2177-2184). IEEE.

Mo, H., Chen, B., & Luo, W. (2018). Fake Faces Identification via Convolutional Neural Network. In *Proceedings of the 6th ACM Workshop on Information Hiding and Multimedia Security* (pp. 43–47). ACM.

Mohammed, H., Clarke, N., & Li, F. (2016). An automated approach for digital forensic analysis of heterogeneous big data. *Journal of Digital Forensics. Security and Law*, *11*(2), 9.

Moradi, M., & Zulkernine, M. (2004). A Neural Network Based System for Intrusion Detection and Classification of Attacks, *Proceedings of International Conference on Advances in Intelligent Systems*, 148-04.

Moualla, S., Khorzom, K., & Jafar, A. (2021). Improving the performance of machine learning-based network intrusion detection systems on the UNSW-NB15 dataset. *Computational Intelligence and Neuroscience*.

Mousavi, S. S., Schukat, M., & Howley, E. (2016, September). Deep reinforcement learning: an overview. In *Proceedings of SAI Intelligent Systems Conference* (pp. 426-440). Springer.

Muniswamy-Reddy, K. K., Macko, P., & Seltzer, M. I. (2010, February). Provenance for the Cloud. In FAST (Vol. 10, pp. 15-14). Academic Press.

Nachar, R., Inaty, E., Bonnin, P. J., & Alayli, Y. (2020). Hybrid minutiae and edge corners feature points for increased fingerprint recognition performance. *Pattern Analysis & Applications*, *23*(1), 213–224.

Narkhede, S., Baraskar, T., & Mukhopadhyay, D. (2014, March). Analyzing web application log files to find hit count through the utilization of Hadoop MapReduce in cloud computing environment. In *2014 Conference on IT in Business, Industry and Government (CSIBIG)* (pp. 1-7). IEEE.

Nassif, A. B., Shahin, I., Attili, I., Azzeh, M., & Shaalan, K. (2019). Speech recognition using deep neural networks: A systematic review. *IEEE Access: Practical Innovations, Open Solutions*, *7*, 19143–19165. doi:10.1109/ACCESS.2019.2896880

Nataraj, L., Mohammed, T. M., Manjunath, B. S., Chandrasekaran, S., Flenner, A., Bappy, J. H., & Roy-Chowdhury, A. K. (2019). Detecting GAN generated fake images using co-occurrence matrices. *Electronic Imaging*, *2019*(5), 532–1.

Ng, H. W., Nguyen, V. D., Vonikakis, V., & Winkler, S. (2015, November). Deep learning for emotion recognition on small datasets using transfer learning. In *Proceedings of the 2015 ACM on international conference on multimodal interaction* (pp. 443-449). 10.1145/2818346.2830593

Ng, T. T., Chang, S. F., Hsu, J., & Pepeljugoski, M. (2005). *Columbia Photographic Images and Photo realistic Computer. Graphics Dataset.* ADVENT Technical Report Columbia University.

Ng, T. T., Chang, S. F., Hsu, J., Xie, L., & Tsui, M. P. (2005). Physics-motivated features for distinguishing photographic images and computer graphics. In *Proceedings of the 13th annual ACM international conference on Multimedia* (pp. 159–164). ACM.

Nguyen, H. H., Tieu, T., Nguyen-Son, H. Q., Nozick, V., Yamagishi, J., & Echizen, I. (2018). Modular convolutional neural network for discriminating between computer-generated images and photographic images. In *Proceedings of the 13th International Conference on Availability, Reliability and Security* (pp. 1-6). Academic Press.

Nguyen, T. T., Nguyen, C. M., Nguyen, D. T., Nguyen, D. T., & Nahavandi, S. (2019). *Deep Learning for Deepfakes Creation and Detection.* arXiv 2019, arXiv:1909.11573.

Nicolescu, R., Huth, M., Radanliev, P., & De Roure, D. (2018). Mapping the values of IoT. *Journal of Information Technology, 33*(4), 345–360. doi:10.105741265-018-0054-1

Nyarko-Boateng, O., Asante, M., & Nti, I. K. (2017). Implementation of advanced encryption standard algorithm with key length of 256 bits for preventing data loss in an organization. *International Journal of Science and Engineering Applications, 6*(03), 88–94.

Okpe, O. A., John, O. A., & Emmanuel, S. (2018). Intrusion detection in internet of things (IoT). *International Journal of Advanced Research in Computer Science, 9*(1), 504–509. doi:10.26483/ijarcs.v9i1.5429

Omar, M. K., & Hasegawa-Johnson, M. (2002, May). Maximum mutual information based acoustic-features representation of phonological features for speech recognition. In *2002 IEEE International Conference on Acoustics, Speech, and Signal Processing* (Vol. 1, pp. I-81). IEEE.

Othman, S. M., Ba-Alwi, F. M., Alsohybe, N. T., & Al-Hashida, A. Y. (2018). Intrusion detection model using machine learning algorithm on Big Data environment. *Journal of Big Data, 5*(1), 1–12.

Panchal, G., Samanta, D., & Barman, S. (2019). Biometric-based cryptography for digital content protection without any key storage. *Multimedia Tools and Applications, 78*(19), 26979–27000.

Papernot, N., Faghri, F., Carlini, N., Goodfellow, I., Feinman, R., Kurakin, A., Xie, C., Sharma, Y., Brown, T., & Roy, A. (2018). *Technical Report on the CleverHans v2.1.0 Adversarial Examples Library.* arXiv: 1610.00768.

Papernot, N., Mcdaniel, P., Jha, S., Fredrikson, M., Celik, Z. B., & Swami, A. (2016). The Limitations of Deep Learning in Adversarial Settings. *Proceedings of the IEEE European Symposium on Security & Privacy.*

Patidar, S., & Bains, I. S. (2020, August). Web security in IoT networks using deep learning model. In *2020 Third International Conference on Smart Systems and Inventive Technology (ICSSIT)* (pp. 848-855). IEEE.

Peng, F., Zhou, D. L., Long, M., & Sun, X. M. (2017). Discrimination of natural images and computer generated graphics based on multi-fractal and regression analysis. *AEÜ. International Journal of Electronics and Communications*, *71*, 72–81.

Peng, J., Kang, S., Ning, Z., Deng, H., Shen, J., Xu, Y., ... Liu, L. (2020). Residual convolutional neural network for predicting response of transarterial chemoembolization in hepatocellular carcinoma from CT imaging. *European Radiology*, *30*(1), 413–424.

Pevny, T., Bas, P., & Fridrich, J. (2010). Steganalysis by subtractive pixel adjacency matrix. *IEEE Transactions on Information Forensics and Security*, *5*(2), 215–224.

Piva, A. (2013). An overview on image forensics. *International Scholarly Research Notices*, •••, 2013.

Povar, D., & Geethakumari, G. (2014, September). A heuristic model for performing digital forensics in cloud computing environment. In *International Symposium on Security in Computing and Communication* (pp. 341-352). Springer.

Priyadarsini, P. I., Leela, P. S., & Jyothi, B. (2021). Towards Intelligent Machine Learning Models for Intrusion Detection System. *Turkish Journal of Computer and Mathematics Education*, *12*(5), 643–655.

Quan, W., Wang, K., Yan, D. M., & Zhang, X. (2018). Distinguishing between natural and computer-generated images using convolutional neural networks. *IEEE Transactions on Information Forensics and Security*, *13*(11), 2772–2787.

Quick, D., & Choo, K. K. R. (2013). Digital droplets: Microsoft SkyDrive forensic data remnants. *Future Generation Computer Systems*, *29*(6), 1378–1394. doi:10.1016/j.future.2013.02.001

Quick, D., & Choo, K. K. R. (2013). Forensic collection of cloud storage data: Does the act of collection result in changes to the data or its metadata? *Digital Investigation*, *10*(3), 266–277. doi:10.1016/j.diin.2013.07.001

Rabiner, L. R. (1992). Speech recognition based on pattern recognition approaches. In *Digital Speech Processing* (pp. 111–126). Springer. doi:10.1007/978-1-4757-2148-5_5

Radanliev, P., De Roure, D. C., Nicolescu, R., Huth, M., Montalvo, R. M., Cannady, S., & Burnap, P. (2018). Future developments in cyber risk assessment for the internet of things. *Journal of Comput. Ind.*, *102*, 14–22. doi:10.1016/j.compind.2018.08.002

Radanliev, P., De Roure, D. C., Nurse, J. R. C., Mantilla Montalvo, R., Cannady, S., Santos, O., Maddox, L. T., Burnap, P., & Maple, C. (2020). Future developments in standardization of cyber risk in the Internet of Things (IoT). *SN Appl. Sci*, *2*(2), 201–212. doi:10.100742452-019-1931-0

Radford, A., Metz, L., & Chintala, S. (2016). Unsupervised Representation Learning with Deep Convolutional Generative Adversarial Networks. *Proceedings of the 4th International Conference on Learning Representations.*

Raghavan, R., & John Singh, K. (2022). An enhanced and hybrid fingerprint minutiae feature extraction method for identifying and authenticating the patient's noisy fingerprint. *International Journal of System Assurance Engineering and Management*, 1-14.

Ragkhitwetsagul, C. (2016, October). Measuring code similarity in large-scaled code Corpora. In *2016 IEEE International Conference on Software Maintenance and Evolution (ICSME)* (pp. 626-630). IEEE. 10.1109/ICSME.2016.18

Rahmouni, N., Nozick, V., Yamagishi, J., & Echizen, I. (2017). Distinguishing computer graphics from natural images using convolution neural networks. In *Proceedings of the 2017 IEEE Workshop on Information Forensics and Security (WIFS)* (pp. 1–6). IEEE.

Ranzato, M., Poultney, C., Chopra, S., & LeCun, Y. (2007). Efficient learning of sparse representations with an energy-based model. In *Advances in Neural Information Processing Systems* (pp. 1137–1144). MIT Press.

Rayson, P. E., Mariani, J. A., Anderson-Cooper, B., Baron, A., Gullick, D. S., Moore, A., & Wattam, S. (2017). Towards interactive multidimensional visualisations for corpus linguistics. *Journal for Language Technology and Computational Linguistics, 31*(1), 27-49.

Real and fake face detection. Kaggle. (2019, January 14). Retrieved from https://www.kaggle.com/datasets/ciplab/real-and-fake-face-detection?resource=download

Redmon, J., Divvala, S., Girshick, R., & Farhadi, A. (2016). You only look once: Unified, real-time object detection. *Proceedings of the IEEE conference on computer vision and pattern recognition*, 779-788. 10.1109/CVPR.2016.91

Ren, S., He, K., Girshick, R., & Sun, J. (2015). Faster r-cnn: Towards real-time object detection with region proposal networks. *Advances in Neural Information Processing Systems*, 91–99.

Reshma, K., Priyatharishini, M., & Nirmala Devi, M. (2019). Hardware trojan detection using deep learning technique. In *Soft Computing and Signal Processing* (pp. 671–680). Springer. doi:10.1007/978-981-13-3393-4_68

Rodríguez-Félix, D., Aragon-Noriega, E.A., Cisneros-Mata, M., Guevara-Aguirre, D., & Alcántara-Razo, E. (2018). *Management strategies for sustainable fisheries*. Academic Press.

Roopak, M., Tian, G. Y., & Chambers, J. (2019, January). Deep learning models for cyber security in IoT networks. In *2019 IEEE 9th annual computing and communication workshop and conference (CCWC)* (pp. 0452-0457). IEEE. 10.1109/CCWC.2019.8666588

Rossler, A., Cozzolino, D., Verdoliva, L., Riess, C., Thies, J., & Nießner, M. (2019). Faceforensics++: Learning to detect manipulated facial images. In *Proceedings of the IEEE/CVF international conference on computer vision* (pp. 1-11). IEEE.

Ruan, K., Carthy, J., Kechadi, T., & Baggili, I. (2013). Cloud forensics definitions and critical criteria for cloud forensic capability: An overview of survey results. *Digital Investigation*, *10*(1), 34–43. doi:10.1016/j.diin.2013.02.004

Saikia, S., Fidalgo, E., Alegre, E., & Fernández-Robles, L. (2017, September). Object detection for crime scene evidence analysis using deep learning. In *International Conference on Image Analysis and Processing* (pp. 14-24). Springer. 10.1007/978-3-319-68548-9_2

Salama, U., Varadharajan, V., & Hitchens, M. (2012, June). Metadata based forensic analysis of digital information in the web. In *Annual Symposium of Information Assurance and Secure Knowledge Management* (pp. 9-15). Academic Press.

Saleem, S., Subhan, F., Naseer, N., Bais, A., & Imtiaz, A. (2020). Forensic speaker recognition: A new method based on extracting accent and language information from short utterances. *Forensic Science International: Digital Investigation*, *34*, 300982.

Santos, N., Gummadi, K. P., & Rodrigues, R. (2009). Towards Trusted Cloud Computing. *HotCloud*, *9*(9), 3.

Saranya, R., & Prabhu, S. (2016). Image encryption using RSA algorithm with biometric recognition. *Int. J. Adv. Trends Comput. Sci. Eng.*, *5*(11), 19149–19154.

Saraswathi, K., & Balasubramaniam, R. (2010). Biocryptosystems for authentication and network security-a survey. *Global Journal of Computer Science and Technology*, *10*, 12–16.

Saravanan, S., & Maheswari, B. U. (2014). Analyzing Large Web Log Files in A HadoopDistributedCluster Environment. *International Journal of Computer Technology & Applications*, *5*, 1677–1681.

Schmidhuber, J. (2015). Deep learning in neural networks: An overview. *Neural Networks*, *61*, 85–117. doi:10.1016/j.neunet.2014.09.003 PMID:25462637

Schöttle, P., Schlögl, A., Pasquini, C., & Böhme, R. (2018). Detecting Adversarial Examples – a Lesson from Multimedia Security. In *Proceedings of the 26th European Signal Processing Conference (EUSIPCO)* (pp. 947–951). Academic Press.

Shabtai, A., Moskovitch, R., Elovici, Y., & Glezer, C. (2009). Detection of malicious code by applying machine learning classifiers on static features: A state-of-the-art survey. *Information Security Technical Report*, *14*(1), 16-29.

Shaheed, K., Mao, A., Qureshi, I., Kumar, M., Abbas, Q., Ullah, I., & Zhang, X. (2021). A systematic review on physiological-based biometric recognition systems: Current and future trends. *Archives of Computational Methods in Engineering*, *28*(7), 4917–4960.

ShanmughaSundaram, M., & Subramani, S. (2015). A measurement of similarity to identify identical code clones. *The International Arab Journal of Information Technology*, 735–740.

Shariati, M., Dehghantanha, A., & Choo, K. K. R. (2016). SugarSync forensic analysis. *The Australian Journal of Forensic Sciences*, *48*(1), 95–117.

Sharif Razavian, A., Azizpour, H., Sullivan, J., & Carlsson, S. (2014). CNN features off-the-shelf: an astounding baseline for recognition. In *Proceedings of the IEEE conference on computer vision and pattern recognition workshops* (pp. 806-813). IEEE.

Shengli, K., Jun, Z., Guang, S., Chunhong, W., Wenpei, Z., & Tao, L. (2015). The Design and Implementation of the Attendance Management System based on Radio Frequency Identification Technology. *International Conference on Electronic Science and Automation Control.*

Shilpashree, S., Lingareddy, S. C., Nayana, G. B., & Sunil, K. G. (2019). Decision Tree: A Machine Learning for Intrusion Detection. *International Journal of Innovative Technology and Exploring Engineering*, *8*, 1126–1130.

Shin, H. C., Roth, H. R., Gao, M., Lu, L., Xu, Z., Nogues, I., Yao, J., Mollura, D., & Summers, R. M. (2016). Deep convolutional neural networks for computer-aided detection: CNN architectures, dataset characteristics and transfer learning. *IEEE Transactions on Medical Imaging*, *35*(5), 1285–1298. doi:10.1109/TMI.2016.2528162 PMID:26886976

Shullani, D., Fontani, M., Iuliani, M., Al Shaya, O., & Piva, A. (2017). *VISION: A video and image dataset for source identification. EURASIP Journal on Information Security.*

Simonyan, K., & Zisserman, A. (2014). *Very deep convolutional networks for large-scale image recognition.* arXiv2014, arXiv: 1409.1556.

Siniscalchi, S. M., Svendsen, T., & Lee, C. H. (2009, April). A phonetic feature based lattice rescoring approach to LVCSR. In *2009 IEEE International Conference on Acoustics, Speech and Signal Processing* (pp. 3865-3868). IEEE. 10.1109/ICASSP.2009.4960471

Srinivasan, C. R., Rajesh, B., Saikalyan, P., Premsagar, K., & Yadav, E. S. (2019). A review on the different types of Internet of Things (IoT). *Journal of Advanced Research in Dynamical and Control Systems*, *11*(1), 154–158.

Srivastava, N., Hinton, G. E., Krizhevsky, A., Sutskever, I., & Salakhutdinov, R. (2014). Dropout: A simple way to prevent neural networks from overfitting. *Journal of Machine Learning Research*, *15*(1), 1929–1958.

Stamm, M., Bestagini, P., Marcenaro, L., & Campisi, P. (2018). Forensic camera model identification: Highlights from the IEEE signal processing cup 2018 student competition. *IEEE Signal Processing Magazine*, *35*(5), 168–174.

Sudiro, S. A., & Yuwono, R. T. (2012). Adaptable fingerprint minutiae extraction algorithm based-on crossing number method for hardware implementation using FPGA device. *International Journal of Computer Science, Engineering and Information Technology, 2*(3).

Sudiro, S. A., Paindavoine, M., & Kusuma, T. M. (2007, June). Simple fingerprint minutiae extraction algorithm using crossing number on valley structure. In *2007 IEEE Workshop on Automatic Identification Advanced Technologies* (pp. 41-44). IEEE.

Sung, A. H., & Mukkamala, S. (2003). Identifying Important Features for Intrusion Detection Using Support Vector Machines and Neural Networks. *Proceedings of the 2003 Symposium on Applications and the Internet (SAINT'03.*

Surajkanta, Y., & Pal, S. (2021). A Digital Geometry-Based Fingerprint Matching Technique. *Arabian Journal for Science and Engineering*, *46*(4), 4073–4086.

Szegedy, C., Zaremba, W., Sutskever, I., Bruna, J., Erhan, D., Goodfellow, I., & Fergus, R. (2013). *Intriguing properties of neural networks*. arXiv 2013, arXiv:1312.6199.

Szegedy, C., Liu, W., Jia, Y., Sermanet, P., Reed, S., Anguelov, D., Erhan, D., Vanhoucke, V., & Rabinovich, A. (2015). Going deeper with convolutions. In *Proceedings of the IEEE Conference on Computer Vision and Pattern Recognition* (pp. 1–9). IEEE.

Szegedy, C., Vanhoucke, V., Ioffe, S., Shlens, J., & Wojna, Z. (2016). Rethinking the inception architecture for computer vision. In *Proceedings of the IEEE conference on computer vision and pattern recognition* (pp. 2818–2826). IEEE.

Tallón-Ballesteros, A. J., & Riquelme, J. C. (2014). Data mining methods applied to a digital forensics task for supervised machine learning. In *Computational Intelligence in Digital Forensics: Forensic Investigation and Applications* (pp. 413–428). Springer. doi:10.1007/978-3-319-05885-6_17

Tang, Y. (2013). *Deep learning using linear support vector machines*. arXiv 2013, arXiv:1306.0239.

Tewari, R. K., & Ravikumar, K. V. (2000). History and development of forensic science in India. *Journal of Postgraduate Medicine*, *46*(4), 303. PMID:11435664

Thakur, M. R., & Sanyal, S. (2012). *A multi-dimensional approach towards intrusion detection system.* arXiv preprint arXiv:1205.2340.

Thandil, R. K., & Basheer, K. M. (2020). Accent based speech recognition: A critical overview. *Malaya Journal of Matematik, 8*(4), 1743-1750.

Thongkamwitoon, T., Muammar, H., & Dragotti, P. L. (2015). An image recapture detection algorithm based on learning dictionaries of edge profiles. *IEEE Transactions on Information Forensics and Security*, *2015*(10), 953–968.

Tokuda, E., Pedrini, H., & Rocha, A. (2013). Computer generated images vs. digital photographs: A synergetic feature and classifier combination approach. *Journal of Visual Communication and Image Representation*, *24*, 1276–1292.

Tolosana, R., Vera-Rodriguez, R., Fierrez, J., Morales, A., & Ortega-Garcia, J. (2020). *DeepFakes and Beyond: A Survey of Face Manipulation and Fake Detection*. arXiv 2020, arXiv:2001.00179.

Tuama, A., Comby, F., & Chaumont, M. (2016, December). Camera model identification with the use of deep convolutional neural networks. In *2016 IEEE International workshop on information forensics and security (WIFS)* (pp. 1-6). IEEE.

Vamsi, V. V. V. N. S., Shet, S. S., Reddy, S. S. M., Rose, S. S., Shetty, S. R., Sathvika, S., & Shankar, S. P. (2022). *Deepfake Detection in Digital Media Forensics. Global Transitions Proceedings.*

Verdoliva, L. (2020). *Media Forensics and DeepFakes: Sn overview.* arXiv 2020, arXiv:2001.06564.

Vigneswaran, R. K., Vinayakumar, R., Soman, K. P., & Poornachandran, P. (2018, July). Evaluating shallow and deep neural networks for network intrusion detection systems in cyber security. In *2018 9th International conference on computing, communication and networking technologies (ICCCNT)* (pp. 1-6). IEEE. 10.1109/ICCCNT.2018.8494096

Vijayanand, R., Devaraj, D., & Kannapiran, B. (2018). Intrusion detection system for wireless mesh network using multiple support vector machine classifiers with genetic-algorithm-based feature selection. *Computers & Security, 77*, 304–314. doi:10.1016/j.cose.2018.04.010

Vijayarajan, R., Gnanasivam, P., & Avudaiammal, R. (2019). Bio-key based AES for personalized image cryptography. *The Computer Journal, 62*(11), 1695–1705.

Vimala, C., & Radha, V. (2015). Isolated speech recognition system for Tamil language using statistical pattern matching and machine learning techniques. *Journal of Engineering Science and Technology, 10*(5), 617–632.

Vinayakumar, R., Alazab, M., Soman, K. P., Poornachandran, P., Al-Nemrat, A., & Venkatraman, S. (2019). Deep learning approach for intelligent intrusion detection system. *IEEE Access: Practical Innovations, Open Solutions, 7*, 41525–41550. doi:10.1109/ACCESS.2019.2895334

Viola, P., & Jones, M. J. (2004). Robust real-time face detection. *International Journal of Computer Vision, 57*(2), 137–154. doi:10.1023/B:VISI.0000013087.49260.fb

Walker, D. (1975). The SRI speech understanding system. *IEEE Transactions on Acoustics, Speech, and Signal Processing, 23*(5), 397–416. doi:10.1109/TASSP.1975.1162726

Wang, H. (2018). *Real-time Face Detection and Recognition Based on Deep Learning* [Master's Thesis]. Auckland University of technology, New Zealand.

Wang, H., & Raj, B. (2017). *On the origin of deep learning.* arXiv preprint arXiv:1702.07800.

Wang, Q., & Zhang, R. (2016). Double JPEG compression forensics based on a convolutional neural network. *EURASIP J. Inf. Secur.*

Wang, B., Yin, J., Tan, S., Li, Y., & Li, M. (2018). Source camera model identification based on convolutional neural networks with local binary patterns coding. *Signal Processing Image Communication, 68*, 162–168.

Wang, X., Zhu, Z., Wang, F., Ni, R., Wang, J., & Hu, Y. (2021). Medical image encryption based on biometric keys and lower–upper decomposition with partial pivoting. *Applied Optics, 60*(1), 24–32.

Wang, Z., & Srinivasan, R. S. (2017). A review of artificial intelligence-based building energy use prediction: Contrasting the capabilities of single and ensemble prediction models. *Renewable & Sustainable Energy Reviews*, *75*, 796–808. doi:10.1016/j.rser.2016.10.079

Widyowaty, D. S., & Sunyoto, A. (2020, November). Accent Recognition by Native Language Using Mel-Frequency Cepstral Coefficient and K-Nearest Neighbor. In *2020 3rd International Conference on Information and Communications Technology (ICOIACT)* (pp. 314-318). IEEE. 10.1109/ICOIACT50329.2020.9332026

Wu, M. N., Lin, C. C., & Chang, C. C. (2007). Brain tumor detection using color-based k-means clustering segmentation. In *International Conference on Intelligent Information Hiding and Multimedia Signal Processing* (pp. 245-250). 10.1109/IIHMSP.2007.4457697

Yan, W., & Kankanhalli, M. (2015) Face search in encrypted domain. *Pacific-Rim Symposium on Image and Video Technology*, 775-790.

Yang, P., Ni, R., & Zhao, Y. (2018). Recapture image forensics based on Laplacian convolutional neural networks. In *International Workshop on Digital Watermarking*. Springer.

Yang, P., Ni, R., Zhao, Y., & Zhao, W. (2019). Source camera identification based on content-adaptive fusion residual networks. *Pattern Recognition Letters*, *119*, 195–204.

Yang, S., Luo, P., Loy, C. C., & Tang, X. (2016). Wider face: A face detection benchmark. *Proceedings of the IEEE Conference on Computer Vision and Pattern Recognition*, 5525-5533.

Yan, W. (2019). *Introduction to Intelligent Surveillance: Surveillance Data Capture, Transmission, and Analytics*. Springer. doi:10.1007/978-3-030-10713-0

Yan, W. (2021). *Computational Methods for Deep Learning: Theoretic, Practice and Applications*. Springer. doi:10.1007/978-3-030-61081-4

Yao, H., Qiao, T., Xu, M., & Zheng, N. (2018). Robust multi-classifier for camera model identification based on convolution neural network. *IEEE Access: Practical Innovations, Open Solutions*, *6*, 24973–24982.

Yao, Y., Hu, W., Zhang, W., Wu, T., & Shi, Y. Q. (2018). Distinguishing Computer-Generated Graphics from Natural Images Based on Sensor Pattern Noise and Deep Learning. *Sensors (Basel)*, *18*, 1296.

Ying, Y., Su, J., Shan, P., Miao, L., Wang, X., & Peng, S. (2019). Rectified exponential units for convolutional neural networks. *IEEE Access: Practical Innovations, Open Solutions*, *7*, 101633–101640.

Yin, H. (2008). The self-organizing maps: background, theories, extensions and applications. In *Computational intelligence: A compendium* (pp. 715–762). Springer.

You, Y., Gitman, I., & Ginsburg, B. (2017). *Large batch training of convolutional networks*. arXiv preprint arXiv:1708.03888.

Yuan, X., Li, C., & Li, X. (2017, May). DeepDefense: identifying DDoS attack via deep learning. In 2017 IEEE international conference on smart computing (SMARTCOMP) (pp. 1-8). IEEE. doi:10.1109/SMARTCOMP.2017.7946998

Yu, I. J., Kim, D. G., Park, J. S., Hou, J. U., Choi, S., & Lee, H. K. (2017). Identifying photorealistic computer graphics using convolutional neural networks. In *Proceedings of the 2017 IEEE International Conference on Image Processing (ICIP)* (pp. 4093–4097). IEEE.

Yu, J., Hu, A., Zhou, F., Xing, Y., Yu, Y., Li, G., & Peng, L. (2019, October). Radio frequency fingerprint identification based on denoising autoencoders. In *2019 International Conference on Wireless and Mobile Computing, Networking and Communications (WiMob)* (pp. 1-6). IEEE.

Yusiong, J. P. T., & Naval, P. C. (2019, April). Multi-scale autoencoders in autoencoder for semantic image segmentation. In *Asian Conference on Intelligent Information and Database Systems* (pp. 587-599). Springer.

Zanella, A., Bui, N., Castellani, A., Vangelista, L., & Zorzi, M. (2014). Internet of things for smart cities. *IEEE Internet of Things Journal, 1*(1), 22–32. doi:10.1109/JIOT.2014.2306328

Zhang, L. B., Zhu, Z. L., Yang, B. Q., Liu, W. Y., Zhu, H. F., & Zou, M. Y. (2015). Medical image encryption and compression scheme using compressive sensing and pixel swapping based permutation approach. *Mathematical Problems in Engineering.*

Zhang, S., Wei, Z., Nie, J., Huang, L., Wang, S., & Li, Z. (2017). A review on human activity recognition using vision-based method. *Journal of Healthcare Engineering, 2017*, 2017. doi:10.1155/2017/3090343 PMID:29065585

Zhao, W., Yang, P., Ni, R., Zhao, Y., & Li, W. (2018). Cycle GAN-Based Attack on Recaptured Images to Fool both Human and Machine. In *International Workshop on Digital Watermarking*. Springer.

Zhao, W., Yang, P., Ni, R., Zhao, Y., & Wu, H. (2018). Security Consideration for Deep Learning-Based Image Forensics. *IEICE Transactions on Information and Systems, 2018*(101), 3263–3266.

Zhu, B. B., Swanson, M. D., & Tewfik, A. H. (2004). When seeing isn't believing. *IEEE Signal Processing Magazine, 21*(2), 40–49.

Zhu, J. Y., Park, T., Isola, P., & Efros, A. A. (2017). Unpaired image-to-image translation using cycle-consistent adversarial networks. In *Proceedings of the IEEE International Conference on Computer Vision* (pp. 2223–2232). IEEE.

Zhu, Q., Yeh, M. C., Cheng, K. T., & Avidan, S. (2006). Fast human detection using a cascade of histograms of oriented gradients. *2006 IEEE Computer Society Conference on Computer Vision and Pattern Recognition (CVPR'06)*, 2, 1491-1498.

Zuo, Z. (2018). *Camera Model Identification with Convolutional Neural Networks and Image Noise Pattern, 2018.* Available online: http://hdl.handle.net/2142/100123

About the Contributors

Alex Noel Joseph Raj (Member, IEEE) received the B.E. degree in electrical engineering from Madras University, India, in 2001, the M.E. degree in applied electronics from Anna University, in 2005, and the Ph.D. degree in engineering from the University of Warwick, in 2009. From October 2009 to September 2011, he was a Design Engineer with Valeport Ltd., Totnes, U.K. From March 2013 to December 2016, he was a Professor with the Department of Embedded Technology, School of Electronics Engineering, Vellore Institute of Technology, Vellore, India. Since January 2017, he has been with the Department of Electronic Engineering, College of Engineering, Shantou University, China. His research interests include deep learning, signal and image processing, and FPGA implementations.

Vijayalakshmi G. V. Mahesh received the B.E. degree in electronics and communication engineering from Bangalore University, India, in 1999, the M.Tech. in digital communication and networking from Visvesvaraya Technological University, in 2005, and the Ph.D. degree from the Vellore Institute of Technology, Vellore, India. She is currently working as an Associate Professor with the BMS Institute of Technology and Management, Bengaluru, India. Her research interests include pattern recognition, machine learning, image processing, and deep learning.

Ruban Nersisson completed his Bachelor of Engineering in Instrumentation & Control Engineering from University of Madras, India in 2001, Masters in Biomedical Signal Processing & Instrumentation from SASTRA University, Thanjavur, India in 2004 and PhD from VIT University in 2018. He has more than 16 years of teaching experience and has served in various Engineering colleges in and out of India. He currently works as an Academic Faculty member in India's number 1 private university VIT University. His research areas are Bio signal Processing, Speech recognition, Machine learning. He has more than 30 research publications in SCI, Scopus indexed journal and National/international reputed conferences on the above-mentioned fields.

Ang Yu's academic and technical background includes RF circuits/electronics, microwave (transmission line based devices), applied electromagnetism, antenna design and analysis for communication systems, electromagnetic forward modeling for radar imaging application, and sensors for structural health monitoring. His approach involves both mathematical modeling, simulation (using commercial software and customized software) and experimental work (doing prototype design, fabrication, and measurement). Dr. Yu has taught courses such as Engineering Mathematics, Electromagnetism, Wireless Communications, and Introductory Electronics. He has mentored graduate and undergraduate students while participating in research projects.

Jennifer Gentry is a Computer Science Assistant in Carolina University's School of Arts & Sciences. Course specialties include software engineering, software programming, operating systems, and databases. She previously taught Computer Science at ECPI University in Greensboro and Online where she taught many various aspects of the industry. Prior to any academic endeavors, Professor Gentry worked as a Project Manager and Senior Structural Engineer at HAECO Cabin Solutions and developed in-house software for the structural engineering department at Sikorsky Aircraft in Stratford, Connecticut.

* * *

Namitha A. R. received Master degree M.Tech in Computer Science and Engineering from Maharaja Institute Of Technology, Mysore in the year 2014, BE in Computer Science and Engineering from BGS Institute of Technology, Mandya in the year 2012. Presently, working as an Assistant Professor in the Department of Computer Science and Engineering in BGS Institute of Technology and has published many articles in National and International conferences. Her area of interest is E-commerce, Big Data, Cloud computing, Cyber Security.

Pinaki Acharjya works at the Techno College of Engineering, Agartala, Tripura, India.

Ayaz Ahmad is working as an Assistant Professor in the Department of Mathematics, National Institute of Technology Patna, Bihar. He has published Many research papers in International Conferences and Journals.

Chandrashekhar Azad has received his MCA from Ranchi University, Ranchi in 2011. In his MCA degree, he has received Gold Medal for Best Master Degree in Professional Courses. He has received Ph.D. from Birla Institute of Technology,

Mesra Ranchi the Department of Computer Science & Engineering in 2017. He has qualified GATE (Computer Science & Information Technology) and UGC NET (Computer Science and Applications) examinations. Currently he is working as an Assistant Professor in the Department of Computer Science and Engineering at National Institute of Technology, Jamshedpur. He has published more than 35 research papers in journals and conferences of international repute.He serves as a reviewer for various international journals and conferences. His primary area of research includes Intrusion Detection System, Meta Heuristic Algorithms, Swarm Intelligence, Data Mining, Feature Selection and Machine Learning.

Subhabrata Barman is an Assistant Professor with the Department of Computer Science & Engineering, Haldia Institute of Technology, West Bengal, India. His research interests are in the field of Wireless Networks, Computational Intelligence, Remote Sensing and Geo-Informatics, Parallel and Grid Computing. He has published research papers at various International and National Journals and Conferences. He is a Professional Member of IEEE, IACSIT, IAENG and a reviewer of International Journal of Wireless Networks (Springer).

Madhab Choudhury is an MTech CSE Information Security student of NIT Jamshdpur.

Pankaj Dadheech completed his Ph.D. degree in Computer Science & Engineering from Suresh Gyan Vihar University (Accredited by NAAC with 'A' Grade), Jaipur, Rajasthan, India. He completed his M.Tech. degree in Computer Science & Engineering from Rajasthan Technical University, Kota and he has completed his B.E. in Computer Science & Engineering from University of Rajasthan, Jaipur. He has more than 16 years of experience in teaching. He is currently working as an Associate Professor & Dy. HOD in the Department of Computer Science & Engineering (NBA Accredited), Swami Keshvanand Institute of Technology, Management & Gramothan (SKIT), Jaipur, Rajasthan, India. He has published 21 Patents at Intellectual Property India, Office of the Controller General of Patents, Design and Trade Marks, Department of Industrial Policy and Promotion, Ministry of Commerce and Industry, Government of India. He has published 4 Australian Patents at Commissioner of Patents, Intellectual Property Australia, Australian Government. He has published 1 German Patent. He has also Registered & Granted 2 Research Copyrights at Registrar of Copyrights, Copyright Office, Department for Promotion of Industry and Internal Trade, Ministry of Commerce and Industry, Government of India. He has presented 53 papers in various National & International Conferences. He has 55 publications in various International & National Journals. He has published 5 Books & 11 Book Chapters. He is a member of many Professional Organizations like the IEEE Computer Society, CSI, ACM, IAENG & ISTE. He has been appointed as a Ph.D. Research Supervisor in the Department of Computer Science & Engineering at SKIT, Jaipur (Recognized Research Centre of Rajasthan Technical University, Kota). He has also guided various M.Tech. Research Scholars. He has Chaired Technical Sessions in various International Conferences & Contributed as Resource Person in various FDP's, Workshops, STTP's, and Conferences. He is also acting as a Guest Editor of the various reputed Journal publishing houses, Conference Proceedings and Bentham Ambassador of Bentham Science Publisher. His area of interest includes High Performance Computing, Cloud Computing, Information Security, Big Data Analytics, Intellectual Property Right and Internet of Things.

Supriya Prashant Diwan is working as an assistant professor at Government College of Engineering, Karad, Satara District, Maharashtra. She graduated at Dr. B.A.M. University (Electronics Engineering), Aurangabad, Maharashtra, India. She secured Master of Technology and pursuing Ph.D. at Walchand College of Engineering, Sangli, Maharashtra, India under QIP Scheme (AICTE). She is in teaching profession since more than 12 years. She has presented number of papers in National and International Journals, Conference and Symposiums. Her main area of interest includes Artificial Intelligence, cloud computing, machine learning Internet of Things and Embedded Control Systems.

Dankan Gowda V. is a Faculty in the Dept. Electronics and Communication Engineering, BMS Institute of Technology and Management, Bengaluru. He obtained his PhD in Electrical Science and Engineering from Visvesvaraya Technological University, Belgavi. He authored Many research papers on Signal Processing, Communication, Vehicle dynamics and IoT. His research interests are IoT and Signal Processing.

Anitha Ruth J. is working as Assistant Professor in SRM Institute of Science and Technology, Chennai with 20 years of teaching experience for undergraduate and post graduate students in Computer Science department. She has a Doctorate degree in Computer Science and Engineering from SRMIST. She' also has completed her Master Degree and Bachelor Degree from university of Madras. She has published her papers over 3 International Journals. She is a member of Indian Science Congress. She has always enjoyed teaching and providing knowledge to the student from different forms of life. Her work experience involved in taking class, begin a counsellor to counsel the students to have a good career. Her research area include Deep learning, Neural network and security.

Swetha K. R. is currently working as Assistant Professor, Department of Computer Science and Engineering, BGS Institute of Technology, Adichunchanagiri University, BG Nagara, Nagamangala Tq., Mandya, Karnataka. She obtained her Master of Engineering in Computer Science from UVCE, Bangalore University, Bangalore. She is perusing PhD at Adichunchanagiri University. Qualified GATE-2009 with 3rd state Rank and 484th all over India rank. Having 10+ years teaching experience in both undergraduate and postgraduate streams. She has published 2 full length papers in IEEE conferences.

Sheetalrani R. Kawale is serving as an Assistant Professor in the Department of Computer Science at the Karnataka State Akkamahadevi Women's University, Vijayapura. She has 19 yrs of teaching experience and pursued PhD in the computer science field. Her area of interest is in networking.

Santanu Koley currently works at the Department of Computer Science & Engineering, Haldia Institute of Technology as a Professor. Dr. Koley does research in Computer Security and Reliability and Information Science.

Puneeth Kumar B. S. is working as an Assistant Professor in the Department of Computer Science, St. Joseph's College (Autonomous), Bangalore. He has published Many research papers in International Conferences and Journals.

Swathi Pai M. is currently working as a Faculty in the Department of Computer Science School of Engineering, Presidency University, Bangalore. She has published Many research papers in International Conferences and Journals.

Sangeetha N. has completed a Bachelor's degree from the University of Madras and Masters from Anna University. She has completed her doctoral research in Image watermarking at Anna University Chennai, Tamil Nadu, India. Her research interests are Image watermarking, authentication, and cryptography.

Thangadurai N. is working as a Professor and Director – Centre for Research and Innovation in Sankalchand Patel University, Visnagar, Gujarat, India. He has obtained his Ph.D. Degree in Wireless Sensor Networks from Bharathiar University, Coimbatore. He has obtained his Bachelor's Degree in Electronics and Communication Engineering from Coimbatore Institute of Technology and Master's Degree in Applied Electronics from Mohamed Sathak Engineering College under Anna University and MBA from Alagappa University. He has more than 20 years of experience in Teaching, Research and Administration. He has authored/co-authored 181 research papers in both International and National Journals and Conferences.

He has supervised 64 numbers of undergraduate and postgraduate students for their project completion and guiding 8 Ph.D. scholars now. 5 research scholars have been awarded for their Ph.D. under his guidance. He is guiding 6 PhD scholars now. He received sponsored research project grant from VGST, ISRO, MSME, DST and AICTE. He has also filed 36 Indian patents into his credit and that are published. Also 2 design patents filed. He got granted one Australian patent and Germany patent into his credit. He has also authored/co-authored 9 books & 6 Book Chapters into his credit. His research interests are Wireless Communication, Satellite Communications, Mobile Adhoc and Wireless Sensor Networks, Biomedical Engineering, Embedded Systems, Optical Communicationand Navigation Systems. He is also a Life member of following professional bodies like ISCA, ISTE, IAENG, and IACSIT. Also, he is a Fellow of IETE and OSI and Senior Member of IEEE. He has received many awards like Best Young Scientist Award-2018, Award for Research Publications from VGST 2016-17, Bharat Excellence Award -2017, and Outstanding Researcher Award – 2016. He worked for ISO, NAAC, and NBA, ABET accreditation and NIRF, GSIRF, QS Ranking.

Sudhansu Sekhar Nanda is an Assistant Professor in Finance & Accounting at Kirloskar Institute of Advanced Management Studies, Harihar, Karnataka. He has ten years of experience in industry and academic. His contribution in the field of Finance gets evident from three books in Finance and more than 30 scholarly research articles published in reputed international and national indexed journals. Dr. Nanda, Ph.D., M.F.C., M.Com, LL.B has an inquisitive mind which made him explore several areas of Finance and Accounting like Capital Market, Merger and Acquisition, Corporate Finance, International Finance and Financial Derivative.

Ramesh P. received the B.E and M.Tech degree in Computer Science and Engineering from JNTU, Hyderabad. He is having a work experience of 16 years in Teaching and 1year in Industry. Published 8 international Journals and 2 National papers. SCJP Certified by Sun Microsystems. He is also member of professional societies like MIE and ISTE.

Ramkumar P. has completed B.E(CSE) at Sri Sairam Engineering College Chennai in the year 2006. He completed M.E. (CSE) at National Engineering College Kovilpatti in the year 2009. He is pursuing Ph D in VTU, He published 3 books also he has published papers in reputed national and international journals. He filled 3 patents.

Prashanta Kumar Patra is working as Officer on Special Duty/Professor in the Department of Computer Science and Application, Odisha University of Technology and Research, Bhubaneswar, Odisha. He has published Many research papers in International Conferences and Journals.

Avudaiammal R. has received her B.E. degree in Electronics and Communication Engineering from Madurai Kamaraj University, India in 1992 and M.E. degree in Applied Electronics from Bharathiar University, India in 2000. She obtained her doctoral degree from Anna University Chennai, India in the year 2013. She is working as a Professor at St. Joseph's College of Engineering, Chennai, India. She has more than 25 years of teaching experience in Engineering Colleges. She has published books on Microprocessors and on Information Coding Techniques. Her areas of interest are in Embedded Network Processing systems, Multimedia Networks, Image processing and Remote sensing. She has about 48 publications.

Shekhar R. is a doctorate in Computer Science from MS University, Tirunelveli, a Postgraduate in Computer Networks and graduate in Computer Science and Engineering from the University of Bangalore. He has professional certifications in Microsoft and Cisco Networking. Dr.Shekhar joined Alliance in 2012 and has since been actively engaged in the areas of teaching, research, training and development. Dr.Shekhar has a vast experience of nearly two decades in teaching and has held many prestigious positions in various reputed institutions. He is a highly versatile teacher in various computer related subjects such as Data Mining, Image Processing, Computer Networks, Artificial Intelligence and many other subjects related to Computer Science. He has guided many postgraduate students in preparing dissertations in various subjects. He has presented papers in national and international forums, published number of articles in journals having high impact factors, and chaired many conferences. Dr.Shekhar has organized various workshops and conferences for highly reputed institutions. He is a lifetime member of ISTE and also holds the membership of various reputed international organizations. He serves as an editorial member of IJICTS, an International journal and has been a reviewer for several national and international journals. He is also a sitting member of different national and international associations in the field of Computer Science.

Uma R. is working as Professor in the Department of Computer Science and Engineering, Sri Sairam Engineering College, Chennai, India, with 25 years of teaching experience for undergraduate and post graduate students in Computer Science Department. She has a Doctorate degree in Computer Science and Engineering from Anna University Chennai, India. She has completed her Master Degree in Computer Science and Engineering from, College of Engineering Guindy, Anna University, India and Bachelor Degree from SRM Engineering College, University of Madras. She has published her papers over 22 International Journals and has one filed patent, text book on Java and one book chapter to her credit. She is a member of IEEE, IACSIT and life member of ISTE. Her current research interest includes Information Retrieval, Data Mining, Deep Learning, and Machine Learning.

Vijayarajan Rajangam completed his Bachelor of Engineering degree in Electronics and Communication Engineering from the University of Madras, in 1998, and a master's degree in Applied Electronics from Madurai Kamarajar University, in 1999. He completed his doctoral research in Image Fusion at Anna University, in the year 2015. He is currently working as a Faculty Member with the Centre for Healthcare Advancement, Innovation, and Research, School of Electronics Engineering, Vellore Institute of Technology, Chennai. He has published 32 research contributions in various SCI/Scopus journals and conferences. His research interests include computer vision, machine learning algorithms for signal and image processing, image fusion, bio-cryptography, emotion classification, and deep learning for image analysis. He is guiding Ph.D. scholars in the field of Medical image analysis.

Kumaraswamy S. is a Professor in Dept. of Computer Science and Engineering, Global Academy of Technology, Bengaluru. He obtained his PhD in Computer Science and Engineering from Visvesvaraya Technological University, Belgavi. He authored few research papers on Cloud Computing and Virtualization. His research interests are cloud computing and storage area networks.

Shani S. Kumar is doing her Masters in Embedded system design at Vellore Institute of Technology Chennai. Her research interest includes Embedded applications and cryptography algorithms

Ansuman Samal is working as a Faculty at Faculty of Hospitality and Tourism Management, Siksha O Anusandhan Deemed to be University, Bhubaneswar, India. He has published Many research papers in International Conferences and Journals.

Sathiya Narayanan Sekar has more than 10 years of academic research experience. His areas of expertise are signal processing, computer vision, machine learning and data analytics. He received his B.E. degree (in 2008) from Anna University, Chennai, India, and his M.S. and Ph.D. degrees (in 2011 and 2017 respectively) from Nanyang Technological University (NTU), Singapore. His Ph.D. thesis focussed on developing novel compressive sensing reconstruction algorithms for sparse signals with partially known information. He was the recipient of the NTU Research Student Scholarship 2011-2015 and NTU-EEE Outstanding Teaching Assistant Award 2014. From October 2015 to April 2018, he served as a Research Associate/Fellow in NTU. The project was on compressive sensing applications to radar imagery and video, and it was funded by Singapore's Ministry of Education. Since June 2018, he is working as an Assistant Professor (Senior Grade) in Vellore Institute of Technology, Chennai.

Lingaraj Sethi is currently associated as research scholar at Department of Computer Science and Engineering, Odisha University of Technology and Research Bhubaneswar.

Hui Wang received her Master's degree from Auckland University of Technology, Auckland New Zealand in 2018, her research interests include human face detection and recognition, intelligent surveillance and deep learning, etc.

Wei Qi Yan is the Director of Centre for Robotics & Vision (CeRV), Auckland University of Technology (AUT), his expertise is in deep learning, intelligent surveillance, computer vision, multimedia, etc. Dr. Yan has published over 250 research papers, his research distinctions include the published Springer monographs: Computational Methods for Deep Learning (2021), Introduction to Intelligent Surveillance (2019), etc. Dr. Yan is the Chair of the ACM Multimedia Chapter of New Zealand, a Member of the ACM, a Senior Member of the IEEE, TC members of the IEEE. Dr. Yan was a visiting professor with the National University of Singapore (NUS, QS Ranking #11), Singapore.

Index

A

B

C

D

E

F

www.ingramcontent.com/pod-product-compliance
Lightning Source LLC
LaVergne TN
LVHW061538290926
849162LV00004B/839